IMPROVING CLASSROOM READING INSTRUCTION

Gerald G. Duffy
Laura R. Roehler

IMPROVING CLASSROOM READING INSTRUCTION
A DECISION-MAKING APPROACH

Photographs by Robert Bawden
Cover photograph by Gerald G. Duffy

RANDOM HOUSE, NEW YORK
THIS BOOK WAS DEVELOPED FOR RANDOM HOUSE
BY LANE AKERS INCORPORATED

First Edition

9 8 7 6 5 4 3 2

Library of Congress Cataloging-in-Publication Data

Duffy, Gerald G.
  Improving classroom reading instruction.

  Bibliography: p.
  Includes indexes.
  1. Reading. I. Roehler, Laura R., 1937–
II. Title.
LB1050.D755 1986   428.4′07   85–19402
ISBN 0–394–35504–0

Designed and composed by The Bookmakers, Incorporated, Wilkes-Barre, Pa.

Manufactured in the United States of America

TO
Danise and Bob
Mike
Susinn and Eddy
Chris
Kathy
Annie
Byrch

Contents

List of Figures xiii
Preface for Students xvii
Acknowledgments xix

Part I *Introduction*

1 *Classroom Reading Instruction: Practice and Promise* 3

THE GOAL OF READING INSTRUCTION 4
THE IMPACT OF THE TEACHER 6
CURRENT INSTRUCTIONAL PRACTICE IN READING 7
WHY READING INSTRUCTION IS CONDUCTED THIS
   WAY 8
BECOMING AN INSTRUCTIONAL DECISION MAKER 14
CONCLUSION 17
SUGGESTED READINGS 18

Part II *Knowledge: The Basis of Instructional Decision Making*

2 *The Reading Curriculum* 21

DESCRIBING READING 21
OUTCOMES OF READING INSTRUCTION 27
BUILDING A READING CURRICULUM 40
CONCLUSION 40
SUGGESTED READINGS 41

3 *Students and Their Reading Growth* 43

STAGES OF DEVELOPMENTAL READING GROWTH 44
CURRICULAR EMPHASES AT VARIOUS STAGES 54
CONDITIONS THAT MODIFY STUDENT GROWTH 58
MAKING DECISIONS ABOUT DEVELOPMENTAL STAGES 62
CONCLUSION 66
SUGGESTED READINGS 67

4 *Components of Instruction and Methodology* 69

THE BACKGROUND TO INSTRUCTION 70
TERMS ASSOCIATED WITH DIRECT INSTRUCTION 78
TERMS ASSOCIATED WITH INDIRECT INSTRUCTION 81
EXAMPLES OF DIRECT AND INDIRECT INSTRUCTION 82
MAJOR APPROACHES TO ORGANIZING READING
   INSTRUCTION 85
A COMBINED APPROACH TO ORGANIZING A READING
   PROGRAM 93
CONCLUSION 95
SUGGESTED READINGS 96

Part III *Organizing for Instruction*

5 *Creating a Literate Environment* 99

CHARACTERISTICS OF A LITERATE ENVIRONMENT 100
COMPONENTS OF A LITERATE ENVIRONMENT 103
CREATING A LITERATE ENVIRONMENT 109
CONCLUSION 113
SUGGESTED READINGS 113

6 *Organizing Instructional Time* 115

STRENGTHS AND WEAKNESSES OF BASALS 116
ORGANIZING THE YEAR-LONG PROGRAM 119
ORGANIZING FOR WHOLE-GROUP INSTRUCTION 121
ORGANIZING FOR SMALL-GROUP INSTRUCTION 123
CONCLUSION 129
SUGGESTED READINGS 131

7 *Collecting Data to Form and to Teach Reading Groups* **133**

WHAT KINDS OF READING GROUPS? 134
COLLECTING DATA TO FORM READING GROUPS 136
HOW TO COLLECT VITAL SIGNS DATA 144
CONCLUSION 156
SUGGESTED READINGS 157

8 *Managing Reading Groups* **159**

PLANNING FOR EFFECTIVE ACTIVITY FLOW 160
ENSURING SUSTAINED STUDENT ENGAGEMENT 169
STEPS IN CREATING A MANAGEMENT SYSTEM 175
CONCLUSION 177
SUGGESTED READINGS 177

9 *Planning and Conducting Reading Lessons* **179**

OBJECTIVES: THE CORNERSTONE OF EFFECTIVE
   PLANNING 180
TYPES OF LESSON PLANS 183
PLANNING INDIRECT INSTRUCTION 184
PLANNING DIRECT INSTRUCTION 188
THE SUBTLETIES OF INSTRUCTION 203
CONCLUSION 211
SUGGESTED READINGS 212

10 *Planning and Conducting Writing Lessons* **213**

WHY IS WRITING IMPORTANT TO READING
   GROWTH 214
THE WRITING CURRICULUM 216
PROVIDING INSTRUCTION IN WRITING 224
INTEGRATING READING AND WRITING 228
PRESSURES ASSOCIATED WITH WRITING
   INSTRUCTION 230
CONCLUSION 231
SUGGESTED READINGS 232

Part IV Conducting Instruction

11 Teaching Preschool and Kindergarten Reading 235

OVERVIEW OF PRESCHOOL AND KINDERGARTEN
  READING 236
DEVELOPING ATTITUDE OUTCOMES 238
TEACHING PROCESS OUTCOMES 243
DEVELOPING CONTENT OUTCOMES 253
INTEGRATING READING AND WRITING 256
CHARACTERISTICS OF AN INSTRUCTIONAL DAY 260
CONCLUSION 261
SUGGESTED READINGS 262

12 Teaching Primary-Grade Reading 265

OVERVIEW OF PRIMARY-GRADE READING 266
DEVELOPING ATTITUDE OUTCOMES 267
TEACHING PROCESS OUTCOMES 273
DEVELOPING CONTENT OUTCOMES 295
INTEGRATING READING AND WRITING 300
CHARACTERISTICS OF AN INSTRUCTIONAL DAY 305
CONCLUSION 306
SUGGESTED READINGS 307

13 Teaching Middle-Grade Reading 309

OVERVIEW OF MIDDLE-GRADE READING 310
DEVELOPING ATTITUDE OUTCOMES 311
TEACHING PROCESS OUTCOMES 318
DEVELOPING CONTENT OUTCOMES 329
INTEGRATING READING AND WRITING 335
CHARACTERISTICS OF AN INSTRUCTIONAL DAY 341
CONCLUSION 343
SUGGESTED READINGS 344

14 *Teaching Upper-Grade Reading* 347

OVERVIEW OF UPPER-GRADE READING   348
DEVELOPING ATTITUDE OUTCOMES   349
TEACHING PROCESS OUTCOMES   357
DEVELOPING CONTENT OUTCOMES   368
INTEGRATING READING AND WRITING   376
CHARACTERISTICS OF AN INSTRUCTIONAL DAY   380
CONCLUSION   381
SUGGESTED READINGS   382

Part V *Special Instructional Problems*

15 *Computers and Classroom Reading Instruction,*
   Michael Kamil   **387**
USES OF COMPUTERS IN READING AND LANGUAGE
   ARTS   388
A BRIEF INTRODUCTION TO COMPUTERS   389
EXAMPLES OF APPLICATIONS IN READING AND
   LANGUAGE ARTS   392
EVALUATING READING AND LANGUAGE ARTS
   SOFTWARE   393
HARDWARE   396
CAUTIONS AND LIMITATIONS OF COMPUTERS   398
WHAT ABOUT THE FUTURE?   399
SUGGESTED READINGS   401
SUGGESTED RESOURCES REGARDING COMPUTERS   402

16 *Exceptional Children and Mainstreaming,* Sandra Michelsen   **405**

INTRODUCTION   406
STUDENTS WITH DIVERSE NEEDS   407
HISTORICAL BACKGROUND OF SPECIAL EDUCATION   408
PL 94-142   409
GENERAL SUGGESTIONS FOR HELPING MAINSTREAMED
   STUDENTS   411

SPECIFIC SUGGESTIONS FOR READING INSTRUCTION 412
THE GIFTED CHILD 416
CONCLUSION 420
SUGGESTED READINGS 420
REFERENCES 421

17 *Special Language Issues,* Maria Torres **423**

MAJOR TYPES OF LANGUAGE DIFFERENCES 424
BLACK ENGLISH 425
BILINGUALISM 427
EIGHT MYTHS ASSOCIATED WITH SPECIAL LANGUAGE
    ISSUES 430
MEETING SPECIAL LANGUAGE NEEDS THROUGH
    BILINGUAL EDUCATION 438
MEETING SPECIAL LANGUAGE NEEDS OF BLACK
    ENGLISH 441
PROVIDING INSTRUCTION FOR SPECIAL LANGUAGE
    SITUATIONS 443
RESOURCES 445
CONCLUSION 446
SUGGESTED READINGS 447
REFERENCES 448

Part VI *Continued Professional Growth*

18 *Continued Professional Growth* **453**

ASSESSMENT PLAN 454
RESOURCES FOR IMPROVEMENT 457
MONITORING AND EVALUATING PROGRESS 460
THE IMPORTANCE OF PERSONAL GROWTH 463
FACING THE REALITIES 464
CONCLUSION 466
SUGGESTED READINGS 467

Glossary **469**
Author Index **479**
Subject Index **483**

List of Figures

2.1 *Outcomes of reading instruction* 28

2.2 *Types of knowledge about how reading works* 33

2.3 *Types of fix-it strategies* 35

2.4 *The reading curriculum* 39

3.1 *Sample curriculum emphases at the Readiness Stage* 44

3.2 *Sample curriculum emphases at the Initial Mastery Stage* 46

3.3 *Sample curriculum emphases at the Expanded Fundamentals Stage* 49

3.4 *Sample curriculum emphases at the Application Stage* 51

3.5 *Sample curriculum emphases at the Power Stage* 53

3.6 *Curricular emphases at various stages* 55

3.7 *The Readiness Stage* 56

3.8 *The Initial Mastery Stage* 56

3.9 *The Expanded Fundamentals Stage* 57

3.10 *The Application Stage* 57

3.11 *The Power Stage* 58

3.12 *Making decisions about the vital signs of reading* 63

3.13 *Making decisions about conditions for reading growth* 66

4.1 *How students interpret classroom work* 72

4.2 *How instruction works* 74

4.3 *Steps in conducting a directed reading lesson (DRL)* 88

5.1 *Steps in establishing USSR in classrooms* 109

6.1 *Steps in reorganizing basal text prescriptions* 124

6.2 *Two forms of the directed reading lesson* 126

7.1   *Sample results of a sociogram*   138
7.2   *Traditional criteria for establishing reading levels*   140
7.3   *A list of 325 basic sight words*   146
7.4   *Types of context clues*   150
7.5   *Some common structural units*   151
7.6   *Common phonic elements*   152
7.7   *Material needed to collect diagnostic data about reading*   155
8.1   *Two ways to create space by organizing classroom desks*   162
8.2   *Sample record-keeping device*   166
9.1   *The format for planning indirect instruction*   186
9.2   *Decisions to make in planning indirect instruction*   189
9.3   *The format for planning direct instruction of process*   190
9.4   *Questions teachers ask when doing a task analysis*   192
9.5   *Criteria for observing direct instruction in process outcomes*   193
9.6   *Criteria for observing direct instruction in content outcomes*   197
9.7   *Sample lesson for teaching prefixes as a strategy for pronouncing
       unrecognized words*   199
9.8   *Decisions to make in planning direct instruction in process*   201
9.9   *Decisions to make in planning direct instruction in content*   202
9.10 *Model of instructional sequence*   210
10.1 *Writing concepts to be developed*   216
10.2 *Feelings to be developed about writing*   216
10.3 *Curriculum goals for functional and recreational writing*   218
10.4 *Stages in the composing process*   220
10.5 *Strategies for the planning stage*   220
10.6 *Strategies for the drafting stage*   222
10.7 *Strategies for the editing stage*   224
10.8 *An example of indirect instruction in writing*   226
10.9 *An example of how to teach a directed writing lesson*   226
11.1 *Instructional emphasis at the Readiness Stage*   236
11.2 *An example of how to teach positive attitudes to preschoolers and
       kindergarteners*   240
11.3 *An example of how to teach print awareness at the Readiness
       Stage*   244
11.4 *Using a listening situation to teach the general strategy for meaning
       getting*   246
11.5 *An example of how to teach oral context to preschoolers and
       kindergarteners*   246
11.6 *An example of how to teach letter sounds*   248

11.7   *An example of how to teach a directed listening activity for content outcomes at the Readiness Stage*   254

12.1   *Instructional emphasis at the Initial Mastery Stage*   268

12.2   *An example of how to teach attitudes in the primary grades*   270

12.3   *An example of how to develop knowledge about how the reading system works*   274

12.4   *An example of how to teach word meaning*   274

12.5   *An example of how to teach sight words*   276

12.6   *An example of how to teach easily confused sight words*   278

12.7   *An example of how to teach context clues as a strategy for figuring out unrecognized words*   280

12.8   *An example of how to teach structural analysis as a strategy for figuring out unrecognized words*   282

12.9   *An example of how to teach phonics as a strategy for figuring out unrecognized words*   284

12.10 *An example of how to teach a directed reading lesson for content outcomes in the primary grades*   298

13.1   *Instructional emphasis at the Expanded Fundamentals Stage*   312

13.2   *An example of how to use indirect instruction to teach attitudes in the middle grades*   314

13.3   *An example of how to develop fluency*   320

13.4   *An example of how to teach students to generate new predictions*   322

13.5   *An example of how to teach students to use visible cues to comprehension*   324

13.6   *An example of how to teach students to use invisible cues to comprehension*   324

13.7   *An example of how to teach a directed reading and thinking lesson to ensure comprehension of recreational text*   332

13.8   *An example of how to use SQ3R to ensure comprehension of functional text*   332

14.1   *Instructional emphasis at the Application Stage*   350

14.2   *Sample projects that can be used as a culminating activity for integrated units*   353

14.3   *An example of how to develop attitudes in the upper grades*   354

14.4   *An example of how to develop understanding of how the reading system works*   356

14.5   *Propaganda devices*   358

14.6   *Strategies for locating information*   360

14.7   *An example of how to teach students to use locational skills*   360

14.8   *Strategies for taking multiple-choice and essay tests*   362

14.9   *An example of how to teach students to organize and remember what they read*   363

14.10   *An example of how to teach students to read and study efficiently*   363

14.11   *An example of how to teach students to interpret literary devices in comprehending the content of recreational text*   370

14.12   *An example of how to teach students to use QARs to comprehend the content of functional text*   372

14.13   *An example of how to use structured overviews to ensure student comprehension of functional text*   373

18.1   *Teacher self-assessment*   456

18.2   *Professional organizations*   458

18.3   *Professional journals*   458

Preface for Students

This book is written to help you become a professional teacher of reading. Professional teachers are in control of classroom instruction. They make the decisions.

Control comes from knowledge and from a willingness to use knowledge. This book provides the knowledge and sets the expectation that you should use the knowledge to make instructional decisions.

Because the information load is heavy, the book has been carefully organized to assist your learning. Part I starts with an introductory chapter that provides background information about reading instruction as it should be conducted. Part II then provides fundamental background information essential to instructional decision making. This information focuses on *what* you teach, *who* you teach, and *how* you teach. It is the foundation for Part III, which describes how to organize your instruction. The knowledge from the previous three parts is then applied to Part IV, where chapters describe how to conduct instruction with prereaders, primary-grade students, middle-grade students, and upper-grade students. Part V describes special problems you may encounter as a teacher of reading. Finally, Part VI discusses the importance of continuing your professional growth and fine-tuning your decision-making ability throughout your career and suggests ways to do so.

The chapters are not separate and isolated but, rather, are cumulative; that is, each succeeding chapter uses information from previous chapters as a starting point. Similarly, concepts are continually developed throughout the book. For instance, *instruction* is discussed in virtually every chapter, and as the book progresses, the meaning of the term becomes more and more refined as it is used in a variety of contexts and with a variety of examples.

To help you comprehend the content of the book, the following learning aids have been included:

1. *Advance organizers*. Each of the 18 chapters begins with an overview, or *Getting Ready*, section. These overviews are followed by specific *Focus Questions* that direct you to specific information to be learned. Together they will help you activate appropriate background experience needed to understand the chapter content.

2. *Chapter headings and subheadings*. These have been designed to guide your reading. They not only signal where important points are discussed, but wherever possible, they are cued to the focus questions found at the beginning of each chapter.

3. *Figures and Illustrations*. Over 90 summarizing figures have been provided to aid in the review and acquisition of key material. In addition, several photographs in each chapter attempt to help you construct mental pictures of classroom reading instruction.

4. *Chapter conclusions and bibliographies*. Chapter conclusions provide you with a brief review of major themes within each chapter, and end-of-chapter bibliographies, or *Suggested Readings*, offer specific guidance to further exploration of these themes.

5. *Glossary*. A comprehensive glossary is included at the end of the book to make your task of becoming a literate teacher of reading as easy and efficient as possible.

One additional aid could not be built into the book. That is the opportunity for you to use what you learn with real students in real classrooms. Perhaps a supervised field practicum is part of your coursework. If it is, use that situation as an opportunity to test and to apply what you learn in this book. If no such practicum is available, try to arrange classroom visits on your own so that you can observe the teaching of reading and try out the content of this book. The more you use the content, the better you will understand it.

You are embarking on a difficult task. Teaching reading is complex. However, the rewards are satisfying and fulfilling. Hopefully, this book (together with your real-world experience with students) will help you become a professional decision maker who reaps the rewards of being a classroom teacher of reading and literacy.

Acknowledgments

We wish to acknowledge the contributions of the following people who helped make this book possible:

Dr. Beth Ann Herrmann of the University of South Carolina and Mr. Gerald Jennings of the Berrien Springs, Michigan, schools for their careful review of an early version of the manuscript.

Dr. James Hoffman of the University of Texas, Austin, for helpful advice above and beyond the call of duty.

Drs. Michael Kamil, Sandra Michelsen, and Maria Torres for their careful work in developing the Part V chapters.

Linda Vavrus, Janet Johnson, and Susinn Benton for creating test items, the glossary, and the index.

The students in our respective undergraduate reading methods classes who provided helpful advice when using mimeographed copies of early forms of the manuscript.

Karla Bellingar for care and concern in preparing the manuscript at various stages of its development.

PART **I**

INTRODUCTION

Part I consists of a single chapter introducing you to reading instruction as it is currently conducted in many schools and as it can be conducted if teachers are in control of their own instruction. At the end of this unit you should understand this book's purpose and be able to answer questions such as:

1. How do many teachers conduct classroom reading instruction, and why do these practices exist?
2. What do you need to learn to be a teacher who makes decisions?

CHAPTER 1

Classroom Reading Instruction: Practice and Promise

GETTING READY

What do you think of when you hear the term *reading instruction*? Perhaps it stirs a memory of something that happened each school morning when you were in the lower grades. Or perhaps it was a time to read library books, or to struggle with workbook pages and teacher questions about stories in a "reading book." Whatever your previous experiences with reading instruction, they will help you understand what is discussed in this chapter.

This chapter establishes the goal of reading instruction in today's schools, introduces the instructional practices proven most effective in achieving this goal, and reports on the extent to which teachers actually follow these practices. Obstacles to effective instruction are also discussed along with the characteristics of teachers who overcome them. Finally, the rationale of the book is presented so that you can better anticipate and prepare for the content that follows.

FOCUS QUESTIONS

As you read this chapter use the following questions to guide your understanding of what reading instruction is and what it can be.

1. What is the goal of reading instruction?
2. How is reading taught in today's schools?
3. Why is it taught this way?

4. What conditions are necessary in order to become an effective instructional decision maker?
5. What techniques can assist in dealing with classroom complexities?
6. How do teachers maintain cognitive control of instruction?

THE GOAL OF READING INSTRUCTION

In one second-grade classroom a boy was observed working his way through a pile of six or seven worksheets that he had been assigned as seatwork. After much struggle and persistence he finally finished the last one, arranged them into a neat pile, heaved a huge sigh, and said out loud, "I don't know what they mean, but I did 'em."

This anecdote contains a serious message. Reading instruction should produce students who understand and control the reading process. If it does not—if instruction causes students to view reading as a series of tasks rather than a sense-making process—then they will be unable to use reading for either functional or recreational purposes.

To determine whether students understand and control the reading process, teachers interview students following a reading lesson. Consider, for instance, the following second-grade student who was interviewed following a writing lesson on making short sentences into longer ones:

T: How do you make a short sentence a little longer?
S: Well, you add a couple more words that you think would sound good with the sentence and then you have a longer sentence.
T: Okay. Do you have some steps to follow when you do that?
S: What do you mean?
T: Well, when you make short sentences into longer sentences, do you have some steps to follow?
S: You mean, like how to do it?
T: Uh-huh.
S: Like you should circle and underline.
T: Okay, once you have it circled or underlined, then what do you do?
S: Then you just add some words and that makes a longer sentence.

Notice that the student has focused on the procedure of circling and underlining, *not* on understanding how to consciously make short sentences into longer

Students engaged in reading.

ones. In fact, his answer to the last question reflects a belief that simply adding some words (regardless of what words or in what order) is all that is needed.

In contrast, read the following interview response from another second grader who understands how to decode words that have the letters *ou* in them.

> T: What were you learning today?
> S: To pronounce words that have *ou* in them.
> T: Why do you suppose you were learning this skill?
> S: So it could help you decode words with *ou* in them.
> T: How do you use *ou* to decode words?
> S: First, you figure out the *ou* and what it sounds like. *Ow*, like
>   in loud. I'd go l-*ou*-d, loud.

In short, a proper goal of classroom reading instruction is to produce student awareness of how to read. This awareness, in turn, stimulates increased achievement because students are in control of their reading.

THE IMPACT OF THE TEACHER

Students learn what teachers emphasize. If teachers emphasize accurate answer getting and neat circling, students will learn that reading is getting the right answers and circling. If teachers emphasize *how* to make sense out of text, students will learn how to be in control of their reading.

Notice the emphasis on answer getting as opposed to sense making in the following two excerpts from lessons. In the first one, a second-grade oral-reading session, the emphasis is on accurate pronunciation of words rather than on understanding the sense of the message:

T: Okay, Jack, go ahead and read.
S: Now Bobo also —
T: Not *also*, *al-ways*.
S: Always tried to do as he was told. So he picked up the light and put it outside. After time —
T: *Another* time.
S: Another time, Bobo's mother called him from the yard.

Answer getting rather than sense making is also emphasized in the following excerpt from a second-grade reading lesson on main idea:

T: All right, now here are some possibilities for titles for that paragraph. "A Trip Downtown," "The New Shirt," "The Shirt that Didn't Fit." Let me read them again. "A Trip Downtown," "The New Shirt," "The Shirt That Didn't Fit." Now of those three possibilities which one would go best? Annie?
S: "A Trip Downtown."
T: Okay. Tim, what do you think?
S: "The New Shirt."
T: Sharon, how about you?
S: "The New Shirt."
T: I think the girls decided on "A Trip Downtown", and the boys like "The New Shirt." Mainly, what was the story about?
S: A trip downtown.
S: Getting a new shirt.
T: Getting a new shirt, wasn't it?

There is little evidence here of sense making, of how to go about determining the main idea. The teacher calls for answers from students, but offers no strategy for developing those answers. Once again there is no evidence of teacher concern for putting the reader in control.

What could have been done to turn these instructional activities into sense-making episodes? In the first example the teacher could have established that all reading is message getting and that reading is making sense of the message the author is sending. From such a foundation, the teacher could respond to errors such as *also* for *always* and *after time* for *another time* by waiting to see if the student corrects the error without prompting and, if not, asking the student to "see if that makes sense." In the second example the teacher could have established why the main idea is important in getting the author's message, provided a strategy for figuring out the main idea, and taught students to refer to that strategy to determine whether "A Trip Downtown" or "The New Shirt" seemed more sensible as the main idea.

In short, when teachers emphasize mechanical procedures and recitation, students learn to be mechanical; when teachers emphasize sense making and meaning, students learn to understand. Similarly, when instruction focuses on task completion and getting the right answers rather than on message getting and developing conscious reading strategies, students learn to "get done," but not how to comprehend. Once again, students learn what teachers emphasize.

CURRENT INSTRUCTIONAL PRACTICE IN READING

If the proper goal of reading instruction is to put students in control of the reading process—to help them get meaning from written text—one would expect to find comprehension instruction dominating most elementary classrooms. In fact, however, such a sense-making approach to reading instruction is relatively rare. Unfortunately, too many teachers fill their instructional time with activities and procedures. Positive attitudes toward reading and the conscious development of comprehension strategies receive surprisingly little emphasis.

This phenomenon, moreover, appears to be prevalent at all grade levels. For instance, many primary-grade teachers emphasize workbook pages and worksheets without providing any assistance regarding how to do the task or why it is being pursued. The following worksheet directions to students are typical:

> T: I would like to have you read the first paragraph to yourselves and put a line under every word you can see that has the word *play* in it. Even if it has an *s* added to it. We're looking for the word *play*, Okay, Mary?
> S: *Look.*
> T: Okay. There's the word *look*. But we're looking for *play*. John?

S: *Playing.*

T: Yes, *playing* has *play* in it. How about the next one? Sue?

In this example there is both an absence of assistance to students and an emphasis on answer getting. There is no explanation about why the worksheet should be completed or how it contributes to the student's understanding of reading.

A similar pattern is seen in upper-elementary classrooms where teachers ask questions to assess whether students comprehend what was read. The following excerpt from a third-grade reading lesson shows how teachers interrogate during reading without first instructing children in how to comprehend:

S: *(Reading orally)* It was morning. The sun was in the—

T: You can stop there. It was a good morning for doing something. What is it a good morning to do?

S: Jump.

T: Ed, will you read for me?

S: Hop, hop, hop—

T: He is going to talk to a rabbit, isn't he? Is it a small rabbit?

S: No, kind of big. Kind of big and kind of small.

T: It's Bill's turn to read.

S: The rabbit did not look happy. The rabbit had lost two little rabbits on the hill.

T: Why is the rabbit unhappy, Bill?

S: Because he lost two rabbits?

T: He lost two rabbits. Where did he lose them? Katie?

S: On the hill.

T: Okay. Jack will read for us now.

Such question answering in oral reading activities or monitoring of students through worksheets is found in virtually all studies of classroom reading instruction. Teachers at all levels apparently select instructional tasks because the materials are available rather than because they benefit individual students. The driving force is not putting students in control, but rather, occupying their time. Student understanding of how reading works too often becomes a secondary concern.

WHY READING INSTRUCTION IS CONDUCTED THIS WAY

Teachers do not lack dedication and diligence. They follow a mechanical, routinized pattern of reading instruction because of the constraints under which they work. These constraints are discussed in two categories: (1) the complexity of classroom life, and (2) the dominance of the basal reading textbook.

THE COMPLEXITY OF CLASSROOM LIFE

One of the unfortunate myths of the American culture is that anyone can be a teacher. The truth is that being an effective teacher is very difficult, especially if by *teacher* we mean someone who develops a thorough understanding of language and literacy. What makes teaching so difficult is the complexity of managing daily classroom life. Too often these management tasks dominate teachers, leaving little time and energy for instructional development.

What is so difficult about managing classroom life? First, a teacher must organize and smoothly manage the activities of 25 or 30 youngsters for five or six hours every day. It is difficult enough to keep 1 seven-year-old child occupied for five or six hours; it is incredibly more difficult to deal with 25 or 30. Getting so many children organized into cooperative working units so that they attend to academic tasks is more than some people can manage. It is even more difficult when student ability levels are widely varied, as is typically the case.

The social interactions of classroom life also contribute to the difficulty of teaching. One of a teacher's first and most important tasks is to create a socially acceptable environment. To do so, however, is quite demanding given the 25 or 30 distinct personalities who must involuntarily exist in close proximity to each other for extended periods of time.

The problem is further compounded by the fact that, in our society, going to school is a serious business in which schools and teachers are held accountable for student achievement. To ensure this achievement, state and local boards of education require various kinds of achievement tests, and if the test scores are low the teacher is held accountable by parents and school officials. This accountability for good achievement test scores can be handicapping to teachers since achievement growth is affected by many factors outside the teacher's control, and since *what* is measured by tests often differs from the instructional goals of teachers.

Student accountability also adds to the complexity of classrooms. For instance, because students exchange classroom performance for grades, they often avoid responding in order to not make errors, and they negotiate for easy tasks that increase the chances that they will get better grades. Such behavior makes a teacher's job that much more difficult.

Classroom life is made more difficult by the fact that teachers must constantly deal with dilemmas as well as with problems. Whereas a problem is resolvable by rational problem solving, dilemmas have no "right" answers and, consequently, provoke uncertainty. For instance, if a teacher is teaching a reading group of 10 students and notices that 2 are whispering together while something is being explained to another child, the teacher is faced with a dilemma. If the teacher turns attention to the two whispering students, the one being taught suffers; if the whispering is ignored to attend to the student at hand, the whispering tends to spread. It is a dilemma. Similarly, if a teacher is teaching a group of 10 students and it becomes clear that 5 of them understand the task and 5 do not, the teacher is faced with a dilemma. If all 10 are held until they have *all* learned satisfactorily, the 5 who already know the task will lose interest; if the 5 who know it are dismissed, the other 5 may be embarrassed and made to feel stupid. Such dilemmas are endless in the daily life of teachers, and dealing with them makes teaching complex.

The problem of dilemma management is further complicated by the fact that the educational system often conditions teachers to believe that there are simple answers to the problems of instruction. For instance, teachers are often required to use certain instructional materials or certain procedures. These

The classroom is a complex place.

Conducting instruction with a basal textbook (courtesy of Michigan State University).

directives imply that such materials or procedures are panaceas that can solve a teacher's problems. Nothing could be further from the truth. Teaching is too complex; no one set of procedures or materials can possibly anticipate all the situations to be dealt with.

Of all the difficulties of classroom life, however, perhaps none is harder to deal with than the isolation of teaching. Whereas the classroom is a crowded social environment, it is an environment of children, not of adults. Classroom teachers are virtually isolated from other adults during the hours they are teaching; similarly, they are isolated from professional colleagues in other schools and school systems. As such, teachers face a professional loneliness. Trying to cope with the dilemmas and difficulties of classroom life when isolated from their peers adds to the complexity of teaching and classroom life.

These are but some of the factors that make teaching difficult. Contrary to public opinion, not everyone can deal with these complexities and still have the energy left to effectively teach students how language works. For 85 to 95 percent of American elementary school teachers, basal reading texts seem to be the answer.

THE DOMINANCE OF BASAL READING TEXTBOOKS

Whether or not you have recently been in an elementary school, you are probably familiar with the basal reader. It is that carefully structured reading book that typically contains a series of reading selections (fiction, nonfiction, and poetry) and that most of us remember as the focus of our elementary reading instruction. Each child in a reading group has the same book; children in different reading groups usually have different levels within the same series of books. During reading group time the students read the selections in their basal (either orally or silently), discuss the stories with the teacher, and complete the skill exercises in the accompanying workbook.

The basal text thrives for two reasons: First, it works. For teachers who have difficulty dealing with the complexity of classrooms and who consequently have little energy left to plan their own instruction, a basal textbook provides an organizational structure. It tells them what to do, tells them what to say, puts materials in the students' hands to keep them busy, and provides tests to determine whether progress is being made. In the hectic, frantic environment of classroom life it seems to be a lifesaver because by providing routines, procedures, and activities it structures the program and promotes the smooth flow of classroom life.

Second, the basal text thrives because it is accepted. It has been an integral part of the reading scene for so long that many school officials and teachers cannot conceive of conducting instruction without it. Further, there has in recent years been a growing movement toward systematizing and coordinating districtwide reading programs to provide a cohesive developmental sequence from kindergarten to Grade 8. A basal text with its carefully developed levels, cohesive skill sequence, and massive assistance to teachers seems to be tailor-made for providing such a system. In fact, basals are so ingrained in our educational system that even good teachers begin to doubt themselves if they are not religiously following the basal system. The following excerpt is from a letter written by a former student:

> I sometimes feel I am struggling against odds to give my kids a worthwhile reading program. I have tried a different approach this year by balancing basal skills with children's literature. We read anything from Arnold Lobel and Shel Silverstein to Beverly Cleary and Judy Blume. Although I'm aware there is more to reading than the recreational end, I feel a small miracle has taken place with my kids. They sit on the edge of their seats, they laugh out loud, they hold their breath, they get angry, but they can't wait to get to the next page! It never happened that way with the basal stories. Yet, I go through doubtful periods as I leaf through basal manuals wondering what horrible gaps I may be creating in these children's reading development.

This teacher, despite the fact that her students are not only in control of the reading process but are *excited* about it, feels guilty because she is not faithfully and mindlessly following the dictates of the basal system. Such is the pervasiveness of the basal text's influence!

However, despite its systematic characteristics and its apparent usefulness in making classroom life more manageable, basal texts are not a panacea. There *are* problems associated with their use. The first is that, in the process of using a basal to free themselves from some of the complexities of conducting reading instruction, teachers often transfer the responsibility for instruction from themselves to the basal. They expect the basal to provide the instruction, and if students do not learn it is the basal's fault, not the teacher's. In other words, they do not operate on the principle that the teacher makes the difference, but rather on the principle that the basal program makes the difference.

Second, because some teachers assign instructional responsibility to a basal text program, they do not plan instruction themselves. They do what the teacher's edition says to do and make sure that students cover the material. They focus on whether students get the right answer, assuming that correct responses mean that students are learning what the basal says they are supposed to learn. Such teachers seldom try to think of alternatives, because all the prescriptions are presumably in the teacher's edition. One need only read them and follow the directions. Hence, teachers become technicians who follow someone else's plans rather than professionals who make their own instructional decisions.

Finally, the faith teachers place in basals is unwarranted. Basal materials sometimes present information in confusing ways, emphasize rote practice and assessment exercises that promote answer-oriented instruction, and provide exercises that are often misleading and/or inaccurate.

Despite their deficiencies it is unlikely that basal texts will change appreciably in the near future. The reason is simple: they sell the way they are. Because teachers want help in ordering classroom life they request highly structured, answer-oriented basals, and because publishers are profit oriented they willingly provide them. Consequently, teachers will probably continue to use them. However, they should learn to use them well. That means use of basals should be based on the belief that teachers, not basals, make the real difference. Just how much difference teachers make will depend to a large extent on whether they are in control of the basal so that they use it rather than having it telling them what to do. To be in control teachers need to simplify the complexities of classroom life by carefully organizing instruction and implementing efficient classroom management procedures. Only if teachers organize and manage their classrooms efficiently will they have time to think about how to control their instruction and make their own decisions despite the presence of basal textbooks.

BECOMING AN INSTRUCTIONAL
DECISION MAKER

This textbook, then, is designed to help teachers become instructional decision makers when teaching reading. It puts a premium on helping to organize and manage the complexities of classroom life and to direct reading instruction even while using a basal text. Part III, "Getting Organized," provides specific details on how to make such decisions. Before getting into the specifics of instructional decision making, however, it will be helpful to review some of the more prominent characteristics of teachers who are effective decision makers.

First, such teachers think in terms of what students must learn, rather than what tasks they must complete. In reading, the ultimate outcome is for students to be in control of the "real" reading pursued by literate people. Therefore, instruction is not designed to get students to accurately complete skill exercises, but rather to develop literate people who can read whatever is available to them.

Second, such teachers view reading broadly. They see it not as a skill or series of skills or even as a discrete subject, but rather as a component of language in which the purpose is communication.

Third, these teachers understand the motivational aspect of learning to read. While it is important that students learn how to read, it is equally important that they *like* to read—that they read willingly in order to acquire information and enrich their lives.

Fourth, such teachers emphasize cognitive processing and awareness rather than rote memory and accurate answers. Instead of asking pupils, "Are you correct?" they prefer to ask, "How do you know you are correct?"

Fifth, such teachers are not dependent on a basal text. Instead, they view it as a tool, as a foundation, and as a guide, but not as an instructional imperative. Their reading program may begin with a basal text, but they typically modify, adjust, and innovate according to desired goals and individual needs.

Sixth, decision-making teachers know that the teacher's guides that accompany basal texts provide only tasks, activities, and directions. They seldom explain *how* to do a task successfully. Consequently, these teachers work hard at doing task analyses of reading assignments to create explicit instructions concerning *how* to do the tasks.

Seventh, these teachers are not looking for a panacea. They know that reading instruction is complex, that classrooms are complex, and that students and teachers are complex. They know that there can be no cure-all when so many complexities interact. Instead, they see themselves as constantly developing their instructional competence, but realize that they will never have "the answer."

Teacher decision making begins with careful planning.

Finally, because there is no perfect way to teach reading, these teachers never do things exactly the same from year to year. They are constantly thinking, changing, modifying, and innovating; they are always looking for a way to improve their instruction.

In sum, teachers who are effective decision makers are in control because they use professional knowledge rather than follow someone else's prescriptions. They are professionals who make their own decisions, not technicians who follow directions.

Perhaps one way to dramatize this difference is to note the way in which two teachers react when an instructional sequence does not lead to learning. In both examples the teacher has presented a lesson, and the students' answers indicate a lack of understanding. In each case the teacher is faced with the need to spontaneously generate a new explanation. The first teacher is a technician who slavishly follows the prescriptions of the teacher's guide. When the need to explain arises, she does not know what to do, so she continues asking for the correct answer.

> T: When you add an *apostrophe s* to *boy*, it shows that the boy has something. Can you make up a sentence for kittens?

Something belongs to the kittens.

S: There's a basket full of kittens.

T: That's what Jennie was doing over here. You added just an *s*.
That's more than one kitten. This time make it ownership.
Something belongs to this right here. Troy?

S: The kitten always owns the basket.

T: All right, but can you change your sentence around? You're saying the kitten owns the basket. Let's use kitten and basket.

S: Kitten basket.

T: But with the *apostrophe s*.

S: The kitten's basket.

T: The kitten's, that's the kitten's basket. All right. What belongs to
the kitten. Troy?

S: The basket.

In contrast, note the following teacher's response to the same kind of
problem:

T: Connector words are what, David?

S: Two words put together.

T: What are connector words, Josh?

S: Two words hooked together.

T: They are not two words. Maybe I explained that incorrectly. A
connector word is a word that connects one or more ideas.
Okay, in this sentence, "They always walk to school together,
and they always walk home together," there are two ideas.
They always walk to school, and they always come home. Of
the four connector words I put on the board, which word is
connecting the two ideas, David?

S: *And*.

T: *And*. Do you see that? *And*. I have it underlined here. See how
it is connecting the ideas of walking to school together and
coming home together? It is sort of like a bridge that connects
these two. Bridges connect different places, words connect
ideas. Connector words connect ideas.

This teacher is not under the control of the basal. She possesses professional
knowledge about reading and about how to instruct, and she uses this
knowledge analytically to generate a spontaneous explanation. As a result the
students' misconception is corrected, they become aware of how to do the task,
and they achieve.

CONCLUSION

Effective reading instruction requires more than drilling children, more than asking them for correct answers, and more than demanding that directions be followed accurately. Sense making must be constantly emphasized. Students must understand what reading is and how it works, what they are trying to accomplish when they read, *how* to go about getting correct answers, and how to control their own cognitive processing as they read. The emphasis is on thought, not memory; on understanding, not mechanics; on real-world application, not school tasks; and on conscious awareness, not rote response.

Unfortunately classroom reading instruction today rarely emphasizes sense making. Instead teachers tend to take students through basal materials using a recitation format that emphasizes accurate answer getting and artificial reading tasks. Behind this mechanical approach to reading instruction lies their need to cope with the complexity of classroom life. This task itself is so demanding that it becomes their primary objective, and they unwittingly shift their instructional responsibilities to the basal text program. As such, they operate as technicians following directions rather than as professionals thinking and acting for themselves.

This book is based on two principles. First, it assumes that students learn what teachers emphasize. If teachers focus on memory and accurate answers, students learn only facts and focus only on accuracy. If teachers focus on understanding and sense making, students learn to read for understanding and sense making. Second, the most effective teachers do not teach like technicians. They make decisions based on their professional knowledge. Teachers who make instructional decisions are not dominated by the classroom environment; they do not follow the directives of basal texts like a trained technician. Instead they take suggestions such as those presented in this book and try to improve on them.

This textbook is designed to put you in control of your reading instruction despite the realities and constraints of classroom life. If you are in control as the teacher, you will put your students in control of their reading—they will learn to be strategic in making sense of text and will learn to use reading in the real world outside of school.

CHECK YOUR UNDERSTANDING

Now that you have read the chapter, check your understanding by answering the Focus Questions presented at the beginning of the chapter. If you cannot answer one or more of the questions, return to the chapter, find the section that corresponds to the question, and reread.

SUGGESTED READINGS

Alvermann, D. E., & Boothby, P. R. (1982). Text differences: Children's perceptions at the transition stage in reading. *Reading Teacher, 36*(3), 298–302.

Blachowicz, C. L. (1983). Showing teachers how to develop students' predictive reading. *Reading Teacher, 36*(7), 680–684.

Durkin, D. (1984). Is there a match between what elementary teachers do and what basal reader manuals recommend? *Reading Teacher, 37*(8), 734–744.

Kopfstein, R. M. (1978). Fluent reading, language, and the reading teacher. *Reading Teacher, 32*(2), 195–197.

Lehr, F. (1982). Teacher effectiveness research and reading instruction. *Language Arts, 59*(8), 883–887.

Shannon, P. (1982). A retrospective look at teachers' reliance on commercial reading materials. *Language Arts, 59*(8), 844–853.

Singer, H. (1978). Active comprehension: From answering to asking questions. *Reading Teacher, 31*(8), 901–908.

Stern, P., & Shavelson, R. J. (1983). Reading teachers' judgments, plans, and decision making. *Reading Teacher, 37*(3), 280–286.

Wilde, S. J. (1979). The experience and consequences of literacy: A case study. *Language Arts, 56*(2), 141–145.

KNOWLEDGE: THE BASIS OF INSTRUCTIONAL DECISION MAKING

Part II provides the foundation knowledge you need to become an instructional decision maker when teaching reading. This knowledge is divided into three chapters: Chapter 2 on what you teach (curriculum), Chapter 3 on whom you teach (students), and Chapter 4 on how you teach (instruction).

At the end of this unit you should be able to state why these three knowledge sources are important to instructional decision making and to answer questions such as the following:

1. What do you teach in reading, and why do you teach it?
2. What is the normal progression in learning to read, and what conditions affect reading growth?
3. What constitutes instruction, and what are the major approaches to reading instruction?

CHAPTER **2**

The Reading Curriculum

GETTING READY

To be in control of your reading instruction, you must know what to teach. To know what to teach, you must know what reading is. This chapter defines reading, describes the outcomes to seek when teaching reading, and begins to describe what to teach to develop these outcomes.

FOCUS QUESTIONS

As you read this chapter use the following questions to guide your understanding of reading.

1. How does reading work? That is, how do readers get meaning from text?
2. How is reading defined?
3. What is the major outcome of reading instruction?
4. Given the nature of reading, what are the three major suboutcomes of reading instruction?
5. What does a good reader do that a poor reader does not do?
6. How is the reading curriculum organized?
7. What do you teach when you teach reading?

DESCRIBING READING

Traditionally, reading has been described as a series of competencies or skills to be mastered. These competencies represented the reading act when it was broken down into its component parts. For instance, it was logically assumed that the smallest unit in reading was the alphabet letter and its associated sound; hence, descriptions of reading often began with letters and letter-sounds, then progressed to syllables, then to words, then to phrases, then to sentences, and so on. The idea was that the best way to understand reading was to break it down into smaller pieces. Reading instruction consisted of teaching each of these separate parts, because it was assumed that reading would result when all the separate parts had been learned. Given this description, it is understandable why many teachers emphasize isolated skill instruction during reading; it makes sense if reading is a series of skills that, when added together, total reading.

However, this description of reading is inaccurate. Reading is not the performance of a series of independent skills; it is the simultaneous interaction of many abilities. Nor does reading begin with the alphabetic letter and proceed in an orderly progression to meaning. It starts by seeking meaning and uses a variety of sources, including letters, to create meaning. Similarly, reading does not consist of determining *the* meaning in text; it consists of constructing an interpretation of text based on what a reader already knows. Hence, reading is more than simply the sum of a set of component parts or skills.

SCHEMA

Humans organize thoughts and information into categories. All experiences are organized into mental structures called *schemata*. For instance, people have a mental structure for *birds* that reflects all their experiences with birds. Hence, when someone uses the word *birds* people activate their bird schema. Because of their background experiences, their mental structure for birds includes wings, flying, and other distinctive characteristics associated with birds.

Whenever people begin talking about a particular topic, they *compose* (or construct) a message by drawing upon the information they have in that schema. Whenever people listen to someone else talk about a topic, they *interpret* (or reconstruct) the message in terms of what they already know about the topic. The amount of information possessed on a given topic (or organized into a given schema) depends upon experience with or prior knowledge about that topic. The more people know about a topic, the richer their schema is and the better they will understand messages about that topic; the less they know, the more barren their schema is and the less they will understand about that topic. For instance, the authors of this book have a richer schema for reading instruction than students do because, unlike them, they have spent years teaching reading and studying effective reading instruction. Consequently, when the authors read a text on reading instruction they comprehend more and detect a richer network of associations than their students do.

ROLE OF PRIOR KNOWLEDGE

Language is the communication and clarification of thought from one person to another. In the case of this book, the authors want to communicate to the readers their thoughts about reading instruction so the readers' schema will become more like ours. We want the readers to understand reading instruction as we do.

Traditionally, reading educators have assumed that this kind of understanding resulted by pouring information into the minds of students as if they knew nothing about the topic to begin with. However, this is not how comprehension works. Rather than being a pouring-in process, comprehending is an interactive process. Whatever someone hears or reads about a topic

Field trips provide background knowledge that can be used when reading about related topics.

interacts with what that person already knows (or thinks he or she knows) about that topic. For instance, you know much about reading instruction simply by virtue of having gone to school yourself. Your classmates also know much about reading instruction for the same reason. However, none of you know exactly the same thing. Because you went to different schools, for instance, each of you has different preconceptions about reading instruction. When the information from this book interacts with your preconceptions about reading instruction, both you and your classmates actively interpret what you read in terms of what you have previously learned. Consequently, each of you creates slightly different meanings from this text.

THE ROLE OF INFERENCING IN COMPREHENDING

Because comprehension depends on *interpreting* new knowledge in terms of what is already known about a topic, virtually all comprehending is inferential. Whenever a person receives a spoken or written message, that person makes predictions about the intended meaning—predicts what the author is trying to communicate. These inferences are based on four kinds of prior knowledge:

1. Knowledge of letters and words.
2. Knowledge of what is already known about the topic.
3. Knowledge of the author's purpose.
4. Knowledge of the kind of text in which the message is found.

It works like this. First, the letters and words are examined for cues about the topic. People confirm their hypothesis about the topic and then use what they already know about that topic (in terms of their schema for the topic) to predict what the author means. They also make inferences based on what they know about the author's purpose in writing the selection and their own purpose for reading it. Finally, people predict meaning based on what they know about the literary structure being employed by the message sender, knowing, for example, that political speeches produce a different kind of meaning than comedians' dialogues or fables or editorials.

USING STRATEGIC BEHAVIOR WHEN READING

Readers are strategic when making such inferences. That is, they do not construct meaning randomly. A system of language conventions is employed to make sense of text and to monitor the meaning-getting process. When something does not make sense a reader stops, analyzes the situation in terms of what is known about the reading system, and tries to repair the blockage by using a *fix-it* strategy. For instance, if a reader who has a strong background in unions prepares to read a passage entitled "The Strike," a hypothesis develops that the message is going to be about unions and that schema is activated. However, when the first line of text starts out, "When Anne rolled her last ball and got her twelfth strike in a row," the reader will stop, confirm that the message is about a game rather than a union, fix the situation by substituting a bowling schema for the union schema, and continue reading. Such conscious strategic behavior is part of the reading act.

AN EXAMPLE OF HOW READING WORKS

Read the following text for another example of how reading works:

The Rotation

The rotation in a Piper Cherokee occurs at 60 miles an hour. When achieving that IAS, apply back pressure on the yoke and step on the right rudder. Soon you will achieve your best angle of climb.

When reading "The Rotation" you simultaneously used prior knowledge from a variety of sources. You used what you know about letters to identify the words *the rotation* in the title and probably predicted a meaning associated in some way with turn-taking or revolving. However, by the time you had read the first line you had encountered other words (such as *Piper Cherokee* and *60 miles an hour*) which caused you to revise that prediction. If you have enough prior knowledge about airplanes to include Piper Cherokees in your airplane schema, you probably predicted an airplane topic at this point although, unless you have a rich airplane schema, you may not have yet been able to construct a meaning for *rotation*. However, if you knew that this passage appeared in a chapter entitled "How to Take Off and Land a Small Plane," your choice of predictions for *rotation* would be narrowed to airplanes landing and taking off. On the other hand, if this passage appeared in a book on "The Favorite After-Dinner Jokes of Famous Toastmasters," you would start forming hypotheses about where the punch line is in relation to the word *rotation*. You would, in effect, abandon the schema for how to fly an airplane and get your mind in gear for a joke.

People use all these various knowledge sources almost simultaneously, monitoring their sense making as they proceed and being strategic about building sensible meaning. Every time people encounter unknown terminology (such as *IAS*) or a word (such as *yoke*) whose meaning they associate with a totally different topic, they generate new hypotheses. By testing hypotheses that are triggered by their knowledge of the letters, the topic, the purpose, and the text structure, they gradually construct the meaning the author intended for "The Rotation." Depending upon the richness of their small-plane schema, people may correctly infer that *rotation* refers to that point at which the plane first leaves the ground, or they may remain unclear about its precise meaning yet still comprehend the essential message about taking off.

Differences in schema are crucial. For instance, those who built a meaning for "The Rotation" based on a sparse schema for airplanes may get the essential sense of what is happening, but will not have a clear understanding of where the yoke is, what a rudder looks like, what is the best angle of climb, and so on. Most licensed pilots, however, will not only construct those additional meanings but will be critical of the use of the term *best angle of climb* because they will feel it is not precise enough to describe the situation. In short, they go beyond the text passage and make a judgment.

THE ROLE OF TEXT

The purpose of reading is to make sense out of text. The text is what authors create to convey their ideas. That is, authors want to send messages and they compose text to communicate these meanings. The meaning is in the author; the text carries the meaning. In composing text authors use conventions of a language system to signal their meaning to the reader who in turn uses understanding of the conventions of language to reconstruct the author's message from the text. Because the reader operates from a different set of schemata than the author, a slightly different message is usually reconstructed. Again, the meaning is *not* in the text; it is in the mind of the reader who uses the language conventions the writer has provided to reconstruct an interpretation of the author's message. Hence, reading is meaning seeking, tentative, and constructive. Any one sample of text may be interpreted in slightly different ways by different people who bring different meaning to it. For instance, earlier in this chapter the authors said that they are writing this text so that the readers will understand reading instruction in the same way they do. In actuality, however, the readers will not understand it in the same way because they bring to the text different schemata than the authors did when they wrote it.

SUMMARY

Reading is meaning getting, or comprehending the content of a text. Meaning results from the simultaneous interaction of a variety of information sources of which letters and sounds make up but one. Readers seek meaning using their prior knowledge about the letters and the words in a text, the topic, the purposes the text is designed to achieve, and the text structure. These knowledge sources interact simultaneously as readers predict the meaning of a text and gradually reconstruct an interpretation of the message employing fix-it strategies when the sense making breaks down. As a reader encounters and identifies words in a text, schematic associations are activated about the topic. As a reader encounters the literary structure of a text (whether it is set up as an essay or as an epic poem, for instance), expectations are triggered about what will be found in the text. And as a reader understands the author's purpose, the meaning of a text becomes clear. Inferences are made on the basis of these associations and expectations in order to reconstruct a representation of an author's message, and fix-it strategies are employed when text representations do not make sense.

Given this description, it is understandable that reading is not a set of isolated skills to be learned apart from real text in the expectation that meaning getting results when all the separate parts are mastered. Instead, reading is meaning seeking from the very beginning. Further, meaning is built (or reconstructed) by connecting new knowledge in a text with old knowledge from a reader's prior experience. This connecting occurs as a reader generates a series of hypotheses about what an author means. These hypotheses are generated and tested using interacting knowledge sources such as the printed page, a reader's schema, an author's purpose, and the form or structure of the text. Implicit in all this is the concept that readers have positive attitudes about reading because they understand the communication function of language and appreciate the joy and utility of reading. Not only do they construct meaning, they value the role reading plays in their lives. Consequently, reading is defined as follows: *Reading is the reconstruction of the author's printed message for functional and/or recreational purposes.*

OUTCOMES OF READING INSTRUCTION

Chapter 1 states that the major goal of reading instruction is to put students in control of the reading process so they can make sense out of the messages authors attempt to convey. Instruction has been successful if students use reading for functional and recreational purposes and are in control of the process of getting meaning from text.

However, because of the complex nature of reading, this major goal can be broken down into the following three components or subgoals: (1) developing positive responses and concepts that encourage reading growth (*attitude outcomes*), (2) developing an understanding of how the reading system works (*process outcomes*), and (3) developing an ability to use process knowledge to comprehend the message that is the content of a text (*content outcomes*).

Students' attitudes toward reading are a reflection of the experiences they have had with reading. Teachers should provide experiences designed to develop an understanding of what reading is and to develop positive responses to reading. These are called attitude outcomes. The second component is called process outcomes because it focuses on *how* readers get meaning from text — on the language conventions that are used to communicate meaning. Teachers should show students how the reading system works and strategies for fixing up blockages to meaning. The third component is content outcomes because it focuses on understanding and remembering what the text says. Teachers should teach students to get messages from two major kinds of text: functional texts that are written to inform (such as textbooks, newspapers, recipes, and so on) and recreational texts that are written to entertain and enrich (such as novels, poems, fables, and so on).

Developing all three components — a positive attitude toward reading, an understanding of how reading works, and an ability to use this understanding to comprehend text — will produce readers who are in control of the reading process and who can use text for functional and recreational purposes. Figure 2.1 provides a graphic illustration of the outcomes of reading.

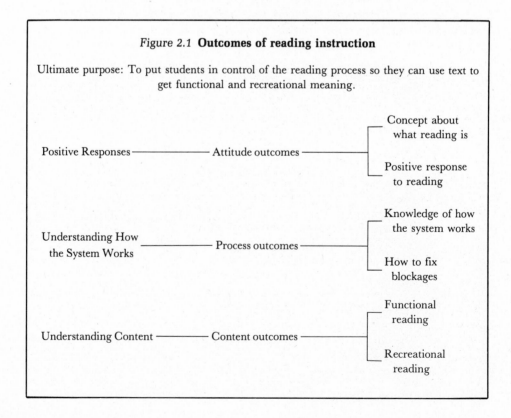

Figure 2.1 Outcomes of reading instruction

Ultimate purpose: To put students in control of the reading process so they can use text to get functional and recreational meaning.

Positive Responses —————— Attitude outcomes ——————
- Concept about what reading is
- Positive response to reading

Understanding How the System Works —————— Process outcomes ——————
- Knowledge of how the system works
- How to fix blockages

Understanding Content —————— Content outcomes ——————
- Functional reading
- Recreational reading

ATTITUDE OUTCOMES

To control the reading process students must have a concept of what reading is and must feel that reading is an activity worth pursuing. A student who has an incomplete or erroneous concept of reading or who perceives reading negatively is unlikely to gain control of the reading process and use it purposefully.

Concept. A concept is the combination of all the characteristics you associate with something. Each concept is organized as a mental structure or schema, as previously described. For each concept a person usually has a word label. The common concept *dog* mentally generates many characteristics because of rich experience with that word. The word *platypus*, however, may generate only a few characteristics because the concept *platypus* is not as rich as that of *dog*. Because each person has had different experiences, each one generates a slightly different set of characteristics for each word. Even a common word like dog results in slightly different concepts or mental pictures because of people's varying experiences with dogs.

Because a concept is the mental combination of all the characteristics associated with a word label, it is dependent upon a person's experiences with

Real reading activities in classrooms build accurate concepts about the usefulness of reading.

the word. In reading, for instance, if the school experience emphasizes worksheets, drill, and correct answers during the reading period, students think reading is worksheets, drill, and correct answers. If, in contrast, the school reading experience emphasizes genuine communication and important meaning getting, making sense out of written messages, and using reading to meet needs and/or to solve problems, students think reading is meaning getting, sense making, and problem solving.

One of the major goals in reading instruction is to help students build the concept that reading is a meaning-getting activity. Such a concept of reading contributes to a positive attitude about reading and to conditions that promote reading growth. To build this concept, teachers should provide students with reading experiences that highlight the fact that text is produced by writers, a writer has a real message to convey, and all reading involves the interpretation of a writer's message. When genuine communication prevails, students think of reading as person-to-person message sending; the inanimate book and printed page are seen as a vehicle authors use to represent meaning; and reconstructing an author's message is the focus.

Similarly, experiences with reading should emphasize the relationship among all the various language modes: listening, speaking, reading, and writing. Students then learn that (1) speaking and writing involve a message sender who composes a message, and listening and reading involve a message receiver who interprets a message; (2) reading and writing are not different subjects but, rather, are closely related; and (3) both reading and writing focus on meaning.

To evaluate students' concepts of reading, collect data about what students think reading is. Do their comments during class discussions reflect an understanding that

1. Reading is message sending and receiving?
2. Someone wrote the message?
3. The reader's job is to interpret the message?
4. Reading and writing are similar to listening and speaking?

If students do not understand what reading is they will be less than enthusiastic about learning to read.

Positive Responses. Because teachers want students to use reading independently for either functional or recreational purposes, they must encourage positive responses to reading. The object is to have students read without outside help, *choose* to read, *like* to read, and use reading for both practical and enriching purposes. In short, teachers want students to feel good about reading.

A positive attitude toward reading is closely tied to one's concept of reading since it is difficult to feel good about something that is improperly or partially understood. A full and accurate concept of reading provides the foundation for a positive response to reading. If students are involved in meaningful reading activities — reading that calls for the interpretation of important and/or interesting written messages — the chance of achieving a positive response is good. The chances become even better when these reading experiences are pleasurable and rewarding, rather than boring "work." Hence, to create a positive response to reading, teachers provide reading experiences that are fun and that reflect the message-sending and message-getting essence of reading.

To evaluate students' positive responses, collect data about how students feel about reading. How often do students choose to read recreational and/or functional materials independently? What evidence is there that they enjoy such reading? If students choose not to read on their own, instruction has not been effective.

PROCESS OUTCOMES

It is important to develop readers who fluently and accurately reconstruct messages from text; that is, they get the author's message with a minimum of difficulty. To accomplish this, teachers not only give students reading material they care about, but also help them understand how they get meaning from that material. Consequently, the second outcome of reading instruction focuses on how reading works. There are two aspects to understanding the reading process: knowledge of how one gets meaning from text when things are going smoothly and how to repair blockages to meaning getting when things are not going so smoothly.

Knowledge of How the Reading System Works. This chapter has already explained that readers get information from text by simultaneously using knowledge about the words, the topic, the author's purpose, and the type of text. Through the interaction of these four sources of knowledge a reader forms hypotheses about meaning, confirms or modifies these as the reading progresses, and gradually constructs an interpretation of the overall message.

Although this interactive process occurs almost instantaneously, for illustrative purposes it is often helpful to create a logical sequence one follows in constructing meaning. This sequence may be described as follows. The reading process begins when readers confront or prepare to confront some text. On the basis of their understanding of the topic (e.g., the rules of baseball) the kind of text employed (e.g., information book), and the author's purpose (to convey the basic procedures in playing the game), readers activate appropriate schemata. In this case schemata are activated for rules of baseball, the structure and format of information books, and how their purposes fit with the author's purpose. The first step, then is to activate schemata relative to the topic, type of text, and author's purpose. In a sense it is a preparatory step in which readers select information needed to make sense out of an author's message.

Second, readers begin identifying each word or group of words on the page, working from left to right and from top to bottom. Third, as the words are identified readers attach personal meaning to each familiar word that fits the context of their understanding of the topic, text type, and purpose. Fourth, as subsequent words are identified readers begin making predictions about the author's intended meaning. These predictions are guided not only by the word meanings but also by other meanings associated with the text (such as understanding the author's purpose) and by syntactic cues (such as sentence order, prefixes and suffixes, and special-purpose words such as prepositions and conjunctions). Fifth, readers begin confirming, rejecting, or modifying the predicted meanings in terms of using their own schemata and the cues imbedded in the subsequent sections of the text. Finally, if the prediction is confirmed, the readers go on; if it is not (if the prediction no longer makes sense in view of subsequent meaning cues), readers use fix-it strategies to repair the blockage so that meaning getting can continue.

This process can be illustrated with the following example.

Time flies. You can't; they fly too fast.*

As you confront the text you begin to activate appropriate schemata. In this case only topical schemata can be activated, because no clues to text type or author purpose are provided. The topic you probably activated was the colloquial reference to how quickly time passes. As your eyes moved across the page from left to right you identified the individual words, made a prediction that the passage was about how quickly time passes, and called upon semantic meanings consistent with the time schema. You probably continued with this prediction until you met the word *they*. At this point your self-monitoring system activated an alarm because there is a syntactic inconsistency between the singular *time* and the plural *they*. You must discard the time prediction, return to the beginning, and initiate a fix-it strategy before text processing can continue.

When readers are consciously aware of how reading works, they can use that knowledge to get meaning. Figure 2.2 shows how readers can check their

---

* Wilson, C. (1983). Teaching reading comprehension by connecting the known to the new. *Reading Teacher, 36*(4), 366–369.

Figure 2.2 **Types of knowledge about how reading works**

Knowledge about words
- instant identification of common words
- having a conceptual meaning for the words

Knowledge about topic
- what is already known
- weaving new knowledge with known

Knowledge about purposes
- author's purpose in creating a text
- reader's purpose in reading a text

Knowledge about text
- type of text (narrative, expository, etc.)
- structure of text (e.g., the *grammar* of the text; whether it is a story, chronological, causal)

Knowledge of how to be fluent
- instant recognition of words
- using knowledge of topic, purpose, and text to predict intonation

knowledge of words in the text, predict meaning by consciously activating what they already know about the topic, and refine these predictions by reference to: (1) their own purposes and those of the author, (2) their knowledge of the text structure, and (3) their knowledge of how the text message should sound when read aloud. Because they understand how reading works, they have a general strategy for comprehending, and they tend to read the text in a smooth and natural-sounding way.

To determine whether students have achieved this outcome, collect data regarding how accurately and how fluently they construct messages from text and how aware they are of the reading strategies they employ. If students are not conscious of how they get meaning, they are not prepared to read independently the variety of texts encountered throughout life.

Strategies That Restore Meaning. Ideally students should always fluently reconstruct meaning using what they know about the words, the topic, the purpose, and the type of text. Realistically, however, they encounter (1) words they can neither identify nor comprehend, (2) ideas they are unable to interpret, and (3) central themes and/or conclusions they are either unable to perceive or lose track of during the course of their reading. In such cases students need fix-it strategies they can use to remove the blockage and restore meaning and fluency.

In order for readers to eliminate problems that disrupt meaning, three conditions must exist. First, they must recognize that the text is not making

Teaching students how to reason with reading skills *(courtesy of Michigan State University).*

sense. As previously noted, this means constantly monitoring comprehension and when meaning is blocked saying something like, "Oh, oh; something is wrong here." Second, they must recognize the source of the blockage, for example, a new word or one whose meaning is unclear, a syntactic inconsistency, or perhaps a theme inference or conclusion that has been missed. Identifying the source of the difficulty usually demands that the student go back over the text just read. Such look-backs are an essential part of strategic reading. Third, they must have a set of fix-it strategies that can be used to remove the blockage and restore fluency.

As noted earlier, there are four kinds of fix-it strategies (see Figure 2.3). These correspond to the typical attempts readers make to generate new meanings once their original predictions have broken down. To illustrate, look again at the text about time.

Time flies. You can't; they fly too fast.

To reiterate, most readers will activate a schema for *time* and will predict that this text is about its swift passage. However, when reading the word *they,* most readers stop and say, "Oh, oh; something's wrong here." Their hypothesis has broken down and they begin searching for a way to fix it up.

The first thing most readers do is ask themselves the question, "Do I know the individual words?" Then they reread the text after first activating a set of word-analysis or decoding strategies that help them determine whether the individual words were correctly identified. To do so they use context strategies (figuring out whether each word makes sense in the sentence), structural analysis strategies (examining prefixed and suffixed words to determine if they were used correctly) and, as a last resort, phonics strategies (sounding the word out letter by letter or syllable by syllable). In the case of *time flies*, you find that you did have the individual words right. You then proceed to a second set of strategies.

For most readers, the second level of fix-it strategy involves activating either knowledge of grammatical structure (*syntax*) or word meanings (*semantics*). For instance, the conflict between *time flies* and *they* causes good readers to activate their knowledge about syntax, to note that the syntactical sequence of *time flies* could be verb-to-noun as well as the more common noun-to-verb order, and then to make the prediction that *flies* may not be a reference to swift movement, but rather a reference to insects. A reader might then predict that the passage is about insects, reread the text, confirm the hypothesis, and

---

Figure 2.3 **Types of fix-it strategies**

Level 1 Strategies for decoding words
- Context (meaning surrounding an unknown word)
- Structural analysis (prefixes, suffixes, root words)
- Phonics (letter sounds)

Level 2 Strategies for generating alternative schemata
- Syntactic knowledge (grammatical structure)
- Semantic knowledge (meaning associated with words, topic, purpose, and/or text type)

Level 3 Strategies for using visible cues
- Syntactic cues
    word order (e.g., noun-verb sequence)
    typographic (e.g., punctuation, italics)
    key function words (e.g., conjunctions, prepositions)
- Semantic cues
    structural analysis (e.g., prefixes, suffixes)
    context (meaning surrounding an unknown segment)

Level 4 Strategies for inferring from prior knowledge
- Topic knowledge (what is being discussed)
- Purpose knowledge (why it is being read)
- Text type knowledge (e.g., expository, narrative, newspaper)

proceed. The same thing happens with word meanings in "The Rotation." Most readers initially ascribe to *rotation* the meanings *turn taking* or *revolution*. However, when predictions based on those meanings break down, a reader tries to think of other meanings and proceeds to test them.

A third set of fix-it strategies is used when neither of the first two restores the meaning. This third set involves looking for visible cues that clarify either syntactic or semantic difficulties and lead to new predictions. They are visible on the printed page. For instance, a reader looks for syntactic cues to meaning by examining word order, typographic cues (punctuation, italicized words, and so forth) and key function words (prepositions, conjunctions, and so forth). Semantic clues to meaning include examination of the structural character of words (prefixes and suffixes) and their context (the meaning surrounding unknown words). In the syntactic category an example of word-order cues (specifically, verb-noun sequence) was seen in *time flies*. An example of typographic cues to meaning can be observed in noticing the difference between *Larry, my brother, went with me*, and *Larry, my brother went with me*. Examples of key function word clues are words such as *first, next*, and *finally* to signal sequence or *because* and *so* to signal cause–effect. In the semantic category, an example of structural characteristics is the difference between *follow* and *unfollowable* or between *approve* and *disapprovingly*. Finally, an example of context is *"A biplane, an airplane with two wings, flies fast,"* in which the semantic meaning of *biplane* is identified right in the sentence.

If meaning is still missing, readers may need to resort to a fourth set of strategies. Rather than searching for visible cues on the printed page, readers may have to look inside themselves for what is known from background experience and then infer. These cues are invisible because, rather than being on the printed page, they are in the reader's mind. Here, the reader asks, "What do I know about this type of text (poem, directions, and the like), the author's purpose, or the topic that would help me repair the meaning blockage? In contrast to the previous category, these clues are mental, imbedded in the reader's available schema knowledge. For instance, if the meaning blockage is in a story, the reader could think about what is know about how stories follow a sequence from setting, main character, problem, events connected to the problem, and problem resolution. Inferences regarding the author's target audience and purpose in writing the text can also provide clues, as can general knowledge of the topic being discussed (facts, themes, judgments, and so on).

Some people think of fix-it strategies as reading skills. Skills, however, are procedures that are memorized and applied rotely rather than tools applied flexibly and adaptively for repairing meaning breakdowns. Consequently, reading skills tend to be used automatically rather than thoughtfully and strategically for fixing blockages to meaning. Students associate such skills with academic tasks such as worksheets or tests, but seldom use them to restore

meaning in real text. Consequently, while basal texts usually refer to these procedures as reading skills, this book will refer to them as *strategies*. They should
be taught as flexible plans to be consciously used to repair meaning blockages,
not as procedures to be automatized.

To assess this outcome, notice when fluency is disrupted whether students
analyze the nature of the blockage, apply a strategy that removes the blockage,
and continue reading fluently. If students are unable to independently repair
breaks in fluency, instruction has not been effective.

CONTENT OUTCOMES

The third major subcomponent of reading instruction is the development of a
reader's ability to get meaning from the text being read. Reading instruction
has a means–ends relationship that is useful in teaching students how reading
works (process outcomes) as a means of getting the text message (content outcomes). This application of process knowledge to text content is discussed in
terms of the two major kinds of text—functional and recreational—found in
elementary schools.

A student reading functional text to understand content.

Functional Text. Functional text is written to convey information. Textbooks are a good example, as well as newspapers, catalogs, recipes, job applications, encyclopedias, and various kinds of written directions. Basal textbooks usually include examples of functional text. For instance, a basal text might include a selection on giraffes taken from an information book entitled "Animals of Africa" or a news article on the space shuttle.

Since it is so important for students to comprehend functional text, effective teachers require students to use textbooks, references sources, newspapers, catalogs, and other examples of functional text found in the real world. When presenting these activities to students, teachers normally guide the reading process to help students get the meaning. They orient students to the specific terminology and any unknown words; provide introductory activities that activate topical schema; provide information about the author's purpose when writing the text and the student's purpose in reading it; and help students anticipate and interpret text structure. In short, they help students activate the four knowledge sources used in getting meaning from text: the words, the topic, the author's purpose, and the type of text.

Recreational Text. Recreational text, written primarily to entertain and to enrich, includes fiction such as short stories, novels, and fictionalized biographies. In this category also are poems, fables, mythology, fairy tales, and other folk literature. To help students comprehend and appreciate recreational text, teachers use recreational text in a variety of activities. Uninterrupted sustained silent reading (USSR) is a widely used activity in which both students and teachers quietly read books of their choice. Other practices include reading aloud to students daily from a short story or novel and having students share their favorite books with each other.

Basal textbooks typically contain numerous selections of recreational reading written specifically for children. When presenting such text to students, teachers normally provide guidance similar to that given for functional text. That is, teachers prepare students for the selection by helping them activate prior knowledge about the words, topic, purpose, and type of text. In addition, teachers often use recreational reading activities to develop students' ability to interpret literary devices such as metaphors and symbolism.

SUMMARY

Reading is defined as reconstructing the author's printed message for functional and/or recreational purposes. A good reader is one who (1) chooses to read independently; (2) understands the general strategy for getting the author's message and consciously uses it to remove blockages to meaning getting; and (3) applies what is known about reading in order to understand content. None of these three outcomes is more important than the others, nor is one prerequisite to another. Rather, all three outcomes develop together and interact in supporting and encouraging reading growth.

Evaluate the effectiveness of reading instruction by collecting data about students' experiences with reading, their general reading strategies, their ability to repair breaks in fluency with appropriate fix-it strategies, and their ability to get meaning from functional and recreational text. Instruction is effective only if students are in control as they read various kinds of text.

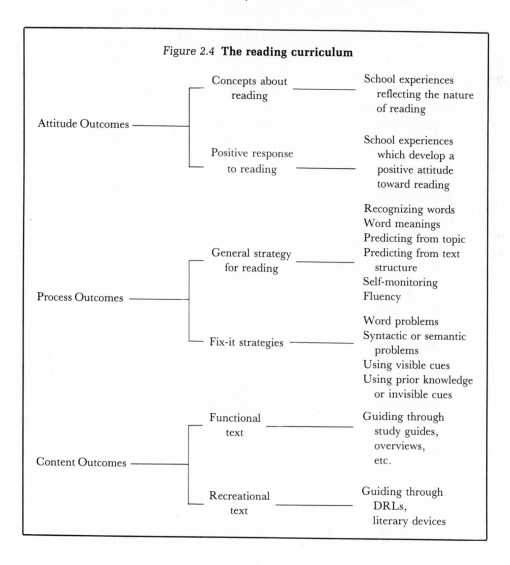

Figure 2.4 **The reading curriculum**

Attitude Outcomes

Concepts about reading —————— School experiences reflecting the nature of reading

Positive response to reading —————— School experiences which develop a positive attitude toward reading

Process Outcomes

General strategy for reading —————— Recognizing words
Word meanings
Predicting from topic
Predicting from text structure
Self-monitoring
Fluency

Fix-it strategies —————— Word problems
Syntactic or semantic problems
Using visible cues
Using prior knowledge or invisible cues

Content Outcomes

Functional text —————— Guiding through study guides, overviews, etc.

Recreational text —————— Guiding through DRLs, literary devices

BUILDING A READING CURRICULUM

Reading instruction is designed to develop attitude, process, and content outcomes. These outcomes are imbedded in the reading curriculum, that is, in the formally developed plans that describe what is to be learned.

Teachers make decisions about the reading curriculum—about *what* to teach in reading—in reference to *why* they teach reading. Because it is important that students understand and enjoy reading, part of the curriculum focuses on this. It is also important that students understand how they get meaning from text, and part of the curriculum focuses on this. Additionally, students must understand the content of various types of texts, and part of the curriculum focuses on helping students get content from functional and recreational text. In short, reading instruction should center around the concepts and attitudes that create positive conditions for the growth of reading ability, the knowledge of how reading works, and the ability to get meaning from text.

A reading curriculum is a direct reflection of the three outcomes to foster in reading. As shown in Figure 2.4 a reading curriculum is designed to achieve each of these outcomes. To develop attitude outcomes, teachers create experiences and activities designed to build desired concepts and positive responses. To develop process outcomes, teachers teach students what to do to generate fluent predictions about an author's meaning and show students how to restore meaning when the predictions are not confirmed. To develop content meaning, teachers guide students in the interpretation of functional and recreational text. Teaching these things develops students who control their own processing of recreational and functional text.

CONCLUSION

The crucial difference between technicians and professionals is that professionals know why they are teaching what they teach. Technicians, on the other hand, teach according to the directions of a teacher's manual or workbook exercise. They do not have a rationale for their teaching. Unless teachers know *why* they teach what they do, it is unlikely that their instructional program will hang together well. The technician's emphasis on isolated tasks, mechanics, and surface answers as discussed in Chapter 1 creates a disjointed and mechanical instructional program. In short, knowing the "why" behind your teaching activities is the first step in becoming a professional decision maker.

A central focus of this book is the emphasis on justifying your instructional decisions in reference to desired reading outcomes. While there are many classroom constraints that limit what you can do and materials you can use, professionals rise above these constraints because they not only know what they are teaching, they know why they are teaching it. They intentionally shape instructional tasks and materials to create desired attitude, process, and content goals. Their mental command of the curriculum puts them in cognitive control of instruction and provides the basis for continuous modification and improvement. It is this cognitive autonomy that the authors want you to develop.

CHECK YOUR UNDERSTANDING

Now that you have read the chapter, check your understanding by answering the Focus Questions presented at the beginning of the chapter. If you cannot answer one or more of the questions, return to the chapter, find the section that corresponds to the question, and reread.

SUGGESTED READINGS

Artley, A. S. (1980). Reading: Skills or competencies? *Language Arts, 57*(5), 546–549.

Auten, A. (1985). Focus on thinking instruction. *Reading Teacher, 38*(4), 454–456.

Babbs, P. J., & Moe, A. J. (1983). Metacognition: A key for independent learning from text. *Reading Teacher, 36*(4), 422–426.

Canady, R. J. (1980). Psycholinguistics in a real-life classroom. *Reading Teacher, 34*(2), 156–159.

Chomsky, C. (1976). After decoding, what? *Language Arts, 53,* 288–296.

Downing, J. (1982). Reading—skill or skills? *Reading Teacher, 35*(5), 534–537.

Fitzgerald, J. (1983). Helping readers gain self-control over reading comprehension. *Reading Teacher, 37*(3), 249–253.

Garner, W. I. (1984). Reading is a problem-solving process. *Reading Teacher, 38*(1), 36–47.

Gemake, J. (1984). Interactive reading: How to make children active readers. *Reading Teacher, 37*(6), 462–466.

Golden, J. M. (1984). Children's concept of story in reading and writing. *Reading Teacher, 37*(7), 578–584.

Guthrie, J. T. (1984). Comprehension instruction. *Reading Teacher, 38*(2), 236–238.

Jones, L. L. (1982). An interactive view of reading: Implications for the classroom. *Reading Teacher, 35*(7), 772–777.

Lipson, M. Y. (1984). Some unexpected issues in prior knowledge and comprehension. *Reading Teacher, 37*(8), 760–764.

Otto, J. (1982). The new debate in reading. *Reading Teacher, 36*(1), 14–18.

Pearson, P. D. (1976, March). A psycholinguistic model of reading. *Language Arts, 53*(3), 309–314.

Rand, M. K. (1984). Story schema: Theory, research and practice. *Reading Teacher, 37*(4), 377–383.

Roney, R. C. (1984). Background experience is the foundation of success in learning to read. *Reading Teacher, 38*(2), 196–199.

Sanacore, J. (1984). Metacognition and the improvement of reading: Some important links. *Journal of Reading, 27*(8), 706–712.

Shuy, R. W. (1982). What should the language strand in a reading program contain? *Reading Teacher, 35*(7), 806–812.

Strange, M. (1980). Instructional implications of a conceptual theory of reading comprehension. *Reading Teacher, 33*(4), 391–397.

Tatham, S. M. (1978). Comprehension taxonomies: Their uses and abuses. *Reading Teacher, 32*(2), 190–194.

Wilson, C. R. (1983). Teaching reading comprehension by connecting the known to the new. *Reading Teacher, 36*(4), 382–390.

CHAPTER 3

Students and Their Reading Growth

GETTING READY

Chapter 2 discussed the goals of reading instruction and developed general guidelines for what to teach in reading. This chapter turns to those who receive reading instruction. First, it describes the developmental reading stages that students move through and the reading curriculum associated with each stage. Then, it discusses the conditions that affect how quickly or slowly students move through these stages. Finally, this chapter suggests an initial diagnostic strategy to help you determine each student's stage of developmental reading growth.

FOCUS QUESTIONS

As you read this chapter use the following questions to guide your understanding of students' reading growth.

1. What are the stages of developmental reading?
2. What is the typical curriculum at each stage?
3. What curricular outcomes tend to get emphasized at various grade levels?
4. What verbal reasoning factors affect the rate of reading growth?
5. What perseverance factors affect the rate of reading growth?
6. How can you determine a student's development reading stage?

STAGES OF DEVELOPMENTAL
READING GROWTH

Imagine a total school population from kindergarten through twelfth grade. Many of the five-year-olds in the kindergarten will be preparing to read, many of the six-year-old first graders will be beginning to read, and so on through the twelfth grade where, hopefully, all students will be literate. Because most students learn to read in a steady, progressive, predictable pattern, classroom reading instruction is often called *developmental reading*. This simply means that the instruction provided in a particular grade is part of a developmental progression. The different points along this line of development are called *stages of developmental reading growth*.

There are many ways to describe and label the stages of developmental reading growth. This book refers to five stages, starting with the earliest development and continuing through high school.

The first level is labeled the *Readiness Stage*, and includes preschool, kindergarten and first grade. At this level most students are not actually reading, but are preparing to do so. Oral-language activities are generally used to help them learn the attitude, process, and content goals needed to begin actual reading. An example of the curriculum taught at this level is shown in Figure 3.1.

Figure 3.1 **Sample curriculum emphases at the Readiness Stage**

I. *Attitude Outcomes*
    A. Concepts—what reading is
        1. Talk written down
        2. Written by someone who is trying to say something
        3. For enjoyment
        4. For getting information
    B. Positive responses—How a student feels
        1. Excitement from reading
        2. Satisfaction from reading
        3. Knowledgeable from reading
II. *Process Outcomes*
    A. Knowledge about how reading works
        1. Words
            a. Developing print awareness of words
            b. Developing letter and word knowledge
        2. Using prior knowledge, purpose, and text structure to construct

meaning in listening situations
- a. Reading involves the use of prior knowledge and clues from the text to predict what the author is going to say
- b. Authors write and readers read for many purposes
- c. Meaning can be predicted if an author's purpose is known
- d. Stories have beginnings, middles, and ends

B. Fix-it strategies
1. Word analysis
   - a. Context (predicting what word fits an oral context)
   - b. Phonics
     - (1) Developing print awareness for letters and letter sounds
     - (2) Auditorily discriminating letter sounds
     - (3) Associating letters and sounds
     - (4) Blending sounds
2. Generating new predictions in listening situations
   - a. From syntax (using word order)
   - b. From semantics (using word meanings)
3. Visible cues to listening comprehension
   - a. To syntax (using word order)
   - b. To semantics (using context to complete oral sentences)
4. Invisible cues to listening comprehension
   - a. Type of text (using story structure: beginning, middle, end)
   - b. Purpose (determining author's purpose)
   - c. Topic
     - (1) Classifying words by a single relationship
     - (2) Making judgments about fantasy or reality

III. *Content Outcomes*
A. Recreational and functional texts
1. Getting meaning from story narratives read to students
2. Getting meaning from simple expository texts read to students

The second level is called the *Initial Mastery Stage* and ordinarily begins in the first grade and continues into the second grade. It is at this stage that most students actually begin to read print. During the Initial Mastery Stage students are able to read preprimers, primers, and other materials associated with beginning reading. At this time students learn the appropriate attitude, process, and content goals with a particular emphasis on word identification. An example of the curriculum taught at this level is shown in Figure 3.2.

The third stage is called the *Expanded Fundamentals Stage* and ordinarily begins in the second grade and continues into the fourth. At this stage a student's reading level expands into second-, third-, and fourth-grade materials due to an increased mastery of the fundamentals of reading. Curriculum emphasis con-

Figure 3.2 **Sample curriculum emphases at the Initial Mastery Stage**

I. *Attitude Outcomes*
    A. Concepts—what reading is
        1. A message written by an author for a reader
        2. For enjoyment
        3. For information
    B. Postive responses—how a student feels
        1. Excitement about reading
        2. Satisfaction from reading
        3. Knowledgeable from reading
        4. Satisfies curiosity by reading
II. *Process Outcomes*
    A. Knowledge about how reading works
        1. Words
            a. Developing word meanings
            b. Recognizing high-utility words instantly
            c. Recognizing easily confused words instantly
        2. Prior knowledge, purpose, and text structure
            a. Authors have specific purposes when they write
            b. Predictions about meanings are more accurate when the author's purpose is known
            c. There are story structures and expository text structures
            d. Text structure, prior knowledge, and author's purpose help to predict and verify meaning
        3. Fluency
            a. Stories are read in a pattern similar to oral language
    B. Fix-it strategies
        1. Word analysis
            a. Context (identifying words using the context of a sentence)
            b. Structural analysis (identifying words using common affixes)
            c. Phonics
                (1) Identifying words by using initial- and final-consonant letter sounds
                (2) Identifying words by using phonogram sound units
        2. Generating new predictions
            a. From syntax (using word order)
            b. From semantics (using word meanings)
        3. Visible cues
            a. To syntax
                (1) Using typographic cues
                (2) Using word order
                (3) Using inflectional endings

(4) Using key words
b. To semantics (using context to identify words and meaning)
4. Invisible cues
   a. Type of text (using text structure and format)
   b. Purpose (determining author's purpose)
   c. Topic
      (1) Making inferences about relationships when key words are stated
      (2) Classifying words and phrases
      (3) Making judgments about content of message
III. *Content Outcomes*
  A. Recreational text (getting meaning from story narratives)
  B. Functional text (getting meaning from simple expository text)

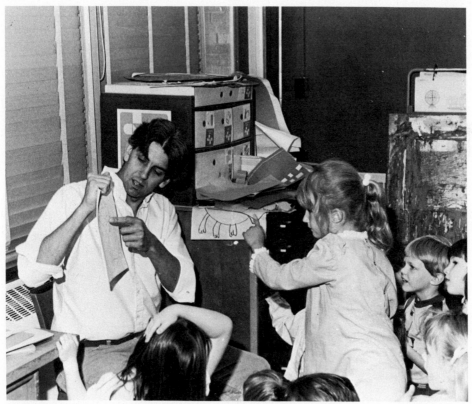

Students at the Readiness Stage engaged in prereading activities.

tinues to include attitude, process, and content outcomes, but the emphasis on word identification diminishes and the emphasis on comprehension increases. An example of the curriculum taught at this level is shown in Figure 3.3.

The fourth stage of developmental reading growth is called the *Application Stage* and ordinarily begins at about the fourth grade and continues into the eighth grade. It is called the Application Stage because students are greatly involved not only with basal reading textbooks but also with textbooks for other curricular areas, such as social studies, science, and mathematics. They apply what they have learned about reading to these other content areas. At this stage emphasis is on attitude, process, and content outcomes that support such application. An example of the curriculum taught at this level is shown in Figure 3.4.

The fifth stage of developmental reading growth is called the *Power Stage.* It typically begins in the eighth grade and can continue long after formal schooling ends. It is called the Power Stage because students can handle almost any kind of reading. Because it typically occurs at the postelementary school level, the Power Stage is not emphasized in this book. However, the curricular emphasis shifts at this level, particularly as it relates to functional reading typically encountered in high school. An example of what is typically taught at the Power Stage is listed in Figure 3.5.

First-grade students at the Initial Mastery Stage reading beginning reading books.

Figure 3.3 **Sample curriculum emphases at the Expanded Fundamentals Stage**

I. *Attitude Outcomes*
    A. Concepts—what reading is
        1. Communciation between a writer and a reader
        2. For enjoyment and information
        3. Predicting meaning
        4. Sense making
        5. A tool
    B. Positive responses—how a student feels
        1. Excitement from reading
        2. Satisfaction from reading
        3. Knowledgeable from reading
        4. Curious from reading
        5. A sense of power from reading

II. *Process Outcomes*
    A. Knowledge about how reading works
        1. Words
            a. Recognizing high-utility words instantly
            b. Recognizing easily confused words instantly
            c. Developing word meanings, including multiple-meaning words
        2. Prior knowledge, purpose, and text structure
            a. The meaning of several sentences can be predicted using what is known about the topic
            b. Predictions about meaning are based on what is known about the topic combined with what is known about the words, the purpose, and the text structure
            c. Good readers know their purpose for reading the text and the author's purpose for writing it
            d. Different kinds of meaning are conveyed by different kinds of text
            e. There are many types of text structures (e.g., stories, articles, poems, letters)
        3. Fluency
        Expressive text is read in a pattern reflecting the intonation intended by the author
    B. Fix-it strategies
        1. Word analysis
            a. Context (identifying words using the context of surrounding sentences)
            b. Structural analysis
                 (1) Identifying words by analyzing compounds
                (2) Identifying words using contractions
            c. Phonics (identifying words using phonograms and vowel generalizations)

    2. Generating new predictions
       a. From syntax (using word order)
       b. From semantics (using word meanings)
    3. Visible cues
       a. To syntax (using key words to note phrase relationships)
       b. To semantics (using context to predict sentence meaning)
    4. Invisible cues
       a. Type of text (using text structure and format)
       b. Purpose (determining author's purpose)
       c. Topic
          (1) Making inferences about relationships when no key words are stated
          (2) Classifying sentences
          (3) Making judgments about word choice within a message
    5. Study skills
       a. Locating information in order to understand
       b. Organizing information in order to understand
       c. Reading text efficiently
III. *Content Outcomes*
   A. Recreational text
     1. Getting meaning from various forms of expressive text
     2. Getting meaning from various literature genre
   B. Functional text
     1. Getting meaning from expository text (e.g., textbooks)
     2. Using question–answer relationships (QARs) to get meaning

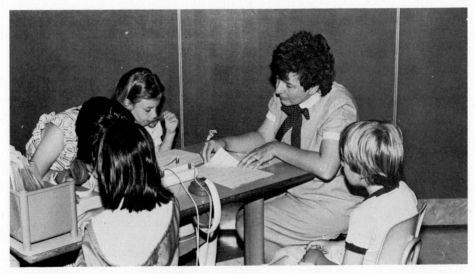

Third-grade students at the Expanded Fundamentals Stage learning how to comprehend.

Figure 3.4 **Sample curriculum emphases at the Application Stage**

I. *Attitude Outcomes*
   A. Concepts—what reading is
      1. Authors have purposes for writing text; readers have purposes for reading text.
      2. Reading can clarify knowledge, feelings, and attitudes
      3. Reading can expand knowledge, feelings, and attitudes
      4. Reading is a valuable tool
      5. Reading meets needs
   B. Positive response—how a student feels
      1. Excitement from reading
      2. Satisfaction from reading
      3. Knowledgeable from reading
      4. Curious from reading
      5. A sense of power from reading
II. *Process Outcomes*
   A. Knowledge about how reading works
      1. Words
         a. Recognizing instantly 95% of the words encountered in text
         b. Developing word meanings
      2. Prior knowledge (the meaning of paragraphs can be predicted using knowledge of topic)
      3. Purpose (reading makes the most sense when the purpose of the writer and the reader coincide)
      4. Text structure (various kinds of text have various structures that can be used to predict meaning)
      5. Fluency (functional text is read in sense-making units)
   B. Fix-it strategies
      1. Word analysis
         a. Context (identifying words using the context of the paragraph)
         b. Structural analysis (identifying words through recognition of common prefixes and suffixes)
         c. Phonics (using syllabication to identify words)
      2. Generating new predictions
         a. From syntax (using word order)
         b. From semantics (using word meanings, including multiple meanings)
      3. Visible cues
         a. To syntax (using key words to note paragraph relationships)
         b. To semantics (using context to predict and verify paragraph meaning)
      4. Invisible cues
         a. Type of text (analyzing text into meaningful units)
         b. Purpose (verifying purpose through content)
         c. Topic

              (1) Classifying paragraphs
              (2) Drawing conclusions from paragraphs based on prior knowledge
              (3) Making judgments about text in reference to prior experience
        5. Study skills
           a. Locating information in order to understand
           b. Organizing information in order to understand
           c. Reading content efficiently

III. *Content Outcomes*
    A. Recreational text
        1. Getting meaning from various forms of expressive text
        2. Getting meaning from various literature genre
    B. Functional text
        1. Getting meaning from expository and content-area text
        2. Using question–answer relationships (QARs) to get meaning from content
        3. Getting meaning from text containing heavy conceptual loads

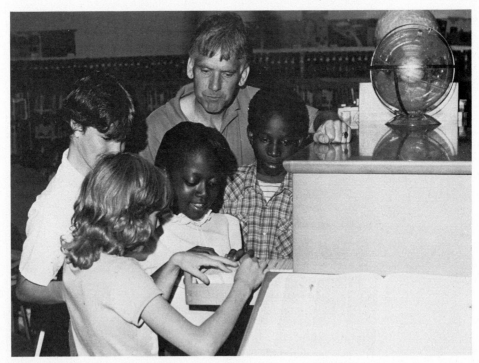

Sixth-grade students at the Application Stage learning to use study skills.

Figure 3.5 **Sample curriculum emphases at the Power Stage**

I. *Attitude Outcomes*
    A. Concepts—what reading is
        1. Can clarify knowledge, feelings, and attitudes
        2. Can expand knowledge, feelings, and attitudes
        3. Is a valuable tool
        4. Meets needs
        5. Can solve problems
    B. Positive responses—how a student feels
        1. Excitement from reading
        2. Satisfaction from reading
        3. Knowledgeable from reading
        4. Curious from reading
        5. Powerful from reading
II. *Process Outcomes*
    A. Knowledge about how reading works
        1. Words
            a. Continued development of instantly recognized words
            b. Continued development of word meanings
        2. Prior knowledge
            a. Determines the concept for a word and the meaning we attach
               to text
            b. Can be used to predict and synthesize meaning across types of
               text
        3. Purpose (text can be read for a reader's selective purposes)
        4. Text structure (text can be analyzed by structure, which provides
           clues to meaning)
        5. Fluency (text is read in sense-making units according to purpose and
           structure)
    B. Fix-it strategies
        1. Word analysis
            a. Context (identifying words using context of the selection)
            b. Structural analysis
                (1) Identifying words through recognition of less common
                    prefixes and suffixes
                (2) Identifying words through recognition of Greek and
                    Latin roots
            c. Phonics (none)
        2. Generating new predictions
            a. From syntax (using word order)
            b. From semantics (using word meanings)
        3. Visible cues
            a. To syntax (using key words to note relationships among
               selections)

        b. To semantics (using context clues to predict and verify meanings)
    4. Invisible cues
        a. Type of text (verifying meaning through text structure)
        b. Purpose (verifying purpose through content)
        c. Topic
            (1) Classifying across selections
            (2) Drawing conclusions
            (3) Making judgments based on experience and values
    5. Study skills
        a. Locating information in order to understand
        b. Organizing information in order to understand

III. *Content Outcomes*
    A. Recreational text
        1. Getting meaning from various forms of expressive text
        2. Getting meaning from various literature genre
    B. Informational text
        1. Getting meaning from expository and content-area text
        2. Using question–answer relationships (QARs) to get meaning from content-area text
        3. Getting meaning from text containing heavy conceptual loads

In summary, this book organizes the reading curriculum in terms of both the desired outcomes and the various stages of developmental reading growth. Curriculum developers use these two categorical schemes to decide what should be taught to the average, normally progressing student at any given grade level. Professionals who make instructional decisions (rather than following the dictates of a teacher's manual) need to know what constitutes a normal developmental sequence in reading to evaluate both the validity of the curriculum provided in the basals and the progress of students.

CURRICULAR EMPHASES AT VARIOUS STAGES

As Figure 3.6 illustrates, the relative emphasis given the three curricular outcomes varies according to the stages of developmental growth even though all three outcomes are treated at every developmental stage. For instance, a kindergarten teacher would expect to emphasize attitudes almost 50 percent and content less than 25 percent of the time whereas a twelfth-grade teacher would reverse this emphasis. Similarly, the emphasis within any particular outcome varies from one developmental level to another. The emphasis on content goals is greatly recreational at the Readiness and Initial Mastery levels where story narratives are frequently used and is greatly functional at the Application and Power levels where expository text is emphasized. The emphasis on process is emphasized at the Initial Mastery and the Expanded Fundamentals levels where many fix-it strategies are taught, and focuses more on knowledge of how the language system works at the higher levels. The emphasis on attitudes stresses developing a concept of reading at the early stages, but emphasizes creating a positive response at the later stages.

Another way to think about the relative curriculum emphasis at various stages of developmental reading growth is shown in Figures 3.7–3.11. These figures illustrate which outcomes are introduced, which are stressed, and which continue to be developed at each stage of growth.

Although all the curricular outcomes are taught at each stage of developmental reading growth, each stage is characterized by its particular curricular emphasis. When teaching a particular grade level, teachers need to know what that particular emphasis is. Chapters 11 through 14 on conducting instruction are organized to reflect these curricular emphases.

Figure 3.6 **Curricular emphases at various stages**

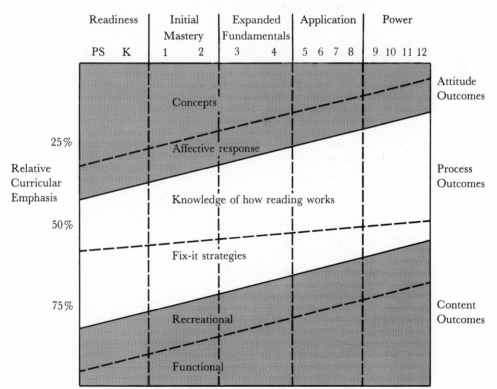

Figure 3.7 **Readiness Stage**

Outcomes	Relative Emphasis
Attitude Outcomes	
Concepts and positive responses	Stressed (in listening comprehension)
Process Outcomes	
Knowledge about how reading works	
Words	Stressed (print awareness)
Prior knowledge, purpose, and text structure	Introduced (listening comprehension)
Fix-it strategies	
Word analysis	Stressed (print awareness)
Generating new predictions using visible clues and using invisible clues	Introduced (in listening comprehension)
Content Outcomes	
Recreational and functional text	Stressed (in listening comprehension)

Figure 3.8 **Initial Mastery Stage**

Outcomes	Relative Emphasis
Attitude Outcomes	
Concepts and positive responses	Stressed
Process Outcomes	
Knowledge about how reading works	
Words	Stressed
Prior knowledge, purpose, and text structures	Stressed
Fluency	Introduced
Fix-it strategies	
Word analysis	Stressed
Others	Introduced
Content Outcomes	
Recreational and functional text	Stressed

Figure 3.9 **Expanded Fundamentals Stage**

Outcomes	Relative Emphasis
Attitude Outcomes	
Concepts and positive responses	Stressed
Process Outcomes	
Knowledge about how reading works	
Words	Continued development
Prior experience, purpose, and text structure	Continued development
Fluency	Stressed
Fix-it strategies	
Word analysis	Continued development
Generating new predictions using visible and invisible cues	Stressed
Study skills	Introduced
Content Outcomes	
Recreational text	Stressed
Functional text	Stressed

Figure 3.10 **Application Stage**

Outcomes	Relative Emphasis
Attitude Outcomes	
Concepts and positive responses	Continued development
Process Outcomes	
Knowledge about how reading works	
Words, prior knowledge, purpose, text structures	Continued development
Fluency	Continued development
Fix-it strategies	
Word analysis, generating new predictions using visible and invisible cues	Continued development
Study skills	Stressed
Content Outcomes	
Recreational text	Stressed
Functional text	Stressed

Figure 3.11 **Power Stage**

Outcomes	Relative Emphasis
Attitude Outcomes	
Concepts and positive responses	Continued development
Process Outcomes	
Knowledge about how reading works	
Words, prior knowledge, purpose, text structures	Continued development
Fluency	Continued development
Fix-it strategies	
Word analysis, generating new predictions using visible and invisible cues and study skills	Continued development
Content Outcomes	
Recreational text	Stressed
Functional text	Stressed

CONDITIONS THAT MODIFY STUDENT GROWTH

There is a danger in discussing stages of developmental reading growth because it may create the impression that all students develop "normally." First-grade teachers may expect all their students to be at the Initial Mastery Stage, third-grade teachers may expect all of their students to be at the Expanded Fundamentals Stage, and so on. Such is not the case. A more accurate expectation is that some of the students at each grade level will follow a normal developmental reading progression, but others will not. In fact, one of the factors that makes classroom teaching so complex and difficult is that the students, whereas alike in age, are at varying stages of developmental reading growth and therefore cannot be taught the same things simultaneously. In one third grade, for instance, it is not unusual to have 25 students of which only 15 are at the Expanded Fundamentals Stage where you would expect to find normal third graders. Of the remaining 10 students, 5 may be developing slower than normal and still be in the Initial Mastery Stage whereas the other 5 may be developing faster than normal and be in the Application Stage. Translated into reading levels this means that of the 25 students in this third grade, there could be 2 reading in a first-grade basal; 3 reading in a second-grade basal; 8 reading in the easier of the two third-grade basals; 7 reading in the harder of the two third-grade basals; 3 reading in a fourth-grade basal; and 2 reading in a fifth-grade basal. If each student is to receive appropriate instruction, six different reading groups would be necessary.

Classroom teachers must understand this reality in order to make good decisions about reading instruction. The first step is to understand why the variance in normal reading growth occurs. To some degree, differences can be attributed to varying quality of instruction. However, even when instruction is excellent, differences in student progress occur. Consequently, it is important to understand the factors affecting varying rates of progress.

VERBAL REASONING

A student's ability to understand and respond to instruction is influenced by an aptitude for verbal learning. Some people learn to read faster than others simply because they have an aptitude for reading. Just as some people have an aptitude for mechanics or mathematics or poetry writing and others do not, some people have more aptitude for learning to read than others. There is nothing wrong with either the fast developers or the slow developers, it is just that some have more aptitude in that area than others. We call this aptitude *verbal reasoning*.

Background experience influences verbal reasoning and, ultimately, reading development. Some students come to school with rich experiences that enhance verbal reasoning. They have been to many different places, they have had a variety of vicarious experiences through the media, they have encountered many different ideas and concepts, their oral vocabulary is rich and varied, and their families value accepted school behavior. Conversely, other students have seldom been outside their immediate neighborhood, they have had limited vicarious experiences, they have been exposed to few ideas and concepts, their oral vocabulary is limited, and their families may not value accepted school behavior. Since reading involves constructing meaning using prior knowledge and text information, students with rich background experience can be expected to construct meaning easier and progress faster in learning to read than students whose background experience is sparse.

Similarly, culture and cultural variations influence one's aptitude for learning to read. Our society includes children from various cultural backgrounds, including white middle class, Mexican, black, Vietnamese, small town, and urban to mention but a few, and they must all learn side by side. Even when language is no problem, each culture may have its own traditions and its own expectations for how to do things. The ways of one culture are not better than the ways of another, they are just different. Some cultures, however, are tied more closely than others to what is considered appropriate school behavior. For instance, the expectations associated with school materials, rules, and teacher attitudes may be new to students from certain minority cultures. Conversely, students whose cultural tradition matches the expectations of schools have less trouble adapting to the materials, rules, and teachers because of background familiarity with the way things are done. For instance, the Oriental cultures revere teachers and teacher–student interactions that are very formal; consequently, Oriental students sometimes have difficulty adjusting to the more informal teacher–student interactions typically found in American schools. These cultural differences may affect verbal reasoning and, ultimately, progress in learning to read.

Language variations of several kinds influence students' aptitude for understanding and responding to instruction. For instance, it is not unusual in many American schools to find students from immigrant homes who do not speak English at all. Since they speak whatever language is spoken in the home, these students have difficulty with the verbal reasoning associated with instruction and move more slowly through the developmental stages. Similarly, some students have dialects that differ greatly from the dialect used for instruction. This, too, will occasionally impede students' movement through the developmental stages. Special language problems such as these are discussed in greater detail in Chapter 16.

Keep in mind that differences in developmental reading growth are found in all classrooms and may stem from factors that influence students' verbal reasoning. You will see such differences in every class you teach. They must be taken into account in order to understand why some students are learning more quickly than others.

PERSEVERANCE

Verbal reasoning problems account for some differences in the rate of developmental reading growth, but they do not account for all. Perseverance also explains some differences in the rate of reading growth. There are four conditions that affect perseverance: *expectancy, self-concept, motivation,* and *interest.*

Expectancy is the most influential condition since all humans tend to do what is expected of them. Children from homes where reading and learning is valued tend to have positive expectations regarding learning to read. Because important people in their lives expect them to learn to read, they *do* learn to read. This phenomenon is called a *self-fulfilling prophecy* because humans tend to fulfill the expectations set for them.

Teachers also set expectations that quite often are subtly communicated. For instance, by regularly calling on certain students more than others, by regularly praising some students more than others, and by setting slightly higher academic standards for some students than for others, a teacher creates the expectation that certain students are smarter and capable of learning more than others.

Communicating expectations can be insidious. Teachers can communicate negative or positive expectations without knowing they are doing so. For instance, in a classroom having both male and female students, teachers may unconsciously work harder with students of the same gender thereby setting more positive expectations for the favored group and less positive expectations for the other group. Such positive and negative expectations influence students' perseverance and, ultimately, the rate of developmental reading growth. The students for whom positive expectancies are set tend to persevere and, hence, to learn to read faster than those for whom negative expectancies are set.

Self-concept is closely related to expectations. It refers to the image that people hold of themselves. If a student has a positive self-image, the chances for normal developmental reading growth are good; if a student has a negative self-image, the chances for normal developmental reading growth are not as good. People's positive and negative self-images are closely related to expectation because they develop their self-images from their perceptions of what other people think of them. If families and teachers set high expectations for students, they tend to develop positive self-images. If families and teachers set low expectations for students, or expect them to be ineffective or unimportant, they tend to develop less positive self-images. The more positive a self-image, the more confidence there will be in attacking difficult tasks such as learning to read. Hence, a positive self-image helps a student persevere in moving through the stages of developmental reading growth.

Both motivation and interest also influence a student's perseverance. Interest refers to a student's response to the *topic* being pursued. For instance, a student who responds more positively to the topic of baseball than to the topic of race cars has more interest in baseball. By arranging instruction to include topics that are of interest to students, teachers can increase their perseverance; that is, students will be more tenacious in pursuing tasks.

Motivation refers to a student's response to the activity being pursued. For instance, a student who responds more positively to problem-solving activities than to memory activities will be more motivated when doing problem-solving activities. A student who responds more positively to composing activities than to copying activities will be more motivated when composing than when copying. Also, certain activities are often preferred because students know they can complete them successfully. By arranging instruction to include activities that motivate students, teachers can increase their perseverance. The key to both interest and motivation is a student's response — the more positive a student's response to topic and activity, the more perseverance there will be in pursuing the reading task. When there is more perseverance there is a better chance that normal progress will be made.

To summarize, a student's rate of progress through the stages of developmental reading growth is greatly influenced by both perseverance and verbal reasoning. Both are necessary for learning to read. Therefore, since students possess different amounts of verbal reasoning and perseverance, expect them to move through the stages of developmental reading growth at different rates of speed, even if the instruction provided is excellent.

MAKING DECISIONS ABOUT DEVELOPMENTAL STAGES

If there are stages of developmental reading growth, and if students in any particular classroom move through these at different rates, then each classroom will contain students from several stages. How can teachers determine at what stage each student is and, if appropriate, the reasons why a student is moving faster or slower than expected?

One reading specialist argues that a student's health as a reader can be determined by checking the vital signs of reading, just as the physical health of a person can be determined by checking the vital signs of the body.* The vital signs of reading health are the three curricular outcomes specified in Chapter 2. If a student (1) has an accurate concept of what reading is and responds positively to reading (attitude outcomes), (2) understands how reading works and possesses fix-it strategies (process outcomes), and (3) can get content meaning from functional or recreational text (content outcomes), then the student is a "healthy" reader. If, however, a student is deficient in one or more of these categories, a problem exists.

To make decisions about a student's reading health, teachers use knowledge about the goals of reading (the vital signs) and knowledge about what constitutes normal progress for the student's age (stages of developmental reading growth). A checklist such as the one shown in Figure 3.12 can be modified to fit each stage of developmental reading growth and can be used as a tool in deciding about a student's vital signs. For each student the teacher checks *yes* or *no* in the left-hand column for each of the vital signs at a particular stage of developmental reading growth, making the necessary decision on the basis of data collection techniques such as those listed in the right hand column. If *yes* is checked for each vital sign at that developmental level, a student can be said to be a healthy reader at that stage of reading growth.

Similarly, if a student is not at the developmental stage normally expected

* Sherman, G. (1985). A personal communication. Michigan State University.

Figure 3.12 **Making decisions about the vital signs of reading**

Student's name: _____

Student's age and grade: _____

What would be the student's *expected* stage of developmental reading growth? _____

Does the student exhibit the vital signs of healthy reading associated with the stage of reading growth that is normal for that age and grade?

What data should I collect to find out the answers to these questions?

I. Attitude Outcomes

A. Concept of what reading is

____ yes ____ no Understands that reading is meaning getting?

____ yes ____ no Has a rich concept regarding the function of reading?

Interview student about reading.
Observe how student makes use of reading.
Observe student's response to reading.

B. Positive response

____ yes ____ no Has positive feelings toward reading?

____ yes ____ no Likes to read?

Interview student.
Observe student during free time, reading times, etc.
Observe student's response to various kinds of reading situations.

II. Process Outcomes

A. Knows how reading works

____ yes ____ no Knows most words instantly?

____ yes ____ no Has concepts for the words met in reading?

____ yes ____ no Uses prior knowledge to predict meaning?

____ yes ____ no Uses author's purpose to predict meaning?

____ yes ____ no Uses knowledge of text structure to predict meaning?

Listen to student read text at grade level.
  Are 95% of the words recognized instantly?
Select words from text materials and ask student to use them orally in sentences.
Give student several reading tasks and ask student to tell you how meaning is obtained and how words, topic, purpose, and text structure are used.

____ yes ____ no Reads with fluency?

Listen to how the student reads orally and check whether what is read sounds smooth and natural.

Figure 3.12 **Making decisions about the vital signs of reading** (continued)

B. Uses strategies to restore meaning

    1. Word analysis

____ yes ____ no Analyzes unknown words using context? | Give student a sentence that can be read but has a word missing. Is the missing word correctly predicted?

____ yes ____ no —using structural analysis? | Give student words with affixes. Are the words correctly identified?

____ yes ____ no —using phonics? | Give student nonsense words containing phonic elements that should be known at that level. Are the words correctly pronounced?

    2. Generates new predictions

____ yes ____ no Uses syntactic cues to look back and generate new predictions? | Give student passages to read that are somewhat difficult and have student read them out loud. When student encounters difficulty, observe whether student looks back and starts over with a new prediction. Ask student questions to see if student is consciously making new predictions.

____ yes ____ no Uses semantic cues to look back and generate new predictions?

    3. Visible cues
        To syntactic meaning

____ yes ____ no Constructs meaning using typographic cues? | Give student a paragraph with typographic cues and have student tell how these were used to construct meaning.

____ yes ____ no Uses roots and affixes? | Give student affixed words and have student explain how the meaning of the root word was changed.

____ yes ____ no Uses key words? | Give student a grade-level paragraph with relationships signaled by key words and ask student questions regarding the relationships.

        To semantic meaning

____ yes ____ no Uses context? | Give student a grade-level sentence with one unknown word and ask student to predict what the unknown word means.

    4. Invisible cues
        Text type

____ yes ____ no Analyzes text and text structure? | Give student samples of text and ask student to tell you what clues they offer for meaning.

Figure 3.12 **Making decisions about the vital signs of reading** (continued)

        Purpose

____ yes ____ no Matches author purpose   Give student sample of text and ask student
                 with reader's purpose?   to identify author's purpose, student's own
                                                        purpose, and how these relate to meaning
        Topic   getting.

____ yes ____ no Constructs meaning by   Give student a list of grade-level words and
                 classifying?   have student classify them into categories
                                       and label them.

____ yes ____ no Infers from gist?   Have student read a grade-level paragraph
                                        and ask questions that require inference
                                       from gist.

____ yes ____ no Infers relationships?   Have student read a grade-level paragraph
                                        in which relationships are inferred and ask
                                        questions about the relationships.

____ yes ____ no Draws conclusions?   Have student read a grade-level paragraph
                                        and ask questions that require drawing
                                       conclusions.

____ yes ____ no Makes judgments?   Have student read a grade-level paragraph
                                        and ask questions that require making
                                       judgments.

III. Content Outcomes

A. Functional reading

____ yes ____ no Reads and understands   Give the student samples of functional text
                 expository text?   and check understanding by having
____ yes ____ no Reads and understands   student summarize and/or answer
                 directions?   questions about text context.
____ yes ____ no Reads and understands
                 specialized kinds of
                 functional text
                 (recipes, application
                 forms, etc)?

B. Recreational reading

____ yes ____ no Reads and understands   Give student samples of recreational text and
                 stories?   check understanding by having student
____ yes ____ no Reads and understands   summarize and/or answer questions about
                 poems?   text content.
____ yes ____ no Reads and understands
                 specialized kinds of
                 narratives (fantasy,
                 folk literature, etc.)?

Figure 3.13 **Making decisions about conditions for reading growth**

Student's name: _____

Student's age and grade: _____

What do the vital signs say is the student's stage of development growth? _____

Conditions affecting reading growth	What data should I collect?
Perseverance	
____ yes ____ no Has a positive expectation?	Interview student.
____ yes ____ no Has a positive self-concept?	Observe student's behavior and interactions.
____ yes ____ no Is interested?	Observe what topics student chooses to pursue.
____ yes ____ no Is motivated?	Observe what activities student chooses to pursue.
Verbal Reasoning	
____ yes ____ no Has an aptitude for verbal learning?	Check general achievement history; note oral language; check extent of oral vocabulary.
____ yes ____ no Has experience background?	Interview student about various topics and depth of understanding.
____ yes ____ no Has cultural background?	Interview student and parents; make home visit.
____ yes ____ no Has language variations?	Converse with student.

for a person of that age, a teacher can use the checklist in Figure 3.13 to make decisions regarding why the discrepancy exists. This checklist lists (1) the verbal reasoning and perseverance factors that influence the rate of reading progress and (2) suggestions for collecting data for each of the conditions. For a student who is not making satisfactory progress, there will invariably be _no's_ checked for certain factors influencing verbal reasoning and/or perseverance. Hence, a teacher can use knowledge about factors that modify normal reading development to make decisions regarding why a student's progress is unusually fast or slow.

CONCLUSION

For many students, reading ability develops at a steady rate and in predictable stages. Each stage of normal reading growth is characterized by the type of reading task a student is able to perform. Whereas there is a normal rate of progress through the various reading stages, not all students progress at this rate. Faster developers are characterized by aptitudes and background conditions that support verbal reasoning and perseverance and allow them to capitalize on instruction. Slower developers lack some of these aptitudes and supporting conditions.

To be an effective teacher, you must monitor vital signs and use your knowledge of normal patterns of reading growth to make decisions about a student's reading placement in a particular classroom. Similarly, use your knowledge about vital signs to make initial decisions about what aspects of the reading curriculum should be emphasized and about what factors are influencing students' verbal reasoning and perseverance.

CHECK YOUR UNDERSTANDING

Now that you have read the chapter, check your understanding by answering the Focus Questions presented at the beginning of the chapter. If you cannot answer one or more of the questions, return to the chapter, find the appropriate section that corresponds to the question, and reread.

SUGGESTED READINGS

Anselmo, S. (1978). Improving home and preschool influences on early language development. *Reading Teacher*, *32*(2), 139–143.

Criscuolo, N. P. (1979). Effective approaches for motivating children to read. *Reading Teacher*, *32*(5), 543–546.

Evans, J. R., & Smith, L. J. (1976). Psycholinguistic skills of early readers. *Reading Teacher*, *30*(1), 39–43.

Fredericks, A. D. (1982). Developing positive reading attitudes. *Reading Teacher*, *36*(1), 38–40.

Heathington, B. S., & Alexander, J. E. (1984). Do classroom teachers emphasize attitudes toward reading? *Reading Teacher*, *37*(6), 484–488.

Lang, J. B. (1976). Self-concept and reading achievement — An annotated bibliography. *Reading Teacher*, *29*(8), 787–793.

Mass, L. N. (1982). Developing concepts of literacy in young children. *Reading Teacher*, *35*(6), 670–675.

Omotoso, S. O., & Lamme, L. L. (1979). Using wordless picture books to assess cross cultural differences in seven year olds. *Reading Teacher*, *32*(4), 414–419.

Pieronek, F. T. (1980). Do basal readers reflect the interests of intermediate students? *Reading Teacher*, *33*(4), 408–415.

Roettger, D. (1980). Elementary students' attitudes toward reading. *Reading Teacher*, *33*(4), 451–453.

Weeks, T. E. (1979). Early reading acquisition as language development. *Language Arts, 56*(5), 515–521.

Wixson, K. K. et al. (1984). An interview for assessing students' perceptions of classroom reading tasks. *Reading Teacher, 37*(4), 346–352.

CHAPTER **4**_____

Components of Instruction and Methodology

GETTING READY

Previous chapters focused on understanding reading—its nature, goals, and developmental stages. But you must also know *how* to teach reading, and that is the focus of this chapter. First, this chapter differentiates between direct and indirect instruction and then describes various approaches to instruction and how each one organizes the reading program. Finally, the combined approach to reading instruction recommended in this book is described.

FOCUS QUESTIONS

As you read this chapter use the following questions to guide your understanding of how to teach reading.

1. What is the distinction between teaching and instruction?
2. What is the definition of instruction?
3. How is instruction distinguished from practice, application, and assessment?
4. What are indirect and direct instruction?
5. What are the major approaches to reading instruction?
6. How does each approach shape the organization of the reading program?
7. What are the distinguishing features of the instructional approach recommended in this chapter?

THE BACKGROUND TO INSTRUCTION

Learning intended curricular outcomes is what schooling is all about. In reading the intended outcomes are the attitude, process, and content goals described in Chapters 2 and 3. Learning occurs when a student develops or changes (1) an attitude about reading; (2) an understanding about how reading works, and/or (3) a particular meaning from a text. Learning attitude, process, and content outcomes can develop whether teachers are present or not; in fact, it can happen without schools. Many children learn much about reading before they enter school. However, students—especially low-aptitude students— seldom learn all they need to learn outside school. To ensure that all children learn the desired reading goals in a reasonably uniform way, schools provide instruction.

THE DISTINCTION BETWEEN TEACHING AND INSTRUCTION

Teaching is a global term encompassing much of what a teacher does in the course of the school day. *Instruction* is a more specific term that focuses only on what the teacher does to intentionally create desired curricular outcomes. The first step in understanding instruction, therefore, is to distinguish between what teachers do to create desired curricular outcomes and what they do to keep their classes moving smoothly, to keep up morale, to make children feel good about themselves, and so forth.

CHARACTERISTICS OF INSTRUCTION

There are three characteristics of instruction. First, it is an *intentional effort* by the teacher to provide students access to the information needed to develop a particular curricular goal. Second, it uses *pedagogical strategies* designed to help develop the intended goal. These pedagogical strategies include some kind of work and a description of how to do that work. The work may be traditional school activities such as completing written assignments or reading particular pages in a book or nonacademic activities such as free reading or putting on a play. Whatever the work is, however, the teacher chooses it as a method of developing the attitude, process, or content outcome being taught. A teacher gives a presentation to provide students with information about how to do the task—how to achieve the attitude, process, or content outcome being taught. A presentation may be direct and overt or indirect and covert, but in either case, it is designed to help students achieve the goal and is part of the teacher's pedagogical strategy. Third, instruction involves a dynamic and subtle *interaction between teacher and students*. Because students come to an instructional setting with some degree of prior knowledge and experience (a schema) for what is being taught, they inevitably interpret the work and the teacher's presentation of it. After "sizing up" the work and the teacher's presentation in light of their prior knowledge, students restructure the situation to fit their understanding of this kind of work and their perception of what the teacher really wants them to do. The lesson then progresses, and in the absence of any further interaction between teacher and students, students learn what they have interpreted the task to be, which is not necessarily what the teacher had in mind (see Figure 4.1).

To ensure that students interpret what the teacher says in ways that lead to the intended curricular goals, instruction must include interaction between teacher and students (see Figure 4.2). That is, students must be given an opportunity to act upon their interpretation of what the work and the presentation meant; the teacher must then note the response, decide how the students have restructured, elaborate upon the original presentation, and give the students another opportunity to respond. This cycle of asking students for responses, noting their restructuring, elaborating on the presentation in light of the student's interpretation, and then asking for another response repeats itself until the students demonstrate the attitude, process, or content outcome being taught.

Instruction is characterized by the intention to provide information, the use of pedagogical strategies, and teacher elaboration during interaction with students. Instruction is like building a bridge between a student and a curricular goal that will lead the student to the achievement of the outcome. These bridging experiences consist of work that a teacher intentionally structures so the students think about a goal in a certain way. It starts with a teacher deciding upon the outcome to be achieved and then creating and demonstrating the classroom work designed to achieve this outcome. The student actively sizes up or interprets the work. In short, the student is not a passive recipient of instruction but, instead, is an active interpreter of instruction.

After interpreting the task at hand, the student performs the work accordingly. What is learned is the interpreted outcome, not necessarily the intended one. For instance, a teacher who wants students to learn letter sounds may assign a ditto sheet that requires students to draw lines from each letter to a picture of an animal whose name begins with that letter sound. However, when the teacher presents this work, the students may decide that the task is to finish the ditto sheet, not to learn the letter sounds. Acting upon this interpretation, they may relate the letters and pictures in ways other than letter-sound associations and use these to guide their line drawing. As a result, they may complete the dittos but may not learn the letter sounds as the teacher intended.

Figure 4.1 **How students interpret classroom work**

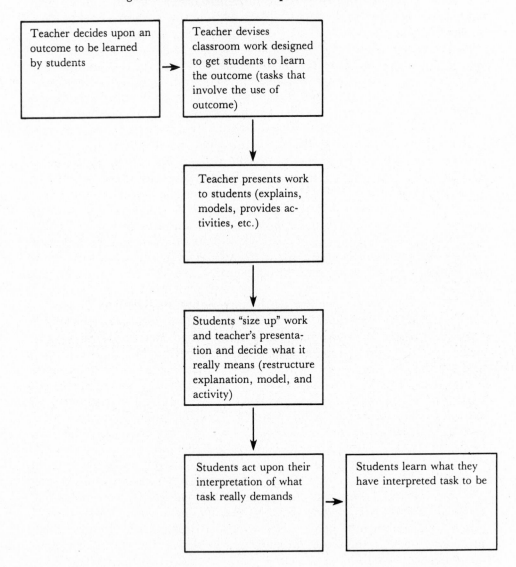

SOURCE: Modified from Doyle, W. (1984). Academic work. *Review of Educational Research, 53*(2), 159–199.

To combat such misinterpretation, a teacher structures a series of interactions with students. Each interaction offers a window into the students' minds, allowing the teacher to interpret how the students have restructured the task and to provide elaboration as appropriate. Consequently, successful instruction is as dependent upon these spontaneous elaborations as it is on initial presentations or appropriate work. For instance, in the example of the ditto sheet task, teacher–student interactions would reveal that students were not learning what was intended, and the teacher could spontaneously provide elaborated explanations to guide student restructuring. Similarly, assigning students to independently read text chapters or to complete computer console activities is not always desirable because neither allows for the teacher–student interaction that is such an important aspect of good instruction.

To summarize, instruction can be defined as a teacher's intentional use of academic work, presentations, and interactive exchanges that provide the information students need to understand and achieve desired curricular outcomes.

The teacher plays a prominent role in direct instruction.

Figure 4.2 **How instruction works**

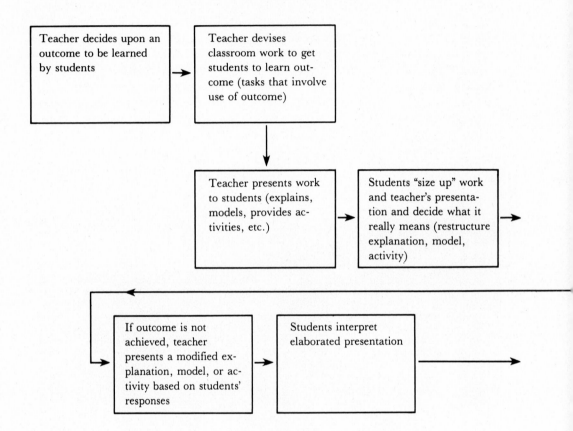

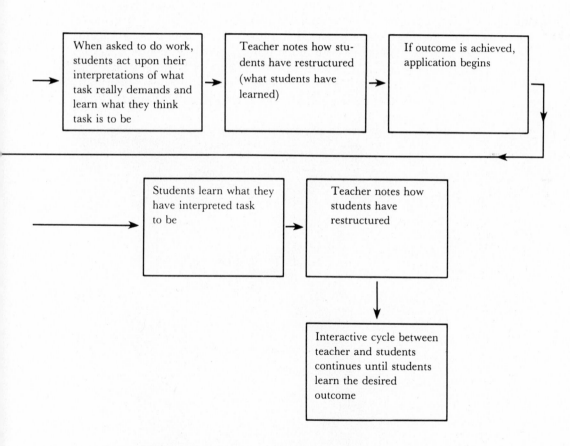

SOURCE: Modified from Doyle, W. (1984). Academic work. *Review of Educational Research, 53*(2), 159–199.

THE DISTINCTION BETWEEN
DIRECT AND INDIRECT INSTRUCTION

Instruction can be direct or indirect. That is, teachers can be more or less overt in presenting work to students. When teachers instruct *directly* they assume a highly structured, active, and dominant role in which *teacher talk* is relied upon to ensure that students interpret the work in the intended way and achieve the desired outcome. This kind of instruction is frequently used to create process and content outcomes.

In contrast, when teachers instruct *indirectly* they depend more on a structured environment than on teacher talk. That is, the activities themselves communicate and shape the students' interpretations of the task and lead them to discover the outcome. The prearranged environmental conditions are assumed to contain self-evident information needed to understand and achieve the curricular goals, and the teacher takes a much more covert role. There is, for instance, much less teacher talk. A strength of this approach is the student interest and motivation that comes with independent (or semi-independent) pursuit of activities. A weakness is that because students are not working as closely

Students' tasks are completed independently of direct teacher supervision in indirect instruction.

with a teacher there tends to be less teacher–student interaction. This means that the teacher has less opportunity to monitor and correct students' restructuring. As a result, indirect instruction is more frequently used to develop the concepts and the positive responses associated with the attitude outcomes of a reading curriculum and is less frequently recommended for the process and content goals that require closer teacher monitoring.

Direct and indirect instruction are not mutually exclusive. Rather, instruction is a continuum ranging from extreme examples of direct instruction through gradually diminishing amounts of teacher intervention to a point where a teacher does not directly intervene at all. Hence, any particular instructional episode may be more or less direct or indirect depending upon how much the teacher intervenes or how much the environment and/or the activity is relied upon to supply the information.

Whether instruction is direct or indirect, however, it always reflects the intention of the teacher, involves some kind of academic work — a presentation of information — and involves one or more interactions. The more direct the instruction, the more a teacher takes responsibility for directly providing information about what is to be learned; the more indirect the instruction, the more the information is assumed to be implicit in the environment or the activity. There is always interaction with students, although it is much more evident with direct instruction where it is generally verbal. With indirect instruction the initial involvement tends to be between the environment and the student and is less dependent on teacher talk. Teachers observe student responses during indirect instruction and elaborate upon explanations if needed, but their interaction is usually less systematic.

SUMMARY

The first important step in learning to teach reading is knowing when teachers are providing instruction and when they are not. Teachers *are* providing instruction when they intentionally devise strategies and interactions that provide students with the information needed to develop a specific curricular goal. Teachers are *not* instructing when they engage in classroom activities that are not intentionally designed to develop specific curricular outcomes. This does not mean that noninstructional classroom activities are unimportant. On the contrary, they are crucial to the smooth operation of a classroom. Collecting the milk money, taking the lunch count, supervising recess, consoling an injured child, scolding a misbehaving student, and countless other activities that make up the daily classroom routine are essential for effective classroom operations. Such activities are a part of teaching, but they are not examples of instruction since the teacher is not intentionally using professional knowledge to create specific curricular outcomes.

To summarize, instruction is the term used to describe what the teacher intentionally does to create specific curricular outcomes. It can be more direct, in which case teachers assume an overt, active, and dominant role in presenting and guiding the work, or it can be more indirect, in which case teachers assume a more covert role by creating an environment that leads students to discover curricular outcomes, particularly those associated with attitude goals. Whether instruction is direct, indirect, or at some midpoint on the continuum, the teacher intends that students interpret the task in ways to ensure they will learn the intended curricular outcome.

TERMS ASSOCIATED WITH DIRECT INSTRUCTION

Four distinct types of instructional behaviors tend to be associated with direct instruction. They are *assessment, explanation, practice,* and *application.*

ASSESSMENT

Assessment involves the collection of data to be used in making decisions and it is crucial to all instruction, especially direct instruction. Teachers cannot make good decisions about instructional objectives unless they assess student performance. Good objectives must be realistically matched to current performance levels, and consequently good teachers constantly collect data about how well students are doing. They use these data to make decisions about what students do or do not understand and what their instructional needs are.

Data can be collected either formally (using standardized tests) or informally (using teacher-made measures). Whereas clinicians and reading specialists make much use of formal tests, most classroom teachers rely on informal data collection. That is, they observe their students, question and talk with them, examine their written work, and make instructional decisions from these data. For instance, in the description of how instruction works (see Figure 4.2), the teacher's observation of students' restructuring is an example of assessment that relies on informal data.

Assessment is a prerequisite to instruction. That is, it occurs before instruction begins. As with instruction, assessment is intentional and strategic — teachers must know what to assess, how to assess it, and how the resultant data can be used to guide instruction. Its unique function is to collect information about what to do next in instruction. The suggestions in Chapter 3 about how to collect vital-signs data are good examples of assessment.

EXPLANATION

Explanation plays a particularly crucial role in direct instruction. It is during explanation that a teacher provides the information students need to develop an *understanding* of what is being taught. Since direct instruction is targeted mainly at process and content outcomes, most explanations develop an understanding of either how reading works or how to get content meaning from various texts.

Explanation is verbal assistance. It provides the "how-to" bridge between not knowing and knowing. During presentations a teacher explains by modeling and demonstrating. During the interaction following the presentation a teacher explains by elaborating, clarifying, questioning, and creating analogies. The explanation plays a major role in determining how students will interpret a task, because students tend to think about tasks in the same way that teachers talk about them. In short, students learn what teachers emphasize.

Explanation consists of two parts. The first is the *presentation* — a series of brief teacher statements about what is to be learned, why it is to be learned, and how to do it. The presentation usually includes explicit teacher modeling of how to do a task and, as such, relies greatly on teacher talk. The second is the *interaction* between teacher and students as the teacher gradually shifts to the students the responsibility for doing and understanding a task. This is normally accomplished by providing a series of trial responses to a task; students complete succeeding items in a series with less and less assistance from the teacher (with less and less teacher talk and more and more student talk). The intent is to gradually transfer the responsibility of the task to the students so they are able to do it without teacher assistance. The interaction part of instruction calls for much flexibility from the teacher, since students constantly modify explanations in terms of their prior experience. During interaction teachers must spontaneously elaborate upon their explanations to help students restructure information in the intended way.

PRACTICE

Practice is repetition. Its function is to make habitual the task developed during explanation. Whereas explanation develops initial understanding of how to do a task, practice solidifies that understanding. For instance, explanation may result in an understanding of how to figure out the theme of a story, while practice makes the strategy a habit. Practice is frequently characterized by repetition and drill while explanation is characterized by information giving and sense making.

When teachers want to give students practice, they usually assign controlled text. That is, they give students text that has been intentionally structured to include many repetitions of whatever knowledge or strategy is being taught, because it would be difficult to find natural text (such as a library book) that includes sufficient examples. In many reading classrooms students practice with controlled text such as workbook pages and/or ditto sheets in which they respond several times to a similar kind of task. Controlled text is efficient and easy to use, but it does not encourage transfer to natural text. Since the ultimate goal is application to real reading, natural text is often more useful for practice despite the relative scarceness of examples.

Whereas explanations must be teacher led, practice can be either guided by a teacher or unguided. Practice is guided when teachers directly supervise students' practice. For instance, when teachers monitor each student's response during the interactions following explanations or when they listen to each student read aloud during the reading group, they are conducting guided practice. It is unguided when teachers have students complete practice independently. For instance, teachers are conducting unguided practice when they give students unsupervised seatwork, assign practice sheets for homework, or give students free reading.

As with explanations and assessment, practice is part of the bridge the teacher provides during direct instruction to help the student achieve the desired outcome. It is intentional (the teacher decides what the practice is to be) and strategic (the practice is carefully designed to solidify a specific curricular outcome). However, practice is distinct from explanation. Explanation comes first and then practice solidifies what has been explained and understood. Because it would be foolish to practice something one does not understand, explanation is a prerequisite to practice.

APPLICATION

Application is use within natural settings. Its function is to help a student transfer what has been learned from an instructional setting to a real world setting. Whereas explanation develops students' understanding of an outcome, and practice provides repetition in using the outcome in a somewhat artificial situation (the text is controlled rather than natural), application applies what has been learned to natural settings. For instance, explanation helps students understand how to figure out the meaning of an unknown word from context, and practice helps students use what has been learned in workbooks, basal selections, or on ditto sheets, but application ensures that students will use what has been learned in real reading, that is, functional and recreational text. Instruction in process outcomes, for example, is most successful when it begins with natural text so that students can see from the beginning the application of their learning.

Application can be distinguished from assessment, explanation, and practice by its function. If a teacher's intention is to develop initial understanding, it is explanation; if a teacher's intention is to solidify understanding, it is practice; if the teacher's intention is to test understanding, it is assessment; and if the teacher's intention is to help students transfer understanding to real reading, it is application.

SUMMARY

Direct instruction is associated with the following four instructional behaviors: assessment, explanation, practice, and application. Teachers use these instructional behaviors most frequently when developing process and content outcomes.

TERMS ASSOCIATED WITH INDIRECT INSTRUCTION

Indirect instruction is typically used to develop the concepts and positive responses associated with the attitude goals specified in Chapter 2. In contrast to direct instruction in which the teacher plays an overt role by providing verbal explanation, controlled practice, and guided application, indirect instruction requires an environment that does the presenting for the teacher. Using indirect instruction, a teacher builds a *literate environment* (see Chapter 5) that creates an atmosphere or context that stimulates the desired attitude outcomes. A teacher orchestrates three aspects of the environment to create these outcomes — the *physical,* the *social–emotional,* and the *intellectual.*

THE PHYSICAL ENVIRONMENT

The physical environment refers to what is seen in the classroom. It includes such things as seating arrangements, types of furniture, decorations on the wall, work that is displayed, and bulletin boards. Teachers can structure a physical environment to stimulate a specific reading goal. For instance, a positive response to reading could be developed by including in the physical environment lots of attractive books and inviting places to read them, such as bean bag and easy chairs. This physical environment invites children to pause and to relax with books. Such an arrangement is an intentional and strategic design to create an understanding and appreciation of reading. It can therefore be called instruction or, more specifically, a form of indirect instruction.

THE SOCIAL–EMOTIONAL ENVIRONMENT

The social–emotional environment refers to the social interactions that occur among classroom participants. For instance, a teacher may wish to develop the concept that reading is a form of communication between reader and writer similar to the speaker–listener relationship. To accomplish this the teacher may pair students together to exchange first oral and then written messages. The teacher, in this case, does not directly explain the communicative nature of language but, instead, arranges a social activity that demonstrates that all language is a process of message sending and message getting. Such teacher orchestration of a classroom's social-emotional environment is an example of indirect instruction.

THE INTELLECTUAL ENVIRONMENT

A teacher also uses the intellectual environment to create desired reading outcomes. The intellectual environment refers to the expectations, challenges, and interests that teachers set, as well as to their modeling role. For instance, teachers who want to develop the notion that reading is an enjoyable leisure-time activity may provide specific times for pleasure reading and personally participate in reading books during that time. Or, a teacher may set aside time to read a story to the students. The instruction is not overt; there is little or no direct teaching about how to enjoy books, nor is the pleasure reading or listening to the story perceived as practice. Instead, the teacher arranges for the environment to carry the message that reading is an enjoyable leisure-time activity. This is indirect instruction.

SUMMARY

Instruction is indirect when the teacher intentionally orchestrates various aspects of the classroom environment in ways that lead students to specific outcomes. While it may not appear that teachers are engaged in instruction when they are sitting and reading a library book or quietly observing students interacting in pairs, they really are. Such activity is intentional, it involves work, a strategy for presenting the work, and interactions with students as they pursue it. It is, therefore, an example of instruction. Specifically, it is indirect instruction, because the teacher assumes a relatively passive and covert role and permits the environment to do the instructing.

EXAMPLES OF DIRECT AND INDIRECT INSTRUCTION

Both direct and indirect instruction are intentional efforts by teachers to create specified outcomes; both employ work, presentations, and interactions with students and both are teacher led. The difference is one of degree. In direct instruction a teacher intervenes in a more direct and straightforward manner to create the desired outcome; in indirect instruction a teacher's intervention tends to be more subtle. Good teachers use both direct and indirect instruction. The decision to employ direct or indirect instruction depends upon two things. The first is the desired curricular outcome. If a teacher wants to develop an understanding of reading or good feelings about reading as an activity, indirect instruction is usually best. If a teacher wants to develop knowledge about how reading works or the ability to get content meaning from a text, direct instruction usually works best. The second condition is the aptitude of the student. If a student learns to read easily, indirect instruction is often effective; however, if a student has difficulty learning to read, better results are usually obtained with direct instruction. Consequently, a teacher's decision to use direct or indirect instruction depends upon the curricular goal and the aptitude of the students being taught.

EXAMPLES OF INDIRECT INSTRUCTION

The attitudes students develop about reading usually result from indirect instruction. The following illustration, in which a relatively indirect form of instruction is used to develop good feelings about how reading can enrich our lives, is typical.

In this example the teacher follows a three-step plan. First, the teacher engages the students in book sharing. Children's books that typically stimulate a sense of wonder are collected—examples include McCloskey's *Time of Wonder*, Sperry's *Call It Courage*, L'Engle's *Wrinkle in Time*, and Lewis' *Moment of Wonder*. The teacher displays these prominently in the classroom, reads certain excerpts aloud, and features the theme of wonder on a bulletin board. This sharing is the work.

Second, the teacher discusses with the students the books and their potential for enrichment. This is the presentation. To an observer, the discussion looks casual, informal, and unplanned. In reality, however, the teacher has deliberately selected the books, carefully selected which segments to read, and planned what to say to students to draw unusual experiences described in the books to their attention.

Third, the teacher involves the students themselves in choosing and reading books, guiding them as they talk about passages that stimulate interest, and reinforcing classmates who respond positively to the chosen passages. This is student interaction. This three-step sequence looks casual, but it has been deliberately planned to get students to appreciate the way books can produce a sense of wonder.

Another powerful example of indirect instruction is an activity called uninterrupted sustained silent reading, during which both teacher and students read quietly from a book they have chosen. The object is to build a positive attitude toward reading by getting students used to reading a book of their choice for a specified period of time. Again, a casual observer may see this as noninstructional because it does not look like the teacher is instructing. In fact, however, this is instruction because the teacher has intentionally orchestrated the environment to provide students with an opportunity to develop a positive response to reading.

Instruction in both these examples is relatively indirect. Although it appears to be spontaneous and unstructured, in reality it is carefully planned (even though it looks casual), teacher led (but not dominated), and strategic (involving strategies about the work, presentations, and interactions).

AN EXAMPLE OF DIRECT INSTRUCTION

Because direct instruction is particularly useful in developing fix-it strategies, this outcome is used to illustrate a relatively direct form of instruction. Specifically, the example involves figuring out the meaning of an unknown word using context clues. Learning how to use this strategy becomes the work. In contrast to the indirect instruction just illustrated, direct instruction does not look casual. The teacher plays the role of a strong leader, and the teacher's strategic use of professional knowledge is obvious.

The lesson format consists of six stages and includes both a presentation and an interaction. The first three stages are the presentation. First, there is an introduction to a basal reader selection that will be read in this lesson. Second, there is an introduction to the reading strategy that will be applied to the selection. This includes teacher statements about what is to be learned, how it is to be applied, and what the student needs to attend to. While this takes only one and one-half minutes or so, the statements are very explicit. Being explicit and brief comes from knowing your content and being well prepared to deliver instruction. Third, there is teacher modeling. The teacher specifies "the secret" to using the strategy, models it by explaining how to figure out the meaning of an unknown word, and summarizes by having students review the steps involved. The time is brief, but the statements are explicit. Again, the importance of teacher knowledge and preparation cannot be overemphasized.

The next stage is the interactive stage, in which the teacher assesses student restructuring of the lesson and monitors their use of the strategy, gradually moving them from being other-directed (directed by the teacher) to being self-directed (using the strategy without help). The teacher retains control initially, but gradually moves from directives, to questions, to supportive feedback as students begin interpreting the task correctly and using the strategy on their own. The interactive stage is where teacher knowledge is especially apparent because, when students misinterpret and respond incorrectly, only a knowledgeable teacher is able to generate spontaneous reexplanation that redirects the students' thinking in the desired direction.

Once students can use the strategy without assistance there must also be practice in applying the strategy to text. Some teachers use controlled rather than natural text for such practice. However, guided application is recommended, in which the teacher uses a basal text story or other sample of text to model how the strategy will be used.

The final stage, then, is independent application, which focuses on helping students use the strategy in texts they choose to read. If the teacher sees that students are using the strategy in real reading then the direct instruction has been successful. However, if the strategy is only used when reading basal textbooks or doing workbook pages, direct instruction has not been successful.

SUMMARY

Both direct and indirect instruction are important. A relatively direct form of instruction is most appropriate for teaching specific knowledge about how reading works and for teaching specific content meaning, especially to low-aptitude students. A relatively indirect form of instruction is most appropriate for teaching concepts and developing attitudes about reading. However, there is no set rule for when a teacher should use one or the other form of instruction. In fact, teachers will often use both simultaneously. Suggestions for making decisions about when to use either direct or indirect instruction and specific guidelines for planning such instruction are provided in Chapter 9. The main point now is that, while indirect instruction appears more relaxed, casual, and spontaneous than direct instruction, both are intentional, are teacher led, and employ strategies designed to get students to interpret tasks as teachers intend so that specified curricular outcomes result.

MAJOR APPROACHES TO ORGANIZING READING PROGRAMS

Instruction, whether it is direct or indirect, has to be organized. Teachers call their year-long series of organized reading activities the *reading program.* Every classroom has such a program; that is, every teacher organizes the teaching of reading into a set of year-long activities. The different ways to organize programs are usually discussed in terms of approaches to the teaching of reading. Although there are many such approaches the three major ones are: *the basal text approach, the language experience approach,* and *the personalized approach.* In practice, the basal text approach is used by most classroom teachers.

THE BASAL TEXT APPROACH

As noted in Chapter 1, basal reading textbooks are used in almost all American elementary classrooms. For many teachers a basal textbook is the reading program, and their year-long set of activities come primarily from the teacher's guide that accompanies the basal text.

Publishers invest millions of dollars in developing, packaging, and marketing these instructional materials. About 10 publishers dominate the market, competing fiercely with each other for sales. Despite the competition, however, the differences between the major basal reading programs are marginal. All follow essentially the same format. Each one includes a multilevel series of 15 to 20 books, beginning with readiness books designed to get kindergarteners ready to read print and proceeding through the first stories children read (called preprimers and primers) to texts designed for use in the eighth grade. Usually, a publisher provides two separate books (one slightly more difficult than the other) for use at each grade level. In actuality, however, several levels may be in use in any given classroom at a particular time because of the wide differences in students' reading abilities. This explains why

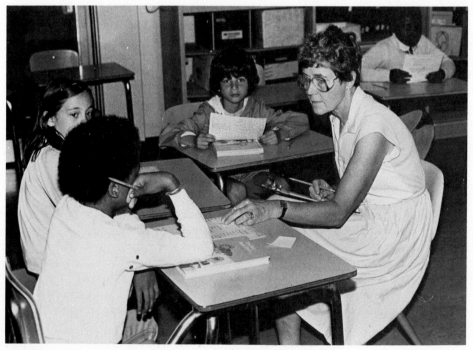

A basal text group in action.

American school children identify each other's relative reading status by asking the question, "What book are you in?"

Each level of a basal reading series includes a student's text with the selections to be read, a workbook with exercises to be completed, and a teacher's edition with extensive teaching directions and suggestions. The teacher's edition for any given level is a massive book that contains in a single volume:

1. Copies of both the selections and the workbook pages that appear in the student's edition.
2. Extensive descriptive material regarding the philosophy of the basal program.
3. Organizational procedures teachers should follow in implementing the program.
4. Specific directions to follow in presenting prescribed skills.
5. Suggested questions to ask when discussing selections with students.
6. Enrichment activities for use as follow-up or culminating activities.
7. Tests that can be used to evaluate student achievement.

In addition, most basal reading series provide supplementary charts, worksheets, games, and other instructional devices useful to a teacher.

Typically, teachers use basal texts in the following way. They call the reading groups together, often referring to the group by the title of the basal text being used (e.g., "Would the Windchimes group come to the reading table now?"). The lesson typically begins with the teacher introducing the reading selection using the suggestions provided in the teacher's edition. The teacher then introduces and teaches the vocabulary words, gives students a purpose for reading the selection, and has them read the story (often orally in the very early grades and silently once students are in second grade or beyond). After the selection has been read, the teacher discusses the content with students by asking questions suggested in the teacher's edition and often has students do oral or silent rereading of certain parts to elaborate on some point. Then the teacher refers to the teacher's edition for suggestions regarding what skills to teach, uses these in introducing the skills, and assigns students to the associated workbook pages to give them practice in the skill. Finally, the teacher closes the lesson using one or more of the teacher's edition suggestions regarding enrichment activities and pupil evaluation. Ordinarily, this series of activities requires three or four days for each selection. The format is often referred to as the *directed reading lesson* (DRL) (see Figure 4.3). Once the cycle is completed with one selection, it is repeated with the next. In this way each basal reading textbook is completed, and reading instruction gets accomplished.

There are advantages to the basal reader system. From the teacher's standpoint, a basal simplifies the complexity of teaching reading. All the goals

---

Figure 4.3 **Steps in conducting a directed reading lesson (DRL)**

1. Introduce the story, provide background, and introduce the new vocabulary words.
2. State a purpose for reading or questions to be answered while reading.
3. Read the story (silently or orally, all the way through or in sections).
4. Discuss the story and oral or silent rereading of sections of the story.
5. Teach the skill(s) using the associated workbook.
6. Provide an enrichment activity or culmination.

---

of reading instruction, all the techniques, activities, and materials are provided and have been organized into managable three- to four-day units that can be taught with a minimum of worry or hassle. Instruction can be routinized and the demands on teachers are lessened. When one considers the complexity of the classroom as noted in Chapter 1 this advantage is compelling.

However, the basal also has disadvantages. First, because the basal is organized into a set of routine activities, teachers tend to conduct instruction in a technical manner; they assign the instructional responsibility to the basal and become technicians who follow directions rather than professionals who maintain control of their own instruction. Second, because of the emphasis placed on the stories in the basal, teachers tend to believe that all children learn how to read simply by reading. While high-aptitude students sometimes learn to read by reading, low-aptitude students seldom do. They need instruction in the attitudes, process, and content outcomes. Basal instruction, however, emphasizes content outcomes—the teacher teaches the story—not the positive attitudes needed for reading growth or the strategies used to make sense of the story. Third, despite the emphasis on stories, basal programs provide little opportunity for sustained reading of text. Instead, reading is often disrupted by the need to respond to teacher questions or by requests to read orally in turn. Finally, basals emphasize isolated workbook-type activities more than real comprehension outcomes and as a result tend to convey the impression that reading is a mechanical process of answer getting rather than a cognitive process of making sense out of an author's message.

To summarize, a basal textbook is used to organize the reading program in most elementary classrooms. In fact, many schools mandate the use of a particular basal series, and teachers are expected to follow its sequence and prescriptions with little or no variation. However, whereas basals possess many strengths, they also have serious weaknesses. Even if one is mandated as "the" reading program, adjustments need to be made to account for the weaknesses.

THE LANGUAGE EXPERIENCE APPROACH

When using a basal textbook approach, instruction is organized around the short reading selections contained in a commercially prepared book designed for a given grade level. The language experience approach, in contrast, is organized around students' experiences that are translated into written text and then read. Consequently, students read unique material that describes familiar content (personal experiences) using familiar words. Students are in control of comprehension because the words, prior knowledge, author purpose, and text structure (see Chapter 2) are all personalized.

The language experience approach is most frequently associated with beginning reading. However, because of the dominance of the basal text approach, it is seldom used exclusively. More than any other approach it emphasizes the interrelationships among the language modes. It starts with experiences (such as a field trip), continues with oral language (students talk about the field trip and listen to others express their thoughts), results in a written product (the talk about the field trip is written down) and culminates in students reading what they have written (their own stories). Students learn the

A teacher using the language experience approach.

role of reading within the overall language system: that thoughts can be communicated in spoken messages, that what can be spoken can be written down, and that what is written down can be read.

In the early grades the language experience approach involves taking dictation from children, since young students cannot yet write. In later grades, of course, students do their own writing. Language experience stories for primary grades are frequently composed in groups using patterns of development like this:

1. Discuss an experience with students (e.g., a holiday, the weather, a story they read, or any other common experience).
2. Suggest that the students' ideas be written by the teacher on large experience chart paper displayed at the front of the room.
3. Direct students to suggest a title and a first line.
4. Solicit subsequent contributions from others in the group.
5. When complete, read the product orally to the group.
6. Directs students to read the story to you.
7. Have students copy the story for themselves and illustrate it.
8. The resulting book becomes part of the growing library of material students can read.

Language experience stories for upper-elementary grades are somewhat different in that students can write and do not need to copy a group story. The pattern for upper grades usually follows this type of sequence:

1. Discuss an experience with students (e.g., a field trip, a sporting activity, a visitor to the classroom, an adventure they have had).
2. Brainstorm with students about ideas regarding the topic (e.g., sequences of action, descriptive words, conclusions).
3. Write ideas so they can be seen visually (e.g., on a chalkboard).
4. Guide students in developing an opening and possible plot or sequence of events.
5. Have students complete their own stories.
6. Edit completed stories (editors can be students or teachers).
7. Prepare final copies as books for room, school, or home libraries.

The language experience approach has many advantages. It emphasizes the language concepts that undergird reading (the relationship between reading and writing, for instance). It also puts students in control of the reading process (they know the words because they were used in the oral discussion, they have the prior knowledge because it is based on a shared experience, and they understand both the author's purpose and the text structure because it was self-written). In addition, it is always fresh and motivating, since the experiences that are the basis for the stories are real, not contrived. As such, it may well be the best single approach to reading instruction.

However, there are disadvantages to language experience. The most serious one is that it does not have the built-in organization of materials and activities found in the basal text. Instead, teachers and children generate all the reading materials, and teachers are totally responsible for creating both the curricular structure and the necessary materials. A teacher's organizational task is therefore very difficult. As a result, energy demands on teachers are high.

Another disadvantage is its great emphasis on indirect instruction. Although effective for developing the concepts and feelings associated with attitude goals, the language experience approach is less effective in developing knowledge of how reading works and the ability to get content meaning from text, especially for low-aptitude students. Direct instruction is most effective in developing these outcomes, and there is little emphasis on direct instruction when using language experience.

A final disadvantage is that very few schools allow teachers the latitude to use the language experience approach as the primary means for organizing the reading program. Instead, they either mandate a specific basal text or provide several different basals, thereby setting the expectation that a reading program should be organized around basal materials and activities.

THE PERSONALIZED READING APPROACH

Personalized or individualized reading programs reflect the concept of self-selection in which children choose the library books they wish to read and the words they wish to learn. Students read these selections independently, and the teacher instructs each student through individual conferences. During these conferences the teacher discusses the book currently being read by the student, assesses the student's needs and achievements, and provides individual instruction. Because students must be independent readers in order to employ this approach, it tends to be associated with the middle and upper grades. Again, however, because of the dominance of the basal texts, personalized reading is seldom used exclusively.

To incorporate personalized reading instruction into a classroom:

1. Start collecting a variety of books. For the average classroom, try to collect 100 books, or at least 3 different books per pupil. If there are not enough available in your school, borrow, trade, and ask for donations.
2. Set up an interesting library area with a rug, pillow, and some fur-

niture. Try to arrange the books with the covers facing the
students.

3. Teach your students the Rule of Thumb. If they are primary age
   tell them to select a page in the middle of the book and begin
   reading it silently. Each time they miss a word, they should put up
   a finger. If five fingers are up before the page is finished, the book
   is too hard. Older students can just count up to five words
   missed.
4. Teach them to get books quietly.
5. Teach them how to get help with a word. They could go to the dictionary, an aide, experience charts, other books that they know, a
   friend, the teacher, or they could try to figure it out.
6. Teach them to prepare for a conference with the teacher by:
   a. Selecting a book.
   b. Reading silently to themselves or reading aloud to a friend.
   c. Signing up for the conference.
7. During the conference, which should last 5 to 10 minutes, discuss
   with the student interesting information, author's purpose, and how
   the story can be applied to other situations. Finally, have the student
   read a portion of the story aloud in order to check performance.
8. Meanwhile, the rest of the class is reading its books or doing an
   original activity to follow up something they have read. Examples
   of creative activities are writing for a class newspaper, keeping track
   of books, choral reading, dramatization, writing letters, and
   creative writing.
9. Occasionally you may form temporary groups to work on a particular curricular goal.

The personalized approach to reading has many advantages. It is highly
motivating, since the students are personally involved in selecting their
materials. Vocabulary control is not imposed by an outside source; instead,
students expand their vocabulary as they read a variety of books. This approach promotes personal interaction between students and the teacher, and,
most important, it encourages the reading habit, promoting reading as real and
not as some boring school task that has no relation to the real world.

Personalized reading also has disadvantages, however. There is a lack of
emphasis on process and content outcomes. Fix-it strategies, for instance, are
not taught systematically, but are taught when the learner needs them in relation to self-selected materials. It takes a highly skillful teacher to determine
needs as quickly and as accurately as demanded by this approach, and it takes
a highly organized teacher to find the time to conduct conferences and also to

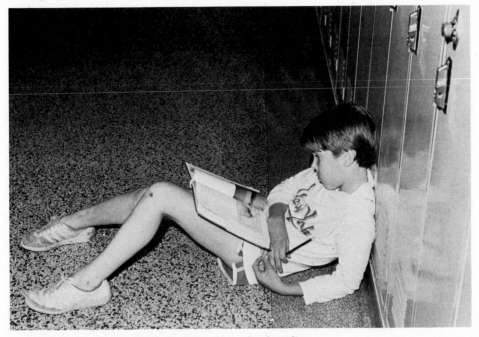

Each student chooses a reading book for personalized reading.

teach the process and content outcomes once the need is recognized. Most teachers feel that they cannot do this adequately. The demands of the classroom are just too great.

While the personalized reading approach is seldom used as the only reading program in a classroom, elements of it are often incorporated into existing programs. For example, many classrooms have regular free-reading periods in which students select what they read and occasionally conference with the teacher about them. The USSR technique mentioned earlier is a good example.

A COMBINED APPROACH TO ORGANIZING A READING PROGRAM

Each approach to reading instruction has advantages and disadvantages. None is totally satisfactory in itself. Consequently, many professional teachers use a combination of approaches to organize the reading program.

The foundation of most combined programs is the basal text because most teachers are in schools where there is an expectation that basals will be used. Furthermore, most teachers feel the need for the organizational routines and structure that accompany the basals. Because basals are often mandated (explicitly or implicitly) and because most teachers appreciate their organizational comfort, they are the basis of most reading programs.

Since basals provide the foundation of most reading programs, these programs take on certain profiles. First, a portion of the allocated instructional time is usually devoted to selections in one or another level of the adopted basal series. Second, a teacher normally uses some form of the directed reading lesson (see Figure 4.3) to guide students through the selections in the basal and uses direct instruction to teach the process outcomes prescribed by the basal text. Third, because the basal text emphasizes process and content goals, these are emphasized during the basal reading time. Finally, instruction is delivered to reading groups formed on the basis of ability, with each group using that level of the basal series that matches their reading level.

By making a basal the foundation of the reading program, certain structures and routines get established — reading groups, directed reading lessons, and direct instruction. If this is the total program of reading instruction, however, it will be out of balance. Process and content outcomes get emphasized, but the concepts and feelings associated with the attitude outcomes do not. Consequently, features of the language experience approach and the personalized reading approach can be combined with the basal approach to create a balanced program of instruction.

Balancing the program is achieved by deliberately allocating time for attitude goals. Once the time is scheduled, the teacher uses language experience and personalized approaches to achieve the outcomes. For instance, a portion of each school day can be scheduled for uninterrupted sustained silent reading. In addition, the teacher can occasionally use this time to develop the feelings and concepts associated with postive attitudes. The teacher can also plan frequent language experience activities in which each student creates text based on a real experience and then reads it. Such activities are used to develop the students' conceptual understanding of reading's relationship to language, the relationship between reader and writer, and the communicative function of language.

Hence, a balanced reading program is not organized around a single approach to instruction, but around a combined approach. At the core of this combined model is a basal textbook and direct instruction. Added to this core activity are daily personalized reading activities and frequent language experience activities to develop the attitude outcomes. Instruction occurs both directly (with the basal text activities) and indirectly (with the language experience and personalized reading activities). The teacher uses each approach to develop specific reading goals.

HOW TO USE INSTRUCTION AND APPROACHES

Direct and indirect instruction and the various approaches to reading instruction are not synonymous. Teachers use the approaches as ways to organize their overall reading program; in contrast, they use direct and indirect instruction to organize the daily lessons within the over all program. For instance, a teacher who uses the basal text approach or the language experience approach or the personalized approach organizes the year-long reading program primarily around basal materials or student written materials or children's literature. Within this overall pattern, however, they may organize individual lessons around either direct or indirect instruction. When making decisions about instruction, therefore, first make a global decision regarding the approach (or combination of approaches) to be employed and then make a series of daily decisions about which objectives should be taught directly and which should be taught indirectly.

CONCLUSION

This chapter provides a foundation for making fundamental decisions about instruction. For instance, you now have a concept for instruction and for the terms associated with direct and indirect instruction. As a result, you should be able to recognize whether a teacher is instructing or is engaged in a noninstructional activity. Similarly, you should be able to recognize whether a teacher is explaining, providing practice, assessing, or guiding application. Further, you should be able to distinguish between direct and indirect instruction and to determine which kind of instruction is most appropriate for the various curricular goals associated with reading. You should also be able to think now about organizing yourself in terms of the major approaches to reading instruction and how you would teach reading with each approach — whether direct or indirect instruction would be emphasized, what tasks would be performed, what the typical activities would be, and what curricular outcomes would be emphasized with particular approaches. Finally, you should be able to visualize how you would teach reading using a combined approach — how each approach would be used to achieve certain goals, how you would assess whether the outcomes had been achieved, what form your instruction would take at various times and with various activities, and so on.

CHECK YOUR UNDERSTANDING

Now that you have read the chapter, check your understanding by answering the Focus Questions presented at the beginning of the chapter. If you cannot answer one or more of the questions, return to the chapter, find the section that corresponds to the question, and reread.

SUGGESTED READINGS

Allen, E. G., & Laminack, L. L. (1982). Language experience reading—It's a natural! *Reading Teacher, 35*(6), 708–714.

Allen, R. V. (1968). How a language experience program works. In E. C. Vilscek (Ed.), *A decade of innovations: Approaches to beginning reading.* Newark: International Reading Association.

Ashton-Warner, S. (1963). *Teacher.* New York: Bantam Books.

Blair, T. R. (1984). Teacher effectiveness: The know-how to improve student learning. *Reading Teacher, 38*(2), 138–142.

Bridge, C. A., Winograd, P. N., & Haley, D. (1983). Using predictable materials vs. preprimers to teach beginning sight words. *Reading Teacher, 36*(9), 884–891.

Duffy, G., & Roehler, L. (1982). The illusion of instruction. *Reading Research Quarterly, 17*(3), 438–445.

Farrar, M. T. (1984). Asking better questions. *Reading Teacher, 38*(1), 10–20.

Guthrie, J. T. (1983). Students' perceptions of teaching. *Reading Teacher, 37*(1), 94–95.

Hall, M. (1979). Language-centered reading: Premises and recommendations. *Language Arts, 56*(6), 664–670.

Hare, V. C. (1982). Beginning reading theory and comprehension questions in teachers' manuals. *Reading Teacher, 35*(8), 918–923.

Hunt, L. C. (1971). Six steps to the individualized reading program (IRP). *Elementary English, 48*(1), 27–32.

Lambie, R. A., & Brittain, M. M. (1983). Adaptive reading instruction: A three-pronged approach. *Reading Journal, 37*(3), 243–248.

Mallon, B., & Berglund, R. (1984). The language experience approach to reading: Recurring questions and their answers. *Reading Teacher, 37*(9), 867–871.

Roehler, L., & Duffy, G. (1981). Classroom teaching is more than opportunity to learn. *Journal of Teacher Education, 32*(6), 7–13.

Roehler, L., & Duffy, G. (1982). Matching direct instruction to reading outcomes. *Language Arts, 59*(5), 476–481.

PART III

ORGANIZING FOR INSTRUCTION

Because teaching is complex and difficult, it requires much organization. Part III provides information about how to get organized. Specifically, it describes how you can organize the classroom environment, the instructional time, the reading groups, and the lessons in both reading and writing.

At the end of this unit you should have an understanding of the level of organization demanded of professional teachers, and you should be able to answer questions such as the following:

1. What organizational decisions need to be made to prepare for reading instruction?
2. What can teachers do to ensure that they are adequately organized?

CHAPTER 5

Creating a Literate Environment

GETTING READY

What students think about reading is tied to the environment in which they learn to read. If the environment emphasizes nonliterate drill and repetition tasks, one concept develops; if it emphasizes literate activities involving books, libraries, and writing, a different concept develops. Reading should develop in a literate environment, and this chapter describes how to create such an environment in the classroom. Creating this environment is a crucial part of getting organized for reading instruction because it is the basis for the attitude outcomes.

A literate environment encompasses the physical, intellectual, and social-emotional environments. This chapter discusses these three environments and provides you with a plan for preparing and using them to help create desired reading outcomes.

FOCUS QUESTIONS

As you read this chapter use the following questions to guide your understanding of what creates a literate environment.

1. Why is a literate environment necessary?
2. What composes the physical environment?
3. What composes the intellectual environment?
4. What composes the social-emotional environment?
5. How do you prepare to use a literate environment for indirect instruction?

CHARACTERISTICS OF A LITERATE ENVIRONMENT

In a literate environment a classroom is permeated with examples of literacy and language in action — *real* language and *real* literacy. For instance, instead of the traditional situation in which the teacher talks and everyone else is quiet, a literate environment encourages various kinds of student communication, both oral and written. Similarly, instead of limiting written material to textbooks, many other kinds of printed materials are used, including trade books, magazines, comic books, catalogs, recipes, and newspapers. Also, rather than teaching writing as a separate subject with an emphasis on neatness and accuracy of script, writing is integrated into reading activities along with speaking and listening.

In a global sense, then, a literate environment provides numerous opportunities for students to encounter and participate in real language and literacy experiences, thereby increasing the chances that they will develop an accurate concept of reading and a positive feeling about it. Teachers deliberately create these opportunities in the form of indirect instruction in order to achieve desired attitude outcomes. This does not mean that direct instruction is ignored or that basal textbooks are not used. Rather, it means that a teacher uses some of the instructional time in reading for activities associated with a literate environment. Indirect instruction conducted in a literate environment depends on certain characteristics, which are described below.

LANGUAGE INTEGRATION

First, indirect instruction used within a literate environment reflects all four language modes: listening, speaking, reading, and writing. It is unusual to use one language mode without another. What is heard was spoken by someone; what is read was written by someone. There is always an audience when someone speaks or writes, even if it is only one's self. People receive information through listening or reading and send information through speaking or writing. People can get or give information through oral modes (listening or speaking) or through printed modes (reading or writing). In short, language is an integrated process and reading — the focus of this book — is but one of the language modes. It is not an isolated skill but rather is part of a language system. Even though this book concentrates on reading, remember that it is only one of the modes and does not stand alone. In fact, an important characteristic of a literate environment is the integration of reading with other language modes. That is, the activities found in a literate environment reflect all the language modes.

FORMAL AND INFORMAL LANGUAGE

Second, indirect instruction found in a literate environment reflects both casual and highly controlled language use. For instance, there are times when language is used without much prior thought. People speak and the words start coming. People listen and the words are understood. People read and focus on the gist rather than the details or write not for an audience but to simply organize their thoughts. Part of language use involves determining whether the information to be received should be listened to carefully or casually; whether it should be read for fun or for information; whether to speak as if to neighbors or to an unknown group; whether to write a letter formally or as a note. People can impose careful thought on their language or just let it occur. In the classroom teachers need to create an environment where all students not only use language freely but also carefully and strategically.

THE PROMINENCE OF WRITING

Third, indirect instruction found in literate environments makes much use of writing. This book has mentioned that because reading is but one part of an integrated language system there should be many classroom activities in which reading tasks are integrated in natural ways with listening, speaking, and writing. However, of all the language modes there is a particularly close relationship between reading and writing. In the primary grades dictation and class-developed stories created by the students and printed by the teacher provide opportunities to illustrate the reading–writing connection. In the middle grades written comments of students' reactions to books read are placed in accessible areas for other students to peruse when selecting a new book to read. In the upper grades story patterns of favorite books can provide the structure for creating new stories or articles. Group discussions of books that carry a similar theme can be summarized for class newspapers. In short, writing should be prominent in a literate classroom.

Consider the relationship between reading and writing. The obvious connection is the text — the array of printed symbols that represent the message being conveyed. The text is composed by a writer who has a message to communicate and who uses the conventions of written language to represent that message. In a sense the writer creates a blueprint of the message to be communicated. This blueprint is then "read" by readers — that is, readers use an understanding of how language conventions work and their prior knowledge about the words, topic, purpose, and text structure to interpret the blueprint, reconstructing a meaning from the text. When the system works well, readers reconstruct the message that the writer intended.

Clearly, there is a close relationship between a writer and a reader — between the composing process and the reading process. The more classroom activities emphasize this relationship between writer and reader, the more accurate a student's concept of reading will be and the more positive will be the attitude toward reading. Consequently, writing is an important part of the literate environment.

THE QUALITY OF INDEPENDENT ACTIVITIES

Fourth, the small-group patterns that characterize reading instruction depend on large amounts of seatwork that can be completed independent of teacher supervision. The content of this independent work should follow naturally from a literate environment and can be set up as individual work, work in pairs, or small group work. Individual student activities can include independent reading for information or pleasure, journal writing for reflective or expressive purposes, opportunities to practice newly acquired strategies or knowledge, and/or assessment of any of the three goals of reading instruction. Work in pairs can include shared oral reading, think-aloud activities to develop reasoning abilities, peer tutoring, reciprocal learning opportunities, and "author's-chair" activities in which student authors are interviewed about their creativity

Print plays a prominent role in a literate environment.

and craftmanship. Small-group activities can include collaborative group assessment of stories and articles, creative drama development and practice, teacher-made games for habituating strategies and skills, and cooperative group discussions of other content areas.

In contrast, it is not unusual in many elementary classrooms to see a different kind of independent activity. Instead of working in a literate environment that emphasizes meaningful language, students sit at desks completing piles of ditto and practice sheets geared to habituate isolated skills and bits of knowledge. Learning is viewed primarily as receiving information and committing it to memory. Communication is at a minimum, and the purpose of seatwork seems to be simply the completion of a task, with little concern for understanding or remembering.

Quality independent activities are a necessary condition for a literate environment. The activities must be tied closely to instructional goals, reflect a two-way communication system, and provide ample opportunities for developing positive attitudes and concepts about reading.

COMPONENTS OF
A LITERATE ENVIRONMENT

There are many ways to create a literate environment. Printed words can decorate the classroom walls, and books, magazines, and pamphlets can be scattered about. Social interactions between teachers and students should occur frequently. Word power and dependence on the printed word should be openly acknowledged. These activities as well as others are part of the literate environment.

Teachers create a literate environment by planning the physical, intellectual, and social–emotional environments. The physical environment should reflect the importance of print, with books and various forms of printed matter evident everywhere. The intellectual environment should consist of mental challenge. The social–emotional environment should encourage socialization through the use of language. When the physical, intellectual, and social–emotional environments are filled with meaningful language, a literate environment results.

THE PHYSICAL ENVIRONMENT

To establish a physical environment conducive to literacy, print must be everywhere. In most areas in America print guides and challenges everyday lives. A trip to the store is guided by Stop signs, Yield signs, Walk and Don't Walk signs. Printed sales slips record our purchases and are kept track of in checkbooks. Billboards and written advertisements challenge and entice people to try certain products. Consumer magazines assist people in selecting the best products. Editorials persuade people to consider a certain point of view, and books and magazines provide challenges, enticements, and entertainment.

A similar environment can be created in the classroom. Print can be displayed prominently and used in a variety of ways. Classroom rules, directions, and procedures can be printed and displayed. Students can be encouraged to verify uncertainties by referring to a printed reference. Print can be used for recreational activities (free reading, choral reading, sharing of poetry, and so forth) as well as for reference (checking a recipe when doing a class cooking project or reading directions for assembling something the class has ordered). Displays of printed language can issue challenges to the students. Thought-provoking questions can be placed around the room on bulletin boards, chalk boards, and display tables, with answers printed close by or directions for where to find the answers printed with the questions.

A teacher also draws students' attention to the integrative nature of language usage—to the way all the language modes are used for communication. Students learn what teachers emphasize; if teachers talk about the integrative nature of language, students will become aware of it. Consequently, the physical environment includes not only the prominent display of print but also tangible envidence of its relationship with other language modes.

THE INTELLECTUAL ENVIRONMENT

A literate environment cannot be based on the physical environment alone; an intellectual environment must accompany it. A teacher orchestrates the intellectual environment by creating challenges. This is done by setting expectations, modeling, and capitalizing on students' interests and motivation.

Expectations. Challenges always involve the possibility of failure; the trick is to choose the right amount of challenge. Part of choosing the right challenge lies with the concept of expectations.

The expectations of other influence how people view themselves. Consequently, the expectations teachers communicate to students can lead them to believe that they can become literate. Do a teacher's words and actions convey negative feelings about risk taking, or do they convey trust and the feeling that it is okay to fail when trying something new because people often learn from their mistakes? Do a teacher's words imply that only perfection is acceptable, or rather, that they value ever closer approximations as a student moves toward a final goal? Teachers should set the expectation that everyone can learn, learning takes time, and failures and mistakes are inevitable and are not reasons to

Literate environments promote real reading.

quit. By setting positive expectations, a teacher makes it easier for students to accept challenges and to persevere in completing them.

Teachers communicate expectations about language as well as about people. For instance, in talking with students teachers establish expectations regarding the integrated nature of language by ensuring that what is written will be read by someone, emphasizing that language is a tool for conveying information, ideas and experiences, and ensuring that reading is seen as one of the four language modes, not as an isolated skill.

Modeling. Modeling, a powerful tool for learning, influences everyone at all levels of development. At a very early age children watch others and then do what they see them doing. Much early learning comes from emulating a model, a tendency that teachers can use to develop a strong intellectual environment. Teachers can model the reading of books and how reading is used. They can model the need to communicate in writing (with the principal's office, other teachers, parents, and students). In short, teachers should make an effort to model all possible uses of the written word.

It is important to distinguish modeling from demonstration. With modeling students have the opportunity to do as the model did. With demonstration, although information is presented, the student has no opportunity to perform the task. The distinction is important when developing an intellectual environment. If bulletin boards, worksheets, and learning centers are intended as models, students must be given the opportunity to try whatever is being modeled. For instance, if a bulletin board poses a set of questions about the natural world, students must be shown how to find the answers. This might be done by connecting the questions to various literary sources where the answers can be found.

Interests. Interests, the third factor to be considered in the development of the intellectual environment, refers to the wide range of topics that students are curious about and want to explore. Dinosaurs, tornadoes, horses, and unexplained events fall into this category for many children. When teachers want students to use language (especially reading), high-interest topics such as these can be used to create challenges that students are willing to pursue.

One strategy is to have the students themselves become resident experts on topics of interest to them. Each student selects an interest area such as whales, doll making, or computers and becomes the class expert through exten-

Teachers model recreational reading as part of the intellectual environment.

sive reading. All questions on the topic are then directed to that student. This is also an excellent way to illustrate the integrative nature of language since all four language modes are typically used when the resident experts are consulted.

Motivation. Motivation is the desire to pursue a particular activity. It should not be confused with interests, which involve attraction toward particular topics. Motivation refers to a person's feelings toward an activity associated with a topic. A student could have an interest in dolphins, but not be motivated to write a three-paragraph paper on dolphins. Motivation is the immediate urge to do something whereas interest is a long-abiding curiosity. To motivate students, teachers use activities that students want to be involved in.

Most students also possess a set of internal motivators that, when activated by well-chosen activities, produce a positive attitude toward the activity and result in higher achievement. One such internal motivator is choice. Whenever students are provided a choice of activities, motivation is activated. Choice can include the selection of two or three activities or topics from many, a language mode to use (listen or read, speak or write), or the time to complete the activities.

A second internal motivator is the opportunity to act like an adult. For instance, most students enjoy opportunities to pretend being a teacher, whether it is with pairs of students, a small group of students, or an entire class. This internal motivator can be used with many different types of activities.

A third internal motivator is the opportunity to alter language. Activities such as creating new definitions for words (*illegal* is a sick bird, *bull dozer* is a sleeping bovine) are helpful, as are creating new words for definitions (a very fast car is a *zoommobile* or an awesome football team is the *terror machine*).

Another internal motivator is the opportunity to create language through poems, stories, and/or articles. For instance, a sixth-grade student created the following story patterned after Remy Charlip's *Fortunately*.

> Fortunately I had a friend.
> Unfortunately he died.
> Fortunately there was a funeral.
> Unfortunately it was sad.
> Fortunately there were flowers.
> Unfortunately I wish there were more.
> Fortunately everyone was there.
> Fortunately so was I.
> Fortunately I want to be just like him.

Similarly, Michael, a second-grade student, created the following paragraph as part of an activity that encouraged him to create language:

All about Computers

by Michael

I will answer five questions about computers.

What are the five main parts of a computer? The five main parts of a computer are the control unit, the arithmetic unit, memory devices, input devices, and output devices.

Where did the word computer get its name? The computer got it's name from compute.

Why do computers punch holes? The holes are for computers to read.

What does COBOL stand for? COBOL stands for common business oriented language.

Is there any such thing as a computer language? Yes, COBOL is a computer language.

Whenever any of these internal motivators are activated, the possibility of student engagement and success is enhanced.

One example of how the intellectual environment can be organized using expectations, modeling, interests, and motivation is with uninterrupted sustained silent reading. As mentioned in Chapter 4, USSR is a good example of indirect instruction designed to develop attitude goals. The technique is deceptively simple: students and teachers read books of their choice individually for a sustained period of time each day. The purpose is to get students "hooked" on reading and to offer sustained opportunities to practice real reading. It works because it sets an expectation that all students will read; it includes modeling by the teacher and emulation of that model by students; the interest of every student is accounted for through individual choice of books; and motivation is accounted for through choice of what to read, how much to read and how to follow up on the reading. The steps in establishing USSR in the classroom are listed in Figure 5.1.

THE SOCIAL–EMOTIONAL ENVIRONMENT

Literacy and the social–emotional environment are closely related. Literacy is the communication of ideas and, as such, is a social event that is influenced by the emotions of the communicators. Hence, when building a literate environment teachers attend to such factors as social interactions and collaborative sharing.

Social Interactions. The quality of the social interactions accompanying reading activities influences feelings and concepts about reading. For instance, when students discuss a book together (such as Sendak's *Where the Wild Things Are or*

Figure 5.1 **Steps in establishing USSR in classrooms**

1. Establish a spot in the room for a library.
2. Gather three to five books per child that range in topic, difficulty, and so forth.
3. Include magazines, newspapers, comics, catalogs, and so forth.
4. Have every child choose something to read.
5. Keep the first session short — 5 minutes or less.
6. Make each succeeding session longer by 1 minute until the desired length of time is attained.
7. Change the books in the room library periodically (usually every month or so).
8. Have the children keep some sort of record of what they're reading, but do not give grades, establish competitions for the most books read, and so forth.
9. Periodically you and the children share what you have read and talk about the nature of reading as it relates to what is being read. Keep these sessions very informal.

White's *Charlotte's Web*), they not only have the opportunity to express their own concepts and feelings but to hear others expressing theirs. As a result of this social interaction, they modify their own feelings and concepts and achieve more attitude goals. Social interactions help promote the understanding that reading is communication and that communication brings satisfaction.

Collaborative Sharing. Collaborative sharing is a specialized type of communication that assists in developing positive attitudes about reading. In collaborative sharing each member of a group has an assigned responsibility. One student is the manager, another the recorder, another the researcher, and so on. Group size is determined by the number of responsibilities, but the usual number is three or four. The manager keeps the group on task and makes certain everyone participates, the recorder keeps a written record of the interaction, and the researcher goes back to the original source of information when needed. If any group member has difficulty, all group members help. Since everyone has a responsible role to play within the group, social interactions bring high status to everyone, not just to those who already enjoy it. This sharing of high status by all increases the feeling that reading is satisfying and enriches the concept that reading, writing, talking, and listening are all elements of communication.

CREATING A LITERATE ENVIRONMENT

Planning a literate environment starts with the three goals of reading instruction developed in Chapter 2. The teacher first decides what curricular goals to

Purposeful oral interaction is at the heart of the social–emotional environment.

work toward, then builds a literate environment designed to support these goals. Use the following steps when building a literate environment.

1. Decide upon the outcomes you wish to develop. Those that relate to attitude outcomes are best developed through activities associated with a literate environment. For these outcomes the environment plays the dominant role, whereas with the process and content outcomes the teacher plays the dominant role. For instance, using the curriculum statements specified for attitude outcomes in Figures 3.1 through 3.5, select the ones you wish to achieve with your class. At the primary level, you might select feelings such as *reading satisfies the need to know* and concepts such as *reading is for getting information.* At the later elementary level, you might select feelings such as *reading helps you feel good about yourself and others* and concepts such as *reading is a tool that can clarify knowledge, feelings, and attitudes.* The curriculum goals you select depend on the developmental stage and the needs of the students. However, you must select the curriculum goals before establishing activities to develop those goals.

2. Allocate sufficient time for the instruction. Time is connected to learning; that is, the more time given to an outcome, the more that is learned, and the less time allocated, the less that is learned. The activities in the literate environment must be allocated sufficient time if the goals are to be achieved.

3. Use the principles of indirect instruction. Organize activities such as learning center, classroom libraries, and visual displays to indirectly lead students to the achievement of the outcomes.

4. Use the physical, the intellectual, and the social-emotional environments to create the desired environmental conditions necessary to achieve your curricular goals.

    a. *Physical environment.* At the primary level a cooking center and a science center can have written directions. The classroom library can have books prominently displayed that provide either information or enjoyment. A bulletin board can be titled "The Wonders of the Animal World" and can contain pictures of such wonders as the sixteen foot white shark or flying squirrels. These can be accompanied by questions requiring written answers. At the upper elementary level activities can include a science center or an anthropological center involving a dig or the development of a time capsule. A classroom library that has books prominently displayed with additional information on digs or time capsules and a bulletin board displaying the products or the progress of a dig can also be developed. The range and variety of outcome directed activities is limitless.

    b. *Intellectual environment.* At the primary level elements of the intellectual environment (expectations, interests, motivation, and modeling) can be developed in several ways. A cooking center and science center can include the expectation that all students use them. The interests of specific students (such as octopuses or kangaroos) can be the topics in the science center. Pictures can be used to stimulate motivation and you can model the desired outcome. At the upper levels similar procedures can be employed. For instance, the anthropological center can include the expectation that all students will be involved, the student experts can be called on for help, any developing interest in digs or other related activities will be included, and you will model the desired outcomes.

    c. *Social–emotional environment.* Social interactions and collaborative sharing support the goals selected. At the

Reading to children is another important part of the literate environment.

primary level, for instance, time can be allocated for informal social interactions about the work in the center. More
formal interactions among students can occur in collaborative endeavors where tasks and outcomes are
predetermined by you and implemented by the groups. At
the upper levels, the same plan can occur. Time can be
allocated for formal and informal social interactions and
collaborative groups involving the anthropological center.

5. Match groups to specific activities and outcomes. During indirect
instruction in a literate environment students normally work in
small groups or as individuals. At times, however, you may wish to
explain certain procedures to the whole class. Some groups may be
formally established, as with collaborative groups, but many will be
informal.

6. Monitor activities in terms of desired outcomes. Once a literate environment has been planned and is operating, monitor its effectiveness. Activities that do not lead to the desired outcome can be
dropped and more effective activities substituted.

CONCLUSION

The environment in which students learn to read can have a major impact on what they learn. Therefore, you should plan and build classroom environments that promote a meaningful and exciting concept of reading.

CHECK YOUR UNDERSTANDING

Now that you have read the chapter, check your understanding by answering the Focus Questions presented at the beginning of the chapter. If you cannot answer one or more of the questions, return to the chapter, find the section that corresponds to the question, and reread.

SUGGESTED READINGS

Auten, A. (1983). The ultimate connection: Reading, listening, writing, speaking — thinking. *Reading Teacher*, *36*(6), 584–587.

Berglund, R. L., & Johns, J. L. (1983). A primer on uninterrupted sustained silent reading. *Reading Teacher*, *36*(6), 534–539.

Boodt, G. M. (1982). Up! up! and away! writing poetry in the reading class. *Language Arts*, *59*(3), 239–244.

Coody, B., & Nelson, D. (1982). *Successful activities for enriching the language arts*. Belmont, CA: Wadsworth.

Duffy, G. G. (1967). Developing the reading habit. *The Reading Teacher*, *21*, 253–256.

Evans, H. M., & Towner, J. C. (1975). Sustained silent reading: Does it increase skills? *The Reading Teacher*, *29*, 155–156.

Gentile, L. M., & McMillan, M. M. (1978). Humor and the reading program. *Journal of Reading*, *21*(4), 343–349.

Hamilton, M. C. (1974). Read aloud to children. *Instructor*, *84* 129–130.

Hamilton, S. F. (1983). Socialization for learning: Insights from ecological research in classrooms. *Reading Teacher*, *37*(2), 150–156.

Holbrook, H. T. (1982). Motivating reluctant readers: A gentle push. *Language Arts*, *59*(4), 385–390.

Hubbard, R. (1985). Second graders answer the question "Why publish?" *Reading Teacher*, *38*(7), 658–662.

Janney, K. P. (1980). Introducing oral interpretation in elementary school. *Reading Teacher*, *33*, 544–547.

Jennings, M. (1978). *Tape recorder fun*. NY: David McKay.

Langer, J. A. (1982). Reading, thinking, writing and teaching. *Language Arts*, *59*(4), 336–341.

Mager, R. (1969). *Developing attitudes toward learning.* Palo Alto, CA: Fearon, p.37.

Manna, A. L. (1984). Making language come alive through reading plays. *Reading Teacher, 37*(8), 712–717.

Martin, C. E., Cramond, B., & Safter, T. (1982). Developing creativity through the reading program. *Reading Teacher, 35*(5), 568–572.

McCracken, R. A. (1971). Initiating sustained silent reading. *Journal of Reading, 14*, 521–524; 582–583.

McCracken, R. A., & McCracken, M. J. (1978). Modeling is the key to sustained silent reading. *Reading Teacher, 31*(4), 406–408.

Mendoza, A. (1985). Reading to children: Their preferences. *Reading Teacher, 38*(6), 522–527.

Mikkelsen, N. (1982). Celebrating children's books throughout the year. *Reading Teacher, 35*, 790–795.

Miller, G. M., & Mason, G. E. (1983). Dramatic improvisation: Risk-free role playing for improving reading performance. *Reading Teacher, 37*(2), 128–131.

Moore, J. C., Jones, C. J., & Miller, D. C. (1980). What we know after a decade of sustained silent reading. *Reading Teacher, 33*(4), 445–450.

Nessel, D. D. (1985). Storytelling in the reading program. *Reading Teacher, 38*(4), 378–381.

Odland, N. (1979). Planning a literature program for the elementary school. *Language Arts, 56*(4), 363–367.

Radencich, M. C. (1985). Books that promote positive attitudes toward second language learning. *Reading Teacher, 38*(6), 528–530.

Seaver, J. T., & Botel, M. (1983). A first-grade teacher teaches reading, writing, and oral communication across the curriculum. *Reading Teacher, 36*(7), 656–664.

Sides, N. K. (1982). Story time is not enough. *Reading Teacher, 36*(3), 280–283.

Wagner, B. J. (1979). Using drama to create an environment for language development. *Language Arts, 56*(3), 268–274.

Wetzel, N. R., Davis, L., & Jamsa, E. (1983). Young authors conference. *Reading Teacher, 36*(6), 530–533.

CHAPTER 6

Organizing
Instructional Time

GETTING READY

The scarcity of time, more than any other single thing, makes classroom teaching difficult. There are many things to do and not enough time to do them. You must achieve all three reading outcomes, know the individual students and their stages of developmental reading growth, structure a literate environment in the classroom, and employ direct and indirect instructional techniques. Even the best teachers are hard pressed to provide adequate instruction for all three outcomes when they have only five hours of reading time a week with which to work.

The situation is further complicated by the fact that in most school systems a basal textbook is mandated. Because it is mandated, teachers often expect that *all* reading goals can be accomplished during the time devoted to the basal text materials, despite publishers' warnings that this is not so. Further, the complexity of daily classroom life (mentioned in Chapter 1) tends to make teachers focus on routine management tasks rather than on decisions about how to achieve the three goals of reading. Such "teaching like a technician" involves following the prescriptions of the teacher's guide without making decisions about what to teach, how much time to allocate, and how to teach it.

This chapter helps you avoid teaching like a technician by showing you how to organize your time so that the three major goals of reading can be accomplished despite basal textbooks and other constraints of classroom life. To accomplish this, you must first have a literate environment in place, as described in Chapter 5. Then you must know what the strengths and shortcomings of the basal text are and how to compensate for the shortcomings while capitalizing on the strengths. This chapter provides a plan for doing so. It explains how to establish year-long goals and how to achieve specific outcomes through large-group and small-group instruction.

FOCUS QUESTIONS

As you read this chapter use the following questions to guide your understanding of how to organize your time.

1. Summarize the strengths and weaknesses of a basal text reading program.
2. What three kinds of organizational decisions do teachers make in order to ensure that all three reading outcomes are achieved?
3. Considering a year-long curriculum, how can you ensure that adequate instructional time is allocated to all three outcomes of reading?
4. How can you be sure that the goals for each outcome are specified?
5. What organizational patterns should you keep in mind regarding large-group reading instruction?
6. What organizational patterns are helpful when thinking about basal text units?
7. What is the organizational pattern for organizing a basal text lesson?
8. In organizing a classroom reading program, approximately what proportion of the total instructional time is devoted to the basal text program?
9. What proportion of the total instructional time is devoted to each of the three major outcomes of reading?

STRENGTHS AND WEAKNESSES
OF BASALS

As mentioned in Chapter 1 and again in Chapter 4, a basal textbook has many appealing characteristics. Its sequential lessons provide a structured progression in which (1) the gradually increasing difficulty of each level expedites the process of grouping students according to ability, (2) the prescriptions in the teacher's guide provide valuable suggestions for teaching, (3) the reading selections are written to appeal to students at that level, and (4) the accompanying workbook and practice pages provide numerous activities to keep students occupied. The overall impression is that an entire reading program is contained right there in the materials and that all a busy teacher has to do is follow the prescriptions of the teacher's guide to ensure that students achieve all the outcomes of reading. Despite appearances, however, the comprehensiveness of a basal program is an illusion. It *seems* to be so, but it is not. There are three reasons for this.

ATTITUDE OUTCOMES

Although basal texts prescribe many different kinds of activities, they do not give equal treatment to the three reading outcomes. For instance, whereas most basal text programs discuss the need for developing concepts and positive responses to reading, very little instructional time is actually devoted to this outcome. Activities may be suggested, but little is done to help teachers incorporate these suggestions into a busy school day. Even when a basal contains good suggestions about developing attitude goals, other tasks are given priority, leaving little time for attitude development. More emphasis seems to be placed on reading the selections (content outcomes) and on completing the skill activities (process outcomes) than on attitude outcomes.

PROCESS OUTCOMES

At first glance basals seem to place a great emphasis on process outcomes because there are many suggestions in the teacher's guide regarding reading skills. In actuality, however, most of the activities in the teacher's guide focus on the content of the selections rather than on how to get meaning from them. Skills are taught from the standpoint of mastery and automaticity rather than as strategies to be consciously applied when meaning is blocked.

The difference is a major one. To illustrate, consider a typical basal lesson. The first part of the lesson focuses on the story. The lesson begins with an introduction to the story, a discussion of new vocabulary words, the establishment of purpose-setting questions, and the assignment of the pages to be read. No explicit mention is made here of how the reading system works or of how to use such knowledge to get meaning from the text; instead, teachers provide students with background and a "mind set" about the message contained in the selection. After students read the story there is typically a question and answer period in which the teacher quizzes the students on the story. Because these questions focus on what happened in the story, the teacher is checking the students' understanding of the story content, not their understanding of how the reading system helped them get meaning from the text or how strategies were applied when meaning broke down.

The second part of the lesson focuses on skills. The teacher assigns a skill page in the workbook. This assignment emphasizes answer accuracy. Seldom does the teacher ask the students to explain when the skill would be useful in reading text, what blockage situation might occur for which this skill would be useful, how to use the skill strategically when encountering such a situation, or what mental steps to follow when applying the skill in real situations. In short, neither knowledge about how reading works nor strategic application of skills receives much emphasis in a typical basal lesson.

CONTENT OUTCOMES

Basal texts emphasize content outcomes. Many of the suggested instructional activities are directed at answers to what happened in the selection. However, the answers are usually isolated from the process one uses to get the answer. Consider the order in which the basal lessons are typically organized. The first step is to teach the story selection; the second step is to teach the several skills recommended in that section of the teacher's guide, usually by assigning workbook pages. Seldom is there an explicit connection between a story selection and the skills to be taught. In fact, it sometimes seems that the story and the skills stand as separate activities. It is not expected that the skill would be used when reading real text, and no instructional activity is provided to illustrate how this might be done. In fact, skills are typically taught only in the context of the workbook; seldom are they connected to the reading selection in the basal text.

A more logical system would be to connect the targeted skill with the reading selection. For instance, as part of the preparation for reading a story selection, the skill could be introduced and taught with the expectation that it would be used immediately when reading the story. In that way, a teacher provides students with a rationale for why the skill is being taught, illustrates how it can be used strategically in reading the story, and has students apply the skill as they read it. The emphasis is then on application. Rather than being left to the isolation of workbook pages, skills are shown to be tools that have immediate use in real text.

SUMMARY

Whereas people sometimes get the impression that basal programs are complete reading programs, this is not really the case. If a teacher simply follows the prescriptions of a basal program, emphasis will be on the content of the basal reading selections and on skills practice that is unrelated to the selections. Relatively little emphasis is placed on attitudinal goals (even though these may be recommended by the basal teacher's guide) or on direct explanation of how the reading system works. Apparently it is hoped that students will come to an implicit understanding of how the system works while reading the selections. The emphasis is on getting content meaning from the selections in the basal and on teaching the skills as rules and algorithms to be applied automatically. Therefore, basals do not provide a complete and well-rounded reading program and teachers must supplement them by allocating instructional time to all the outcomes of reading. This calls for three kinds of organizational decision making including: (1) the year-long program; (2) large-group instruction, and (3) small-group instruction.

ORGANIZING THE YEAR-LONG PROGRAM

To organize the year-long curriculum, two considerations are essential. First, time must be allocated to the various outcomes, and second, the goals to be accomplished must be specified.

TIME ALLOCATIONS

In most classrooms the reading period occurs first thing each morning and lasts for an hour or an hour and a half. This is the only time allocated to reading instruction. Typically, all this allocated time is devoted to basal text instruction. Usually a teacher meets with three or four reading groups during this time, teaching one group at a time while the other groups do seatwork.

To develop all three reading goals, however, it is necessary to think more broadly about how to allocate time for reading. Because reading permeates all aspects of the school day, reading instruction can be integrated into other school activities; that is, reading goals can be achieved during times other than the hour or hour and a half allocated for reading. In the area of attitudes, for instance, conceptual understandings regarding the communication function of reading can be developed in conjunction with any subject matter; concepts about the reciprocal nature of reading and writing can be developed during a writing period; and positive responses to reading can be developed at any point in the school day when stories and poems are shared. Similarly, certain process outcomes about how the reading system works can be taught from a social studies or science textbook just as well as from a basal reader. Finally, content outcomes can be developed anytime a text is used. In short, reading goals can be developed all day long.

It is also possible to integrate other school content into reading time. Science materials can be read as seatwork during the reading period, stories and poems can be written during reading-group time, and quality books can be shared in collaborative student groups while the teacher is working with another basal text group. Finally, direct and indirect instruction can occur simultaneously. For instance, while the teacher is directly instructing one reading group, other reading groups can be engaged in instructional activities that depend on less direct teacher intervention.

Accomplishing such integration, however, requires careful year-long planning by a teacher. The times when certain goals are to be developed must be identified, and a teacher must consciously allocate additional instructional time beyond the hour or hour and a half that is usually designated. For instance, a teacher must examine the year-long language arts or social studies

Effective teachers make good use of nook-and-cranny time.

curriculum and decide when these objectives can be integrated with reading outcomes. In short, the integration of reading with other content areas does not occur by accident. Teachers consciously allocate instructional time to make the integration happen and by doing so create more instructional time for reading.

Another way to create more reading time is to look for the nooks and crannies of the school day. All school days have dead spots of five or ten minutes duration. It may be a transition from one activity to another, or a short period of time between two special teachers, or any other time that is too short to start a formal lesson. These nooks and crannies are goldmines for teachers looking for extra time for reading. For instance, book sharing and other activities designed to develop positive attitudes can be done at these times. Similarly, such time can be used to provide short periods of direct instruction about how certain words convey emotional connotations, or how we make predictions about what meaning is being communicated, or how to get content meaning from various kinds of texts.

SETTING GOALS

Whereas time allocation is crucial, it is not enough. A teacher must also decide what is to be accomplished during the time allocated. For instance, if a teacher decides that reading can be integrated with the social studies curriculum, specific reading objectives must be planned for the social studies period. Without such conscious goal setting, desired outcomes only occur by accident.

To be effective, teacher should list at the beginning of the school year the broad goals they wish to achieve in each of the three curricular areas. The suggested outcomes for each developmental stage of reading growth listed in Chapter 3 can be helpful. Once teachers have listed the goals for each outcome, they must decide which ones are best achieved through indirect instruction and which through direct instruction. After selecting their goals and appropriate modes of instruction, teachers then assign goals to specific time slots. Goals to be achieved during regular basal text instruction are assigned to that time slot, while others may be assigned to language arts, social studies, or nook-and-cranny time slots. In this way time is allocated for each of the broad goals teachers wish to achieve.

ORGANIZING FOR WHOLE-GROUP INSTRUCTION

Teachers who rely on basal textbooks conduct their reading instruction in small reading groups. However, as previously mentioned, a basal program does not develop all reading outcomes. Some are better taught in large-group situations, either in predetermined time frames or in nook-and-cranny time slots.

Attitude outcomes are particularly responsive to large-group instruction. For instance, language experience activities can often be conducted with an entire class, particularly when the whole class has participated in a field trip, a school assembly, or another special event. A special event provides the stimulus for creating a written message. In creating this message a teacher develops concepts about the message-sending properties of reading, the author–reader relationship, the similarity between constructing meaning when reading and composing meaning when writing, and so on. Similarly, book-sharing activities can be conducted with the entire class. During these sessions the teacher can develop positive attitudes toward reading by modeling, pointing out how certain books stimulate particular emotional responses, noting names of children who are particularly appreciative of literature, and so on.

Large-group instruction is also useful in developing certain process outcomes. For instance, some of the nook-and-cranny time can be used for mini-lessons about how the reading system works. Whenever there is a spare five minutes between activities, teachers can present information to students, showing them how knowledge about the reading process can help them determine an author's intended meaning. Similarly, such times can be used to let individual students demonstrate how they determined meaning in their own

Whole-group instruction is an important part of a reading program.

reading or to allow them to work together to figure out the "real" meaning of a particular text passage. Finally, there are times during a school day when the whole class may read the same text, thereby providing an opportunity to develop content outcomes in a large group.

Although this kind of large-group instruction may look spontaneous, good teachers carefully plan it. For instance, a field trip or other special event may be planned as the basis of a language experience lesson that, in turn, will be used to develop an attitude outcome identified in a year-long plan. Similarly, a teacher may allocate time for book sharing with the intention of developing another attitude outcome. Even process and content instruction may look spontaneous when they occur as space fillers in one of the nooks and crannies of the school day but, in reality, are part of a year-long plan to deliberately use odd moments to develop certain curricular outcomes.

There are several advantages to such large-group instruction. First, it moves reading outside the context of the basal textbook. Because reading is not confined to the selections in a basal and to small groups, students learn that reading fits into virtually all situations. Second, large-group instruction provides the opportunity for students of varying ability levels to contribute together. In contrast to the small reading groups that are formed on the basis of ability, large-group instruction allows good and poor readers to work together. Finally, teachers often find large-group instruction a relaxing change of pace from the routine of daily reading groups. Large groups can be managed more easily because all the students are working on a single task rather than in a variety of situations that require different amounts of supervision.

Because basal texts dominate programs in today's classrooms, teachers sometimes overlook the potential of large-group instruction, especially for developing important attitude goals. To ensure a broad and comprehensive program, however, time should be deliberately allocated for large-group instruction and for the attitude outcomes that basal textbooks tend not to emphasize.

ORGANIZING FOR SMALL-GROUP INSTRUCTION

Large-group instruction is important, but it is not enough. A good reading program must also include small basal text groups that emphasize process and content goals. These require as much careful organization by the teacher as do large groups. Two kinds of decisions are required: how to organize a basal unit and how to organize a basal lesson.

UNIT ORGANIZATION

A unit in most basal textbooks is comprised of several selections that are grouped together and often reflect a theme. For instance, a basal text may have units of five stories each, with the theme of the first unit *courage*, the second *sports,* and so on. While the length of units and the way they are tied together vary from one basal series to another, virtually all basals group selections into units.

Each lesson in a unit typically includes a selection to be read and skills to be taught. In most basals the selection is taught first and is followed by the skill lesson, which tends to isolate the skill from the preceding selection. A teacher can rectify this by reorganizing the instructional sequence so that the skill is taught prior to reading the selection. By doing this the skill can be used when reading the story.

Accomplishing this reorganization is a two-step process. First, a teacher must survey the basal prescriptions for the whole unit, reorganize these prescriptions according to the three goals of reading, and identify the specific instructional objectives to be achieved under each goal. Second, a teacher must decide which objectives to teach with each story.

The first step — that of reorganizing the prescriptions into related groups — is necessary because there is seldom any clear relationship among the skills or strategies taught in a particular unit or between these skills or strategies and the

Figure 6.1 **Steps in reorganizing basal text prescriptions**

1. List all the objectives prescribed by the basal.
2. Group these objectives into three categories according to the three major reading outcomes (attitude, process, content).
3. Delete objectives that do not reflect any of the three major outcomes.
4. Add any objectives the basal fails to prescribe.
5. For each of the three categories of objectives, group together similar objectives (put all phonics objectives together, all comprehension strategies together, and so forth).
6. Examine the lists of similar content within each of the three categories and state an objective for each. The resulting list states your objectives for the unit.

skills and strategies needed to read the selections. For instance, a phonics skill on the initial *ch* digraph may be presented in the same unit with a skill on predicting outcomes. The two do not seem to be related in any obvious way, nor do the basal selections to be read in the unit call for the use of either *ch* digraphs or predicting outcomes.

Although some teachers follow such random prescriptions faithfully, professionals try to impose a more sensible organization on the unit. They list what the basal prescribes for the unit, organize these objectives into categories reflecting the three reading outcomes, add objectives that the basal text may have neglected, and eliminate any prescriptions that ought not to be taught or do not relate to the three outcomes.

Once all the prescribed objectives have been categorized by outcome and any additions have been made, the teacher groups together those objectives that go together. For instance, in the process category the teacher groups all the word-identification strategies together, all the comprehension strategies together, and so on. Then the teacher further organizes each of these process groupings into subunits (such as phonics skills, context skills, and structural analysis skills in the word-identification category). When finished with this categorizing, a teacher knows precisely what is to be taught in each of the three outcome categories, and within each category, there is a list of the curricular objectives that go together. These clusters of similar content are then restated as objectives for that unit. Figure 6.1 illustrates the steps involved in reorganizing basal content.

Once teachers have identified the objectives to be taught in a basal unit, they must then decide which objective goes with which selection. This often means that they must move a skill from its place in the basal and teach it in a different story. For instance, it is not unusual for a basal textbook to prescribe a lesson on determining word meaning through the use of prefixes without having any prefixed words in the accompanying selection. Consequently, that particular selection cannot be used to teach prefixes, so the teacher must move the prefix lesson to another place in the unit where there is a selection containing prefixed words. By matching objectives and selections the teacher ensures that curricular objectives will be taught in the context of their application to real reading rather than in isolation.

LESSON ORGANIZATION

Once teachers have organized a basal unit so that specific objectives are matched to specific selections, they are ready to organize individual lessons. The first step is to decide whether to teach a content or a process outcome, since each one has its own organizational scheme.

Two Lesson Plan Formats. A teacher who decides to have students focus on the content of the selection organizes the lesson using the steps of the directed reading lesson. As mentioned in Chapter 4, there are six steps to the standard DRL:

1. Introduce the story by activating appropriate background experience and introducing new vocabulary words.
2. Set the purposes for reading the selection.
3. Have the students read the section silently or orally.
4. Discuss the selection in terms of the purposes discussed in Step 2.
5. Teach the prescribed skills.
6. Close the lesson by summarizing the content and/or by involving students in an enriching activity.

If a teacher's objective is to develop a process outcome, however, an eight-step modification of the DRL sequence is used:

1. Introduce the selection and the special vocabulary.
2. Introduce the process outcome to be applied when reading the selection.
3. Model the process outcome.
4. Guide student acquisition.
5. Set the purposes for reading the selection.
6. Have the students read the selection silently or orally.
7. Discuss the content of the selection and how the process outcome was used while reading it.
8. Close the lesson.

Figure 6.2 **Two forms of the directed reading lesson**

Standard DRL		Modified DRL	
Step 1	Introduce selection (activate schema and special vocabulary)	Step 1	Introduce selection (activate schema and special vocabulary)
Step 2	Set purposes for reading selection (for content understanding only)	Step 2	Introduce knowledge or strategy to be taught
Step 3	Have students orally or silently read selection	Step 3	Model how to use knowledge or strategy
Step 4	Discuss selection (for content understanding only)	Step 4	Mediate student acquisition of knowledge or strategy
Step 5	Teach skills	Step 5	Set purposes for reading selection (include application of knowledge or strategy as well as understanding of content
Step 6	Bring closure to lesson (by summarizing content only)	Step 6	Have students orally or silently read selection
		Step 7	Discuss selection (in terms of both content and application of knowledge or strategy)
		Step 8	Bring closure to lesson by summarizing both content and use of knowledge or strategy

Thus, a process goal becomes the focus of the lesson in contrast to the DRL, which normally emphasizes the content of the section with skills taught as an add-on after the selection has been read. Said another way, the standard DRL focuses on developing an understanding of what went on in the selection in isolation from the skill lesson; the modified DRL focuses on the connection between how one makes sense of text and the application of that understanding to the selection. Figure 6.2 illustrates the similarities and differences in the two forms of the DRL.

Both lesson sequences are examples of direct instruction. A teacher decides at the outset (in reference to the unit plan) what process or content goal to teach with a particular basal selection. The teacher directly assists a student in understanding either what the selection says or how a particular aspect of process can be used to make sense out of the selection. It is as if the teacher is saying:

I know something about how reading works and I'm going to share it with you so you can use it to get meaning from this story we are about to read. I'm not going to keep secret what I know about how to be a good reader and I am not going to make you figure it out by yourself as we go along. Instead, I'm going to make it as clear as possible so you can put it to work in this story and in other things that you read.

Decisions Associated with the Two Lesson Plan Formats. Both lesson plans require teacher decision making. First, a teacher must decide what outcome is desired and how to alter the basal's prescribed sequence accordingly. Once this decision is made, a teacher must fit the basal text prescriptions into the sequence appropriate for either content or process goals.

If the intent is to develop a content goal, decisions focus on using the DRL to guide students in activating appropriate background experience, developing concepts for new words, and ensuring that the message is understood. To make these decisions teachers use their understanding of how readers use knowledge of words, topic, purpose, and text structure to comprehend. They introduce the vocabulary, tell students what the topic of the story or selection is, state the author's purpose in writing it, and cue students to distinctive features of the text structure. The intent is to help students to make

A teacher plans how to reorganize basal text content.

initial predictions about meaning based on what they know about topic, author purpose, and cues provided in the text structure (titles, subtitles, headings, illustrations, and so forth). By getting students to activate appropriate knowledge and to predict on the basis of that knowledge, a teacher gets students ready to comprehend the message of the selection. Consequently, in planning the DRL teachers guide students regarding words, topic, purpose and text structure.

The decisions are somewhat different when developing process outcomes. Whereas the first step in both types of lesson are identical, the second step in process-oriented lessons is to state explicitly what process knowledge or strategy is being taught. This is where the modified lesson plan format begins to depart from the standard DRL. Whereas this statement is often brief, it answers three important questions for the students:

1. It tells them what they will be learning about how reading works.
2. It specifies where the knowledge or strategy will be used (i.e., the teacher states where they will use the knowledge or strategy in the basal selection they are about to read and specifies similar situations where they could use that knowledge).
3. The teacher alerts them to what they must pay attention to in order to learn the knowledge or strategy.

The third step is to model the knowledge or strategy being taught. After stating what is to be learned, when it will be used, and the "secret" to doing it, the teacher says, "Here, let me show you how it's done." Then, using a sample of text, the teacher explains the thinking a student must do to use the knowledge or strategy. This modeling should give the students all the information they need to use the knowledge or strategy when they read. Since the teacher models each step no steps are omitted or glossed over.

No matter how explicitly and thoroughly the teacher models, students must be given an opportunity to try out the knowledge or strategy and to adapt it to their own mental processing. Consequently, the next step is to provide additional text passages similar to those used to model and asks students to "Do as I did." In short, the students follow the teacher's model in using the knowledge or strategy. At first the teacher provides lots of support in the form of cues and directives, but gradually such aids are removed as the student adapts and personalizes the use of the knowledge or strategy. This is a crucial stage in the instructional sequence since it is the students' responses at this stage that reveal misunderstandings about how the knowledge or strategy works. If misunderstandings become evident, the teacher must spontaneously provide explanations to eliminate the confusion and put the student back on the right track. That is why this step is called *guiding student acquisition* — the teacher forms a connecting bridge between the student and the outcome. Whether a student learns to use the knowledge or strategy often depends upon the teacher's sensitivity in performing this guiding or bridging role.

Once students demonstrate an understanding of how to use the knowledge or strategy, the teacher assigns the basal selection for practice. The teacher sets two purposes for reading the basal selection: first, students are given content purposes associated with getting the message of the text; second, they are asked to apply to the selection the process knowledge or strategy they have learned. They then begin reading the selection together, usually silently but sometimes orally (especially in the primary grades). After they have read the selection, the teacher guides the discussion, talking with the students about the content of the story and about how the newly taught knowledge or strategy is applied to it. Finally, the teacher closes the lesson by summarizing both the content of the selection and the process that was taught.

Ultimately, of course, teachers must ensure that students apply the knowledge or strategy in settings other than the basal textbook. The real purpose of reading instruction is to help students become independent readers of real-world materials. This purpose cannot be achieved adequately if students think reading strategies are meant to be used only when reading a basal textbook. Consequently, a teacher's task is not done until a student can apply the knowledge or strategy to natural text.

SUMMARY

The previous section provides two organizational frameworks for planning basal text reading lessons. If the objective is to teach the content of the selection, use the DRL; if the objective is to teach a process knowledge or strategy such as those described in Chapters 2 and 3, use the modified DRL. By using these two organizational plans, teachers can be in control of basal texts and can focus on directly and explicitly developing with students the content and process outcomes of the reading curriculum.

CONCLUSION

Being a professional reading teacher is not easy. The three major outcomes of reading instruction require both indirect and direct instruction and much instructional time. However, there is only a limited amount of instructional time in the school day and much of the time normally allocated to reading instruction is dominated by the basal textbook.

This chapter suggests three organizational patterns or structures that can help you solve this dilemma. The first is a pattern for organizing the year-long

It is important to allocate equal time to the three major outcomes.

curriculum, which emphasizes the allocation of instructional time to each of the three major goals of reading. The second is for whole-group instruction in non-basal settings emphasizing indirect instruction intended to develop the positive attitudes that are the foundation of a good reading program. The last is an organizational plan for basal text instruction in small reading groups emphasizing process and content goals. This plan requires two major patterns: one for reorganizing a basal unit and one for reorganizing a lesson plan format. By using patterns or structures such as these, you impose your own organization on classroom instruction rather than passively following the prescriptions of basal textbooks. Thus, you maintain a focus on the major curricular goals while simultaneously exercising cognitive control over your instruction.

CHECK YOUR UNDERSTANDING

Now that you have read the chapter, check your understanding by answering the Focus Questions presented at the beginning of the chapter. If you cannot answer one or more of the questions, return to the chapter, find the section that corresponds to the question, and reread.

SUGGESTED READINGS

Baumann, J. F. (1984). How to expand a basal reader program. *Reading Teacher,* *37*(7), 604–607.

Charnock, J. (1977). An alternative to the DRA. *Reading Teacher, 31*(3), 269–271.

Crafton, L. K. (1982). Comprehension before, during, and after reading. *Reading Teacher,* 36(3), 293–297.

Gourley, J. W. (1978). This basal is easy to read—or is it? *Reading Teacher,* *32*(2), 174–182.

Helton, G. B., Morrow, H. W., & Yates, J. R. (1977). Grouping for instruction: 1965, 1975, 1985. *Reading Teacher, 31*(1), 28–33.

Hill, S. E. (1985). Children's individual responses and literature conferences in the elementary school. *Reading Teacher, 38*(4), 382–386.

King, R. T. (1982). Learning from a PAL. *Reading Teacher, 35*(6), 682–685.

Shannon, P. (1982). Some subjective reasons for teachers' reliance on commercial reading materials. *Reading Teacher, 35*(8), 884–889.

Swaby, B. (1982). Varying the ways you teach reading with basal stories. *Reading Teacher, 35*(6), 676–680.

Unsworth, L. (1984). Meeting individual needs through flexible within-class grouping of pupils. *Reading Teacher, 38*(3), 298–304.

CHAPTER 7 _____

Collecting Data to Form and to Teach Reading Groups

GETTING READY

The scarcity of time is not the only thing that makes reading instruction difficult. Another difficulty stems from the fact that the students receiving instruction represent various levels of developmental reading growth. If you are teaching a particular grade level (e.g., third grade) and you have 24 students in the class, the reading levels will normally range from beginning reading (about first grade level) to upper-grade reading (about sixth grade level). If you try to teach all 24 children in one large group, the advanced readers will probably get bored and the low-aptitude readers will probably get frustrated. Both will lose interest. By grouping children according to ability, however, each group receives instruction at the appropriate level.

To deal with such individual differences in pupil ability, teachers form reading groups so that students with similar needs are taught together. This chapter recommends two types of groups, describes them, and explains the data-collection decisions that you must make in using such groups.

FOCUS QUESTIONS

As you read this chapter use the following questions to guide your understanding about how to form reading groups and how to plan their instruction.

1. Why are reading groups desirable?
2. What are the characteristics that distinguish collaborative groups?

3. What are the characteristics that distinguish ability groups?
4. How will you assign students to collaborative groups?
5. How will you assign students to ability groups?
6. How will you decide whether a particular basal selection is at a student's reading level?
7. Once groups are formed, why do you need to collect data using the vital signs?
8. How can you determine student needs for attitude, process, and content outcomes?

WHAT KINDS OF READING GROUPS?

Many classrooms have only one kind of reading group—a traditional basal textbook group formed on the basis of reading level. There is a serious weakness in this. Whereas basal textbooks are helpful in developing process and content outcomes, they are less helpful in developing attitude outcomes. Hence, when there are only basal text groups, the instructional emphasis tends to neglect the latter.

This problem can be eased by having two kinds of reading groups. Just as a literate classroom environment must have a variety of activities reflecting the three goals of reading instruction, there must be different grouping patterns to accommodate the various outcomes. Collaborative groups are recommended to promote attitude goals and ability groups to promote process and content goals.

Collaborative groups are temporary and heterogeneous groups in which three or four children of varying abilities work together on a particular project. For purposes of reading instruction the projects in collaborative groups are directed toward attitude goals. For instance, temporary collaborative groups may be formed to create language experience stories; read and discuss certain kinds of books together; discuss themes and issues relating to outside reading; organize and prepare presentations that will be made to the rest of the class or to other classes; produce various kinds of text, such as poetry, drama, letters to the editor, and essays; follow written directions (such as recipes); and engage in a variety of other activities that result in positive responses and conceptual understanding of reading. The group members normally divide up the work according to their particular strengths. Seldom do all the group members perform the same functions or do the same reading. Such grouping is sometimes called *cooperative grouping* because all group members contribute to the completion of the activity.

In contrast, ability groups are homogeneous. Four to eight children are grouped together because they are all working at the same ability level. Conse-

A collaborative group works together on a project.

quently, they can be given the same written material with the expectation that they will all be able to read it and perform the required tasks. Unlike collaborative groups in which each participant contributes to a group goal by performing a different task, ability groups require each member of the group to perform the same tasks to ensure that everyone achieves certain process and content outcomes. For instance, a teacher may emphasize how stories are structured so students can use this as a strategy to predict meaning or may demonstrate a study guide that will help them locate and comprehend salient information in a chapter of their social studies text.

Both kinds of groups are important. Collaborative groups provide opportunities for students to develop the attitude goals of reading whereas ability groups permit teachers to show how reading works and how students can understand the messages in text. The greatest benefit of using both kinds of groups, however, may lie with its potential for neutralizing negative expectations. One of the persistent problems with using only ability grouping is that negative expectations are communicated to the children in the low group. The low-group student is publicly labeled "a dummy." No matter what a teacher may say to soften this label, the fact remains that the child is in the lowest reading group and everyone knows it. These negative expectations are neutral-

A teacher provides instruction for an ability group.

ized somewhat by the use of collaborative groups. In collaborative groups each child is a worthwhile contributor to a heterogeneous group and, consequently, morale and perseverence are maintained.

COLLECTING DATA TO FORM
READING GROUPS

Having two kinds of reading groups means that a teacher must decide how to assign students to groups. The following section describes the data needed to help make these decisions.

DATA FOR COLLABORATIVE GROUPS

A collaborative group must work together to accomplish a goal despite student differences. However, teachers must avoid assigning cliques of "in-group" children to collaborative groups simply because they know how to get a job done. The way to form collaborative groups is to collect data about students' interests, their ability to get along with others, and the current social relationships in the classroom. There are several ways to do this.

The most useful way to collect information is through daily observation. Much can be learned about students simply by watching what they do and say in a variety of situations. Whom do they talk to? Who talks to them? Who are the leaders and who are the followers? Who is being picked on? What interests, strengths, and weaknesses do various children display?

Another useful technique is to use a questionnaire to solicit the students' interests and attitudes. A teacher can administer it as an interview technique in the kindergarten and primary grades or in its written form with more mature students. Such questionnaires should be simple and easy to complete. For instance, sentence-completion tasks such as the following are useful:

My idea of a good time is_____.

The smartest person in the class is _____.

I like _____ because _____.

A teacher collects data about a student's interests.

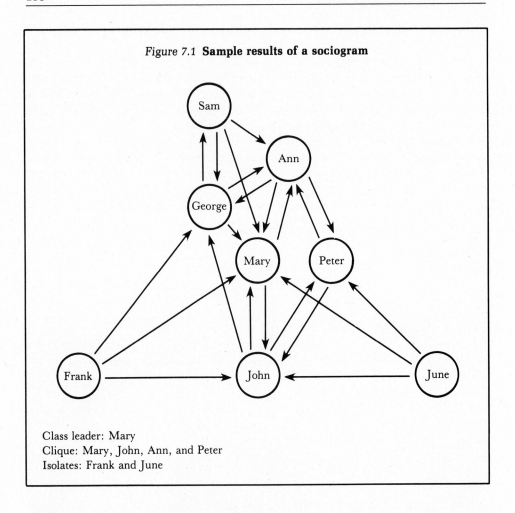

Figure 7.1 **Sample results of a sociogram**

Class leader: Mary
Clique: Mary, John, Ann, and Peter
Isolates: Frank and June

A simple way to collect information is to give students a list of statements and to ask them whether these are true or false about themselves:

I think most of the kids in school like me.

I get nervous when I have to talk in front of the class.

Another useful technique is to talk casually to each of the students. For instance, it is possible to talk with a particular child while supervising recess or while the child is waiting to go to lunch. Because they are so informal and nonthreatening, conversations of this nature can yield valuable information about a student.

Finally, a *sociogram* is often a useful indicator of the social relationships in the classroom. A sociogram is administered by asking students in the class to list the three children that they would most and least want to be with in a group. As shown in Figure 7.1, the results can be plotted to graphically display who the popular children are, who the isolates are, and where the cliques exist. Such information is valuable when forming collaborative groups. For instance, it helps teachers decide where to place isolates, whether to split up a clique, and where to place class leaders. Sociogram data are useful in making a variety of decisions about collaborative grouping.

There is no totally systematic way to form collaborative groups, but because their composition changes from activity to activity teachers must be prepared to organize them frequently. Decisions will be more appropriate if they are based on data gathered about the students, their preferences, their perceptions, and the way other students view them.

DATA FOR ABILITY GROUPS

Since ability groups are composed of students with similar abilities, to form such groups teachers collect ability data. The question is, what kind of ability?

As noted in some detail in Chapter 2, reading is not a set of skills that, once mastered, equal *reading.* Instead, humans store knowledge in mental structures or networks (referred to as schemata) that are applied to text information to form hypotheses. These hypotheses, in turn, either elaborate upon or modify existing schemata. In making and testing these hypotheses a reader uses a variety of strategies based on knowledge of how reading works and how to fix blockages to meaning.

Traditionally, teachers have assessed reading levels by asking students to read aloud progressively more difficult paragraphs and to respond to a series of questions about the content of those paragraphs. For instance, to determine whether a student has a third-grade reading level, we would make an oral reading assignment from the third-grade book and then ask questions about the paragraph's content. If the student is 99 percent fluent in identifying words in the text and 90 percent accurate in answering questions about the passage, that level of text is considered to be the student's *independent reading level;* that is, material from that level can be read by the student without assistance from a teacher or another adult.

Similarly, if a student reads with 95–99 percent fluency in word identification and/or 75–90 percent accuracy in comprehension, that level of text is considered to be the student's *instructional reading level*; that is, material from that level can be read by the student with some assistance from the teacher. If the

Figure 7.2 **Traditional criteria for establishing reading levels**

Frustration Level (text too difficult)	= Student identifies less than 95% of the words and/or is less than 75% accurate in comprehension
Instructional Level (text can be read with guidance)	= Student fluently identifies 95%–99% of the words and is 75%–90% accurate in comprehension
Independent Level (text can be read without assistance)	= Student fluently identifies 99%–100% of the words and is 90%–100% accurate in comprehension

student reads the material with less than 95 percent fluency in word identification and/or less than 75 percent accuracy in comprehension, the material is considered to be at the *frustration reading level*; that is, such material is considered too difficult for the student to read under any circumstances (see Figure 7.2).

Whereas it is comforting to have such quantitative guidelines for determining reading levels, current knowledge about how reading works suggests that this technique may not be completely adequate. A student's reading level is not entirely revealed by the number of the words identified and the number of the questions answered in a sample of graded text. Instead, whether a student can read a passage or not depends upon prior knowledge, on the presence or absence of a schematic structure for the topic being discussed. In other words, an individual's reading level in a particular text depends upon the topic being discussed. A selection on one topic from a typical third-grade book may be easy for one student because of familiarity with that topic, whereas for another child in the same reading group it may be quite difficult because of lack of background information. Similarly, one basal text selection may be fairly easy for a student because it deals with familiar content and the very next selection may be difficult because of its unfamiliarity. In addition, factors such as syntax and special vocabulary can affect text difficulty. Consequently, the practice of establishing independent, instructional, and frustration reading levels can be misleading because it implies a single, static reading level for each child.

In view of these factors, how do teachers assign students to the proper text in a basal series when each book consists of a variety of selections, some of which may reflect a student's background experience and some of which may not? This is a classic example of a teaching dilemma. As with all dilemmas, there is no "right" answer; instead, teachers use what data are available to make the best decision possible and, when additional data become available, remain flexible enough to modify the decision.

For instance, when beginning the school year in September, listen to each student read passages selected from various levels of the basal text series. A third-grade teacher, for instance, might ask the students to read samples of basal text from the first-, second-, third-, and fourth-level books. As the students read, the teacher notes any breaks in fluency. For instance, the teacher listens for intonation patterns that do not match the meaning of the text; words that are miscalled or omitted; words that are inserted or substituted; words that are repeated or identified incorrectly and then corrected; noticeable hesitations that are made before words; ignored punctuation; and any other indications of nonfluent reading. Breaks in fluency that alter the meaning of the text and remain uncorrected by a student should be noted in particular, because such breaks suggest an inability to self-monitor the meaning-getting process.

After the oral reading has been completed, the teacher assesses comprehension by having a student first retell or summarize what the selection was about. If important meaning relationships are omitted, probe with questions designed to assess a student's comprehension of that particular relationship. Following oral reading of successively more difficult passages, examine the students' performance pattern across the various passages. Using the criteria

A teacher collects data about a student's reading level.

for independent, instructional, and frustration levels outlined in Figure 7.2 as a guide (but not as an iron-clad rule), ask and answer questions such as the following:

- What passages did the student read with no apparent difficulty?
- In what passage did the student first begin to show some frustration?
- At what point did the reading become clearly frustrating for the student?
- On the basis of the student's reading performance across these paragraphs, what level basal text seems to be comfortable — not too frustrating and not too easy?

It is sometimes difficult to decide on initial student placements in a basal text despite having listened to each student read. In these cases it is helpful to check other data sources. For instance, a student's previous teacher will know what level text the student was in the year before. Similarly, it is possible to look in students' cumulative record folders for recommendations from other teachers and for the results of other tests.

If placement is still difficult, it is best to follow the rule, When in doubt, go low. For instance, if after listening to a third grader read basal text passages a teacher cannot decide between placement in a second- or third-level book, it is probably best to begin at the second level. By doing so a student's self-concept is protected. If a teacher corrects a faulty initial placement by moving a student to a lower group, that student is bound to feel discouraged. Such experiences can cast a pall on a student's motivation for the remainder of the year. If, however, a teacher begins by making the lower of the two placements and later assigns the student to the higher level, the student will feel encouraged and motivated by the move.

The assessment task is not over, however, once you have assigned students to groups. As previously mentioned, reading ability level is not a static thing, and teachers must continue to collect and act upon fresh data. Because the level of difficulty in a basal text selection depends partly upon a student's background experience regarding the topic, it is necessary to make adjustments for individual students despite the fact that they are all supposedly at a particular reading level. For instance, a selection on sheep herding in the Rocky Mountains will be easier for students who have some prior knowledge about sheep, sheep herding, or the Rocky Mountains. In this sense all students in a group are never reading at exactly the same reading level. Consequently, when assigning students to ability groups, you must continually monitor individual students' prior knowledge as well as keep track of the more traditional measures of word identification and comprehension accuracy.

MONITORING VITAL SIGNS FOR READING GROUPS

In Chapter 3 the concept of vital signs was introduced to illustrate how a teacher can determine each student's stage of developmental reading growth. The vital signs of reading health relate to the three major goals of reading. Students' relative placement is determined by comparing their performance on each vital sign to the expectations established for each stage of developmental reading growth. These performance expectations are listed in Figures 3.1–3.5. A format for making decisions about a student's vital signs in reading is provided in Figure 3.12.

USING VITAL SIGNS TO DETERMINE STUDENT NEEDS

The vital signs were introduced in Chapter 3 in connection with the stages of developmental reading growth. However, teachers apply the same concept when working with reading groups. Whereas collaborative groups are formed according to social relationships, and ability groups are formed according to reading level, decisions about what to teach in both collaborative and ability groups are made by collecting data about each student's performance in relation to the three goals (the vital signs).

To develop attitude outcomes, employ collaborative groups. However, forming the groups and assigning them activities to pursue does not automatically assure the development of appropriate attitude outcomes. Teachers also need to know *which* attitude outcomes the students in the group need. Student need, then, is the key. To illustrate, assume a teacher is teaching a third grade and can use the curriculum normally emphasized at the Expanded Fundamental Stage (see Figure 3.3). If the concept the teacher wants to develop is *Reading is a communication between a writer and a reader*, the collaborative group activity will be different from one emphasizing the concept *Reading is a tool*. Similarly, if a teacher forms collaborative groups to develop positive responses to reading, the activities chosen will differ depending on what kind of positive response the teacher is trying to develop.

Similarly, to achieve process and content outcomes at the same third-grade level, a teacher employs ability groups. However, specific process and content goals will not result simply by moving students through a basal text. Teachers need to know which goals the students in the group need to develop. Referring again to Figure 3.3, instruction in an ability group will differ depending on the desired outcome: Is it for developing instant recognition of easily confused words or for developing an understanding of the different kinds of meanings that are conveyed by different types of text? Similarly, if teachers want to develop content outcomes, the lesson will look different if the intent is to understand the content of narrative poetry rather than of a newspaper editorial.

Consequently, whereas collaborative and ability groups may initially be formed in reference to social relations and reading level, the ongoing objectives for a group are guided by a teacher's assessment of students' vital signs. In collaborative groups, knowledge of each student's attitudinal needs will shape the kinds of activities that are pursued and the way these activities are structured. In ability groups, assessment of students' knowledge about the reading process and their ability to apply this knowledge to text will determine which of the basal text prescriptions to emphasize most and least and what kind of supplemental instruction to provide.

HOW TO COLLECT VITAL SIGNS DATA

Data must be collected to determine which outcomes the students need to develop. Again, the techniques outlined in Figure 3.12 are helpful, as are the lists associated with each stage of developmental reading growth in Figures 3.1–3.5.

ATTITUDE OUTCOMES

To determine a student's conceptual understanding of reading, conduct an interview and ask questions such as: What is reading? Why do people read? What is the purpose of reading? Where did the writing on the page come from? Also, teachers can observe how students use reading. Do they read to solve problems or for pleasure? Do they treat reading as a communication process? Do they understand the relationship between reading and the other language modes, particularly writing? The information obtained from these observations and interviews can then be compared to the typical curricula found at the various stages of developmental reading growth (use Figures 3.1–3.5) to determine which concepts must yet be developed.

Use similar techniques to collect data about students' response to reading. For instance, interviews can be used to ask students what feelings they experience when reading, what they appreciate about reading, how often they read, what their favorite book is and why, and so on. Similarly, teachers can observe whether students choose to read during leisure time, whether they respond emotionally to what is read, whether they seem to value what has been read, and so on. Again, the information obtained can be compared to the attitudinal objectives listed in Chapter 3 for the various stages of developmental reading growth. By comparing data about the students' attitudes with the expectations for each stage of growth, teachers can determine which feelings and appreciations must yet be developed.

PROCESS OUTCOMES

In the process area, it is necessary to find out what students know about how to use words, prior knowledge of topic, author's purpose, and test structure in order to get meaning from text. Teachers also need to know how well student use strategies to repair breaks in meaning.

Teachers need to find out two things about students' word knowledge. First, they need to know what printed words can be identified, since individual words must be recognized in order to predict meaning. This can be determined by having a student read a sample of text at the appropriate reading level and noting all the words that are not instantly recognized, are miscalled, or cause the student to break reading fluency. Another technique is to use a graded list of words. The teacher puts each word on a card and flashes each to the student one at a time (see Figure 7.3). Those the student identifies instantly are *sight words*; those that cause hesitation or cannot be identified must be learned. For a student who is at the readiness level the same technique can be used to determine how many alphabet letters are known, since not many words have been learned.

The second thing teachers need to find out about students' word knowledge is their understanding of the meaning of words encountered in text. To gather this information, a teacher first pronounces a word and then asks the student to use the word orally in a sentence. If the word is used correctly, the student knows the meaning of the word in that context. By identifying what words the student does not know (that is, words that are not recognized in print or for which the student has no meaning), teachers know which words to teach for sight recognition and which to teach for meaning.

To determine whether a student can use the various knowledge sources (words, topic, purpose, and text structure) to predict meaning, a teacher can select a variety of text samples (short story, news article, recipe, and so forth) at a student's reading level and ask the student to talk out loud about how he or she tries to get meaning from these various kinds of text. What the teacher is looking for here is an understanding of how to use words and word meanings as well as knowledge of topic, purpose, and type of text to make and later modify predictions about meaning. While students will not talk about such processes like teachers do, their self-reports reveal whether they have an understanding of how to use knowledge about how the reading system works. By comparing a student's articulated knowledge with that to be developed at each developmental stage (see Figures 3.1–3.5), a teacher can determine what knowledge must yet be developed.

Figure 7.3 **A list of 325 basic sight words**

I	father	write	draw	most	turtle	head
and	make	before	feet	next	more	lie
the	cat	please	many	miss	both	answer
a	get	old	their	nice	bowl	balloon
to	sit	there	your	air	uncle	watch
was	hot	again	over	because	egg	cross
in	but	his	well	careful	hurt	engine
it	an	chair	sure	done	climb	front
of	be	push	into	felt	end	bear
my	they	any	may	heavy	circus	calf
he	for	by	upon	love	kind	eye
white	were	how	color	poor	floor	left
black	out	song	street	also	clothes	minute
red	him	very	does	believe	paw	monkey
green	us	am	family	catch	quite	people
blue	or	day	funny	ear	animal	log
yellow	have	our	bread	lion	every	build
one	new	with	milk	point	turn	soft
two	sad	bigger	more	together	kept	beautiful
three	this	do	away	wild	large	care
four	what	know	doll	tried	noise	year
five	all	put	good-bye	post	wolf	vegetable
six	been	will	could	voice	world	great
seven	her	are	morning	war	worm	picture
eight	much	busy	friend	warm	cried	little
nine	them	just	hurry	wonder	pennies	then
ten	about	apple	ready	breakfast	cabbage	we
saw	too	when	store	feather	cage	did
mother	baby	talk	end	else	heard	surprise
girl	something	today	brother	umbrella	learn	water
look	from	as	ask	nothing	carry	woman
on	house	off	quiet	field	sign	word
after	want	child	read	held	splash	give
get	went	take	school	already	spring	right
is	where	tell	own	quick	station	find
not	door	children	car	always	turkey	would
she	dog	walk	only	roar	soup	ride
who	shall	wash	once	arrow	squirrel	should
boy	pull	first	shoe	bump	wear	listen
go	if	full	bird	country	cover	money

Figure 7.3 **A list of 325 basic sight words** (continued)

good	long	horse	break	elephant	across	hair
like	other	orange	drink	board	bottom	honey
on	laugh	keep	slow	caught	automobile	
some	ball	table	near	early	buy	
you	some	which	match	fire	dear	
jump	pretty	guess	mice	hello	through	
brought	enough	piece	thought	roll	tomorrow	

SOURCE: These sight words are taken from Duffy, G. & Sherman, G. Systematic Reading Instruction, Harper & Row, 1971. If you are using a particular basal reader program, you can develop a similar sight word list for your program by taking the new words introduced at each level (usually found at the back of the teacher's edition) and list them in order of appearance in the basal series.

Teachers also want to determine how fluently a student reads — whether the reading is smooth and whether the voice intonations reflect the author's meaning. To do this, a teacher can ask students to read text orally and note their breaks in fluency. The teacher then must decide whether the fluency breaks are caused by words that are not instantly identified or by a lack of understanding about how to use knowledge of topic, author purpose, and text to predict voice intonations; or a combination of both. Sometimes this decision can be made simply by listening to and observing students as they read. This is especially the case when a fluency break is caused by unidentified words. At other times, however, teachers will want to have students talk out loud about why they make the reading sound a certain way or why they are not reading the text the way the author would say it.

When a reader's predictions about text meaning are confirmed, the text processing continues smoothly. However, when the predictions are not confirmed, the reader stops and says, "Oh, oh, this doesn't make sense" or "Oh, oh, something's wrong here." At this point, the reader must become strategic. That is, the reader must locate the source of the difficulty and apply an appropriate strategy to remove the blockage so that the text processing can proceed. The initial way to determine whether a student uses strategies is by listening to oral reading. When a blockage is encountered, teachers can ask the student to talk out loud about fixing the blockage. In the course of this assessment, teachers are trying to answer three questions:

1. Does the student recognize when a blockage to meaning occurs and stop to figure out what is wrong?
2. Once recognized, can the student determine the source of the difficulty, that is, whether it is an unrecognized word, a word with an unknown meaning, a confusion about sequence, and so on?
3. Once the source of the difficulty has been located, can the student apply an appropriate fix-it strategy? For instance, if the source of difficulty is a word unrecognized in print, can the student retrieve a context strategy, a structural analysis strategy, or a phonics strategy to analyze and identify the word? Such assessment helps determine the students' ability to monitor their reading performances and to retrieve and apply fix-it strategies as needed. As a result, teachers can decide whether they need to emphasize strategies and, if so, which ones.

If enough text is read, students will eventually encounter a variety of blockages that will allow teachers to observe their repertoire of fix-it strategies. However, this is a time-consuming procedure, and for diagnostic purposes it is often efficient to assess strategy usage in more isolated tasks.

For instance, if teachers want to determine whether students have strategies for analyzing words not recognized in print they can build brief assessments that check each of the three ways (context, structure, and phonics) of analyzing unknown words. For instance, to determine whether students can analyze using context, teachers can give them sentences with missing words and ask them to predict the missing word (see Figure 7.4 for types of context clues). To determine whether students can analyze using structural analysis, teachers can give them unrecognized words that can be identified through prefixes and suffixes (see Figure 7.5 for common structural units). To determine whether students can analyze using phonics, teachers can give them nonsense words containing phonic elements that should be known at that level and ask them to pronounce the words (see Figure 7.6 for common phonic elements). In each case, the students should talk out loud about their analysis so that teachers can determine whether or not a strategy is being correctly applied. In so doing, it is possible to determine whether students can use the context, structural, and phonic strategies to analyze unknown words.

Similarly, teachers can build informal assessments to determine whether syntactic and semantic cues are used to remove blockages to meaning. For instance, teachers can create passages similar to the examples about *time* and *rotation* in Chapter 2, in which they deliberately cause a certain prediction to be made, knowing that it will be changed as the student reads further. They can ask students to read the text orally, noting whether they look back when the blockage is encountered. Since teachers have intentionally included syntactic and semantic cues that can be reexamined during the look-back, they can ask students to explain about what cues are being used and how the predictions are being made. This technique gives teachers another check on students' overall awareness of their need to monitor meaning getting while also giving insight regarding their use of syntactic and semantic cues.

Teachers can also create an informal device to assess students' use of visible cues to meaning. For instance, students' use of typographic cues, prefixes and suffixes, and key words can be determined by creating text in which the meaning getting depends upon such visible cues. Teachers can ask students to explain the meaning being conveyed and the way in which the visible cues can be used to figure the meaning out. The following sentence offers an example:

> After the dance, I was unable to smile because Mary, who *was* my friend, played a despicable trick on me.

This sentence allows students to use each of the three major kinds of visible syntactic cues. The comma after *dance* and the commas setting off the phrase *who was my friend*, as well as the italicized *was* are all examples of typographic cues that can be used to figure out what the sentence means. The meaning of the verb *unable* can be figured out from its root and prefix, and the words *after* and *because* are key words, the former because it signals a chronological relationship and the latter because it signals a cause–effect relationship. In addition, this sentence allows students to use other word meanings in the sentence (semantics) to figure out the meaning of the word *despicable*. By asking students to explain about how they get meaning from sentences such as these, teachers can assess their use of visible cues, both syntactic and semantic.

Finally, even though invisible cues cannot be directly observed because they call for a reader's knowledge about topic, author purpose, and type of text, teachers can assess student use of these cues. For instance, teachers can provide samples of various kinds of text and have students use their experience with each kind to predict their meaning. Similarly, teachers can ask them to relate how author and reader purposes influence what meaning will be obtained. A paragraph such as the following can be used to ask for inferences based on the gist of the paragraph and on relationships, and then to ask for conclusions and judgments:

> The camel and his driver were stumbling across the desert. They had not seen an oasis for days. The sun was low on the horizon on the fourteenth day when the driver croaked, "I see one." But he really didn't. It was just a mirage.

After this is read the teacher could ask a classification question such as: "Into what category would you put the words *camel, desert, oasis,* and *mirage*?" A ques-

---

Figure 7.4 **Types of context clues**

1. *Direct Definition Clue:* Unknown word is defined (and/or identified) in the passage.
   Ex: The first goal of a serious photographer is a perfect *exposure*, or amount of light actually hitting the film.
2. *Experience Clue:* Unknown word is defined (and/or identified) by using one's own experience to make a prediction (or inference).
   Ex: The perfect exposure will show the most intricate detail in the picture, down to the thread used to sew on a button.
3. *Synonym Clue:* Unknown word is defined (and/or identified) by reference to a synonym in the text.
   Ex: Maria is a *fortunate* person. I wish I could be as lucky.
4. *Sentence Structure Clue:* Unknown word is defined (and/or identified) by reference to its function in the sentence (whether it functions as a noun, a verb, an adjective, an adverb, and so forth).
   Ex: Our baseball game was cancelled because of *inclement* weather.
5. *Summary Clue:* Unknown word is defined (and/or identified) by reference to the gist of the text.
   Ex: Jenny has had several unhappy things happen to her lately, but she has a *resilient* nature. She has continued to work hard despite her troubles. Even in difficult times, she always seems to be sunny and cheerful.
6. *Mood Clue:* Unknown word is defined (and/or identified) by reference to the mood of the passage.
   Ex: I stood in the hateful slime of the Great Swamp. Before this, I had always felt that there was something beautiful about every place on earth. Now I knew there wasn't. It's *malevolence* seeped around me like a deadly fog. I felt that it's stench of evil and decay brought me a message of ill will.

---

tion designed to elicit inference from gist might be: "Why did the driver want to find an oasis?" A question designed to elicit inferences based on relationships might be: "At what time of day did the driver think he saw an oasis?" A question requiring drawing a conclusion might be: "What caused the driver to think he saw an oasis?" Finally, to determine the ability to make judgments, a question might be: "What do you think the driver could have done to prevent this situation from happening?"

CONTENT OUTCOMES

It is necessary also to determine how well students get meaning from various types of text, of which there are two major types—functional and recreational.

Figure 7.5 **Some common structural units**

Some Common Prefixes

Prefix	Meaning
dis-	not; the opposite of
in-, im-, il-, ir-	not
pre-	before
re-	again, back
un-	not, the opposite of
anti-	against; opposed to; stopping
inter-	together; between
under-	below; beneath

Some Common Suffixes

Suffix	Meaning
-age	act or result of; cost of
-dom	position or rank of being; condition of being
-hood	state or condition of being
-ist	person who does or makes or works

Other Prefixes	Other Suffixes
mal-	-able
mid-	-ian; -an
mis-	-ant
pro-	-ern
super-	-ful
	-ic
	-ly
	-meter

Some Latin Roots

Root	Meaning	Example
cred	believe	credence, credo, incredible
cur	run, flow	current, curriculum
fac, fec	do, make	factory, defect
gen	kind, type	generic, generation
mit, miss	send	admit, dismiss, transmission
scrib, script	write	inscribe, describe, prescription
stat	stand, put in place	stature station
struc, stru	build, prepare	instruct, construction
voc, vok	call	vocal, vocation
volv, vol	roll, turn	evolve, revolve

Figure 7.6 **Common phonic elements**

Consonants: b, c, d, f, g, h, j, k, l, m, n, p, q, r, s, t, v, (w), x, (y), z. The letters b, d, f,
  h, j, h, l, m, n, p, r, s, t, v, w, y, and z have corresponding sounds that are quite
  consistent in English. The letters g and c are not as consistent in that they each
  have *two* commonly associated sounds. One is referred to as hard, (go), (cane)
  and the other as soft, (gene), (certain):

Hard c cat, cow	Soft c cent, city
Hard g good, gone	Soft g gent, gem

Consonant Blends: A consonant blend or cluster is a combination, in one syllable, of two
  or three consecutive consonants each of which represents a distinct sound when
  pronounced. The following blends occur frequently in English:

bl	dr	gl	sc	sp	tr
br	dw	gr	sk	st	tw
cl	fl	pl	sm	str	
cr	fr	pr	sn	sw	

The important concept to remember is that when a blend is pronounced, you
hear distinctly the sound associated with each letter in the blend. This situation
does not occur when discussing consonant digraphs.

Consonant Digraphs: Two consecutive consonants that represent one sound are called
  consonant digraphs. The following are examples of digraphs:

wh	sh	gh	ch	ng	ck	th	ph

It should be noted that *th* may occur with a *voiced* sound as in *th*ere and *th*is or it
may possess a *voiceless* sound as in *th*ing or *th*in. (If your vocal cords vibrate, it is
voiced; if they do not, it is voiceless.)

Silent Consonant: Like vowels, certain consonants can occur with no sound value present
  during pronunciation.

gh (ghost)	h (honor)	ps (psalm)
wr (wrong)	rh (rhubarb)	kh (khaki)
kn (knot)	pn (pneumonia)	gn (gnat)

Vowels: The italicized portion of the words in the following three categories represent
  the vowel sounds that most frequently occur in English:

I	II	III
ate	*am*	*tool*
eel	*end*	*took*
ice	*ill*	*awe*
ode	*odd*	*rain*
use	*us*	*August*

Long Vowels: The long vowels are those represented by the sounds in Column I and the word *tool* in Column III. *Short Vowels:* The short vowels are those represented by the sounds in Column II and the word *took* in Column III. *Digraphs:* Two vowels appearing together that represent one sound are called vowel *digraphs*. The following are examples of the most common vowel digraphs:

ee (meet)	*ea* (easy)	*ow* (grow)
ei (ceiling)	*ai* (rain)	*aw* (awful)
oe (toe)	*oa* (boat)	*au* (August)
ie (pie)	*ay* (play)	*ue* (true)

Diphthongs: Vowel sounds in which the tongue starts in one position and moves rapidly to another are called *diphthongs*. The italicized portion of the following words are considered diphthongs:

> *oil*   *owl*   *boy*   *out*

Schwa: The *schwa* sound can best be described as an unstressed short *u* sound symbolized by /ə/. The *schwa* sound is the most frequently occurring vowel sound in the English language. The italicized vowel in the following *unstressed* syllables stands for the *schwa* sound:

com*a*	beat*e*n	im*i*tate	butt*o*n	column
bedl*a*m	tak*e*n	nostr*i*l	summ*o*n	

Syllable: The word *syllable* may be defined as a pronounceable unit of a word. If the emphasis in defining syllable is directed at the idea of vowel sounds, children will be able to recognize that *all* of the following words have only one syllable because there is only one vowel sound:

> *so*   two   *see*d   charge   stretch   str*ai*ght

Or that the following words contain two syllables because they have two distinct vowel sounds.

> h*o*tel   p*i*cnic   c*ou*ntry   preach*e*r

Phonetic and Syllabic Generalizations: Syllabication rules and phonetic generalizations have been the subject of some controversy at various times throughout the course of educational history. Whereas many of the rules or generalizations are quite useful, the utility of others is open to question. What is of utmost importance is that a teacher of reading be familiar with the commonly taught generalizations and realize the limitations that the various rules have.

Common Syllabication — Phonetic Generalizations:
Syllabication:

1. Most affixes and inflections are syllables:
     un cola, tell *ing*

2. When two consonants in a root are preceded and followed by vowels, a syllabic division *generally* occurs between them:
     bu*l let*, a*f ter*
   (Certain basic reading series have adjusted this rule to state that the syllable division occurs *after* the *second* consonant: ha*pp* en.)

3. When vowels precede and follow a single consonant, a syllabic division *usually* occurs between the preceding vowel and the consonant:
     ho *t*el, po *l*ice.

4. When a root ends in a consonant followed by *le*, the consonant plus *le generally* make up its final syllable:
     tum *ble.*

5. For purposes of syllabication, consonant digraphs *generally* function as if they were one consonant:
     o *ther*

6. For purposes of syllabication, vowel digraphs *generally* function as if they were one syllable:
     de *t*ai*l, aw* ful

Vowel Generalizations

1. When a syllable has one vowel and it is not in final position, the vowel *generally* records its short sound:
     c*a*t, c*u*t, c*o*t, *i*n d*e*x

2. When a syllable has one vowel and it is in final position, the vowel *generally* stands for its long sound:
     m*e*, m*y*, hell*o*

3. When a syllable has two vowels together, the long sound of the first is *common*:
     m*ea*t, t*ai*l

4. The vowel digraph *oo* stands for both a long and a short sound:
     r*oo*m, w*oo*d

Figure 7.7 **Materials needed to collect diagnostic data about reading**

I. Collecting data about attitude outcomes
    A. Interview probes (what will you ask them?)
    B. Checklist for observing students (what will you look for?)
    C. Interest inventory and/or other forms students can complete (what can they tell you?)
    D. Student questionnaire (what can they tell you?)
    E. A record-keeping device
II. Collecting data about process outcomes
    A. Knowledge of how the system works
        1. Word knowledge
            a. Sight words
                graded list of high-utility words
                graded oral-reading paragraphs
            b. Word meaning
                list of words from the text that may be unknown
        2. Use of various knowledge sources
            a. Sample of various types of text
            b. Interview probes designed to get students to talk out loud about how they get meaning
        3. Fluency
            a. Graded oral-reading paragraphs
            b. Interview probes designed to get students to talk out loud about how they know when to change voice intonations
        4. A record-keeping device
    B. Strategies to remove blockages
        1. Sample graded paragraphs
        2. Interview probes designed to get students to talk out loud about how they fix blockages
        3. Analyzing unidentified words
            a. Sentences in which unidentified words are signaled by various context clues
            b. Sentences in which unidentified words are signaled by structural analysis
            c. Nonsense words containing phonic elements to be tested
        4. Look-backs for syntactic and semantic clues
            a. Sentences and paragraphs that cause a blockage for which there are syntactic and semantic cues to remove the blockage.
        5. Use of visible cues
            a. Sentences and paragraphs containing explicit syntactic cues (typographic cues, structural units, and key words) and semantic cues (context)

6. Use of invisible cues
    a. Samples of various types of text
    b. Interview probes designed to get students to talk out loud about
       how they used their prior knowledge to get meaning
7. A record-keeping device
III. Collecting data about content outcomes
  A. Functional text
    1. Various kinds of functional text appropriate for students' stages of
      developmental reading growth
    2. Probes designed to determine students' comprehension of the text
  B. Recreational text
    1. Various kinds of recreational text appropriate for students' stages of
      developmental reading growth
    2. Probes designed to determine students' comprehension of the text

To assess students' ability to understand various kinds of text, teachers need to listen to students read the kinds of functional and recreational text appropriate for a developmental level. At the third-grade level, for instance, it might be appropriate to determine how well students get meaning from informational text such as social studies texts, directions to games, sections of the newspaper, and simple encyclopedia entries. At the same level it might be appropriate to determine how well they get meaning from recreational text such as children's realistic fiction, narrative poetry, fantasy, and fables.

To assess a student's comprehension of functional and recreational texts, teachers follow basically the same procedure described earlier for determining comprehension of graded oral-reading paragraphs. First, students should be given an opportunity to retell or summarize the selection. The teacher then asks specific questions regarding those facts, concepts, or relationships that were omitted in the retelling. If students demonstrate understanding of the various types of functional and recreational text typically found at that level, they are healthy readers regarding the content goal. If, however, comprehension gaps are found in the reading of certain types of text, instructional assistance must be provided.

Suggestions regarding the materials needed to collect diagnostic data about reading are provided in Figure 7.7.

CONCLUSION

One of the most difficult tasks you will face as a classroom teacher will be organizing the class so that all students receive appropriate instruction. Because teaching each student individually, while ideal in theory, is much too time consuming and results in too little instructional time for each individual student, most teachers strike a compromise by organizing students into groups. This allows for more individualization than teaching the whole group, but does not spread the teacher too thin.

Two types of groups are recommended. Collaborative groups are particularly useful for developing the attitudes goals. To assign students to temporary collaborative groups, collect data about each student's personal and social status, and place together students who are diverse but compatible. Ability groups are particularly useful for developing process and content outcomes. To form ability groups, first collect data about each student's word identification and comprehension at successive reading levels and then assign each student to an instructional reading level (the level that is neither too hard nor too easy). Then assign students to the basal text level that matches the student's instructional reading level. Once you have assigned a student's basal text, however, continue to collect data about the student's schema for the topic discussed in each basal selection, since lack of prior knowledge could cause certain selections to be frustration material.

After you have assigned students to groups, continue to collect data in order to decide what specific objectives must be taught in the groups. Such data collection is guided by the concept of vital signs. Specific techniques are used to determine what students in each group need to learn about each of the three major goals of reading.

The importance of data collection cannot be overemphasized. Decisions about group placement and about instructional emphasis are made in reference to what students can do now and what they must yet learn to do. It is this willingness to continually collect fresh data as the basis of instructional decision making that is one of the principal characteristics of professional teachers.

CHECK YOUR UNDERSTANDING

Now that you have read the chapter, check your understanding by answering the Focus Questions presented at the beginning of the chapter. If you cannot answer one or more of the questions, return to the chapter, find the section that corresponds to the question, and reread.

SUGGESTED READINGS

Baumann, J. F., & Stevenson, J. A. (1982). Understanding standardized reading achievement test scores. *Reading Teacher*, *35*(6), 648–654.

Baumann, J. F., & Stevenson, J. A. (1982). Using scores from standardized reading achievement tests. *Reading Teacher*, *35*(5), 528–532.

Black, J. K. (1980). Those "mistakes" tell us a lot. *Language Arts, 57*(5), 508–513.

Brecht, R. D. (1977). Testing format and instructional level with the informal reading inventory. *Reading Teacher, 31*(1), 57–59.

Bristow, P. S., Pikulski, J. J., & Pelosi, P. L. (1983). A comparison of five estimates of reading instructional level. *Reading Teacher, 37*(3), 273–280.

Haller, E., & Waterman, M. (1985). The criteria of reading group assignments. *Reading Teacher, 38*(8), 772–781.

Hu-pei Au, K. (1977). Analyzing oral reading errors to improve instruction. *Reading Teacher, 31*(1), 46–49.

Johnson, M. S., & Kress, R. A. (1965). *Informal reading inventories*. Newark, DE: International Reading Association.

Marshall, N. (1983). Using story grammar to assess reading comprehension. *Reading Teacher, 36*(7), 616–620.

McKenna, M. C. (1983). Informal reading inventories: A review of the issues. *Reading Teacher, 36*(7), 670–679.

Pflaum, S. W. (1979). Diagnosis of oral reading. *Reading Teacher, 33*(3), 278–284.

Silvaroli, N. J. (1975). *Classroom Reading Inventory*. Dubuque, IA: William C. Brown.

Wulz, S. V. (1979). Comprehension testing: Functions and procedures. *Reading Teacher, 33*(3), 295–299.

CHAPTER 8

Managing Reading Groups

GETTING READY

Once you have determined your grouping patterns and planned the allocation of your instructional time, you must be able to get students on task during reading time and keep them there. This means that you must have a system for managing the classroom. This chapter presents techniques for ensuring student time on task. It is divided into two major parts. Since a teacher's success as a manager depends upon careful planning, the first section focuses on what you should think about when creating an efficient classroom management system. The second section focuses on what you should do to maintain student engagement once instruction begins.

FOCUS QUESTIONS

As you read this chapter use the following questions to guide your understanding of classroom management.

1. What management behaviors do you want to implement and maintain?
2. What classroom patterns do you want to implement and maintain?
3. What materials should you collect and organize?
4. How can you best organize your classroom?

Physical arrangements help with management.

PLANNING FOR EFFECTIVE
ACTIVITY FLOW

Successfully engaging students on tasks demands a smooth flow of classroom activity, which is dependent upon the physical arrangement of a room, the patterns teachers use, and their behaviors in managing the academic content of reading.

PHYSICAL ARRANGEMENT

If teachers plan to use both large- and small-group instruction in an average sized room, then space becomes a problem. Many teachers find that the traditional rows of seats take up too much space, and they use clusters of seats instead. Other teachers use a large rug in the middle of the room for whole-group instruction and have students sit at independent learning centers around the edges for beginning and closing exercises. There are many ways to physically arrange a classroom. The only limitations are the dimensions of the room and the limits of a teacher's creativity. Some teachers are very elaborate and use portable screens, old furniture, large floor pillows, and hanging screens as part of the physical setting. Some simply move the existing furniture. Others organize the room into a noisy half and a quiet half. Listening centers, reading centers, and study areas are in the quiet half, whereas the interaction areas—the physical activity areas and the small-group instruction areas—are in the noisy half. Whatever the arrangement, when teaching small groups teachers should place themselves where they can see the entire room. This allows them to monitor those students who are not in their group while also helping the students in the small group to remain attentive. Figure 8.1 shows two ways to create space by organizing classroom desks. Organizing student desks into rows means that much of the floor space is devoted to rows. Space for learning centers and other activities can be created by eliminating rows.

PATTERNS

When teachers work with a reading group, the students not in the group must work independently. For students to work independently, there must be firmly established patterns or routines that both the teacher and the students agree on. For instance, if a teacher wants students to independently complete a workbook page or a practice game during the reading period, the teacher should provide them with a pattern to follow. It is vital that these patterns be understood and used frequently enough to become habits that operate without direct teacher supervision. Patterns are needed for independent activities, safety-valve activities, procedures, and interaction between teacher and students.

Independent Activities. It is necessary to provide independent activities for students who are not in the participating reading group. While a teacher teaches a small group, the others work by themselves on activities such as reading for pleasure, applying skills, practicing skills, reading basal stories, completing science or social studies assignments, creative writing, or practicing oral and written language skills. These independent activities can be completed individually as seatwork or at centers located in various spots within the room.

Assume that a teacher wants to develop a classroom library and reading center as an independent activity to involve students when they are not in a small group. Decisions need to be made about where to put the library and reading center, what types of books to include, what types of furniture to use, and what patterns will govern its use. The teacher might bring in shelves that are easily accessible to the students, a piece of carpeting or a rug to mark the reading center, several bean bag chairs, and several large pillows for comfortable reading. Books could be filed on shelves alphabetically or by interest areas (mystery books, horse stories, stories of today's world, and so forth). The pat-

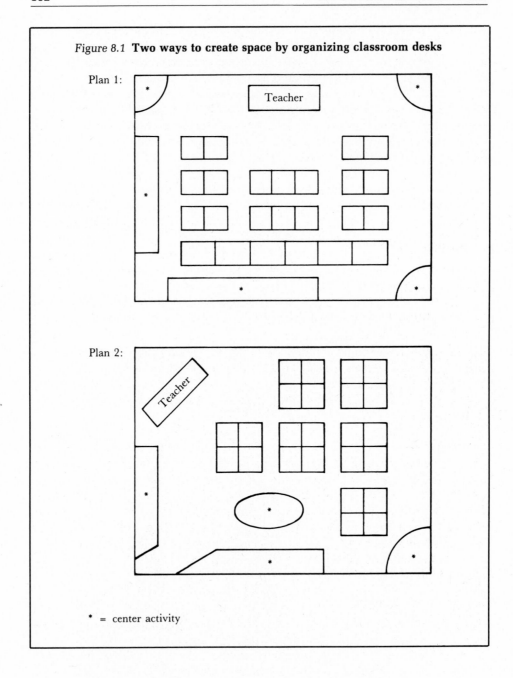

Figure 8.1 **Two ways to create space by organizing classroom desks**

Plan 1:

Teacher

Plan 2:

Teacher

* = center activity

terns for its use may include considerations such as: Where can students read in the room? How are books to be returned? How long can a student stay in the center? Can students return to their seats whenever they wish? Are there follow-up activities? Can students choose whether to work in the center or at other places? These patterns need to be decided and then practiced until they are automatically followed by the students. These decisions should be made and patterns understood prior to conducting reading groups. Giving attention to such detail may seem mundane, but it is crucial to the success of independent activities.

Safety Valves. The first step in managing a classroom is creating independent activities for students to pursue while the teacher is teaching small groups. However, teachers must be prepared for students to finish their assignments at various times. Some will get done before reading-group teaching is finished, and if this has not been anticipated, disruption may result. Consequently, teachers should plan safety valves that students can fall back on when they finish their independent work.

Safety valves usually take the form of learning centers or activities that students can participate in at any time. They are different from independent

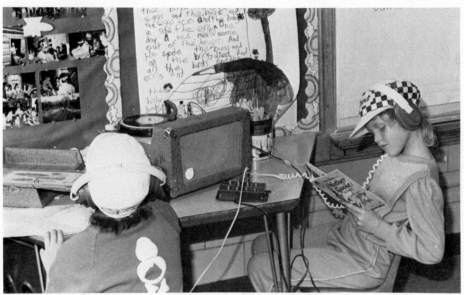

Independent activities and safety valves help teachers manage well.

activities because they do not change daily, they are not always associated with the ongoing academic work in the classroom, and students think they are fun. For instance, appropriate safety valves could include recreational reading, writing in journals, vocabulary games, phonic games, chess or backgammon, art centers, or anything else that appeals to both the teacher and the students. The important thing is that they can be completed with little teacher assistance.

Procedural Patterns. Procedural patterns include routines on how to start, change, keep track of progress, and stop. Each of these patterns should be carefully established.

How-to-start patterns are used to get initial information, such as directions and opening procedures, to the students. One way to handle this is to provide mailboxes for each student, with each mailbox containing directions for the period and other needed information. Some of these directions can be duplicated on ditto sheets to minimize preparation time. The direction sheets tell the student what to do first, second, and so on. Using such a technique saves time and gets students engaged more quickly. For nonreaders, how-to-start procedures can make use of color. A manila folder that has been folded to form a pocket can hold needed materials according to colors that correspond to the different centers. Clothespins that are numbered and color coded can also be used. The intent is to have students well informed about procedures in order to get them on task as quickly as possible. For instance, students can go to their mailboxes, pick up their directions and needed materials, return to their designated places, look at their directions, and begin. This minimizes transition time and increases instructional time.

After the how-to-start patterns are developed, patterns for how to change are required. The options here are as varied as teacher preferences. Activities can be changed on a signal from the teacher or when students have completed an activity. If students change activities independently, one of the problems will be unfinished activities. For some activities, such as reading or ditto sheets, interruption poses little problem. However, an independent activity involving complicated steps (art projects, science experiments, and so forth) may create a problem. Teachers can circumvent this by offering independent activities that can be interrupted during the reading period only. However a teacher decides to change activities, students need to know the patterns for change and to be able to implement them independently.

Once the reading period has started and is running smoothly, teachers need a way to keep track of students' activities. There are many ways to keep records efficiently. A good record-keeping device should not be bulky or cumbersome. It should require little time or effort to record students' progress, and it should provide an immediate picture of where each student is in relation to desired reading outcomes. It should also assist in the development of reading groups. Further, it should allow the teacher and the students to see progress. The thing to remember is that it should be manageable in size and easy to use, while providing a good visual image of the students, outcomes, objectives, and activities.

A record-keeping device used with success consists of graph paper and a loose leaf notebook (see Figure 8.2). Arrange the students' names down the side of the paper and make divisions across the top for each of the three major goals. Within each square in each curricular category, list the objective for that outcome. As objectives are assessed, taught, retaught, practiced, or applied, note this in the squares for that objective. The notebook should be kept handy to record events or behaviors as they occur. The teacher should decide who can record information in the notebook and inform students of the patterns for keeping track of progress.

Contracts are also useful for keeping track of reading progress. The teacher and the students develop a contract, which may vary in length of time for completion (several days, a week, and so on). The completed contract is a record of what the student intends to complete and has completed, and it can be placed in each student's folder.

Turning routines over to students aids management.

Figure 8.2 **Sample record-keeping device**

	Attitudes			Process					Content	
	Reading as communication	Reading as a tool	Positive response to reading	How reading works	Strategies: word analysis	Strategies: new predictions	Strategies: explicit cues	Strategies: implicit cues	Functional text	Recreational text
Mary										
John										
Sue										
Frank										
Allen										

Whatever techniques are used, students should keep as many of their own records as possible. This eases a teacher's time problem and gives the students a continued awareness of their own progress in reading.

It is important to establish patterns for putting away materials, storing incomplete activities, and handing in completed activities at the end of the reading period. This requires that all students know where various materials belong and what kinds of filing systems and storage arrangements are being used. Prior to fully implementing a reading program, a teacher needs to develop such how-to-stop patterns.

Interaction Patterns. Interaction patterns include procedures for socialization among students and between the teacher and students. Socialization is an important factor in any elementary school classroom, and it occurs with or without teacher forethought. In order to make socialization effective, teachers need to develop patterns for its use.

There is no single way to manage interaction in the classroom. Major guidelines are that some sort of patterns be established and that the teacher adjust these patterns for particular students and situations. One way to regulate interaction is to divide the classroom into a noisy half and a quiet half as mentioned earlier. All verbal communications occur in the noisy half, leaving the quiet half relatively noise free. Other teachers, because of personal preference or special circumstances, confine social interaction to a designated center, where students may go to talk, or to a communication center, such as a listening center or a drama center, where interaction has a set purpose.

Regardless of the patterns and the amount of verbal interaction a teacher establishes, there will never be enough for some students. Establishing times for written interaction can help alleviate this difficulty. For instance, each person in the room may have a mailbox where messages can be left allowing all members of the classroom to interact via letters or notes. The patterns specify when mail can be left and when students and teachers can pick up and read their mail.

After the interaction patterns for independent activities have been thought through and planned, teachers can develop interaction patterns for small-group instruction. Efficient reading instruction depends upon a smoothly operating group. There should be a section of the room that is designated as the small-group learning area. Students should know that they are to come to this section quickly and with any needed materials. Teachers should also have their materials ready and be prepared to instruct. Finally, just as a way is needed to get started in independent activities, a way is also needed to get started in small-group instruction. The use of some sort of signal is helpful in getting the group started quickly.

Many teachers find that the use of a buffer helps minimize interruptions during small-group instruction. A buffer is another adult or a student who handles unanticipated situations while the teacher is teaching a group. Ideally, the buffer would be a trained paraprofessional or teacher's aide, but it could also be a parent who has volunteered time. The buffer could also be a high school student who has been released from school to help with such duties. Another source is students from higher grades in the same school. Finally, the buffer can be a student assistant from your own classroom. Responsibilities include handling minor problems such as unexpected interruptions and directions for assignments, supervision of practice activities, participation in learning games, listening to students read aloud, completing assessment activities, correcting papers, and generally providing any kind of nonprofessional classroom assistance.

Summary. When establishing patterns, it is important to be clear and consistent about expected behaviors. This requires careful planning. It is also important to remember that students have a much more difficult time unlearning a pattern and then learning a new one than learning one initially. Once a pattern is set, it becomes a permanent part of a classroom routine. Because of the many patterns that are needed and the limits to their sanity, teachers want to make sure that the patterns that get started are the ones they want. It will be necessary to give much directed assistance early in the school year (including models, walking students through the patterns, talking over modifications, and dress rehearsals), but this assistance will diminish as the patterns become established. Once the reading period is running smoothly, teachers can begin instruction with confidence that students will be engaged on task.

ACADEMIC MANAGEMENT OF READING CONTENT

Before instruction starts, certain decisions need to be made about managing the reading content. The following six decision areas are particularly important:

1. Lessons should focus on academic content.
2. Teachers need to be aware of students' personal concerns.
3. Teachers need to accurately assess skill levels and provide learning tasks of appropriate difficulty.
4. Teachers need to know how to focus attention.
5. Teachers need to know how to provide appropriate challenges.
6. Teachers need students to be responsible and cooperative.

First, the focus should stay on targeted academic content during a lesson. If it is a process lesson, the focus ought to be on the process; if it is a story being read for enjoyment, the focus ought to be on the content of the story; if it is a lesson on developing a concept of reading, the focus ought to be on that concept. This means that teachers must resist students who try to steer them into discussions of other topics. If teachers want students to learn what the lesson is designed to teach, teachers must keep the focus on that content.

Second, teachers need to be sensitive to students' personal concerns. The focus may be on academic content, but the students' personal concerns need to be woven into lessons. For instance, when a lesson is on tornadoes, and students are in an area where tornadoes occur, teachers should be aware of their worries about tornadoes.

Third, teachers need to determine the instructional level of students and to create learning tasks that challenge them intellectually. Teachers must know which curriculum goal they are working on and where the students are with regard to that goal. For instance, if the goal is to develop an understanding that reading involves making predictions and confirming or modifying those predictions, and students have never worked on this goal, a teacher can assume that they are at an initial learning phase. If students have worked on this goal in previous years, the teacher needs to estimate whether they are still in the initial learning phase or in a subsequent one, if they need more presentation, just practice, or guided application. In any case, the more precise a teacher can be in assessing needs, the easier it will be to match activities to developmental levels and thereby ensure a high degree of task engagement.

Fourth, a teacher must know how to focus students. To focus attention, the targeted outcome must be clearly established in the students' minds. If the outcome is a memory task, the students' attention should be focused on the salient features of a memory task; if the outcome is a procedural task, students' attention should be focused on the procedural steps, and so on. Once teachers know what the outcome requires, they need to focus students on this information.

Fifth, teachers need to provide appropriate challenge for students. If they can do a task without assistance, there is no challenge. If they cannot do the task even with appropriate assistance, then the challenge is too great. Providing the appropriate challenge means selecting a learning task where the students need assistance and can benefit from that assistance.

Finally, teachers need to cultivate student responsibility and cooperation. The ultimate goal of schooling is to have all students responsible for their own behaviors and actions. Classrooms characterized by responsible behavior create an optimum environment for learning. Similarly, each member of a group is affected by the other members of the group. Cooperative behaviors allow a group to make decisions and move ahead. Within the classroom, many decisions are group decisions and cooperative behavior creates optimum conditions for achievement.

ENSURING SUSTAINED STUDENT ENGAGEMENT

The first step in organizing for instruction is to allocate as much time as possible to the three major curricular outcomes. Younger students will become engaged just because a teacher wants them to, but older students rarely do so. In both cases it is necessary to keep students engaged once instruction has started. The following discussion of teacher behaviors that encourage continued student engagement is divided into those behaviors that apply to all or most teaching situations and those that relate to specific problems.

GENERAL TEACHER BEHAVIORS

Six general teacher behaviors that help maintain student engagement on task are discussed below.

First, students should be accountable for all work, whether it is completed independently or in groups. Once work has been assigned, it should be completed. If students are not held accountable for completing their work, they find other things to do. This means that a teacher must correct and provide feedback for all academic work assigned in the classroom. Such attention to student accountability helps ensure engaged time on task.

Second, all students should not only be attentive but actively involved during instruction. It is not enough to have their eyes on the teacher. In order to keep their attention, a teacher must actively involve them in thinking, observing, doing, listening, speaking, reading, or writing. The hardest activities to sustain are thinking, listening, and reading. After students have thought for a moment or two, or listened or read for a short time, they should be allowed to speak or write. Continued active involvement requires opportunities both to receive information (listen, observe or read) and to express information (speak, act or write). Younger children can sustain only short periods of receiving and giving information whereas older children can sustain their involvement for longer periods of time.

Third, seatwork should include both teacher-assigned activities and student-choice activities. Seatwork can be completed either individually, in pairs, or in small groups. The activities assigned can vary from practicing newly learned skills, to applying activities, to reading and writing, to informal assessment activities. In any case, variety is important. To develop positive attitude outcomes, seatwork could include reading books, magazines, or newspapers, with students choosing the type of reading material as well as the time and place of the activity. To develop the concept that reading is a tool for gaining information, teachers can structure a voluntary information-gathering activity for a social studies assignment. Other seatwork, however, would be teacher directed, such as an assessment activity to determine if the students need to learn a particular reading strategy or need practice on a particular strategy.

Fourth, the pace should be adjusted to the needs of the students. High-aptitude students can move quickly; low-aptitude students go more slowly. For both, however, the pace should be brisk enough to keep the students' attention, but not so brisk that the students become frustrated and stop attending. Pace can be expedited by breaking instruction into small steps that can be easily understood by the students. Clarifying the purpose or the usefulness of the lesson also encourages brisk pace, because students understand why they are doing a task.

Fifth, success rates for students should be high. Generally, the success rates should be above 80 percent. All students, but particularly low-aptitude students, must have high success rates in order to maintain a high level of perseverance. Students persevere and remain engaged on task when success is high; as the failure rate increases, they get discouraged and engagement on task diminishes rapidly.

Finally, engagement is associated with frequent opportunities to respond. Students need to speak, write, or do in order for learning to occur. Frequent response opportunities encourage learning because it is only through responses that you can determine student understanding and provide the positive feedback that solidifies learning.

To summarize, student engagement on tasks can be increased by holding students accountable, involving them, providing a variety of seatwork, ensuring brisk pacing, ensuring success, and having frequent responses.

SPECIFIC TEACHER BEHAVIORS

You will use many of the general teacher behaviors noted above whenever you teach. However, some teacher behaviors relate only to specific problems of student engagement, such as those that help initiate engagement in an activity and help sustain that engagement.

Helping Students Become Engaged. To help students become engaged, teachers must get their attention. They can do this by using verbal statements, written statements, or some type of an attention-getting device such as a bell or a signal drawn on the board. Once students are attentive a teacher can establish the procedures for the activity. It may be necessary for them to remain in their seats, to form a large circle on the rug, or to complete an activity in small groups at learning centers. Whatever procedures apply, the students need to know them early in the activity.

Student engagement is also promoted by providing thorough, lucid directions for a task they are to complete. Most elementary-age students can only keep a limited number of things in their minds at one time. This means that teachers can only give three or four directions at a time; otherwise, there will be students who cannot complete the work without help. Therefore, it is sometimes necessary to provide direction for the first half of a task and then for the second half, or to provide written directions that supplement oral direction. Remember, however, that written directions are more easily followed when they reflect an established pattern of behavior. By providing directions within the limits of the students' memory capacity and according to established patterns of behavior, teachers help them become engaged.

How teachers distribute materials can also effect engagement. If they pass

Teacher specificity about directions aids management.

out materials before directions are provided, the chances are good that some students will pay more attention to the materials than to the directions. Many problems can be avoided if teachers give directions first, then distribute materials.

After everyone knows what is to happen and what their role is, they then need a signal to begin the activity. Although a teacher can simply tell them to begin, an established signal helps ensure that all students will begin at the same time.

Once started, engagement is enhanced if students' personal needs have been considered. For instance, are the activities pleasant ones from the students' point of view? Do they understand the teacher's rationale for the lesson and concern for their work? Is there variety in the activities and are there opportunities for students to express themselves about the lesson content? Are student concerns heard and clarified? Is appropriate student behavior reinforced? By attending to personal needs such as these, a teacher helps ensure sustained student engagement on tasks.

Question asking also helps students become engaged because it allows students to demonstrate their understanding of the lesson and helps them be attentive during it. For instance, if teaching a content lesson, a teacher should ask questions to activate knowledge about the topic of the story. If teaching a process lesson, a teacher should ask questions to activate knowledge about the target strategy. Questions serve a dual role of helping students to become engaged and preparing them to understand the focus of the lesson.

In summary, initial student engagement is enhanced if a teacher is able to get their attention, give thorough, lucid directions before distributing materials, signal when to begin, consider their personal needs, and ask questions to ensure their understanding of the lesson. When these behaviors are used at the beginning of a lesson, the likelihood of student engagement is increased.

Helping Students Sustain Engagement. Just as there are teacher behaviors that help students become engaged, there are others that help students maintain that engagement. This requires a teacher who can sense a pending break in the activity flow and can do something to prevent its occurrance. Conversely, a teacher who lacks such sensitivity allows the break to occur and then has to restore the activity flow and student engagement. Obviously, the teacher who can prevent such breaks will have students who learn more because they were engaged longer.

There are a number of teacher behaviors that help maintain activity flow. The first one relates to the steps within the lesson. Lessons should be broken into small steps to keep the cognitive demands within the capabilities of the students. The size of the steps varies with the age and aptitude of the students.

Second, a sensitive teacher looks for signals that a group is not working well together and quickly deals with potential problems before the activity flow is disrupted. Often the students' body postures signal that off-task behavior is about to occur. Similarly, students' eyes or the type of noise coming from a group signals a need for teacher assistance. When a teacher is alert and can assess a group's problem before a disruption occurs, it can be solved without a break in the activity flow.

Breaks in activity flow can also be prevented by letting students know what to do with completed work. If everything has to pass through the teacher's hands, valuable instructional time is lost. If students have to ask the teacher what to do with their work, activity flow is broken. Established patterns for turning in work and recording the results aid in sustaining activity flow.

A teacher's use of humor and affection can also help to sustain engagement because it releases the tension associated with concentration, fear, and insecurity. Students who are working hard benefit from a moment of humor, as do students who want to work hard but do not quite understand the task and those who experience a high degree of anxiety during a lesson. However, teachers must be cautious in their use of humor. Sarcasm can make a situation worse, as can laughter directed at a particular student. Make sure that the humor is funny to all the students. Similarly, teachers must use affection wisely. All students need to know that they are important, but artificial affection is quickly spotted and is usually conterproductive to a good atmosphere. Honest affection, in contrast, makes everyone feel good and aids in developing feelings of belonging. Both humor and affection help students sustain engagements.

Teachers can also sustain student engagement by monitoring their involvement in lessons. Everyone, but especially low-aptitude readers, need to be checked and to receive appropriate feedback. Regardless of the focus of the lesson, the only way to determine students' understanding is to monitor their responses. This monitoring helps sustain engagement on task. While monitoring, teachers can move near potentially disruptive students and use nonverbal signals such as a lifted eyebrow or a finger on their lips as a way to head off disruptions. Redirection away from inappropriate behavior and toward the expected behavior, reinforcement of appropriate behavior, removal of potential distractions, and assisting students who are showing signs of frustration are other ways of combating disruptions.

Teacher interactions with students also help sustain engagement. When they stop to talk with students, they should talk about the activity at hand. If a group of students is completing a task about favorite books, the teacher should talk about that assignment. If they are taken off task by discussing something else, it creates a break in engagement, a situation that is often hard to repair.

Teacher sensitivity to students' constraints also helps sustain engagement. This includes sensitivity to intellectual limits, where the content demands more than the students can deliver; to emotional limits, where the content is so unrelated that students have no interest in learning; to concentration limits, where no matter how exciting the lesson is the students have been attending for too long. Teachers who are sensitive to the constraints on their students' learning abilities can use that knowledge to stop lessons before a break in the activity flow occurs.

Sustained engagement is also aided by planned, brief breaks. Few people can concentrate on a task for long periods without an opportunity for the brain to rest. Therefore, breaks are necessary if students are to sustain attention to the lesson. However, long breaks allow students to engage in something entirely new. Consequently, short breaks are favored because they allow rest while minimizing the possibility that attention will wander.

In summary, it is important to remember that students will vary in their ability to remain engaged. A room that is uncomfortable will shorten the engagement time as will an exciting upcoming event. Hunger will shorten engagement, whereas high motivation and interest will lengthen it. The trick is to use the teacher behaviors known to be successful in sustaining high engagement rates while also being sensitive to the students' needs.

STEPS IN CREATING
A MANAGEMENT SYSTEM

This chapter focuses on how to enhance student engagement during lessons. However, the organization and management of a reading program requires the melding of many little pieces. It is a difficult task, but the following guide offers structured assistance. A teacher can adapt these steps in developing a personalized management system.

Step 1 (prior to the opening of school and the assignment of your students)

1. Using the three outcomes of reading instruction as a guide, develop curriculum goals for the year.
2. Within each curriculum goal, collect and categorize activities for assessment, instruction, practice, and application.
3. Develop a teacher resource file for oral reading, independent reading, interest grabbers, independent activities, safety valves, guided application (basals, other commercial activities), and room arrangements.
4. Collect and categorize books and other printed material by interest and general reading levels to be used for independent reading, interest grabbing, and guided application.
5. Develop student activity card files for learning centers, independent activities, safety valves, and interest grabbers.
6. Collect and develop informal and formal assessment tools, including graded oral-reading paragraphs, games, and interest inventories.
7. Develop a general pattern for reinforcement that can be adjusted after you know your students.
8. Develop patterns for how-to-start procedures.
9. Develop patterns for how-to-change procedures.
10. Develop patterns for keeping-track-of-student procedures.
11. Develop patterns for the optional activities (independent activities and safety-valve activities).
12. Develop patterns for how-to-stop procedures.
13. Develop patterns that allow for interaction among you and your students.
14. Develop the general role of the buffer and the steps in training the buffer.

15. Develop your philosophy about approaches (basals, language experience, and personalized reading) to reading instruction and how the three outcomes can be integrated into your philosophy. What balance will you strike in developing these three outcomes?

Step 2 (prior to the opening of school, after you have been assigned a specific classroom)

1. Continue to develop curriculum goals and activities for the three outcomes of reading instruction. Collect source books, activity cards, assessment tools, materials for instruction and application, and lists of recreational books. Develop procedures for the various patterns for the buffer, and refine your philosophy of reading instruction.
2. Develop a floor plan for the physical arrangement of your classroom.
3. Make an inventory of the materials and facilities you have for the coming school year.

Step 3 (after the school year begins)

1. Implement instruction for developing attitude outcomes.
2. Implement patterns for procedures and interactions.
3. Implement independent activities and safety valves.
4. Implement the role of the buffer.
5. Evaluate progress so far, including patterns and procedures.
6. Determine the reading preferences of each student.
7. Initiate plans for students to begin developing their own lifelong reading habits.
8. Administer the informal and formal assessment devices for yearlong needs.
9. Implement instruction for developing process and content outcomes.
10. Evaluate the progress of your reading program to date.

Step 4 (continued growth and evaluation)

1. Continue to develop materials, ideas, sources, a library, patterns, and a teaching style. Be alert for ways you can vary safety-valve activities as the year progresses and be alert for new ideas and materials. Try not to alter the patterns established for safety valves.
2. Continue to evaluate the ongoing reading program. Are your ex-

pectations reasonable? Are patterns developing as expected? Are positive attitudes and an understanding of reading being established? Are content outcomes being achieved? Are you implementing and maintaining the reading program as successfully as you want?

CONCLUSION

Students do not learn targeted outcomes when they are not engaged on task. Consequently, a crucial professional skill is the ability to implement a classroom management system that maximizes student engaged time. This chapter provides a number of suggestions that have proven to be effective.

However, effective instruction is more than getting students engaged on task. It also involves a qualitative dimension. Technicians tend to devote all their thoughts and energies to management. To avoid this, the most effective teachers automatize the principles of management so they do not have to think about it very often and are free to concentrate on improving the quality of instruction. In the final analysis your goal is to get management under control so you do not have to think about it and, instead, can think about quality instruction.

CHECK YOUR UNDERSTANDING

Now that you have read the chapter, check your understanding by answering the Focus Questions presented at the beginning of the chapter. If you cannot answer one or more of the questions, return to the chapter, find the section that corresponds to the question, and reread.

SUGGESTED READINGS

Burns, M. (1981). Groups of four: Solving the management problem. *Learning*, 10, 46–51.

Casteel, C. P. (1984). Computer skill banks for classroom and clinic. *Reading Teacher*, *38*(3), 294–297.

Chernow, F. B., & Chernow, C. (1981). *Classroom discipline and control: 101 practical techniques*. West Nyack, NY: Parker.

Fleet, A. C., Hurst, A. W., & Mackay, M. E. (1976). Expanding the classroom with study areas. *Reading Teacher*, *30*(1), 33–38.

Forgan, H. W. (1977). *The reading corner*. Santa Monica, CA: Goodyear.

Klein, M. L. (1979). Designing a talk environment for the classroom. *Language Arts, 56*(6), 647–656.

Morris, R. D. (1979). Some aspects of the instructional environment and learning to read. *Language Arts, 56*(5), 497–502.

Nevi, C. N. (1983). Cross-age tutoring: Why does it help the tutors? *Reading Teacher, 36*(9), 892–898.

Welch, F. C. & Halfacre, J. D. (1978). Ten better ways to classroom management. *Teacher, 96,* 85–86.

Wood, K. D. (1983). A variation on an old theme: 4-way oral reading. *Reading Teacher, 37*(1), 38–41.

CHAPTER 9

Planning and Conducting Reading Lessons

GETTING READY

There is much for teachers to do in getting organized for reading instruction. As mentioned in previous chapters, you must organize a literate environment, organize instructional time, collect and organize data to form reading groups, and establish procedures and routines to ensure student engagement on reading tasks.

When all these things are done, there remains one more crucial organizational step: to plan and to conduct lessons. This chapter tells you how to organize reading lessons using both indirect and direct instruction.

FOCUS QUESTIONS

As you read this chapter use the following questions to guide your understanding about reading lessons.

1. Why are instructional objectives so important?
2. What is the purpose for each of the three parts of an instructional objective?
3. What decisions must you make to plan indirect lessons?
4. What decisions must you make to plan direct lessons?
5. What is the purpose of a task analysis?
6. Why must teachers consider the subtleties of instruction as well the lesson format?
7. How does lesson planning serve to organize instruction?

OBJECTIVES: THE CORNERSTONE OF
EFFECTIVE PLANNING

Regardless of whether a teacher is planning a lesson using indirect or direct instruction, the most important single characteristic of effective planning is a clearly stated objective. The objective guides a teacher's decision making in planning and conducting the lesson.

Chapter 6 discussed the scarcity of instructional time. One way to ensure the best use of time is to make sure that each lesson has a specific outcome. For instance, if teachers are conducting a lesson using indirect instruction, they should know precisely what concept or positive response they are trying to achieve; if they are conducting a direct instruction lesson, they should know precisely what process or content goal they are trying to achieve. When they do, the lesson has a focus. Teachers know what they are trying to accomplish, and because they do, the students are better able to accomplish it. Consequently, for any reading lesson taught a teacher should *always* be able to answer the questions: "Why am I doing this? What is the outcome I am after? What should students be doing differently after this lesson?" An inability to answer questions like these is often the sign of a technician who is following a prescription in an unthinking way.

THE ABSENCE OF OBJECTIVES

Focus and purpose are not always found in elementary classrooms. Sometimes teachers conduct global, unfocused activities such as oral round-robin reading (in which each student reads aloud in turn while the teacher listens) or reading stories independently followed by rote question-and-answer sessions. The expectation is that the students, while engaged in such activities, will learn to read. Whereas this sometimes works with high-aptitude students, average- and low-aptitude students need more focus.

Often, however, teachers have difficulty avoiding global, nonfocused activity. First of all, these lessons have the advantage of being easy to manage—students can be monitored and controlled with no difficulty. Second, global activities conform to what the public and many nonprofessionals believe reading instruction to be. When students read orally in turn or read silently and answer questions, everything looks orderly, and orderly activities are frequently equated with learning. Third, the planning required for these activities is minimal. It takes only minutes to get an unfocused lesson together; it takes much longer to plan a lesson with a focus. Finally, these lessons ensure activity flow that will fill up the available instructional time. The one thing a teacher does *not* want is a gap in activity during the school day, since such gaps are vacuums that students inevitably fill (often with undesirable activities of their own).

In short, teachers sometimes think in terms of activities to fill the instructional time rather than in terms of objectives that guide the development of specific outcomes. Regardless of how much or how little we may sympathize with the reasons why teachers emphasize activities instead of objectives, the fact remains that a lesson conducted without an objective is effective only by accident. To intentionally develop the goals of reading instruction, teachers must state what they are trying to accomplish.

STATING OBJECTIVES

A good instructional objective is a carefully structured statement that has three parts.

Student Behavior. The first and most important part is a description of what the students will be able to do following successful instruction. For instance, while teaching an attitude outcome such as appreciation of free verse, a teacher might want the students to voluntarily select free verse poems to share with the class, something that they do not now do. The objective will be: *The student will voluntarily select free verse poems to share with the class.* If a process goal such as the use of prefixes to figure out the meaning of unknown words is being taught, the teacher might want the students to tell both the meaning of the unknown prefixed word and how the prefix was used to figure out the meaning. So the objective will be: *The student will state the meaning of previously unknown prefixed words and the thinking used to determine the meaning.* If a teacher is teaching a content outcome such as reading a history chapter for information about the causes of the Civil War, the objective will be: *The student will read the chapter and state the three causes of the Civil War cited by the author.* In each case, the teacher is creating a descriptive statement of what the students should be able to do following instruction. The targeted student behavior must be observable in order to evaluate whether or not it has been achieved.

Conditions. The second part of a good instructional objective should specify the conditions for using what was taught. In reading, this means a real reading situation, since isolated instruction is seldom useful and is sometimes harmful. For instance, for the poetry objective the teacher wanted the students to voluntarily select poems to share with the class. Consequently, as part of the classroom's literate environment, a display of free verse poetry books can be set up. The objective would be appended by the following statement of the condition under which the desired student behavior would occur: *Given a display of free verse poetry in the classroom, the student will voluntarily select free verse poems to share with the class.* That is to say the desired learning has occurred if the student can be observed voluntarily reading free verse poetry during class. If, however, a teacher wants the student to read free verse during free time at home, then home reading must be specified as the condition that best indicates an appreciation of free verse poetry.

When teaching a prefix lesson, a teacher wants students to use prefixes to figure out the meaning of unknown words when reading books of their choice. Consequently, the amended objective might now read: *Given self-selected text in which unknown prefixed words are encountered, the student will state the meaning of the unknown words and the thinking used to determine the meanings.* Here the teacher is saying that it is not good enough that the student use prefix knowledge to figure out words on workbook pages or ditto sheets but must be seen using the strategy with self-selected text as evidence that the desired learning has occurred.

Finally, when teaching about the causes of the Civil War, the amended objective might read: *Given the history textbook and a study guide that helps locate passages dealing with the causes of the Civil War, the student will read the chapter and state the three causes of the Civil War cited by the author.* Here the teacher is saying that the desired learning should occur in the classroom with guided assistance.

The Criterion. The final part of a good instructional objective is a statement of how often the desired learning has to be seen for the teacher to accept it as learned. In the case of appreciating free verse, one reading of a selection could indicate that learning has occurred. Consequently, the objective could be stated: *Given a display of free verse poetry in the classroom, the student will voluntarily select at least one free verse poem to share with the class.* In the case of the prefix strategy, most teachers would not feel comfortable with only a single completion. Therefore, the objective might be stated: *Given self-selected text in which unknown prefixed words are encountered, the student will state the meaning of the words and the thinking used to determine the meanings on at least five occasions.* For the content objective, a teacher may decide that since a study guide has been provided the student should identify all three causes. Consequently, the objective might be stated: *Given the history textbook and a study guide that helps locate the passages dealing with the causes of the Civil War, the student will state the three causes cited by the author.*

SUMMARY

The hallmark of effective instruction is a teacher's awareness of what is being taught. Specifically, the outcome focuses the lesson both for the teacher and for the student. The best way to specify an outcome is to state what the student should be able to do, the conditions under which it should be done, and the criterion that will be an acceptable indication of desired learning. With an objective clearly stated, the lesson is off to a good start.

TYPES OF LESSON PLANS

Most reading instruction is more or less indirect or direct. Indirect instruction, which is used primarily to develop attitude outcomes, frequently makes use of language experience activities and personalized reading and almost never makes use of basal textbooks. It is often conducted in large-group settings, but when small groups are used they tend to be collaborative rather than ability groups. The literate environment supports both direct and indirect instruction, but it supports indirect instruction in particular since the objectives of indirect instruction are achieved more through interaction with the environment than with the teacher. Indirect instruction is usually activity centered and often looks spontaneous and unplanned. However, it is actually planned very carefully. An objective is stated and a format is followed. Usually the format begins with an activity, moves to a discussion of the activity, and then moves to another activity.

Direct instruction, in contrast, is used primarily to develop process and content goals. It frequently uses basal textbooks or other commercially prepared materials and is seldom associated with language experience activities or personalized reading. It is almost always conducted in small groups formed on the basis of ability. Direct instruction relies heavily on teacher interactions with the student; consequently, although the literate environment has an influence, the instructional responsibility is much more dependent on the teacher than the environment. The instruction is task centered rather than activity centered, in that a teacher assigns academic work and directs that work in a conscious effort to create specific outcomes. As with all instruction, an objective is stated. If the goal is a process outcome, the lesson format has the following eight steps:

1. Introduce the basal text selection.
2. Introduce the knowledge or strategy being taught.
3. Model the strategy.
4. Guide student acquisition.
5. Set purposes.
6. Read silently or orally.
7. Discuss the selection.
8. Close the lesson.

Getting students involved in indirect instruction requires careful planning.

If the goal is a content outcome, the lesson format follows the steps of the directed reading lesson:

1. Introduce the basal selection and the vocabulary words.
2. Set purposes for reading the selection.
3. Read the selection.
4. Discuss the selection in terms of the purposes set.
5. Close the lesson.

Direct and indirect instruction are used to create different goals, and each employs distinctly different pedagogical strategies for achieving those outcomes. To plan either kind of instruction, teachers must have a basic format from which planning decisions can be made. Illustrations of how to use the respective formats for indirect and direct instruction follow.

PLANNING INDIRECT INSTRUCTION

When using indirect instruction, a teacher structures the environment so that students will interpret tasks in ways that lead them to specific attitude outcomes. A teacher's role tends to be less intrusive than in direct instruction, and the activity the students are engaged in takes prominence. Hence, the planning format for indirect instruction revolves around an activity.

STEPS IN PLANNING INDIRECT INSTRUCTION

Ultimately, students engaged in indirect instruction work independently without any assistance from the teacher. However, as mentioned in Chapter 4, instruction can be thought of as a continuum from direct to indirect. At one extreme, indirect instruction means no teacher intervention at all. However, there are many times (especially when new activities are being introduced) when instruction is indirect in that students learn the intended outcomes incidentally even though teacher direction is evident. This type of lesson is described here.

There are three major steps in the planning format for this kind of indirect instruction. First, the teacher involves the students in an activity. Usually, this activity is associated with the literate environment, but it is chosen because of its potential for leading students to a specific outcome identified in the teacher's objective. Second, the teacher discusses the activity with the students. This discussion focuses student attention on the desired outcome, although the teacher refrains from being overtly directive. Finally, the teacher involves students in another activity. (See Figure 9.1.) This follow-up activity is related to the first one and gives students an opportunity to further develop the concept or positive response that was discussed in the second step.

This three-step format is typical of many indirect instruction lessons. For instance, teachers use uninterrupted sustained silent reading to develop positive attitudes toward reading and the concept that reading is enjoyable and rewarding. If the activity is observed for a week or more, it will become apparent that the USSR activity often follows the three steps. The activity is the reading. Periodically the teacher will hold informal discussions with students about the books they are reading (or a book the teacher is reading) with the intent of focusing them on positive responses and on the concept that reading is enjoyable and rewarding. Then, following the discussion, the students return to the reading activity. Hence, over a period of time, the USSR activity follows the three-step planning format of activity–discussion–activity.

Similarly, the typical language experience lesson is often organized around the three-step format. For instance, the teacher may want to develop the twin concepts that reading and writing are related and written text conveys an author's message. To do so, an activity in the form of a field trip to the fire station is organized (perhaps in conjunction with a social studies unit on community helpers). Upon returning from the field trip, the teacher discusses with the students the desirability of thanking the firemen for their help, shaping the discussion so that students understand that their message can be effectively

Figure 9.1 **The format for planning indirect instruction**

First: Involve students in an *activity* that has potential to develop a specific attitude outcome.

Second: *Discuss* the activity with students to get them thinking about the attitude outcome.

Third: Involve students in another *activity* to further develop the attitude outcome.

communicated through writing. The teacher and students then move to the next activity, in which the students dictate a note of thanks that the teacher records on a sheet of language experience paper and then sends to the firemen. Again, the three-step format of activity–discussion–activity has guided the teacher's organization of indirect instruction.

ANALYZING PLANNING DECISIONS

Indirect instruction is deceptive and often looks spontaneous and inventive. Teachers who use indirect instruction well are often thought of as creative because they seem to be so innovative on the spur of the moment.

However, most good indirect instruction is not spontaneous but carefully planned. There is creativity, but it is found not in the teacher's ability to "think on the spot" so much as in the ability to make planning decisions that ensure a smooth instructional flow toward a desired objective. To illustrate the kinds of planning decisions that must be made, it is helpful to examine a sample lesson that is relatively indirect.

Assume that a teacher is teaching a second-grade class. The teacher has observed that the students do not understand that stories have a structure that can be used to predict meaning and that they have difficulty seeing the relationship between reading and writing. The teacher wants to change this situation.

The first decision is to make the instruction more indirect than direct because the desired outcomes are conceptual ones that are best achieved through environmental experiences. Also, the teacher is influenced by the fact that almost all the students in the class need to achieve these conceptual outcomes and a large-group setting seems more efficient than repeating the instruction in each of the small ability groups. Consequently, because the teacher wants the student to have experiences that cause them to associate reading with predicting and with writing, and because large-group instruction seems most efficient, the teacher thinks more in terms of indirect instruction than direct instruction.

The second decision involves translating outcomes into an objective. The teacher wants the students to understand that reading stories involves predicting meaning based on the story structure and that reading and writing are related. These outcomes must be translated into observable student behaviors that can be stated as objectives. The teacher decides that to observe the students writing a story in which they use story structure to create the meaning would be evidence that both outcomes were being achieved. Therefore, the teacher states the objectives as follows: *After a story has been read to them, the students will write their own story using a story structure similar to the first story.* The writing of the story is the behavior reflecting the targeted outcome, the conditions are that it should be modeled on the story that was read to them, and the criterion implied is that the writing of a single story will be an indication that learning has occurred.

The third decision is to identify what happens at each step of the three-step format. The first step (activity) is to read the students a story that uses a common story structure in a format that they can easily repeat. The second step (discussion) is to discuss with the students (1) the various parts of the story structure and how they can use these parts to predict meaning, and (2) how, if a reader uses structure to predict meaning, the writer can use it to build meaning. The last step (activity) is another activity in which students use the first story as a model to write a new story.

Next the teacher faces a series of decisions about each of the three steps of the lesson. The first step involves selecting an appropriate story and deciding how to introduce it to the students. In selecting the story, the teacher must be sure that it will be enjoyable for second-grade students and that it reflects the structure employed in most stories. A book such as Mercer Mayer's picture and words book called *There is a Nightmare in My Closet* could be selected. Second graders love it, and it follows the familiar story structure of setting, character, problem, a series of events relating to the problem, and a resolution of the problem. In introducing the story, the teacher decides to read it once for enjoyment and then to read it again during the discussion to point out the story parts.

To expedite identification of the story parts, the teacher decides to show students the pictures most closely associated with a particular part of the story and decides on key statements that must be made to ensure a smooth discussion and on any support materials (chalkboard illustrations, handouts, and so forth) that might help achieve the outcomes. Once the story parts are identified, the teacher prepares the students for writing by modeling how the same story parts guide an author in writing a story like Mayer's.

For the third part of the lesson, the students are invited to use the same story parts to create a story like Mayer's. To ensure that the task does not become overwhelming and therefore frustrating, the teacher gives each student a booklet, and on each page is written a component of story structure to guide them (the first page is for *setting*, the second for *character*, the third for *problem*, and so forth). Further, the teacher elicits a story idea from each student before they begin writing, thereby ensuring that no one is left without a story to write.

At the conclusion of the lesson, the teacher assesses its success by determining which students attained the performance specified in the objective. Those students who wrote their own story using the model story structure have achieved the conceptual understanding that reading involves predicting and that there is a strong relationship between reading and writing. (See Figure 9.2.)

A follow-up activity employing indirect instruction might emphasize the interrelated nature of reading and writing by having students read the books they have written to younger children. The first decision in this lesson involves the choice of indirect instruction. Since the goal of having students better understand the interrelated nature of reading and writing involves developing a concept about reading and writing, indirect instruction seems appropriate. The objective could be stated in the following way: *Given a self-authored story, the student will read the story to younger children.* The three-part lesson format for indirect instruction would consist of the following: (1) students read their own stories; (2) the teacher discusses with students how to introduce their stories to younger children; and (3) students introduce and read their own stories to younger children. A fourth decision would involve ways of helping students be successful. The teacher would discuss with the students what they need to do to ensure that the younger children understand their stories. The discussion might emphasize the need to rehearse the story out loud, how to show the illustrations, and what the younger children might need to know before the story is read. The last decision regarding the assessment of success would be to have the students evaluate how the reading went and how well they predicted what the younger children would need to know.

SUMMARY

Good indirect instruction is the result of good planning, despite the fact that it often appears to be a spontaneous, nonacademic activity. When teachers are involved (as is the case with some indirect instruction), a format of activity–discussion–activity is followed, involving a number of conscious decisions. The effectiveness of indirect instruction is closely tied to the care with which teachers make these decisions.

PLANNING DIRECT INSTRUCTION

When using direct instruction to achieve process and content goals, a teacher assumes a more overt instructional role. The task is defined for students by a

---

Figure 9.2 **Decisions to make in planning indirect instruction**

1. Decide to be more indirect than direct in achieving the outcome.
2. Specify the outcome as an objective.
3. Decide upon the three-part format of activity–discussion–activity.
4. Decide what you will say or do to facilitate the outcome at each of the three major points of the lesson.
5. Assess your success in achieving the desired outcome.

---

teacher's verbal mediation; that is, the teacher directly and explicitly explains to students how to use a reading strategy or how to extract content from the text. Hence, the planning for direct instruction of process revolves around using a strategy to make sense out of text, and the planning for direct instruction of content revolves around what information or understanding the student is to extract from the text.

DIRECT INSTRUCTION FOR PROCESS OUTCOMES

The planning for direct instruction of process goals consists of the eight steps described in the lesson organization section in Chapter 6: introducing the basal selection, introducing the knowledge or strategy to be taught, modeling the knowledge or strategy, guiding student acquisition, setting purposes, silent or oral reading, discussion and closure. (See Figure 9.3.)

The difference between teaching a process outcome in more or less indirect or direct ways can be illustrated through the earlier objective that dealt with predicting meaning by using story structures. The intent was to create experiences which associate reading with the practice of making predictions based on common story structures. This same general goal can be taught as a process outcome. By choosing to teach it as process, a teacher wants students to consciously use their knowledge of story structures to predict meaning.

Figure 9.3 shows the eight-step format to use in developing this consciousness. However, first use the organizational plan described in Chapter 6 to reorganize the content of the basal into units where similar content is taught together. Then state the objective something like this: *Given an appropriate basal text, the student will state how story structure was used to make predictions about meaning in each of five different stories.* Instruction will be effective if students can show how they used story structure to predict meaning in five different basal text stories.

Once the objective is stated, a teacher can begin planning the lesson using the eight-step format. The first step is to select a basal text story in which story structure can be applied. The teacher introduces the story by giving the students background information that activates their prior knowledge about the

Figure 9.3 **The format for planning direct instruction of process**

First: Introduce the basal text selection to which the targeted process will be applied by activating appropriate schema about topic, vocabulary words, and author purpose.

Second: Specify the knowledge or strategy to be taught, its use in real text, and what must be attended to.

Third: Model the thinking you want students to employ in applying the knowledge or strategy.

Fourth: Mediate the students' initial attempts to apply the knowledge or strategy, gradually shifting to them the responsibility for doing the thinking.

Fifth: Set purposes for reading the basal text selection, including both its content and the knowledge or strategy to be used when extracting the content.

Sixth: Read the section silently or orally.

Seventh: Discuss the selection in terms of its content and the knowledge or strategy used to extract the content.

Eighth: Close the lesson by having students summarize both the content of the selection and the knowledge or strategy used.

topic in the story, develops the vocabulary associated with this topic, and gets them thinking about the author's purposes for writing the story (whether it is to inform, to entertain, to provide a moral lesson, or whatever). When teaching word meanings, a teacher relates the unknown words to the students' prior experiences (i.e., the unknown word *tundra* could be explained by comparing it to a large barren area in the students' environment, such as a large vacant lot).

Next, the teacher introduces the process element that will be used while reading the story. In this case, it is knowledge of story structure and how it can be used to predict meaning. In this section of the lesson the teacher tells the students explicitly what reading skill they will be learning, where in the basal text selection they will apply it, and what they must attend to in order to learn it. This introductory step requires that teachers do a *task analysis* that, as the name implies, is an analysis of the task being taught. Its purpose is to arm teachers with specific information about thinking students do when applying reading knowledge or a strategy.

A task analysis has four steps: identifying the outcome, identifying the language principle that can be used to achieve the outcome, identifying the features of the principle that are necessary for its use, and identifying the sequence in which these features are applied. The features and sequence identified in the task analysis become the mental process, or thinking, the teacher wants students to consciously apply when using knowledge to make sense of

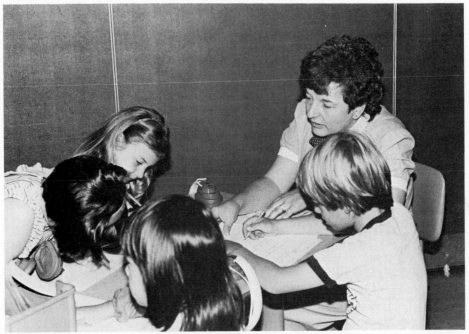

Direct instruction of process objectives involves teacher modeling and appropriate interaction with students.

text. (See Figure 9.4.) In the previous example, the outcome was the conscious use of story structure to make predictions about what will happen in a story; the language principle is the common story format*; the features are the elements of the story structure; and the sequence is identifying the story part, noting the information contained there, and using that information along with general information about the topic to predict what will happen next.

Once the knowledge of story structure has been introduced, the teacher should model its use. This is a crucial step since it is during modeling that teachers actually show students how good readers consciously apply knowledge of story structure to make predictions. Whereas they might use visual aids and other devices at this stage, the best way for teachers to model is by explaining their own thinking processes. When teaching story structures, for instance, a teacher selects a sample story and starts by saying, "When reading this story, I first look at setting, characters, and problem. I see that it is about . . . ." In short, teachers make explicit the mental process identified in the task analysis

---

* The common story format consists of (1) an introduction that includes a setting, main character, and a problem, (2) events related to the problem, and (3) resolution of problem.

Figure 9.4 **Questions teachers ask when doing a task analysis**

What is the outcome I am after? What do I want the students to be able to do?

Is there a language principle or a convention of language I can rely on to achieve that outcome?

What do readers pay particular attention to as they think about the principles or conventions to achieve the outcome?

What sequence do readers follow in thinking through the task and achieving the outcome?

Result: A mental process, consisting of features and a sequence that students can use as a starting point when trying to make sense of text.

by showing students exactly how to use it. In so doing, a teacher ensures that students have a model to follow as they attempt to use the knowledge. They are not left to figure it out for themselves.

In the next step, the teacher mediates student acquisition of the learning objective by providing guided practice. Mediation includes much assistance at first with a gradual lessening as students begin to catch on. For instance, a teacher will initially provide students with many statements that direct their use of the knowledge or strategy, as well as cues and highlighting (such as underlining or pointing to particular elements) that assist them in thinking through the process. Gradually, these statements become questions and the cues are withdrawn until the students are thinking with no assistance.

In teaching story structure, for instance, a teacher gives students sample stories and asks them to use story structures to predict meaning and to explain how they do so. Initially, the teacher may point to each of the three major story parts and make prompting statements regarding the next step in making predictions. As students do their thinking out loud, the teacher listens for knowledge of story structures and provides assistance whenever students exhibit confusion regarding its use in the meaning-getting process. Gradually, the teacher provides less and less assistance as students begin using the mental process independently. (See Figure 9.5.)

Once students demonstrate an understanding of how the knowledge is used, the teacher guides them in applying it to the basal story that was introduced at the beginning. Typically offered as purposes for reading the basal text story are the content of the story itself and the opportunity to apply the knowledge or strategy being taught. In a story structure lesson, for instance,

---

Figure 9.5 **Criteria for observing direct instruction in process outcomes**

	Yes	No

I. *Beginning of the Lesson*

Does the teacher
—state clearly what strategy is to be learned?
—show when and where the strategy is applicable to real reading?
—list the sequence of steps in the strategy?
—model the mental process for applying the strategy?
—think out loud as technique for modeling?
—make clear that there may be alternative strategies?

II. *Middle of the Lesson*

Does the teacher
—have an adequate number of suitable examples?
—restate the goal throughout the lesson?
—use techniques to focus students' attention on the features of the mental processing?
—gradually ask students to do more and more of the processing without any help?
—respond with assistance when students' misconceptions or restructuring lead to confusion?
—reward students for awareness of the process rather than right answers?
—give each student an opportunity to verbalize the entire strategy?
—make frequent reference to the mental processing being employed?

III. *Close of the Lesson*

Does the teacher
—have students summarize the lesson?
—show when and where the strategy is applicable in real reading?
—provide or allow alternative strategies when appropriate?
—provide for student practice?
—guide students in using the strategy when reading real text (in the basal, the content-area text, during USSR, and so forth)?

the teacher will not only talk to students about the content of the story itself but will tell them that the story follows the same three-step format they have learned about and that they should use the thinking process they have practiced to make predictions about content while reading the story. Then the teacher has the students read the story with these two purposes in mind.

In the case of story structures the teacher may wish to combine the reading and the discussion by having a story read in three sections corresponding to the three major story parts and, as students finish each section, discuss with them their predictions about what will happen next. In any case, the teacher monitors their application of what was taught and then closes the lesson by having them summarize both the story content and the way story structures were used to predict that content.

Once the knowledge or strategy has been successfully applied to a basal story, teachers must still transfer the learning to other settings. For instance, they remind students to use the knowledge of story structures when doing uninterrupted silent sustained reading. Other activities in the literate environment can also be used to accomplish this transfer. A particularly useful technique is to have students write their own stories using the three-part story format. This not only reinforces the knowledge taught but also strengthens their understanding of the reading-composing relationship.

As can be seen, teaching story structures by direct instruction is significantly different from teaching story structures in a more indirect way. The planning format used for direct instruction of process outcomes is different, requiring careful task analysis, explicit teacher explanation, and careful teacher mediation and guidance throughout.

DIRECT INSTRUCTION FOR CONTENT OUTCOMES

The lesson format for direct instruction of content goals is similar to that for direct instruction of process goals, but there are differences. When teaching to process goals, teachers want students to develop an awareness of how the reading process works and to use this awareness to consciously monitor and control their reading. When teaching to content goals, however, teachers are less concerned with whether students understand how they get meaning; instead, they just want to make sure that the message is understood. If, in the process of getting the author's meaning, students begin to understand how the reading system works, that is a bonus. The intent, however, is simply to ensure that students understand the message in the functional or recreational text being read.

To illustrate, it is helpful to go back to the process example involving the conscious use of story structures to predict meaning in text. A content lesson involving the same story might at first appear similar, but in reality, it would be different in several significant ways. For instance, if the lesson is taught for content outcomes, the story—not the structure of the story—becomes the focus of the lesson. Story structure would not be taught, although you might ask questions about the story in a sequence that parallels the story structure. In a process lesson, however, the selection is important not because it contains important content but because it affords an opportunity to apply a reading strategy to real text. In the case of story structure the selection is chosen because students can use it to predict meaning using the newly learned story structure strategy. Hence, in the content lesson the objective is to to understand the message, whereas in a process lesson the objective is to consciously use a reading strategy to understand the message.

Content lessons are also different from process lessons in the kind of direct instruction provided. In a process lesson the teacher attempts to make visible the thinking processes used to make sense out of text. In the previous illustration, for instance, the lesson focused on how thinking about story structure can affect comprehension. In a content lesson, however, the teacher focuses on the topic to be discussed, the author's purposes, and the information that should be gleaned from the text. Perhaps questions are asked of students that reflect the structure of stories, but the expectation is that students will answer with infor-

Teacher teaching a directed reading activity for content outcomes.

mation about the content of the story, not with descriptions of how they used story structures to make sense out of the text. Both lessons are good examples of direct instruction, but one focuses on the thought processes needed to get meaning from text whereas the other focuses on the information contained in the text.

The lesson plan formats for direct instruction of process and content outcomes are also different. Because content must be used in both lessons, the first step is virtually identical in the two lessons — the teacher introduces the story to be read, focusing on the topic and the prior knowledge the student must activate to comprehend the content. Vocabulary is emphasized in this first step because understanding the content depends on understanding the words associated with the topic. Hence, the teacher carefully teaches the meaning of the words associated with the topic.

Although content and process lessons are similar in this first step, the subsequent steps differ greatly. In a process lesson the teacher carefully explains how the targeted reading strategy works and how it is to be applied to the story. In a content lesson, however, the teacher moves directly to the story, carefully stating the purposes for reading the selection (the value of the information contained in the text) and providing whatever study aids (guides, notes, summaries, etc.) students might need. Conversely, in a process lesson the purpose is not so much to get the content as to learn a reading strategy. The differences continue as the students read and discuss the text. In a process lesson the discussion deals with how the reading strategy was used to make sense out of the selection, whereas in a content lesson the discussion deals with getting pertinent information from the text. Similarly, the lesson closure differs. In a content lesson only the content is summarized; in a process lesson both the content and the strategy used to understand the content are summarized.

In sum, direct instruction for content differs greatly from direct instruction for process despite similarities in the lesson plan format. To be effective, teachers must first decide if they are developing an understanding of content or an understanding of how to use a reading strategy to make sense out of content. Only when this decision is made should they proceed with planning and conducting the lesson. (See Figure 9.6.)

ANALYZING PLANNING DECISIONS

Like all good instruction, direct instruction requires careful planning, whether the goal is in process or content. Teachers must have a clear concept of what the intended outcome is and have firmly in mind the techniques and examples to be used. This does not mean that direct instruction involves no spontaneity on a teacher's part. To the contrary, unanticipated student responses frequently require teachers to spontaneously modify their lesson plans "in flight."

However, such interactive decision making is only effective if the planning decisions which preceded them are carefully developed. The better prepared teachers are, the more likely it is that they will be able to spontaneously create good responses to unanticipated happenings.

To illustrate the planning decisions in direct instruction of process,

---

Figure 9.6 **Criteria for observing direct instruction in content outcomes**

	Yes	No

I. *Beginning of the Lesson*

Does the teacher

- —state what is to be done and why?
- —activate appropriate schema or prior knowledge?
- —develop the key vocabulary words?
- —discuss the author's purpose in writing the text and the students' purposes in reading it?
- —prepare students for the structure of the text and account for any difficulties in the text?
- —ensure that students know what content they are looking for as they read (theme, causal relationships, details, and so forth)?

II. *Middle of the Lesson*

Does the teacher

- —guide students' reading?
- —ensure that students are directed to relevant, rather than irrelevant, parts of the text?
- —ask clearly sequenced questions that relate to the content purpose stated at the beginning?
- —supplement the text with study guides or other devices designed to ensure student achievement of the content objective?
- —relate students' experiences to the text?
- —monitor student understanding of the text?

III. *Close of the Lesson*

Does the teacher

- —summarize the lesson in terms of the content purposes established at the beginning?
- —highlight important content in the text?
- —check to determine that students' schema about the content have developed in acceptable ways?
- —relate the content to the students' lives?
- —encourage students' points of view?

---

assume once again that a teacher is teaching a second-grade class. The teacher notices that prefixes is one of the skills suggested by the basal text being used by one of the groups and that the students in that group cannot figure out the pronunciation of an unrecognized prefixed word. Since teacher assessment indicates a need for instruction, the first decision is made: teach prefixes.

Second, the teacher decides what kind of instruction to use. Since the desired outcome is to have students use prefixes to repair blockages to meaning caused by unrecognized words, the teacher is teaching a process outcome. Since process goals are better taught by direct than by indirect instruction, the teacher decides to use direct instruction.

Third, the teacher decides to state the outcome as an instructional objective: *Given a text containing unrecognized words having a known root prefixed by* dis- *or* un-, *the student (1) will figure out how to say the unrecognized word and (2) will explain the thinking used to figure out the word in each of the five samples of real text.*

The fourth decision is to do a task analysis of how readers think through the process of figuring out the pronunciation of unknown words having prefixes. The teacher knows the outcome is to consciously apply a strategy to pronounce unrecognized prefixed words; the language principle is that new words can be built by adding prefixes and suffixes; and a sequence to follow in identifying a prefixed word could be (1) identify the root, (2) identify the prefix, (3) separate the two, (4) pronounce each separately, (5) pronounce them as one word, and (6) see if the word makes sense in the sentence.

The fifth decision is to select a text that will give the students a real opportunity to apply the strategy. Usually basal text stories are used, although you must ensure that the basal selection does indeed contain prefixed words that the students might not recognize so there is really an opportunity to apply the strategy. If there is no text situation and a teacher teaches the strategy in isolation, students may never learn to apply it to text.

Sixth, the teacher collects examples that can be used when explaining the strategy. There must be examples to use for modeling and examples students can use to try out the strategy. Not only must there be enough examples, they must all be ones that respond to the strategy.

Seventh, the teacher must decide what to say during the course of the lesson. Since direct instruction is greatly dependent upon the ability to explain things, it is necessary that the teacher plan what to say. This does not mean that everything must be written out ahead of time. It does mean, however, that the teacher should think carefully about what needs to be said, make notes about the sequence of the explanation, decide on key statements, decide on what to display on the chalkboard, decide on what material (if any) students should have in hand during the explanation, and so on. It is helpful to use the eight-step lesson format for direct instruction to guide your thinking in this regard. Figure 9.7 is an illustration of what a carefully stated lesson on prefixes looks like when it follows this format.

Finally, a teacher must assess the effect of instruction and decide whether it was successful or not. Did students learn to use prefixes? Do they exhibit the behavior specified in the objective? In this regard, it is sometimes useful to interview students following instruction. If, after the lesson is over, students can answer the questions What were you learning to do? When would you use it in real reading? How do you do it? the lesson probably has been successful. (See Figure 9.8.)

Figure 9.7 **Sample lesson teaching prefixes as a strategy for pronouncing unrecognized words**

1. Introducing the Basal Text Lesson

Today we are going to read a story about a monkey that lived in the zoo. How many of you have been to the zoo? What do you see at the zoo? We are going to read about the monkeys that lived in the zoo and the special problem a monkey named Clyde had with his brothers and sisters. Now in this story there are some hard words that you have never had before. Here's one right here *(shows students)*. Here's another *(shows students)*. I'm going to teach you a strategy for figuring out these words and others like them so that when you come to them in the story you will be able to figure them out yourselves and go right on finding out about what happens to the monkey.

2. Introducing the Strategy

Sometimes when you are reading you run into a word you don't recognize, like the words I just showed you that are in the story we'll read today. Because you don't recognize it, you can't understand the story. So you need to stop and figure out the word. Today I'm going to show you how to figure out unrecognized words that have prefixes on them. At the end of the lesson, you will have a strategy for pronouncing unrecognized words in your basal text story or in other books that begin with the prefix *dis-* or *un-*. This strategy will help you figure out the pronunciation of prefixed words so you can continue getting the author's meaning despite these hard words. In order to do this you need to look for the root word, then look for the *dis-* or *un-*. Then you separate the two, pronounce each one separately, then say the prefix and the root together.

3. Modeling

I'll explain how I figure out words like these. You'll do this in a moment, so pay attention to the way I figure these words out. Let's say that I'm reading along in my basal story, and

I run into the word *unhappy*. If I've never seen this word before, I say to myself, "Oh, oh. I need to figure this word out if I'm going to continue getting the author's meaning." So I stop, look at the word, and think about what strategy I can use to make sense out of this word. I see that it is a prefixed word, so I think about a prefix strategy. I find the root *(circles it)*. I separate the root from the prefix *(draws a line between them)*. Then I pronounce the prefix — *un-*. Then I pronounce the root — *happy*. Then I say the two parts together — *unhappy*. Then I put the word back into the sentence in the story to make sure it makes sense. Now let's review what I did. You tell me the steps I followed, and I'll list them up here on the board. Susie, what did I do first? Yes, first I . . . *(writes on board)* . . . then I . . . *(writes on board)* . . . .

4. Mediating Students' Initial Attempts to Apply the Strategy

Using Directives and Cues: Can you use my strategy to figure out unrecognized words? Let's try one and I'll help you. Let's assume that you are reading your story and you come to this unknown word *(writes* dislike *on the board, circling the prefix and root and drawing a line between them)*. Let's see if you can use the strategy I used to figure out this word. You have two things to help you: the steps in the strategy listed on the board here *(points)* and the circles and lines in the word you're trying to figure out here *(points)*. Mary, show me how you use the strategy to figure out this word. *(Mary responds by starting with the recognition of a break in meaning-getting caused by an unknown word and by going through the steps of the strategy aloud, ultimately identifying the word as* dislike *and checking to see if it makes sense in the sentence.)*

Using Questions and Faded Cues: Okay. That was good because you thought about how to figure out words that begin with the prefixes *dis-* or *un-*. Now let's see if you can do the same thing when I give you less help. I'm going to erase from the board the steps of my strategy and you see if you can use a strategy of your own that is like mine. And when I put our word *(writes* unkind*)* on the board, I'll just circle the prefix and root, but leave off the dividing line *(circles prefix and root)*. Now, Sam, what would you do first to figure out this word? Can you show me how you'd figure out the word? *(Sam responds by just pronouncing the word.)* You said the word correctly, Sam, but I don't know whether you were doing the thinking correctly. What did you do first? Talk out loud so I can hear how you figured that word out. *(Sam responds, stating the steps he used.)* That's good, Sam. You stated the steps you used to figure out the word correctly. This strategy doesn't work all the time, because some of our words look like words with prefixes but really aren't. *(The teacher illustrates the word* under *and directs the students)* See if this word can be pronounced using our prefix strategy. *(The teacher leads them through the process showing the students where the strategy doesn't work and why.)*

Using Fewer Cues: (The teacher continues to elicit responses from the students, but gradually fades the amount of assistance until the students are doing all the thinking without help and are figuring out the prefixed words independently. The teacher provides other examples of words to which the strategy doesn't apply, such as unless, *having the students state whether the strategy works and why.)*

Using Supportive Feedback and No Cues: Okay. Now before I give you practice in doing this alone, let's make sure we all know how to figure out words like these. *(The teacher has students tell how they figured out prefixed words when no cues are provided and also provides nonexamples for contrast.)*

5. Setting Purposes for Reading the Basal Selection

Now we are going to read the story about the monkey named Clyde. We talked about the fact that Clyde had a problem with his brothers and sisters and we want to find out what that problem was and whether you have had similar problems in your house. There are some hard words in this story that you haven't seen before. When you come to these words, say to yourself, "Oh, oh. I'm going to have to figure this word out." Then see if your prefix strategy will work and, if the hard word does have a prefix, use what we learned about figuring out prefixed words to figure out the word in the story.

6. Reading Silently or Orally

(The teacher has the students read the story orally in primary grades but almost always silently in the middle and upper grades.)

7. Discussing the Story

(The teacher leads a discussion in which questions are posed about both the content and the application of the prefix strategy while reading the story. The intent is to assess whether students understood the content and the application of the prefix strategy.)

8. Closing the Lesson

(The teacher closes the lesson by having students summarize what happened in the story and how the prefix strategy was used to help understand the story. The teacher may also do some kind of culminating, enriching, or broadened language experience activity at this stage to bring closure to the lesson. Closure should also include a statement such as the following.) All right. Now that you have successfully used the prefix strategy to figure out hard words in the basal text story, you have to be sure to use it in other things you read. What other things do you read where you could use this strategy? What if you ran into an unknown word during USSR? Could you use this strategy in that situation? Can you tell how you would use the prefix strategy in reading a newspaper?

Figure 9.8 **Decisions to make in planning direct instruction in process**

Assess to determine whether students need to learn the knowledge or strategy.
Decide whether to use direct or indirect techniques.
State the learning as a specific instructional objective.
Do a task analysis of what you want the student to be able to do.
Select a text in which the knowledge or strategy can be used.
Select examples to be used for your own modeling and for student practice.
Decide on the substance of what you will say and on the sequence of the lesson,
   following the eight-step format for direct instruction in process.
Assess your instruction and decide whether it was effective.

Figure 9.9 **Decisions to make in planning direct instruction in content**

Decide whether the selection is worth reading.

State an objective for the content knowledge you want students to learn.

Analyze what the students need to know about the words, topic, purpose, and text structure in order to get the content knowledge.

Decide how you will aid students in using the words, topic, purpose, and text structure to get the content knowledge.

Decide the sequence of the lesson and what you will say in the lesson.

Decide how you will evaluate whether the lesson has been a success.

The decision patterns are similar when teaching a content outcome. However, rather than starting with a skill contained in the basal, a teacher starts with a selection that needs to be read. The first decision to make is whether a selection is worth reading. Then the teacher decides why it is worth reading and develops an objective describing what student behavior will indicate that the targeted content has been understood. Instead of doing a task analysis as with a process outcome, the teacher analyzes what knowledge sources (words, topic, purpose, and text structure) the student might use to get meaning from the text. On the basis of this analysis the teacher decides what learning aids to provide the students to ensure that they get the targeted content. Such aids might take the form of teacher explanation or it could be paper-and-pencil tasks such as study guides that focus them on the right section of the text or on certain relationships being developed by the writer. In any case, the teacher must decide how to talk to students during the lesson. Finally, as with the process lesson, it is necessary to decide how to evaluate the success or failure of the lesson. (See Figure 9.9.)

SUMMARY

Direct instruction is not a matter of planning an instructional script and then reading it to students. It is a carefully developed, well-structured and explicit effort to achieve particular curricular outcomes with the particular group of students being taught at the moment. Such careful planning is essential for two reasons. First, teaching students how to make sense from text is a complex and difficult task. If teachers do not think carefully about what they are trying to do and how they will do it, the instruction can become jumbled and confusing. Second, all instruction demands that, during instruction, teachers be able to respond spontaneously to students' unanticipated responses while still maintaining an instructional focus on the intended outcome. Such focused spontaneity is not possible unless careful planning has been done beforehand. Consequently, good planning is crucial to effective direct instruction.

THE SUBTLETIES OF INSTRUCTION

The foregoing suggestions for planning lessons are essential and practical. However, good lesson planning is not simply a matter of following a format. Just as good instruction involves subtleties that make planning a constant challenge, good planning requires subtle distinctions and decisions, some of which are described here.

LESSON LENGTH

Many people think of lessons as confined to a definite length of time, usually a single class period. However, lessons are seldom started and finished in a single day. Therefore, when planning either indirect or direct instruction, what is planned often extends over several class periods, even if everything goes perfectly.

In reality, however, things seldom go perfectly. No matter how well a teacher plans, something always needs improving. Consequently, a lesson plan initiated one day will often be modified overnight and presented again in order to clarify points of confusion. Often the second day of instruction will begin with a review of the first day and, depending upon the review, will either move on to the next phase of the lesson or remain at the first phase. As a result, lesson plans are not permanent documents. They are constantly being tinkered with, modified, adjusted, and improved to meet the needs of students. This tinkering requires careful teacher attention and subtle decision making.

INTRODUCING THE LESSON

Direct instruction requires that students be told what the lesson is about at the outset. However, when the targeted outcome is the use of a strategy, three factors complicate the seemingly simple task of introducing the lesson.

First, there is the difficulty of translating skills into strategies. It is easier to introduce a lesson on *main idea* by saying, "Today, we are going to learn about main ideas," rather than saying, "Today, we are going to learn how to figure out the main message the author is trying to convey." The distinction is subtle, but crucial. If students are to learn how to be strategic readers, teachers must emphasize strategic thinking, not knowledge *about* the skill or rote procedures to be automatized.

Second, it is easy to think in terms of separate and isolated lessons.

However, lessons cannot be isolated from one another. Instead, each lesson is a minor variation of similar ones that have been previously taught. All share certain characteristics: the goal of sense making, active student thinking, student use of text and prior knowledge to predict, and student confirmation or rejection of predictions based on whether the result makes sense in context. Consequently, progress is greatest when common themes are emphasized instead of teaching isolated lessons. Again, the difference is subtle, but crucial.

Third, skill instruction is sometimes separated from skill application. Being a good reader means understanding where and when to use the strategies that have been learned. Hence, teachers should specify when a strategy is to be used in real reading. For instance, rather than saying that a strategy "will make you a better reader," it is better to start with a passage from real text, illustrate how one might lose the gist of such a passage, and state that "this strategy will help you fix situations like this when they happen to you." Again the distinction is subtle, but crucial.

SHOWING STUDENTS HOW

All lesson plan formats include a section in which the teacher explains and demonstrates what is being learned. It is variously called the presentation section, the development section, or the modeling section. Whatever it is called, the presentation must reflect three subtle distinctions.

First, the desired outcome must be kept firmly in mind. For instance, if the object is to teach a strategy, the teacher must not get sidetracked into the story's content. In a content lesson, the emphasis is on knowing what happened in the story. A process lesson, on the other hand, focuses not on the answers to story questions but, rather, on how to figure out the answers. Consequently, explanations must focus on the process of figuring it out, not on the answer itself. This is a subtle distinction because we use text to illustrate strategies and, in the process, often end up emphasizing story content. For instance, note what happens in the following lesson where a main idea strategy was being taught, but student responses indicate that they did not understand how to figure out the main idea. The teacher used a paragraph about bears hibernating in the winter to reexplain.

> T: Let's talk about animals that hibernate. You know what hibernate means, right? What does *hibernate* mean?
> S: *(Inaudible)*
> T: Okay, animals that sleep through the winter, right? Now, what are some animals that might hibernate?
> S: A bear.
> T: Okay, a bear.

S: Rabbit.

T: Rabbit.

S: Fox.

T: I'm not sure about all the animals. Squirrels, okay. But don't you see squirrels out in the winter?

S: Yeah.

S: Yeah.

T: Then are they hibernating?

S: No.

S: Yeah.

T: Maybe they do. I don't know. Maybe that is something that I should check out, too.

At this point, the teacher realized that she was not teaching students a strategy for figuring out a main idea but was focusing on story content about animals that hibernate. She tried to shift to a focus on the strategy for figuring out main idea by generating the following nonexample:

T: Okay, let's say we were talking about those animals that hibernate, and I said, "Oh, many, many animals sleep through the winter. Some of the animals are bears. Bears hibernate in cages. And I talk about bears, but then all of a sudden I say, "Fish swim in the sea."

S: How do fish hibernate in that cold water?

T: I didn't say they hibernate. I said, "Fish swim in the sea." "Birds fly south." Is that about animals that hibernate?

S: No.

S: Yeah.

T: No. So, would this be included in my paragraph?

S: No.

T: No. So, what is a main idea? A main idea is a group of sentences that do what?

S: *(In chorus)* Hibernate.

Despite this teacher's best efforts, instruction failed because she slipped into discussing the content of the story when she meant to emphasize how to figure out the main idea. Maintaining a focus on the intended outcome is the crucial component of effective instruction.

A second subtlety in lesson presentations involves showing students how to do something. Because reading is an invisible mental process, it cannot be demonstrated like a swimming instructor demonstrates a new stroke. Reading instruction, instead, involves making visible the thinking that led to the answer. To do this, a teacher can say aloud the mental steps performed when using the strategy (or which the teacher has analyzed to be the steps a novice would need to use). This talking out loud models the thinking. Hence, it is helpful to say, "When *I* use this strategy, I think first about the important words. For instance, in this paragraph, I read along and identify these words as important. Then I . . . ." Doing this allows the students initially to do as the teacher does when employing the strategy. Such modeling is a crucial part of explanation. Without it, students may not know how to begin the task.

A third subtlety in making effective presentations requires that teachers not be *too* prescriptive. No one knows precisely how humans process information. The best that teachers can do is to analyze their own thinking, show the students what they do, and encourage the students to adapt this model for themselves. Allowing for student adaptation is the subtle part. The model must be descriptive, not prescriptive. Say, "Here is a way I think about this problem. Now I want to see if you can use my demonstration to help you solve similar problems." Do not say, "Here is *the* way; you must employ it as I do."

MEDIATING STUDENT ACQUISITION

A major part of a process lesson is the interactive phase, sometimes called *guided practice*. It is here that teachers attempt to move students gradually to the point where they can use strategies independently. As in the other sections of the lesson, subtle verbal distinctions are crucial.

Explanation implies that a teacher does all the talking. However, when that happens, learning does not occur. There must be a gradual transition from teacher modeling to student control. The subtlety involves how quickly or slowly to effect this transfer. Moving too quickly leaves students unclear about what to do; moving too slowly is boring. In order to control this transfer process, teachers can probe for how students get their answers, emphasizing mental processing rather than answer accuracy. For instance, when they direct a student to the main idea of a paragraph, it is better to ask, "How do you know what the main idea is?" than to ask, "What is the main idea?" If students show understanding of how to use the strategy, the lesson can progress; if they do not, more explanation is needed.

If student responses indicate a misunderstanding of the strategy, a reexplanation must be spontaneously generated. Such reexplanation is difficult because it requires instant decision making. For instance, in the following illustration taken from a main idea lesson, the teacher read a paragraph to the group, then proceeded as follows:

> T: Now, of these three titles, which one would be the best main
>   idea? Mary?

S: A trip downtown.
S: A trip downtown.
T: Okay, John, what do you think?
S: The new shirt.
T: Bob, what was your choice?
S: The new shirt.
T: Joan, what about you?
C: A trip downtown.

At this point, it is clear that the students have not understood the teacher's explanation. The situation calls for an elaboration or a reexplanation of how one figures out the gist of a paragraph. Instead, the teacher says:

T: I think the girls decided on a trip downtown and the boys like the new shirt. Mainly, what was the story about?
S: A trip downtown.
S: Getting a new shirt.
T: Getting a new shirt, wasn't it?

Mediating student learning is a subtlety of instruction that requires on-going assessment of student responses (courtesy of Michigan State University).

The teacher does try to elaborate by referring to what the story was mainly about. However, it is not explicit. Compare it to the following spontaneous reexplanation adapted to fit this example:

T: We seem to have some confusion. The main idea is the author's major message in the paragraph. Look at the paragraph here on the chalkboard. What words did we say were important in this paragraph? Sam, can you read them?

S: *Store, shirt, buy, long-sleeved, downtown mall.*

T: Good. Now, the topic of all these words—that ties them together—is what? Mary?

S: They're all about a new shirt.

T: Good. The new shirt is what it's about. That's the topic. Now I've got to think about what the author's major message is regarding the new shirt. So I think to myself, "What does the author want me to understand about the new shirt? What is his main message to me?" To do that, I think of how these words and sentences can be combined into a message. When I think about them together, it's more than just a new shirt. Let's combine them like this *(writes on the board)*. What message ties all these words together? John?

S: It's about how to buy a new shirt.

T: Right. There are many words in paragraphs, but we have to decide what the main message is—what idea ties it all together. How did you know what ties this paragraph together, John?

S: I looked for words that would tell me what the topic was and then thought about what the author wanted me to understand about that topic—about the shirt.

This spontaneously generated reexplanation is more helpful than the first example because it's more explicit. This difference, though subtle, is crucial.

It is not unusual at this stage in the lesson to use various kinds of highlighting to focus student attention on salient features of the strategy. For instance, a teacher may use the chalkboard and underline key words, draw arrows from one meaning relationship to another, circle particular structures, or write out steps to help students learn to use the strategy. However, the teacher must ensure that students learn the intended outcome, not the cues and prompts (such as the teacher's underlining or the steps in the procedure). Again, the distinction is subtle. A teacher can be very explicit about salient features, steps, and sequences, but in the process unintentionally make reading into a mechanical activity of rote memory rather than a strategic, sense-making activity.

PRACTICE

All lesson plan formats call for practice. All practice calls for repetition of a task to make it habitual. Here, again, the subtleties are crucial. The first subtlety in the practice part of the lesson is choosing the proper form of practice. Most teachers employ workbooks or ditto sheets, but these tend to isolate the learning. Since the object is to get students to use strategies in reading real text, it is recommended that practice occur in guided reading of real text — for example, in the basal text selection, the social studies text, or some other appropriate material. Then the learning can be practiced in a context similar to that in which it will ultimately be used.

The second subtlety involves the nature of the practice activities assigned students. In traditional basal instruction, students are asked to read and answer questions and are then assigned grades based on the number of correct answers. When teaching reading strategies, however, teachers are more interested in the thinking processes students go through to get the answer than in the answer itself. Good practice activities, therefore, call for repetitive use of the *thinking* involved. The outcome is thoughtful, not automatized, application.

The third subtlety involves the student behaviors teachers choose to reward. Since they want to develop a strategic approach to text, they should praise students for "knowing how they know." There is a subtle distinction between being praised for thinking strategically and being praised for getting the right answer. The most effective instruction praises the former.

TRANSFER TO REAL READING

Application is the most neglected part of all lessons. When teaching for strategic reading, application requires more than an opening statement regarding the strategy's usefulness or a general reminder regarding the possibility of using it in a basal story. Application must include a genuine reading situation in which, once a meaning breakdown occurs, students can be guided through their storehouse of knowledge and strategies, select the appropriate one, fix the difficulty, and continue processing text. The subtlety here involves the ability to help students recognize when a strategy is called for, access the proper one, use it in a real situation, and determine whether the strategy worked or not. This part of the teacher's explanation is perhaps more crucial than any other.

SUMMARY

Using lesson plan formats helps guide a teacher's planning of indirect and direct instruction. They provide a structure that aids decision making as a teacher plans. However, good instruction also involves subtle distinctions that must be

Figure 9.10 **Model of instructional sequence**

Mandate

Basal prescribes a skill

Planning

Teacher translates that skill into a strategic process (decides what problem it will solve)

Teacher decides when the student will need to use the strategy

Teacher decides on the mental processing (steps) in using the strategy

Teacher assesses the basal prescription for:
- description of the strategy
- usefulness of the strategy
- how to do it

Teacher assesses the basal selection for:
- opportunities to practice and apply the strategy
- cues for when to call for the strategy

Teacher decides how to sequence an explanation for using the strategy

Presentation

Teacher describes the strategy and how it is used

Teacher models recognizing when the strategy would be useful — the cues that tell when the strategy is needed

Teacher models the mental processing (steps) to be followed when using the strategy and checking results for sense

Interaction

Students interpret what they think the teacher's explanation really means

Teacher provides examples of situations that call for use of the strategy

On the basis of their interpretations, students verbalize:
- how they recognized that the strategy is needed
- their versions of using the mental processing modeled by the teacher

Teacher monitors and assesses students' verbalizations of how and when they use the strategy over a number of trials (examples)

If students' verbalizations are correct, teacher gives supportive feedback for using the process correctly and moves to guided application in connected text

If students' verbalizations are incorrect, teacher provides reexplanation and clarification of inaccuracies

Application

Teacher provides connected text that calls for use of the strategy and guides students' application of strategy in that text

Teacher provides opportunities for independent reading and reminds students to apply the strategy when that kind of problem is encountered anticipated during planning. If teachers follow lesson plan formats as a rote procedure of filling in the appropriate categories, instruction will be boring and ineffective. If, however, teachers use lesson formats as a guide and think about the subtleties of the task, the student, and the application to text as they plan, instruction will be more successful and will also be more interesting and relevant.

CONCLUSION

Lesson planning is a crucial organizational step in conducting instruction. However, it is a complex and difficult task that is not to be taken lightly. A good way to review the lesson planning task while also reminding you of the complexity of lesson planning is to study Figure 9.10.*

Chapter 4 discussed instruction in terms of the interaction that occurs between a teacher and students (see Figure 4.2). Figure 9.10 is an elaboration on this teacher–student interaction and illustrates the instructional sequence. Note that the model begins with a skill prescribed by the basal text. Immediately the teacher makes decisions about how to recast the skill as a strategy, where it will be used, what mental process is demanded, and so on. Once planning is completed, the teacher follows the plan during the presentation and the early part of the interaction. However, as the interaction proceeds, the teacher monitors student interpretations of the explanation, deciding spontaneously on elaborations and reexplanations that can be used to help students restructure the learning in terms of the desired outcome. This interactive process and the need for spontaneous decision making continues into the application stage. In short, the plan only takes the teacher to a certain point and then creative instructional response is required. This is the ultimate subtlety.

To some it may seem discouraging to expend so much effort on planning a lesson only to have to modify it during interaction. However, there is another way to view it. In the first place, your success in responding spontaneously during the interaction and application is directly tied to how carefully you planned. The better you plan, the more sure you are of what you are doing and the better you can respond to students' restructuring of your explanations. Secondly, the blend between preparation and creativity seen in Figure 9.10 is the heart of teaching. You will never be replaced by machines or by scripts, because no machine or script can anticipate how students will restructure explanations. Only thinking professionals can do that. This is the reason why teachers must be decision makers.

* The contribution of Dr. Roy Wesselman at Michigan State University in the development of Figure 9.10 is gratefully acknowledged.

CHECK YOUR UNDERSTANDING

Now that you have read the chapter, check your understanding by answering the Focus Questions presented at the beginning of the chapter. If you are unable to answer one or more of the questions, return to the chapter, find the section that corresponds to the question, and reread.

SUGGESTED READINGS

Allington, R. L., & Strange, M. (1977). The problem with reading games. *Reading Teacher, 31*(3), 272–274.

Atwell, A. A., & Rhodes, L.K. (1984). Strategy lessons as alternatives to skill lessons in reading. *Journal of Reading, 27*(8), 700–705.

Gambrell, L. B. (1980). Think-time: Implications for reading instruction. *Reading Teacher, 34*(2), 143–146.

Guthrie, J. T. (1982). Teacher effectiveness: The quest for refinement. *Reading Teacher, 35*(5), 636–638.

Guzzetti, B. J., & Marzano, R. J. (1984). Correlates of effective reading instruction. *Reading Teacher, 37*(8), 754–758.

Isaacs, M. L. (1979). The many facets of language arts: Helps and handbooks for lesson planning. *Language Arts, 56*(5), 577–580.

Johns, J. L. (1982). Does our language of instruction confuse beginning readers? *Reading Psychology, 3*(1), 37–41.

Kitagawa, M. M. (1982). Improving discussions or how to get the students to ask the questions. *Reading Teacher, 36*(1), 42–45.

Pearson, P. D. (1985). Changing the face of reading comprehension instruction. *Reading Teacher, 38*(8), 724–738.

Riley, J. D. (1979). Teachers' responses are as important as the questions they ask. *Reading Journal, 32*(5), 534–537.

Sadow, M. W. (1982). The use of story grammar in the design of questions. *Reading Teacher, 35*(5), 518–522.

Shake, M. C., & Allington, R.L. (1985). Where do teachers' questions come from? *Reading Teacher, 38*(4), 432–438.

Wixson, K. K. (1983). Questions about a text: What you ask about is what children learn. *Reading Teacher, 37*(3), 287–294.

CHAPTER 10

Planning and Conducting Writing Lessons

GETTING READY

Chapter 1 made the point that professional teachers view reading as part of a larger language process. Chapter 2 emphasized the interrelationship between reading and writing. In Chapter 4 the relationship between reading and writing was again pointed out while discussing the language experience approach and its strength in highlighting the reader–writer relationship. The relationship was again emphasized in Chapter 5 when suggestions were made for creating a literate environment as a means of integrating all the language modes.

In sum, reading is an integral part of the total language process and should be taught in close association with oral language (listening and speaking) and writing. Because both reading and writing are based on print, their relationship is particularly important. Consequently, reading instruction should be closely tied to writing instruction.

This chapter describes the intended outcomes of the writing curriculum as they relate to the reading outcomes developed in Chapter 2. It describes the role of indirect and direct instruction and of a literate environment in achieving these goals, and suggests how you can use planning formats similar to those developed in Chapters 6 and 9.

FOCUS QUESTIONS

As you read this chapter use the following questions to guide your understanding of how to develop, organize, and implement writing instruction as part of your reading program.

Writing is closely related to reading.

1. Why is writing an important aspect of good reading instruction?
2. How do you conceptualize a writing curriculum?
3. What are the intended outcomes of a writing program?
4. What is the role of indirect instruction in developing writing outcomes?
5. What is the role of direct instruction in developing writing outcomes?
6. What are some examples of good writing instruction in elementary schools?
7. What are some of the Do's and Don'ts of teaching writing in elementary schools?

WHY IS WRITING IMPORTANT TO READING GROWTH?

Writing is important to reading growth for three reasons. First, both readers and writers use the same set of written language conventions. Writers must understand and manipulate the conventions of text in order to compose a message that readers can reconstruct by using these same conventions. Thus, students' understanding of these conventions is enhanced when they use them in writing as well as in reading.

Second, there is a close relationship between what readers do and think as they reconstruct meaning from text and what writers do and think as they compose text. For instance, both good readers and good writers understand that the essence of written language is to communicate a message to someone who does not have to be physically present to receive it. The act of composing and the act of reconstructing meaning both require a search for sense making that involves an empathy for the other person; a monitoring of the sense-making process as it proceeds; and the use of strategies — to clarify meaning (in the case of writing) and to reconstruct meaning (in the case of reading).

Third, writing is important to the development of reading because a good writing program increases the amount of time spent with text. No matter how much time is spent in the reading program, student development will be enhanced if additional time is devoted to composing text, a task that requires much the same kind of thinking.

Writing, then, is important to the development of effective readers. Good teachers of reading work hard to integrate writing instruction into their reading programs.

Positive writing attitudes depend upon meaningful writing activities (courtesy of Michigan State University).

Figure 10.1 **Writing concepts to be developed**

1. Students understand the reader–writer relationship.
2. Students understand that a writer is the first reader.
3. Students understand that writing is message sending.
4. Students understand that writing is to clarify one's own thoughts.
5. Students understand that writing is directed to an audience.
6. Students understand that the audience is both self and others.
7. Students understand that writing and speaking both involve sending messages.
8. Students understand that writing, other than for self, involves a distant audience.
9. Students understand that audience feedback in writing is more delayed than audience feedback in speaking.
10. Students understand that writing is both recreational and informational.

Figure 10.2 **Feelings to be developed about writing**

1. Students feel they have worthwhile information to share.
2. Students enjoy writing for both recreational and functional purposes.
3. Students feel satisfaction with both recreational and functional writing.
4. Students find writing rewarding.
5. Students feel powerful because of writing.

THE WRITING CURRICULUM

Just as the ultimate outcome of reading instruction is student control of the comprehension process, the ultimate outcome of the writing program is student control of the *composing* process. Students should know how to compose the functional and recreational messages they wish to write. To develop such conscious control, teachers must help students develop positive attitudes toward writing, content knowledge to be communicated, and an understanding of how the writing process works.

ATTITUDE OUTCOMES IN WRITING

Just as reading growth depends upon good attitudes about reading, writing growth depends upon good attiudes about writing. These attitudes reflect concepts about writing that grow from positive experiences with writing.

Concepts about writing are closely related to concepts about reading. Students should understand the reader–writer relationship; that is, they should understand that writers are the first to read composed text, writing is message sending and always involves an audience, the audience can be one's self as well as others, writing is similar to speaking except that the audience is not physically present, and writing fulfills both functional and recreational needs. See Figure 10.1 for examples of concepts about writing.

Similarly, students should have positive experiences with writing. They should associate writing with enjoyment and fulfillment (see Figure 10.2) rather than with fear, work, and defeat. To develop accurate concepts and positive experiences you must provide students with writing experiences that are sensible, useful, pleasant, and reasonably natural. If not—if their writing experiences are meaningless, useless, unpleasant, and contrived—they will develop inaccurate concepts and negative attitudes toward writing.

CONTENT OUTCOMES IN WRITING

Writing content is whatever message the writer wants to send. In the largest sense, content outcomes are what is said in the various kinds of functional and recreational texts students compose. For instance, students should be able to compose such functional texts as business letters, friendly letters, simple expository text, reports, newspaper articles, and formal term papers. Recreationally, students should be able to compose dairies, journals, stories, poems, riddles, and jingles, among others. See Figure 10.3 for examples of curriculum goals.

Knowing what to write includes putting the message in the correct format. Each kind of functional and recreational text has a conventional structure to follow. For instance, there is an accepted format for a business letter, a short report, a news article, a short story, various kinds of poetry, and so on. Students should know these structures and be able to compose text within them.

Before composing various kinds of text, however, the content of the message must be decided upon. Writing depends upon having something to say; that is, upon having a message to send. When students have clear and meaningful reasons for writing, they seldom have difficulty knowing what to say. Consequently, content goals focus on identifying a purpose for writing and on how to generate a message from that purpose.

Content goals should also include distinguishing between writing for one's self and writing for others. The content of personal writing (diaries, journals, reflections, recipes, and so forth) is different from the content of writing produced for an outside audience. Personal writing need not be as concerned with clarity or with adherence to the conventions of language, since there is little chance that writers will fail to understand their own messages even when inaccuracies are present. When writing for others, however, both clarity and language conventions must be maintained to assist the reader in reconstructing the message. In short, the writing curriculum should help students (1) identify

---

Figure 10.3 **Curriculum goals for functional and recreational writing**

1. Students identify the need for a message.
2. Students identify the purpose of a message.
3. Students identify the audience for a message.
4. Students select appropriate text formats.
5. Students use appropriate text formats.

---

the message they want to send, (2) distinguish between writing for one's self and writing for others, and (3) teach them the formats associated with the various kinds of functional and recreational text.

PROCESS OUTCOMES IN WRITING

Process outcomes focus on helping students understand and control the writing process and are divided into two categories: knowledge of the stages in the composing process and strategies for implementing each stage.

Knowledge of the Stages of Writing. To understand how writing works, students must first know what stages writers go through in composing text. All writers must plan, draft, and edit.

The planning stage emphasizes reflection. A writer decides upon the purpose of a message, the central meaning to be conveyed, and the supportive information to be included. An important part of the planning stage is to think about who will read the message and how the message will have to be stated in order to make sense to that audience. For instance, when writing about a sophisticated topic for a sophisticated audience, elaborate background information is not needed. If, on the other hand, an audience is relatively unsophisticated about a topic, it will probably be necessary to build a background before launching into the central message. Consequently, the planning stage must take into account the intended readers' values, concepts, experiences, and schemata.

The planning stage also includes organizing the message into an appropriate text format. For instance, when composing a story, it is helpful to outline the setting, the main character, the character's problem, the series of events that occur, and the resolution of the problem. When composing a news article, all the relevant information is placed in the first paragraph, and certain details are assigned to subsequent paragraphs. Planning is especially crucial when the audience is someone other than one's self, since the text structure helps the reader reconstruct the message.

The second stage in composing text is the drafting stage. Here, a writer composes a message in rough form. At this stage, the writer concentrates on producing a coherent text in which the ideas fit together to convey the intended message and a cohesive text in which the central message is maintained throughout the text. Coherence and cohesiveness are important whether the writer is producing functional or recreational text.

The third stage of writing is editing. Here a writer acts like a reader and critically reads his or her own text. In doing so, the writer tries to anticipate where the reader might have difficulty reconstructing the intended meaning. While all stages of the composing process are important, editing is particularly important because it is here that the message is honed and polished to ensure that a reader makes the interpretations the writer intends. Editing encompasses all aspects of the writing process. For instance, the writer edits the content, audience, and format developed in the planning stage; the coherence and cohesiveness developed in the drafting stage; as well as the finer points of expression such as word and phrase choice, punctuation, grammatical accuracy, and spelling. Figure 10.4 summarizes the stages in the composing process.

Students need to know that whereas good writers move through stages when writing, these stages are not necessarily linear. Writers often move from

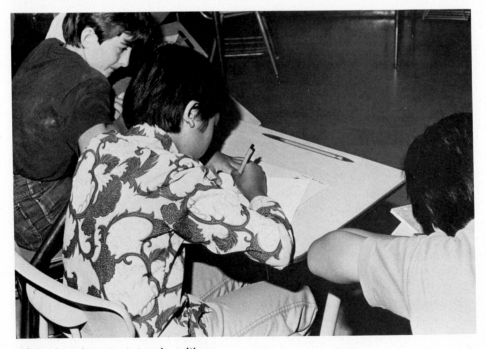

Editing is an important stage in writing.

Figure 10.4 **Stages in composing process**

Planning

1. Writers gather information for message content.
2. Writers focus the gathered information.
3. Writers organize the gathered information.

Drafting

1. Writers compose coherently by following a structure for recreational or functional text.
2. Writers compose cohesively by using transitions between words, sentences, paragraphs, and sections.

Editing

1. Writers critically read their draft(s) from the point of view of their intended audience.
2. Writers critically read their draft(s) for coherence and cohesion.
3. Writers critically read and edit their draft(s) for mechanics.

Figure 10.5 **Strategies for the planning stage**

Strategies for gathering information

1. Interview
2. Observe
3. Listen
4. Read
5. Brainstorm for feelings and knowledge

Strategies for focusing the gathered information

1. Group and label information
2. Set purpose for message
3. Determine audience for message

Strategies for organizing information

1. Choose and apply an appropriate literary structure (a story structure, a news report structure, and so on)

planning to drafting and back again before all the planning is complete. Similarly, editing often occurs before the writing stage is complete. This is particularly true when writing for an audience other than one's self. Nevertheless, the typical progression is as follows. A writer plans for the content, the audience, and the basic organizational structure; this plan is then used to produce a coherent and cohesive first draft; the draft is then edited for content, clarity and the conventions of written language, a process which often results in several new drafts. These stages should be taught at the earliest language experience writing in the Readiness Stage through the writing of detailed research papers at the Power Stage.

Strategies to Be Used at Each Stage. Strategy use in writing is similar to strategy use in reading. Readers consciously monitor their understanding of an author's message, stopping when there is a blockage and activating a strategy to repair it so that the meaning getting can continue. Writers follow a similar sequence. Although the composition process frequently progresses smoothly and efficiently, a writer may encounter blockages at any of the three stages of composition. When such a blockage occurs, the writer calls on a planning, drafting, or editing strategy to remove the blockage.

   At the planning stage the strategies fall into three categories. First, if the problem is a lack of content or information about what to write, a writer must be taught how to get the necessary information. Information can be gathered by brainstorming, reading, interviewing, and/or observing. However, an important distinction must be made here. When children complain that they do not know what to write about it is often because the writing task is not meaningful to them — it is busywork. In such cases the problem is not a lack of information, but rather, a meaningless assignment, and the solution is to give them a good reason for writing rather than strategies for getting more information. However, if the writing assignment involves a real message that will be sent to someone and the student lacks information, then information-gathering strategies must be taught.

   The second category of planning strategies involves focusing on what is to be said. These strategies often involve clarifying the purpose of the writing and can be accomplished by grouping or categorizing gathered information. Finally, the planning stage calls for organizational strategies such as outlining, in which related concepts are grouped together in a chosen text structure. An illustrative list of the strategies associated with the planning stage are provided in Figure 10.5.

   Drafting-stage strategies focus on how to create coherence and cohesion in the message. For instance, when a writer feels that a message is not sufficiently coherent, the age-old format of wrapping an introductory and summary state-

---

Figure 10.6 **Strategies for the drafting stage**

Strategies for creating coherence

1. Follow text structures when writing (formats for stories, poems, reports, articles, and so on)
2. Follow the plan of
   —introduce
   —tell
   —summarize
3. Use headings and subheadings

Strategies for creating cohesion

1. Build transition signals
   —between sentences
   —between paragraphs
   —between sections
2. Create summaries
   —to review
   —to forewarn

---

ment around the central message is a reliable way of obtaining coherence. It can be adapted to both functional and recreational text (although it is most often associated with expository writing) and can be used to add coherence to paragraphs, sections, and entire texts. Another strategy for making expository text coherent is the careful use of headings and subheadings to guide the reader, whereas for recreational text the students can follow a story structure that includes illustrations, flashbacks, and foreshadowing.

Strategies for ensuring cohesion include inserting transition statements between paragraphs and sections and inserting signal words that key the reader to how one section of text relates to another. Another strategy that can be used to achieve cohesion in functional text is to include periodic summaries to remind readers of key points, concepts, or the main idea and in recreational text to remind them of the problem, the sequence of events relating to the problem, or the theme. Figure 10.6 summarizes the strategies writers can be taught to use at the drafting stage.

It is at the editing stage that the author's message is honed and polished to ensure that the reader will reconstruct the intended meaning. Editing requires a writer to play two roles simultaneously because, when editing, the writer is also a reader and looks for places where the text might be confusing. When these are encountered, strategies are employed to fix up the writing and to prevent any blockage. Although organizational characteristics are sometimes modified, most editing focuses on the sentence and word level. For instance, writers use synonym and thesaurus strategies to make more precise word choices; syntactic strategies to improve meaning through word order; punctuation strategies to help the reader "say it like the author intended," and spelling strategies to help the reader identify the words. These strategies are often referred to as the *mechanics of writing* and are sometimes incorrectly taught as skills to be memorized, such as synonym and antonym drills, sentence diagramming, punctuation drills, and weekly spelling tests. When taught in this way, students seldom apply these mechanics to the actual task of composing. When taught as strategies to be used when editing a real message to be sent to someone, however, these mechanics suddenly become more meaningful and useful. Figure 10.7 summarizes editing strategies that writers can be taught.

In short, the curriculum of writing involves teaching students information about how the writing process works, just as the reading curriculum involves teaching information about how the reading process works. In both cases the intent is to produce students who are in cognitive control of the communication process and can apply appropriate strategies to repair actual or potential blockages to meaning getting.

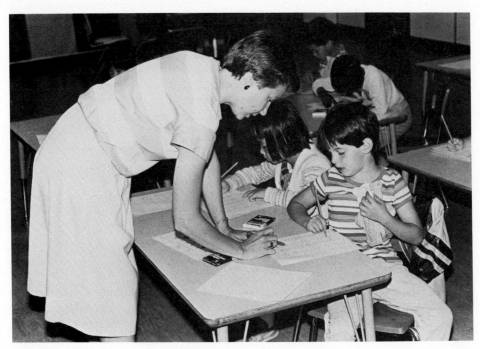

A teacher helps a student with a writing task.

Figure 10.7 **Strategies for the editing stage**

Strategies for editing over-all organization from the perspective of audience
1. Background knowledge
2. Developmental age
3. Knowledge of text structure

Strategies for editing word choice using
1. Synonym strategies
2. Thesaurus strategies

Strategies for editing mechanics using
1. Grammar strategies
2. Spelling strategies
3. Punctuation strategies

SUMMARY

The writing curriculum has much in common with the reading curriculum. Just as teachers try to develop attitude, process, and content outcomes in reading, they try to develop attitude, process, and content outcomes in writing. Just as the content of the message is the central issue in reading, the content of the message is the central issue in writing. Just as we want students to be in control of the comprehension process in reading, we want students to be in control of the composition process in writing. Consequently, when teaching writing, good teachers develop attitude, process, and content outcomes with the intention of creating writers who control their composing efforts.

PROVIDING INSTRUCTION IN WRITING

To provide instruction in writing, the teacher uses a decision-making structure much like the one described for reading lessons. It begins with an objective and is achieved using either direct or indirect instruction.

OBJECTIVES FOR WRITING INSTRUCTION

As with reading lessons, writing lessons begin with objectives keyed to the ultimate outcome of developing cognitive control of the communication process. To determine how well students control the total writing process, teachers begin by assessing the smaller but related attitude, process, and content outcomes. For instance, teachers will assess students' concepts and feelings about writing, their ability to plan and to use knowledge of the writing stages, and their ability to use editing strategies. As with reading, student attainment of these subgoals gives teachers an indication of where students stand in relation to the ultimate outcome.

Once objectives are decided upon, the teacher formally states them using the criteria previously cited for reading (see Chapter 9). That is, the teacher describes the desired student behavior, the conditions under which that behavior can be observed, and the criterion that will be an acceptable indication of learning. Students' writing ability can be intentionally developed only when a teacher has decided upon an objective and the resulting instruction can be precise only if the teacher has consciously stated what the students are to do, under what conditions, and to what degree.

USING INDIRECT INSTRUCTION

Indirect instruction is used to develop the attitude and content outcomes of writing. It frequently revolves around language experience activities or classroom projects, and is closely associated with the literate environment a teacher has created.

As described in Chapter 5, the literate environment consists of classroom activities that use language for real purposes, just as literate people do outside school. When teaching writing, this means that the teacher creates an environment in which there are frequent opportunities for real writing. In this environment invitations are made and RSVPs received, greeting cards are designed and written, notes are passed, recipes are recorded, stories are written, letters are sent and received, records are kept, posters are designed, signs are painted, displays are labeled, newspapers are printed, poems are published, plays are written and performed, and thoughts are solidified. In short, the literate environment uses writing in a variety of natural ways.

These natural writing situations are used by teachers to develop both attitude and content goals. Regarding attitude outcomes, real and meaningful writing activities help students develop accurate concepts of what writing is, its purposes, and the properties that characterize good writing while also helping them develop positive feelings about writing. Regarding content outcomes, natural writing activities give students real purposes for writing. Because these purposes are not contrived, students seldom find themselves with nothing to write about. On the contrary, the activities within a literate environment provide both functional and recreational content that can be shared.

Indirect writing lessons follow the same decision-making pattern and lesson format as described in the previous chapter for indirect instruction in reading. After deciding to use indirect rather than direct instruction to achieve an attitude or content objective, a teacher develops the lesson using the three-

---

Figure 10.8 **An example of indirect instruction in writing**

Step 1: Activity

After brainstorming have each student write to "Dear Abby" with a particular problem selected from those listed during brainstorming. The objective is to develop the concept that writing is message sending.

Step 2: Discussion

Discuss the activity with students, getting them to focus on the concept that writing is message sending.

Step 3: Activity

After brainstorming have students pretend they are "Abby" and answer their friend's letter. The written responses are returned to the students who wrote the initial request for help.

Figure 10.9 **An example of how to teach a directed writing lesson**

BACKGROUND

Assume that you have a group of students who do not know how to write from varying points of view. For instance, they often switch the pronouns that signal the person telling the story (I—first person, you—second person, he, she—third person) and use words with both positive and negative connotations when describing the same person. The following is a lesson plan to teach how to write from a specific point of view.

LESSON SEQUENCE

1. Imbed the writing strategy in an actual writing task. Read a poem such as "For Sale," by Shel Silverstein, in *Where the Sidewalk Ends*. Discuss reactions to the poem, how the brother was feeling, and what events might have made him want to sell his little sister. Then focus on changing the point of view by examining how the little sister might have felt about being sold. Prepare them for writing a letter as the little sister in which *her* point of view is expressed.
2. Introduce the point-of-view writing strategy by telling your students they will learn how to signal point of view with pronoun usage and connotative words. State that consistent pronoun usage indicates whose view is being presented (first, second, or third person). State that readers determine what a writer's view is by use of con-

notative words ("crying and spying sister" in the poem signals negative connotation).

3. Model point of view by taking a sentence such as,"The dog walked down the street." Add a second sentence with a third-person pronoun, "He chased a cat." Show how you can make the sentences signal whose point of view is being taken by adding adjectives to the sentence: "The lazy and unkempt dog walked down the street" or "The sleek groomed dog walked down the street." Revise the second sentence to say, "He chased the snarling, spitting cat," or "He chased the well-tempered, friendly cat." Show how you used third person to signal point of view and connotative words to convey whose point of view you were taking.

4. Mediate student acquisition of the point-of-view strategy by providing simple sentences and helping the students select pronouns and connotative words that are consistent for some point of view. Gradually reduce assistance until the students can write point of view sentences that are consistent and contain connotative words. Have students explain the point-of-view chosen and the connotative words that signal that viewpoint.

5. Return to the poem. Reread it and go over the events that might have caused the older brother's anger. Discuss how his little sister might have felt about the same events. List some connotative words she might have used to communicate her feelings. Have students pretend to be the little sister and write a point-of-view letter explaining to a friend the events that led to her brother's trying to sell her.

6. Discuss the letters, noting examples of consistent pronoun usage and connotative words.

7. Review what students have learned about how to write from a consistent point of view.

step format of activity–discussion–activity. The chosen activity indirectly promotes the desired outcome, the discussion clarifies it, and the follow-up activity reinforces it.

As with all indirect instruction, such writing instruction often looks spontaneous and unplanned. That is because the activity often dominates the instructional setting. For instance, the students are so involved in writing their letters, or in designing their greeting cards, or in preparing their class newspaper that their growing appreciation and conceptual understanding of writing often goes unnoticed. However, despite appearances, indirect instruction is deliberate and planned; skillful teachers simply make it look spontaneous. For an example of indirect instruction in writing, see Figure 10.8.

USING DIRECT INSTRUCTION

Direct instruction in writing is used almost exclusively to develop process objectives. It is conducted in close association with the real writing activities pursued in the literate environment, but often involves small groups of students who need help with a particular part of the writing process. In direct instruction, the teacher assumes an overt role, focusing the lesson on a particular aspect of writing and demonstrating how and when to do it.

As with any instruction, direct instruction in writing process calls for carefully specified objectives. A teacher must decide whether to teach about the stages of writing or to teach fix-it strategies to use when things are not going well. In either case, a good task analysis is in order (see Figure 9.4). By virtue of having done a task analysis, a teacher can describe for the students the features they should attend to and the mental sequence they should follow when engaged in a particular aspect of the composing process.

When actually teaching a lesson in writing process, follow a lesson format similar to the reading format described in Figure 9.3. However, instead of teaching from a basal text story, substitute a writing activity. The first step involves introducing the students to an actual writing task they are to complete. Then introduce them to the knowledge or strategy to be applied to that writing task. Model the targeted knowledge or strategy and then mediate the students' acquisition by providing application opportunities with gradually decreasing assistance. Next, return to the writing assignment and make sure the students apply what was taught as they compose the message. Discuss their completed writing, noting both the message they have conveyed and their application of the targeted process. Finally, close the lesson by having them review what they have learned about how to consciously control their writing. Figure 10.9 is an example of how direct instruction can be used to develop writing process outcomes.

A teacher's decisions when planning direct instruction in the writing process are similar to decisions when planning direct instruction in reading. Data must first be collected to assess whether the students need to learn the knowledge or strategy, and other decisions must be made regarding (1) type of instruction, (2) specific objectives, (3) task analysis, (4) a specific writing task, (5) modeling activities, (6) guided practice activities, (7) mediation behavior, and (8) task evaluation data.

In writing, then, direct instruction is used to develop process outcomes. The intent is to teach students the stages of writing and the strategies that can be used at each stage to achieve conscious control of efforts to compose functional and recreational text.

SUMMARY

Both direct and indirect instruction are crucial to instruction in writing. Indirect instruction develops the attitudes and suggests the content that is the essence of writing. Direct instruction puts students in conscious control of the writing process. The two kinds of instruction work together to create the ultimate outcome of putting students in control of composing real text.

INTEGRATING READING AND WRITING

Writing is emphasized as part of reading instruction because we know that students become better readers when they are also involved in writing (just as they become better writers when they are involved in reading). It is important, then, that instruction in reading and writing be closely related. Rather than having separate reading and writing periods, it is more effective to integrate the two.

The key to integrating reading and writing lies in the literate environment. If classroom activities involve both reading and writing, integration of reading and writing instruction occurs almost naturally. If, however, classroom reading activities are confined to a basal text, integration is quite difficult. While basal text instruction is an important part of most elementary school reading programs, other kinds of activities can be used to supplement the basal and provide an opportunity to integrate reading and writing. The following examples show ways of accomplishing such integration.

1. Provide students with pictures of an action or event. Have them discuss what happened before, during, and after the action or event. Have students write their responses and post the pictures with the descriptions (good for nook-and-cranny time).

2. Teach students how to create *Think Pinks*, which are two words that rhyme and answer a definition question. For example, an unhappy boy is a *sad lad*; a father who has done something wrong is a *bad dad*; an obese feline is a *fat cat*. Create a file of Think Pinks and read them during nook-and-cranny time.

3. Create concept books. For example, using the concept *money* have students create word lists that describe what money is and give examples of money and how it can be used. These concept books become available for reading when students need help in developing other concepts.

4. Create poetry for reading during sharing time or free time. Use common sporting events. Have students write one line as a spectator and the next line as the participant. Alternate lines.

5. Have students assume they are inanimate objects such as a tennis ball or a pencil sharpener. Discuss how they would view the world and what they would see. Take an event and have students write descriptions from varying objects' viewpoints. Read the descriptions during strategy lessons on point of view.

6. Rewrite history. Select an event from social studies that has recently been studied. Discuss "what if's." What if the pilgrims had missed Plymouth Rock? What if the astronauts had missed the

moon? What if we canceled election day? After brainstorming, have students rewrite history. The resulting books can be used for supplemental reading.

7. Have students create codes and send communications to each other. Communications should be meaningful so that students read the code.

8. Read a story or poem to the students. Have them discuss what happened next. Have them write their descriptions in newspaper article formats.

PRESSURES ASSOCIATED WITH WRITING INSTRUCTION

Chapter 1 mentioned that the conditions of the classroom often conspire to make teachers into technicians rather than professionals. The constraints of the workplace cause teachers to provide certain kinds of instruction even when they know that other forms may be better.

This phenonomena also occurs in writing. This chapter presents an approach to writing instruction based on the concept that writing skills are best taught in the context of real writing tasks. However, many classrooms are organized in ways that discourage this concept. For instance, it is not unusual to teach technical skills such as spelling, punctuation, grammar, capitalization, and handwriting in isolation from each other rather than as strategies to be used during the editing stage to strengthen the clarity of a composed message. The expectation seems to be that students will engage in real writing after they have developed a mastery of these isolated skills.

There is little doubt that the traditional practice of drilling and practicing the technical writing skills in isolation hampers the efforts of teachers who wish to teach these same skills as editing strategies. There is a strong tradition in American education for organizing spelling instruction into weekly word-list tests having little to do with students' real reading and writing; teaching students the nomenclature of grammar so that they can identify nouns, predicates, and dangling participles even though this does not help one compose messages more effectively; having children diagram (or parse) sentences according to function even though such breaking down of sentences is the opposite of the composition process; and using worksheets that require identification of incorrect punctuation and capitalization even though such activity is not representative of real writing. These traditions pressure teachers into following conventional practices.

To combat these pressures, a teacher must learn how to fulfill the traditional expectations while still providing meaningful writing activities. The trick is to integrate conventional activities into the writing program where they will be of use. Because these traditional skill activities are essentially practice and drill, they should be placed in direct instruction lessons following the application of some newly learned process in real writing. Hence, if teachers must teach diagramming and parsing of sentences, they should do it as practice activity *after* they have taught a lesson on how to order words to ensure clarity and *after* students have applied that strategy in a real writing activity. If teachers must have students identify examples of incorrect punctuation on a worksheet, they should assign it *after* they have taught a lesson at the editing stage on how to clarify writing through punctuation and students have applied that strategy in real writing. If teachers must teach mandated lists of spelling words, they should supplement the list with words students are encountering in their real reading and writing.

The strong tradition in American education to teach reading and writing as sets of separate skills to be mastered puts pressure on teachers who wish to teach reading and writing as sense-making activities in which students consciously use language conventions to interpret and compose textual messages. However, it is possible to satisfy the traditional expectations while also developing students who are literate.

CONCLUSION

Reading and writing are closely related, and much of the mental processing done by writers is also done by readers. Instructionally, teachers know that the more students write the more they read, and vice versa. Consequently, it is important that instructional programs for elementary school reading be closely integrated with strong programs for writing.

Achieving such integration, however, requires that teachers allocate time to writing and that these writing activities become an integral part of the literate environment. Teachers must also know that the ultimate goal of writing instruction is cognitive control of the writing process and that all subgoals, instructional objectives, and selected modes of instruction should promote this ultimate objective.

This chapter has been designed to help you with this organizational task. The outcomes are specified, the instructional procedures that promote these outcomes are provided, activities for integrating reading with writing are suggested, and the dangers of teaching traditional writing skills in isolation from real writing activities are cited. Specific suggestions for teaching writing at each of the developmental stages of growth will be provided in the following chapters.

CHECK YOUR UNDERSTANDING

Now that you have read the chapter, check your understanding by answering the Focus Questions presented at the beginning of the chapter. If you are unable to answer one or more of the questions, return to the chapter, find the section that corresponds to the question, and reread.

SUGGESTED READINGS

Chomsky, C. (1971). Write now, read later. *Childhood Education*, *47*, 296–299.

Dionisio, M. (1983). Write? Isn't this reading class? *Reading Teacher*, *36*(8), 746–750.

Gambrell, L. B. (1985). Dialogue journals: Reading–writing interaction. *Reading Teacher*, *38*(6), 512–515.

Gaskins, I. W. (1982). A writing program for poor readers and writers and the rest of the class, too. *Language Arts, 59*(8), 854–863.

Guthrie, J. T. (1984). Learning to write coherently. *Reading Teacher*, *37*(4), 430–432.

Guthrie, J. T. (1984). Writing connections. *Reading Teacher*, *37*(6), 540–542.

Friedman, S. (1985). If you don't know how to write, you try: Techniques that work in first grade. *Reading Teacher*, *38*(6), 516–521.

Heald-Taylor, B. G. (1984). Scribble in first grade writing. *Reading Teacher*, *38*(1), 4–8.

Noyce, R. M. (1979). Another slant on mastery writing instruction. *Language Arts*, *56*(3), 251–255.

Smith, L. B. (1982). Sixth graders write about reading literature. *Language Arts*, *59*(4), 357–363.

Wood, K. D. (1984). Probably passages: A writing strategy. *Reading Teacher*, *37*(6), 494–499.

PART **IV**

CONDUCTING INSTRUCTION

Part IV is the core of this book. The information in Parts I through III provided background for making decisions about reading instruction; now you are ready to apply this information. You are ready to consider how to conduct reading instruction at various grade levels.

There are four chapters in this unit, one for each of the developmental stages typically found in elementary schools. Chapter 11 focuses on the Readiness Stage of instruction for preschool and kindergarten. Chapter 12 focuses on the Initial Mastery Stage associated with Grades 1 and 2, Chapter 13 focuses on the Expanded Fundamentals Stage associated with Grades 3 and 4, and Chapter 14 focuses on the Application Stage associated with Grades 5 through 8.

Each chapter describes the special problems, the curricular emphases, and the instructional techniques associated with reading instruction at those levels. In addition, suggested instructional activities are provided. When you finish reading these chapters, you should be able to answer questions such as the following:

1. What are the unique characteristics of teaching at the preschool–kindergarten level? at the primary level? at the middle grades? at the upper grades?
2. How does the curricular emphasis in reading change from level to level?

3. What are the prevalent techniques used at each level to develop attitude outcomes? process outcomes? content outcomes?
4. What are the unique rewards and difficulties of teaching reading at each of the levels?

CHAPTER **11**_____

Teaching Preschool and Kindergarten Reading

GETTING READY

Traditionally, preschools and kindergartens have emphasized nonacademic outcomes. Instructional activities have focused on helping young children adjust themselves to school, group living, and the social conventions that participants in a school setting must follow. Formal reading instruction or attempts to involve students in actual reading are seldom emphasized, although there is general agreement that preschool and kindergarten should help children get ready for such instruction. Hence, *reading readiness* is emphasized.

Since reading is part of a larger communication process called *language*, reading instruction begins with general instruction in language, particularly language as it is used in genuine communication situations. Such general language instruction is emphasized during the preschool and kindergarten years because it helps get students ready for formal reading instruction. This chapter describes the language instruction provided at this Readiness Stage. It provides a general background, describes the major curricular emphases, and suggests instructional activities to help you develop the intended curricular outcomes.

FOCUS QUESTIONS

As you read this chapter use the following questions to guide your understanding about reading readiness.

1. What special problems are associated with teaching reading to prereaders?
2. Describe what you do in a preschool and a kindergarten to develop attitude outcomes.

3. Describe what you do in a preschool and a kindergarten to develop process outcomes.
4. Describe what you do in a preschool and a kindergarten to develop content outcomes.
5. How is writing integrated into reading instruction at the Readiness Stage?
6. What does a typical instructional day look like in preschool and kindergarten?

OVERVIEW OF PRESCHOOL AND KINDERGARTEN READING

There has been much debate in recent years about how to teach reading in preschools and kindergartens. On one side of the debate are those who argue that the emphasis should be limited to socialization outcomes in which children are taught the personal and social responsibility associated with "going to school" behavior. Here, the major instructional activity looks much like play, and the expectation is that children will learn the socialization outcomes while

Figure 11.1 **Instructional emphasis at the Readiness Stage**

Outcome	Relative Instructional Emphasis	Major Instructional Activity
Attitude Outcome		
Concepts about reading	*Stress:* Reading is talk written down What you are reading was written by someone Reading is for enjoyment Reading is for getting information	Indirect instruction using language experience and USSR activities
Positive responses to reading	*Stress:* Reading is exciting Reading is satisfying Reading results in knowledge	Indirect instruction using language experience and USSR activities
Process Outcome		
Knowledge about how the reading system works	*Stress:* Developing print awareness related to recognizing words instantly Developing letter and word awareness	Direct instruction of letter and word knowledge Direct instruction in how to use knowledge sources for listening comprehension

Figure 11.1 **Instructional emphasis at the Readiness Stage** (continued)

Outcome	Relative Instructional Emphasis	Major Instructional Activity
	Introduce: Using words, prior knowledge, purpose, and type of text to comprehend when listening	
Fix-it strategies	*Stress:* Developing print awareness related to analyzing words Using oral context Discriminating letter sounds auditorily Associating letters and sounds Blending sounds	Direct instruction in using context and print to predict unknown words Direct instruction in repairing blockages to meaning in listening comprehension
Content Outcome		
Recreational	*Stress:* Getting meaning from story narratives that the teacher reads orally	Directed listening activity
Functional	*Introduce:* Getting meaning from simple text that the teacher reads orally	Directed listening activity

engaging in such activities. On the other side of the debate are those who argue that preschool children can learn to read, and therefore, schooling at this level should emphasize formal, systematic instruction in reading.

Whereas the debate still rages in some quarters, most educators have settled on a middle-ground position. In this position both socialization outcomes and reading continue to be emphasized, but reading instruction receives less formal emphasis. Less formal does not mean that there is an absence of direct instruction. In fact, both direct and indirect instruction can be found in good preschool and kindergarten programs. It does mean that there is less emphasis on the trappings of formal education. Basal text reading groups are seldom found in kindergartens or preschools. Similarly, the use of readiness workbooks, although more prevalent than basal texts, are generally frowned upon. Instead, many opportunities are provided to expand background experiences, to communicate about these experiences, to use listening and speaking, to perceive reading and writing as exciting and useful activities, and to understand the graphic nature of written language.

The reading Readiness Stage is actually a broad introduction to language. It seldom looks like the formal "book learning" associated with the basal text reading instruction found in the first grade and above. Instead, teachers structure a learning environment that broadly emphasizes communication. Because most children at this level cannot yet read, the communication is mostly oral and the emphasis is on speaking and listening. The content outcomes focus almost entirely on *listening* to the teacher and other adults read functional and recreational text; the process outcomes stress how comprehension works in *listening* situations; and positive attitudes toward reading are often created by students *listening* to a teacher read good children's literature. The major encounter with written text at the Readiness Stage is usually through language experience stories and the major encounter with reading skills is through instructional activities that develop students' awareness of print and the graphic nature of reading. Figure 11.1 summarizes the instructional emphasis at the Readiness Stage.

DEVELOPING ATTITUDE OUTCOMES

Because positive attitudes are the foundation for learning to read, it is crucial that the child's first encounter with schooling create such attitudes. In fact, a strong case can be made that this is the most important outcome to develop in preschool and kindergarten.

Since many children first encounter reading and writing in preschool and kindergarten, their attitudes toward reading and writing are often determined by what happens to them there. Consequently, preschool and kindergarten teachers try to create reading and writing experiences that will develop accurate concepts and build positive feelings about reading and writing.

The major concept to be developed at this level is the understanding that language is a communication system, and that reading and writing are parts of that system. For instance, it is crucial that students understand from the beginning that what they read is a message from someone else; it is like an oral message except that it has been written down. This basic understanding is fundamental to reading development. Similarly, students should be shown early that reading has an important role to play in their lives, that constructing meaning from text can be both functional (provides information and helps solve problems) and recreational (brings enjoyment and enriches lives). These two concepts—the message-sending nature of reading and its potential rewards—are fundamental to reading success and should be strongly emphasized at the preschool and kindergarten levels.

There should also be a strong emphasis on developing positive feelings about reading. Students should be involved in activities that help them see that reading is exciting, is satisfying, and results in new knowledge. Conversely, if the students' initial encounters with text are boring, frustrating, or of little personal use, negative feelings will result. The importance of creating positive responses cannot be overemphasized.

CREATING A LITERATE ENVIRONMENT

A strong literate environment is crucial to the success of preschool and kindergarten programs. This environment should emphasize meaningful activities, and communication should play an integral role. The intent, as it always is with the literate environment, is to create an atmosphere that encourages the kinds of activities that represent *literacy*. In the preschool and kindergarten, literacy must be viewed in its broadest sense, not only in the realm of writing but in the pursuit of literate activities.

For instance, the physical environment should include tangible evidence of the importance of communication. There should be listening, picture book, writing, and language experience centers. The arrangement of the room

Prereaders can be engaged in indirect instruction.

Figure 11.2 An example of how to teach positive attitudes to preschoolers and kindergarteners

Background   You want your students to develop the concept that reading is talk that has been written down. It is possible to use language experience to develop such a concept. The following example is illustrative.

Activity 1   Arrange a field trip to the fire house, the city hall, or some other community agency. Prepare students for what they are to learn on the trip.

Discussion   In the classroom following the trip, discuss what was learned. Direct the students to the need to thank the people that provided the information. Point out that you could speak your thanks if you saw them, but since you probably will not see them, you can send a note.

Activity 2   Work with your students in writing a thank-you note on experience chart paper. As the note is composed, point out that what they say can be written down, and that what is written down can be read by the receivers of the thank-you note.

---

should promote communication, and the displays in the room should celebrate the products of individual and collaborative efforts to communicate. In short, the physical environment of the classroom should clearly show that the participants are engaged in important and exciting activities that require them to communicate.

Much of the physical environment of a classroom is a reflection of the intellectual environment created by the teacher. If teachers originate and promote exciting class projects, there will be evidence of student engagement in meaningful activities. If teachers set the expectation that students will work collaboratively on these projects, there will be a real need for communication. The strong intellectual environments set by teachers translate into the strong literate environments associated with attitude development.

Finally, a good social–emotional environment in the classroom promotes student collaboration and sharing, both of which maximize opportunities for communication. Teachers guide these activities to develop targeted concepts and responses.

Hence, the literate environment plays a crucial role in preschool and kindergarten. It is through a literate environment that teachers create the atmosphere, activities, and interactions that are associated with literacy. At the Readiness Stage a literate environment is particularly important.

THE MAJOR INSTRUCTIONAL APPROACH

At the Readiness Stage the major instructional approach is language experience. This is true for all three major outcomes, but is particularly true for the attitude outcomes. By engaging in collaborative writing based on common experiences, several reading concepts are highlighted: (1) the communication function of written language, (2) the writer–reader relationship, and (3) the relationship among listening, speaking, reading, and writing. In addition, the creation of real text about meaningful experiences is exciting and satisfying and does much to build positive feelings toward reading.

Consequently, preschool and kindergarten teachers spend much time developing language experience stories with their students. Since these stories are based on real experiences, it is important that teachers organize common experiences that are worth writing about. For instance, they might plan field trips to places of interest in the community, have students share their most exciting experiences with each other, and plan special classroom events, such as parties and plays. Children's literature that is read aloud in the classroom can also be an effective source of language experience stories since they can be the genesis for other stories written collaboratively by the teacher and students.

Once an experience has been selected, a teacher can use it as an occasion for message sending and receiving. For instance, prior to the arrival of visitors in the classroom, the teacher and students can collaboratively write invitations to them, write signs directing the guests to their seats, create posters depicting classroom activities, and write stories for display. Once the activity is over, thank-you notes can be written, journals can be kept, summaries can be created, a report to parents can be generated, or a newspaper can be written that chronicles the events and experiences. Any kind of text associated with the real world can be represented in commonly developed language experience writing in the classroom. Through participation in these activities students develop the concepts and responses that are the foundation for continued growth in reading.

Such language experience activities are examples of indirect instruction. Consequently, teachers plan them using the three-step format for indirect instruction described in Chapter 9. The lesson shown in Figure 11.2 is typical of the indirect instruction for attitude development that can be used in preschool and kindergarten.

ACTIVITIES TO DEVELOP ATTITUDE OUTCOMES

There are many activities you can use in preschool and kindergarten to develop positive attitudes toward reading. The following are illustrative.

1. Have the children write one another short letters that are mailed and then delivered by a child playing the part of a postman. The children then read the letters they have received. Emphasis should be placed on the concept that reading is a tool.

2. Using the special kinds of animal or adventure stories that children are interested in, encourage the children to collect or print words that are essential in reading and in enjoying their particular interests. List these words in a special book to develop positive responses toward reading.

3. Show pictures of some of the same things that students will draw in their books, such as a dog or an airplane. Say, "These pictures tell a story. Do you know what this picture is?" Call on a child as you point to the picture. After the correct response is elicited, ask another child, "What is this picture?" When all the picture details have been discussed, more general questions may follow, such as: "What do you think they are doing? Have you ever seen an airplane land? Where did you see it? Was anyone you know in it?" These questions help students to develop the concept that pictures and words convey information.

Teachers of prereaders provide direct instruction.

4. The covers of children's books may be used for this game. Have students sit in a circle, then hold up a cover and have the students guess what the story is about if it is new, or tell about it if it is familiar. Call on several children to get a variety of stories and ideas. Picture post cards, magazine pictures, and travel pictures may all be used if old covers are not available. The concept that reading is enjoyable and informational is developed.

5. Have the students write or dictate their own stories, which you type in primary type. They may then read their stories and exchange them with the other students. These stories may be bound into books. This helps students develop positive attitudes toward reading.

6. Have the students read poetry. They should read it over until it becomes easy for them, developing the idea that language is fun.

7. Felt-board characters provide an excellent vehicle for storytelling. Using a felt board and teacher- or student-made characters from books, have students talk about the books they have read, developing positive attitudes about reading.

8. Puppets are as much fun to make as they are to operate. A large packing box or a table turned on its side can serve as the stage. Kindergarteners enjoy making small drawings of characters introduced in picture books or storytelling sessions and then pasting them on pencils or sticks to use as puppets. The concept of what reading is as well as positive attitudes toward reading can be developed.

9. Have students write their own concept books (what is round, and so on); this will develop positive attitudes toward reading.

TEACHING PROCESS OUTCOMES

Process outcomes are designed to help students understand how the reading system works and how to fix blockages to meaning when they occur. Since most preschool and kindergarten students are unable to read text independently, the process outcomes taught at this level are preparatory in nature.

HOW THE READING SYSTEM WORKS

Preschool and kindergarten teachers teach students how the reading system works in two ways. First, they use language experience activities to teach about the conventions of print in our language. When constructing language experience stories, they point out the top-to-bottom and left-to-right sequencing

---

Figure 11.3 **An example of how to teach print awareness
at the Readiness Stage**

Background   Your students continually confuse the letters *b* and *d*. You
decide to teach them how to visually examine the letters using
the following plan.

Lesson Sequence

Introduction   Begin by pointing to examples of the letters they are confusing
in the story you have been reading to them. Indicate that being
able to read the story themselves requires their being able to
tell the letters apart and that you are going to show them how
to do that.

Modeling   Explain the way you visually examine print in order to tell letters apart. In the case of *b* and *d*, the visual examination emphasizes left-to-right orientation, with the "stick" of the letter
being encountered first in *b* and the "ball" of the letter being encountered first in *d*.

Interaction with students   Give students several opportunities to distinguish *b*'s from *d*'s in
text. Give them considerable help in the early stages as they
talk out loud about how they are visually examining the letters
and gradually reduce this assistance as they demonstrate a consistent pattern in their visual examination.

Closure   Return to the text you have been reading to them. Point out
the letters again and have them use their strategy to visually
examine the letters and to distinguish between them.

Desired Outcome   Given printed text, students will use the conventional ways of
visually examining text to distinguish letters.

---

of language, that spoken words can be represented by written words, that they
can tell where a word ends because there is a space, that a spoken sentence can
be represented as a printed sentence, and that there are certain conventions
(capital letters and periods, for instance) that signal when a sentence begins
and ends. Also, teachers help children learn that words are made up of letters,
and they teach them these letters. At first, preschoolers and kindergarteners
can see no sense in how letters are formed and easily confuse such letters as *u*
and *n* or *w* and *m* or *d* and *b*. It is important, therefore, that children be shown
how the system of discriminating among letters works. A sample of how preschool and kindergarten teachers teach to these outcomes is provided in
Figure 11.3.

In addition to teaching the conventions of print, preschool and kindergarten teachers also introduce the general strategy for getting meaning from messages. However, at this level, the messages are oral, not written. The teacher reads text to students and shows them how to use words, topic, purpose, and text structure to figure out meaning. For instance, a teacher might read a fairy tale and then talk about (1) how the words in the story provide clues to the topic; (2) how recognizing the topic (or what is talked about) triggers thinking about that topic and predictions based on what they already know; (3) how the purpose (having fun or getting information) makes them listen for certain things; and (4) how their general knowledge of fairy tales helps them predict what will happen next in this fairy tale. Although it is a listening situation, the meaning-getting process is very similar to that used when processing text, and it can be taught as a general meaning-getting strategy. Consequently, when the students get to formal reading, they will already be familiar with this general strategy. Figure 11.4 illustrates how a preschool or kindergarten teacher might structure such a lesson.

FIX-IT STRATEGIES

Preschoolers and kindergarteners do not actually read text when first learning how the reading system works or when learning their first fix-it strategies. Instead, they use listening situations and simulated situations involving language experience stories.

At the readiness level the fix-it strategy that is most emphasized relates to *word attack*—what to do when students encounter a word in print that they have not seen before. This kind of strategy receives emphasis at the readiness level because teachers want to get students ready for its use when they first begin reading books at the Initial Mastery Stage. Two kinds of word-attack strategies are stressed.

First, teachers use listening situations to teach preschool and kindergarten students how to use oral context to predict a word that is unknown or left out. For instance, a teacher may play games with students in which they have to complete sentences such as, "When I went to the store, my mother told me to buy a pair of _____." Similarly, students can be asked to predict words that will fill certain slots in sentences such as, "The _____ went to the fair." In this case, a defensible noun would have to be used, whereas in, "I saw a horse in _____ barn," a defensible article or adjective would have to be used; and so on. By engaging students in such exercises they learn that language is a sense-making activity, and they develop a solid foundation for using context to figure out a word that is unknown in print. The thinking process used by readers is similar to that used by listeners, so

Figure 11.4 **Using a listening situation to teach the general strategy for meaning getting**

Background   As part of getting your students ready to read, you want them to be aware of how to get meaning—how to make predictions about meaning based on our knowledge of the words, topic, purpose, and type of text. Because your students cannot yet read, you develop this outcome in a listening lesson. The following example is illustrative.

Lesson Sequence

Introduction   After reading a story to your students discuss what happened in the story. Ask them how they know what the story means. Tell them you are going to show them how to get meaning from stories.

Modeling   Read sections of the story orally and explain what you think of as you hear the first group of words, how hearing those words causes you to predict a topic, how your knowledge of the topic causes you to expect certain things, how your understanding of the author's purpose and the normal pattern of stories gives you clues to where the story is going, and how these predictions continue to be refined as you hear more of the story.

Interaction with students   Using other story samples, have the students "do as you did." At first, give them much assistance as they try to talk out loud about their thinking while processing text. Gradually diminish this assistance until the students can make predictions about meaning without assistance.

Closure   Read another story having the students explain what happened and how they knew what the story meant.

Desired Outcome   Given oral text, students can explain how their knowledge of the words, topic, purpose, and type of text is used to make predictions about text.

Figure 11.5 **An example of how to teach oral context to preschoolers and kindergarteners**

Background   As part of your effort to get students ready to read, you want them to know how to use context to predict what unknown words mean. The following is an example of how you might teach such a strategy in an oral situation.

Lesson Sequence

Introduction	Select a story to read to the students. Pick a word in the story the students are not likely to know and present it to them. Tell them you are going to teach them how to figure out such words while listening to you read the story.
Modeling	Read aloud a section of the story that contains the word. Explain how you used the other words in the sentence and your own background knowledge to figure out the unknown word.
Interaction with students	Present to students other hard words imbedded in context. Have them talk out loud demonstrating how they used the other words and their experience to predict the meaning of the unknown word. Give them much help initially, but gradually diminish this help as you go along.
Closure	Read the story aloud. Afterward, discuss the story content with them. Discuss how they used their strategy to figure out word meaning while they were listening.
Intended Outcome	Given a listening situation, students will use context to figure out the meaning of unknown words.

listening instruction becomes a preparation for reading. Figure 11.5 provides an example of how to teach oral context.

Another word-attack strategy emphasized at the Readiness Stage is preparation for phonics. In order to use phonics to figure out unknown words encountered in print, students must know the letters, they must be able to distinguish one letter sound from another, and they must be able to associate the correct letter sound with the correct letter in print. Some preparatory work for using phonics occurs in the preschool years and much of it occurs in kindergarten. Most teachers introduce phonics by creating simulated situations in the language experience stories that have been written with students. For instance, while reading a language experience story, a teacher might say to a student, "Let's pretend that you didn't know this word. When you came to it, you would have to stop and try to figure it out. How could you use what you know about the sounds of letters to figure out this word?"

These situations must be simulated because most children, in the process of creating the story, will learn the words in a language experience story as sight words, meaning that they no longer have to figure them out. The simulation, however, will help prepare them for figuring out unknown words when they encounter them in their reading at the Initial Mastery Stage. Having children combine this sounding technique with the context strategy discussed

---

Figure 11.6 **An example of how to teach letter sounds**

Background   As part of your effort to get your students ready to read, you want them to know letters sounds. Then if they encounter a word they do not recognize in print they can use initial consonant sounds together with context to predict the unknown word. Here is an example of how to teach letter sounds.

Lesson Sequence

Introduction   Using a story you have read orally, point out the words and show the students how the words begin with letters they know by name. Say that if they know the sound letters make they can begin to say the words on the page and that you are going to teach them those letter sounds.

Modeling   For each letter in turn, demonstrate how you point at the letter and simultaneously say its sound.

Interaction with students   Have the students copy you, pointing to each letter in turn and saying the sound. At first provide much assistance by pointing to the letter and saying the sound with the students. Gradually reduce such help as the students begin associating the sound each time with the letter.

Closure   Return to the story. Point out the words that begin with the letter sounds. Have students use those sounds and the context of the sentence (which you can read orally) to predict what the word is.

Desired Outcome   Given a word unrecognized in print, students will use the initial letter sound and the sentence context to predict what a word is.

---

previously provides an even stronger preparation for reading since the two strategies in combination are a powerful and efficient way to figure out words unknown in print. Figure 11.6 provides an illustration of how to prepare students for phonics.

ACTIVITIES TO DEVELOP PROCESS OUTCOMES

In preschool and kindergarten most of the activities to develop process outcomes are teacher created. Certain commercial materials may be used (such as word games, worksheets, and so on), but the bulk of the activities grow naturally out of the communication activities being pursued. The following are some illustrative examples of activities you can use to develop process outcomes.

Knowledge Activities

1. Cut an oak tag into cards of handy size, such as 3" × 5" and have the students paste on them pictures cut from old books, magazines, and newspapers. Under each picture print the word or phrase that tells about the picture and print the same word on the reverse side of the card. Give the cards to the students to learn to associate the printed symbol with the picture.
2. Use this activity like Bingo. Each player has a card marked off into 12 square blocks. In each block a sight word is printed. On a small pack of cards, each the size of a block, words are printed. Show the cards one at a time. The student whose card has the displayed word raises her or his hand, pronounces the word, points to it, is given the small card, and places it over the appropriate word. The first student to cover a line of words in any direction is the winner.
3. Have all the words the students learn put into their vocabulary book, *My Word Book*. This book can be illustrated by students or pictures may be cut from other sources and pasted under each word to illustrate it.
4. Labeling is a worthwhile device only if it is made meaningful. When students bring in toys, these can be labeled. Shelves in the classroom closet should be labeled to indicate places for various supplies. Children's hooks in the wardrobe can be labeled, and the children can be encouraged to learn the names of their classmates. Use complete sentences when labeling. For example, "This is a Tonka Truck."
5. Write a jumbled sentence on cards or on the board and have the students reassemble the sentences. Examples:
   baby down slid
   a puppy black and white spots had
6. Place phrase cards along the blackboard ledge. Read one of these phrases and call upon a student to go to the board and pick out the phrase that was read. The student then reads the phrase to the class.
7. Give the students several phrase cards based on a story they have read. Write on the board a question that can be answered by one of the phrase cards. All students who think they have a phrase that answers the question correctly raise their hands. Students first read the question from the board and then the answer from their card.

Write the answer on the board and then write another question to be answered as before. Example: *Charlotte's Web*, by E. B. White, provides phrases such as *Charlotte and Wilbur, at the fair, in the barn*, and so forth. A question could be "Wilbur and Charlotte lived _____?" or "Charlotte said good-bye to Wilbur _____?"

8. Place a large box filled with small objects or pictures before the students. Arrange printed word cards corresponding to the objects or pictures along the blackboard ledge. The children close their eyes and draw an object or picture for which they must then find the corresponding word.

9. Number a large cardboard clockface from 1 to 12 and fit with a large moveable hand. The same number of words or phrases is printed either on the blackboard or on a large sheet of paper. A student is called on, spins the hand, sees the number at which it stops, then reads the corresponding printed word or phrase.

10. Prepare cards with black and white drawings of objects that have a characteristic color. Print directions under the objects are such as: "This is a ball. Color it blue."

11. Show a picture to a group and have the students discuss either the main idea, the figures in the foreground or background, or the colors. Occasionally specific questions may be asked, such as, "What is the little boy holding in his hand?" "Where do you think he is going?" Some students may be able to make up a short story of two or three sentences about the picture while the others listen for the sequence of ideas.

Fix-It Strategies

1. Have students learn sequencing by dividing a large sheet of oak tag into four or six squares. In each square there is a picture showing one part of an action sequence that will be completed in the last picture. The same pictures are also placed on small cards cut the same size as the squares on the large card. The students take the small pictures and assemble them to tell the same story as that on the large sheet.

2. Have students learn letter memory by giving them sheets prepared with short rows of lower case and capital letters. The students are instructed to put a circle around the big letters or the small letters.

AAaa   aaaA   AAAa   aaaA
CCC   Ccc   ccC   CCc   ccc   cCC   CCC
B B B B   B B B B   b b b b
D d D   D D d   d d d   D D D (etc.)

3. Have the students fish for sight words. Fold word cards and pin the open ends together with a large straight pin (care must be taken to use steel pins, or hairpins, because a magnet will not pick up ordinary pins). Place them in a container. The students fish with a piece of string attached to a small magnet and pull out one of the "fish." If they can read the word on the card, they may keep it, otherwise it must be thrown back. Keep records of the number of words correctly read each day.

4. Place pictures of objects that rhyme on the blackboard such as a picture of a *pie* and *sky*, a *hand* and *sand*, and so on. Point to the first picture and ask what it is. "Yes, it is a *pie*. Who can find another picture that rhymes with *pie*?"

5. Say, "We are going to play a new guessing game today. This little boy is Bill." Point to a picture or to a child whose name is Bill. "He lives on a high _____. Who can tell me where Bill lives? It is a word that sounds like *Bill*. Yes, it is a *hill*. Bill likes to sit on the window _____. Yes, *sill*. Who can give me another word that sounds like *Bill* and *sill*?"

6. Perform or have a student perform a short series of acts such as tapping on the desk, lifting a book, and then picking up a piece of chalk. The children are called upon to replicate the acts performed in order to develop auditory memory and sequencing.

7. Have students practice letter recognition by playing concentration. Use six different letters at one time with each letter on two separate cards. Place the 12 cards randomly on the table, letter side down. Students find the pairs and keep each pair they find.

8. Have students use concentration to pronounce letter names. Follow same procedure as Activity 7.

9. Use recorded sound patterns in which each pattern is repeated. Direct students to: (1) listen to a sound pattern, (2) stop the recorder, (3) repeat the pattern, (4) start the recorder, and (5) check their accuracy.

10. Play the *Airport* game with students using a gameboard, a toy airplane, and someone to give the oral sound patterns to each child in turn. If the child reproduces a sound correctly, he or she moves the airplane one space down the runway. As each plane reaches the end it may be flown briefly. The same technique can be used in reverse to return the airplanes to the hangar.

11. Play a game in which students pair off and then take turns clapping two sound patterns to each other. The partner must respond to each pair of sound patterns by identifying them as the same or different. The winner can be determined either by recording the

number each child gets right or by adapting the game to a gameboard like the one described in Number 10.

12. Play the game *Monkey Hear, Monkey Do*, using pairs of players and a gameboard. One child claps or says a sound pattern and the partner mimics it. If the partner is correct, he or she moves forward one space on the gameboard.

13. Play a *Dot-to-Dot* game, using any connect-the-dots picture. Students are paired and one says or claps a sound pattern. The other mimics and, if correct, connects as many dots in the picture as there are sound units in the pattern.

14. Play a remembering game in which one student says a word, the next student repeats it and adds another word, the third student repeats the first two words and adds a third, and so on. Continue until one student cannot remember the sequence. The object is to develop a sequence of words or sounds as long as possible.

15. During story time or reading time purposely distort some word in the story by leaving off its first sound. Stop and say, "Oh, I didn't say that word correctly! What should I have said?" This can be done during any daily oral activity.

Content outcomes for prereaders are often listening activities.

16. Have students bring to class pictures cut from magazines, with each picture or series of pictures showing something that has the same sound at the beginning, end, or middle.

17. Bring in a group of magazine pictures, and direct the students to tell what each picture shows and to sort the pictures according to the common beginning, middle or ending sounds. For instance, all the pictures that begin with the same sound heard at the beginning of *kite* go in one pile, all the pictures that begin with the same sounds heard at the beginning of *top* go in another pile.

18. Spread a group of pictures on the floor. Have a student point to a picture that has the same sound heard at the beginning, end, or middle of the word you say.

19. Play games with students that follow this pattern: "I'm thinking of something on your desk that begins with the same sound heard at the beginning of the word *pig*. What am I thinking of?" This activity can also be adapted to middle and ending sounds.

20. Divide a shallow box into four squares. Place a key picture in each of the top two squares. Provide a student with a group of pictures, directing him or her to sort the pictures and place them in the square beneath the picture with the same sound at the beginning, middle, or end.

21. Make a shutter device out of tagboard in which the opening of the shutter can be controlled. Insert a card that has the letter to be learned at the left, followed by a picture of an object beginning with this sound. Open the shutter to reveal first the letter and then the picture. Have the student form the letter sound with their mouths and blend that sound into the picture name as it is exposed.

22. Give each student a group of pictures, some of which begin with the letter to be worked on and some of which do not. Hold up a letter card and direct the students to hold up any picture they have that begins or ends with the sound of that letter.

23. Give the students a group of letter cards. Each student takes turns saying, "I have a letter. *Money* begins with the letter *m*."

DEVELOPING CONTENT OUTCOMES

As previously mentioned, much preschool and kindergarten language activity is oral. This is especially so of content outcomes. Because students cannot read yet, teachers teach listening comprehension of the content of functional and recreational text. Consequently, what becomes a reading activity at the higher grades is often a listening activity at the Readiness Stage.

Figure 11.7 **An example of how to teach a directed listening activity for content outcomes at the Readiness Stage**

Background   You are reading a story to your students. You want to be sure that they understand what happens to the main character and why it happens. To ensure that they get this content, you guide their listening using a directed listening activity. The following is a sample of such a lesson.

Lesson Sequence

Introduction   Tell the students what you are going to read them. Discuss the setting and the circumstances surrounding the story and elicit student knowledge. Identify any words they may not have heard before and explain their meanings.

Set purposes   Specify the particular things you want the students to listen for.

Oral reading   Read the story and be sure the students are listening for the right information.

Discussion   Discuss what they found out regarding the purposes set at the beginning.

Closure   Have the students summarize what was learned and/or have them use what was learned in a subsequent activity.

Desired Outcome   Given a text that is read orally, students will be able to discuss the story in terms of the specific purposes the teacher has set.

Many students receive their first formal introduction to recreational and functional text at the preschool and kindergarten level. In the recreational text area students should understand the content of simple stories that the teacher reads to them. In the functional text area they should understand the content of simple expository text that the teacher reads to them. In both cases the text should be simple in structure because this is typically the students' first formal encounter with text. Listening comprehension is emphasized because the students have not progressed to the point where they can read text independently.

INSTRUCTION TO DEVELOP CONTENT OUTCOMES

Since the students listen rather than read at the preschool and kindergarten levels, much teaching at this level is conducted through use of the directed listening activity (DLA). This is similar to the standard directed reading lesson (DRL) used with many basal texts (see Chapters 4 and 9). The difference, of course, is that the DRL is used with written text whereas the DLA is used with listening activities.

The DLA works like this. Before reading to students the teacher provides them with an introduction that activates their schema for the topic and develops the meaning of unknown words. With this background established, the teacher then specifies what the students are listening for (sets the purpose). Then the teacher begins reading, stopping periodically to remind the students what they are listening for. Following the reading, the teacher holds a discussion in which everyone shares what they learned, focusing primarily on the purposes that were set at the beginning. Finally, the teacher closes the lesson by having the students summarize what was learned and by engaging them in an activity that applies (or enriches) this learning.

The DLA can be used to guide students' listening of either recreational or functional text. For instance, if a teacher is reading students a recreational story, schemata can be activated regarding the setting and the problem encountered in the story, purposes for listening can be cited, and a discussion can be held following the story to share what was learned about the established purposes. If a teacher is reading a functional text, schemata related to that topic can be activated, purposes can be established, and a discussion can be held regarding those purposes. In both cases student listening is guided and, as a result, there is a greater chance that the content will be understood. An illustration of how teachers use the DLA is provided in Figure 11.7.

Preschoolers and kindergarteners create both functional and recreational text as part of their language experience activities. For instance, language experience activities that result in written invitations, lists of activities the class pursued, or a recipe all are functional text. Similarly, language experience activities that result in stories or poems are recreational text. However, it is seldom necessary for teachers to guide students' understanding of these texts. Because they are created from the students' immediate experiences, they have strong backgrounds for the words used, the topic, the purpose, and the text structure. As a result they usually comprehend the content without guidance.

ACTIVITIES TO DEVELOP CONTENT OUTCOMES

Almost any occasion when you can read functional or recreational text to children can be used to develop content outcomes. The following examples are illustrative.

1. The News Corner may be used for announcements or for news pertaining to the students themselves, such as, "We are going to the

market tomorrow." This leads to an understanding of uses of functional information.

2. Interesting pictures with an explanatory word or two about them in very simple language may be placed on the bulletin board. Colorful book jackets from children's books are also good to use, developing the understanding that reading is recreational.

3. Bulletin boards can be used to show all the enjoyable elements of books such as adventure, excitement, and laughter.

4. Concept books that have been written by the students can be used as functional texts for other students. Concepts can include: What is round? What is soft? What is exciting?

5. Puppets can be used to act out information that has been read to students.

INTEGRATING READING AND WRITING

One of the advantages of the language experience approach is the way it dramatizes the integration of reading and writing. In fact, when students are creating language experience charts and stories to read, they are engaged in writing. This is exactly what happens in preschool and kindergarten. Teachers use the occasions for language experience to develop attitude, process, and content outcomes about writing as well as about reading. Collaboratively developed language experience stories are an ideal place to develop accurate concepts of what writing is and to develop positive feelings about writing as an activity. While actually producing the written text associated with language experience, teachers can demonstrate process outcomes such as how writers use the conventions of language to signal meaning to readers, how authors strategically monitor the text they are producing, and how they use certain techniques to focus, reorganize, and clarify their meaning. Regarding content outcomes in writing, teachers can use language experiences to model how decisions are made in the planning stage about whether the writing is to be functional or recreational and what meaning is to be conveyed.

As important as language experience is, however, it is not the only time that students in preschool and kindergarten engage in writing activities. Very young children enjoy what they call writing even though we might call it doodling. They will sometimes draw a picture of something and put a lot of squiggles on the page, which they describe as "a story I have written." These writing activities are an important part of learning to write. Teachers can use these activities to build important concepts about writing, what people use it for, and how it works, as well as to build positive feelings toward writing.

Writing is an integral and important part of the preschool and kindergarten experience. It is evident both in the language experience activities and in the pretend writing that students engage in at this age. Both kinds of writing activities are important to reading because they provide additional experience with written language that, in turn, strengthen the student's desire and ability to use written text.

There are many ways to integrate the various language modes when teaching preschoolers and kindergarteners. One of the most effective is to teach a unit that carries over several days and develops a variety of objectives. Following is an example of such a unit. The *warm up activities* are used to get things started, *focusing activities* direct attention to the specific task, the *reading-writing activities* are the reading or writing activity itself or a preparation for or followup to the reading or writing activity, and *assessment* is the data collected to determine the effectiveness of the instruction. This particular unit is designed to develop students' awareness of the postal system.

SAMPLE TEACHING UNIT

Postal Awareness

Grade Level: Readiness
Objectives:
1. To become familiar with mail transportation
2. To become aware of the structure and function of letter writing.
3. To write letters to parents and to address envelopes.

Day 1 *Warm-up activity:* Bring a letter to class from a parent or several parents telling about something they like about the class. Discuss how exciting it is to get mail. Read the letter to the class.
Focusing activity: Discuss the letter and lead a discussion to the point where the students decide they want to invite their parents to a tea or coffee.
Reading-writing activity: Construct a group letter telling where and when the parents should come. Read the letter together.
Assessment: During the letter-writing process, assess the students' knowledge regarding the form of a friendly letter. Directly teach form to those students who need it.

Day 2 *Reading-writing activity:* Print the letter to the parents neatly, using letter form.
Assessment: Assess the students' ability to print letters and

Puppet activities help integrate reading and writing.

words found in letters. Directly teach penmanship skills to those students who need it.

Day 3   *Warm-up activity:* Using an overhead or an opaque projector, present a model envelope like the one that will be used to send the letter to the parents.

Focusing activity: Directly teach how to address an envelope.

Reading–writing activity: Students practice on sample paper (same size as an envelope) how to address an envelope to their parents.

Assessment: Assess students' ability to address an envelope. Note whether students know their address. Reteach students who need help in addressing envelopes.

Day 4   *Focusing activity:* Discuss the purpose and structure of the postal system.

Reading–writing activity: Address the envelopes. Take the letters to the mailbox and mail them.

Day 5   *Reading–writing activity:* Draw the route of the students letters. Have them predict when the letters will arrive.

Have them verify the arrival.

Note: A trip to the post office would be appropriate at this time.

Day 6 *Warm-up activity:* Brainstorm with the students about all the interesting things they've been doing in class.

Focusing activity: From the brainstorming list, select activities to show parents during the coffee or tea.

Reading–writing activity: Decide how to show parents work, songs, plays, and so on.

Day 7 *Focusing activity:* With the help of the children, decide what refreshments will be served at the coffee or tea.

Reading–writing activity: The results of the discussion can lead to: (1) reading the recipes in order to make whatever is served; (2) measuring the ingredients they use; and (3) cooperatively serving the refreshments.

Day 8 *Reading–writing activity:* The coffee or tea with parents.

Assessment: Assess the success of the coffee or tea. Did the parents enjoy it? Did the students successfully show the parents what they have learned? Did the letters arrive at their homes? Were the reading and writing uses successful? Was information conveyed?

ADDITIONAL INTEGRATED
READING–WRITING ACTIVITIES

1. Provide some pictures from magazines and have the students write titles to the pictures using skills developed during process instruction. Pictures and titles are put on display for all to read.

2. Read *Weekly Readers* to the students and do writing activities to follow the discussions. This is usually completed as a group activity.

3. Have the students write and illustrate a group story. The words and pictures are placed on a roll and shown as a television program. The words are read as they appear on the "screen."

4. Have the students create class stories following field trips. These are placed in a travel folder and referred to for future trips or for review.

5. Have the students create concept books such as: what is *trying*, what is *big*, what is *old*, and so on. Each student creates a page with a sentence and an illustration.

6. Have the students create a collage with a theme such as *happy*, *sad*, *excited*. Once the collage is created, have the class creates a poem

A typical instructional day includes independent activities.

such as "Happiness is—," "Sadness is—," and so on. Collage and poem should be displayed for reading and enjoyment.

7. Begin an alphabet book for each student with a page for each letter. Add appropriate pictures or illustrations to each page throughout the school year.

8. Read *The House That Jack Built*. Discuss the book's repetitive pattern. Discuss other content. Write a group story using the repetitive pattern.

9. Using a story such as "Jack and the Beanstalk" read the story to the point where Jack wakes up the golden harp. Insert into the story the harp saying "You are as noisy as—" Discuss with students what is *noisy*. Have each student create an ending to the sentence. Read the revised story with each student's insertion.

CHARACTERISTICS OF AN INSTRUCTIONAL DAY

Of all the levels of elementary school, preschool and kindergarten have the most distinctive characteristics for three reasons.

First, almost all public preschools and kindergarten are half-day rather than full-day sessions. Consequently, the total daily allocated time for instruction is typically between two-and-a-half and three hours. This characteristic has several consequences. For the teacher, it usually means two completely different classes in a day, one in the morning and one in the afternoon. This poses a real problem since much language instruction should be individually tailored to students' needs, but when you have 50 to 60 students each day, it is hard to keep track of their individual needs. In terms of planning for individual development, more preparation time is required for the preschool and kindergarten teacher than for teachers at the higher levels.

Another distinguishing characteristic of instruction in preschool and kindergarten is the dominance of playlike activities. Because children at this age cannot read and are not yet socialized into the behaviors associated with traditional schooling, teachers cannot give them traditional seatwork tasks that require independence and good work habits. Instead, teachers find a variety of shorter activities, most of which are fun, such as story sharing, games, and creative drama.

The third distinguishing characteristic of preschool and kindergarten is the absence of designated periods for reading, mathematics, and social studies. Whereas preschool and kindergarten teachers do teach these subjects, the allocated instructional time is not divided by subject. Instead, it is divided by activities (manipulative objects, animals, children's literature, and so on), with each activity often calling for the integrated use of reading, mathematics, and social studies. This allows a preschool and kindergarten teacher to focus on activities that relate to the students' real experiences. It also offers the option of brisk pacing, a crucial aspect of teaching at this level since preschool and kindergarten children have relatively short attention spans and must have a variety of activities in a relatively short period of time.

In sum, the instructional day in preschools and kindergartens is unlike that found at any other grade level. Students do not sit at desks, they do not have reading groups in the traditional sense, they seldom use basal readers, the activities often look like play time, and many different kinds of activities are squeezed into a relatively brief half-day period. Even though the school day looks quite different, teachers at these levels are teaching to the same three categories of outcomes as teachers at the higher levels and are striving to lead students to the same ultimate outcome.

CONCLUSION

Although it is important to have good reading instruction at all school levels, it is crucial at the preschool and kindergarten levels because it serves as the foundation for all the instruction that follows. If you teach at the Readiness Stage, you must help students build a solid understanding of what reading is and positive responses to reading as an activity. If students begin to see the relationship between oral language and written language, can begin to make sense out of the conventions of print, and can use what they know about the language to comprehend (in listening situations) the content of functional and recreational text, they will be in a strong position for continued growth in reading. They should be ready to tackle the more formal reading instruction associated with the Initial Mastery Stage.

CHECK YOUR UNDERSTANDING

Now that you have read the chapter, check your understanding by answering the Focus Questions presented at the beginning of the chapter. If you cannot answer one or more questions, return to the chapter, find the section that corresponds to the question, and reread.

SUGGESTED READINGS

Allen, R. V., & Allen, C. (1976). *Language experience activities*. Boston: Houghton Mifflin.

Bailey, M. H. et al. (1982). Preparation of kindergarten teachers for reading instruction. *Reading Teacher, 36*(3), 307–311.

Blachowicz, C. L. (1978). Metalinguistic awareness and the beginning reader. *Reading Teacher, 31*(8), 875–882.

Burris, N. A., & Lentz, K. A. (1983). Caption books in the classroom. *Reading Teacher, 36*(9), 872–875.

Combs, M. (1984). Developing concepts about print with patterned sentence stories. *Reading Teacher, 38*(2), 178–181.

Degler, L. S. (1979). Putting words into wordless books. *Reading Teacher, 32*(4), 399–402.

Ellis, D. W., & Preston, F. W. (1984). Enhancing beginning reading using wordless picture books in a cross-age tutoring program. *Reading Teacher, 37*(8), 692–698.

Gamby, G. (1983). Talking books and taped books: Materials for instruction. *Reading Teacher, 36*(4), 366–369.

Gentile, L. M., & Hoot, J. L. (1983). Kindergarten play: The foundation of reading. *Reading Teacher, 36*(4), 436–439.

Groff, P. J. (1984). Resolving the letter name controversy. *Reading Teacher, 37*(4), 384–388.

Goodall, M. (1984). Can four year olds "read" words in the environment? *Reading Teacher*, *37*(6), 478–482.

Hall, M. (1976). Prereading instruction: Teach for the task. *Reading Teacher*, *30*,(1), 7–9.

Hoffman, S., & Fillmer, H. T. (1979). Thought, language and reading readiness. *Reading Teacher*, *33*(3), 290–294.

Johnson, T. D. (1977). Language experience: We can't all write what we can say. *Reading Teacher*, *31*(3), 297–299.

Larrick, N. (1976). Wordless picture books and the teaching of reading. *Reading Teacher*, *29*(8), 743–746.

Lass, B. (1982). Portrait of my son as an early reader. *Reading Teacher*, *36*(1), 20–28.

Lesiak, J. (1978). Reading in kindergarten: What the research doesn't tell us. *Reading Teacher*, *32*(2), 135–138.

Reimer, B. L. (1983). Recipes for language experience stories. *Reading Journal*, *36*(4), 396–401.

Templeton, S. (1980). Young children invent words: Developing concepts of "word-ness." *Reading Teacher*, *33*(4), 454–459.

Wiseman, D. L. (1984). Helping children take early steps toward reading and writing. *Reading Teacher*, *37*(4), 340–344.

Zirkelbach, T. (1984). A personal view of early reading. *Reading Teacher*, *37*(6), 468–481.

CHAPTER 12

Teaching Primary-Grade Reading

GETTING READY

Many teachers insist that the first and second grades (the Initial Mastery Stage of developmental reading growth) are the most important grades because it is here that students first receive formal reading instruction. If students are well taught in the first two grades, academic success often follows; if they receive poor instruction in the first two grades, a cycle of school failure that persists in later years is frequently initiated.

This chapter will help you apply principles from previous chapters to the problems of teaching primary-grade reading. It provides you with a background for primary-grade reading instruction, describes the major curricular emphasis in each of the three major outcome areas, and provides instructional suggestions for developing these outcomes.

FOCUS QUESTIONS

As you read this chapter use the following questions to guide your understanding about primary-grade reading.

1. What special problems are associated with teaching primary-grade reading?
2. Describe what you do in the primary grades to develop attitude outcomes.
3. Describe what you do in the primary grades to teach process outcomes.
4. Describe what you do in the primary grades to teach content outcomes.
5. What does a typical instructional day look like in the primary grades?

OVERVIEW OF PRIMARY-GRADE READING

Teaching Grades 1 and 2 places special demands on teachers. Both the students and the curriculum are unique. The students are unique because they are newcomers to formal reading instruction. They may have received reading readiness of the kind described in Chapter 11 while in kindergarten, but a few have actually read a book. It is not until first grade that students become conscious of learning reading skills or strategies. Consequently, it is here that they often form lasting impressions regarding the nature of reading. Primary-grade students, then, are at a particularly sensitive stage in their academic careers, and their teachers have a special obligation to provide experiences that develop positive responses and accurate concepts of reading.

The curricular emphasis in first and second grade is also unique. In addition to attitude goals, the emphasis must also deal with the intricacies of figuring out what the printed squiggles on the page mean. This is because, although reading is the interaction of the four knowledge sources (words, topics, purpose, and text structure), the first knowledge source the reader confronts is

Indirect instruction in the primary grades.

graphic—the letters and words on the page. Therefore, much primary-grade instruction focuses on the letters, their sounds, techniques for recognizing printed words instantly, and techniques for figuring out unrecognized words.

The tension that exists between the need to develop attitude outcomes and to develop the ability to deal with the graphic code is a particularly difficult aspect of primary-grade reading instruction. The experiences students have with reading result in concepts and feelings that stay with them for a lifetime, so the teacher must emphasize the sense-making, meaning-getting, and communication aspects of reading. At the same time, however, initial reading demands the ability to interpret the graphic code—the letters, the sounds of letters, the individual words, and the linguistic system that governs how print represents oral language.

This conflict is the source of much of the "teacher as technician" behavior found among first- and second-grade teachers. The scarcity of time and the pressures of accountability often cause primary-grade teachers to overemphasize word identification to the neglect of attitude outcomes. The basal's relatively heavy emphasis on word identification reinforces this inclination and causes teachers to follow the basal text teacher's guide even more closely.

The unique challenge in teaching primary-grade reading is to create positive and accurate experiences with real reading and language while simultaneously providing a solid foundation in how to interpret the graphemic code. The primary-grade curriculum reflects this conflict, as seen in Figure 12.1. This chapter focuses on how to conduct instruction to develop concepts and positive feelings in attitude outcomes; to develop knowledge sources and word analysis strategies in process outcomes; and to move from directed listening to directed reading in content outcomes.

DEVELOPING ATTITUDE OUTCOMES

As already mentioned, the development of attitudes is a crucial outcome at the Initial Mastery Stage of developmental reading growth. Positive attitudes about reading result from accurate concepts of what reading is and from positive responses to the activity of reading. During first and second grade teachers want students to develop the concepts that reading is (1) a message from an author to a reader, (2) an enjoyable pastime, and (3) useful for getting information. In addition, teachers want students to have good feelings about the act of reading. They want them to feel excitement about reading, to feel satisfaction from reading, to feel more knowledgeable as a result of reading, and to satisfy curiosity by reading. These outcomes are best developed through indirect instruction conducted in the context of a literate environment.

Figure 12.1 **Instructional emphasis at the Initial Mastery Stage**

Outcome	Relative Instructional Emphasis	Major Instructional Activity
Attitude Outcomes		
Concepts about reading	*Stress:* Reading is a message written by an author Reading is for enjoyment Reading is for information	Indirect instruction using language experience and USSR activities
Positive responses to reading	*Stress:* Reading is exciting Reading is satisfying Reading results in knowledge Reading satisfies curiosity	Indirect instruction using language experience and USSR activities
Process Outcomes		
Knowledge about how reading works	*Stress:* Word meanings Sight-word recognition Using words, prior knowledge, purpose, and type of text in combination to predict meaning	Direct instruction of words (using basal text recommendations as a basis) and of how to use the knowledge sources
	Introduce: Reading fluently so that it sounds the way the author would say it	Direct instruction in how to use knowledge about reading to predict how the author would say it
Fix-it strategies	*Stress:* Using context, structural analysis, and phonics (or combinations of these) to figure out words unknown in print	Direct instruction of word-analysis strategies (using basal text recommendations as a basis)
	Introduce: Generating new predictions Using explicit cues Using implicit cues	Direct instruction in repairing blockages to meaning (using basal text recommendations as a basis)

Figure 12.1 **Instructional emphasis at the Initial Mastery Stage** *(continued)*

Outcome	Relative Instructional Emphasis	Major Instructional Activity
Content Outcome		
Recreational	*Stress:* Getting meaning from story narratives	Directed reading lessons using basal text selections
	Continued Development: Listening comprehension in recreational text	
Functional	*Stress:* Getting meaning from simple expository texts	Directed reading lessons using basal text selections
	Continued Development: Listening comprehension in functional text	

CREATING A LITERATE ENVIRONMENT

A literate environment is created by orchestrating the physical, intellectual, and social–emotional environments. In the primary grades, the intent is to establish an atmosphere that emphasizes comprehension while simultaneously supporting a curricular emphasis on letters and words.

The physical environment can support this intent by including special centers where recreational books are displayed, lounging areas where relaxed reading can be done, book-related displays, displays of chidren's writings in the form of language experience stories, collections of class-written books, clusters of messages, and labels on objects throughout the room. Labeling, however, should feature words in context rather than words in isolation. Consequently, a chair would not be labeled *chair*, but *This is a chair*.

The intellectual environment supports the intended outcome by including many genuine reading and writing opportunities. Teachers and students use language experience activities to construct and send messages and are themselves recipients of messages. They establish the expectation that students and teachers will engage in meaningful reading, the teacher will model this reading by leading students in language experience activities, and the students will be given a choice of both topic and activity to ensure interest and motivation.

Figure 12.2 **An example of how to teach attitudes in the primary grades**

Background   You want to develop the concept that reading and writing are related aspects of language communication. You decide to do so by involving students in a language experience activity.

Activity 1   You arrange to take the class on a field trip to a farmer's apple orchard where students are shown how apples are grown, harvested, and marketed.

Discussion   Upon returning to the classroom organize students into collaborative groups, have them discuss what they saw and learned in the trip, have each group develop a thank-you note to the farmer, and then work with the whole group in confining the ideas into a single thank-you note.

Activity 2   You have the students read a recipe for making apple sauce and then engage them in actually making apple sauce from the apples picked at the orchard.

The social–emotional environment supports the outcome by emphasizing working together. This, in turn, encourages the communication and interaction with language that naturally accompanies cooperative efforts. Social interactions and collaborative sharing help students develop attitude outcomes because both oral and written communication is highlighted.

In creating a literate environment, then, a teacher makes a deliberate effort to have students conceptualize reading as a meaning-getting activity that is an integral part of language and to create feelings that will motivate future reading. The physical environment highlights the prominent role of language, the intellectual environment stimulates real language, and the social–emotional environment encourages genuine language interactions. In addition, the graphic code is emphasized because the printed word is displayed everywhere and frequent reference is made to its relationship with oral language.

INSTRUCTIONAL APPROACHES

Of the three major approaches to instruction, the basal text approach is least useful in developing attitude outcomes in the primary grades. Instead, the concepts and responses that support such attitudes are better developed through language experience and personalized reading activities.

Primary teachers emphasize the language experience approach to develop the desired attitude outcomes. For instance, teachers look for opportunities to create text with students in order to indirectly illustrate that reading is a message from an author to a reader. Similarly, teachers create language experiences that demonstrate enjoyable and information-giving aspects of reading. Such activities also get students excited about reading, stimulate feelings of satisfaction and knowledge about reading, and help them satisfy their curiosity.

Similarly, teachers make use of personalized reading activities to indirectly develop the attitude outcomes. Usually, these activities take the form of uninterrupted sustained silent reading or some other kind of free-reading activity. Even though first and second graders are just beginning to learn to read, they can nevertheless choose text to read. Such text may include picture books, wordless books, student-authored language experience books, and others. Participation in these personalized reading activities helps students develop the concepts that authors write to convey messages to readers and that reading can be done for enjoyment and for information. Similarly, such self-selected reading helps students to feel excited and satisfied about what they are reading, that they are gaining knowledge, and that their reading can be a response to curiosity.

Lessons are based on the three-step format for indirect instruction described in Chapter 9 (activity–discussion–activity) and make use of collaborative groups as described in Chapter 5. For instance, assume that a teacher wants the students to feel knowledgeable as a result of reading (positive response) and to understand that reading involves receiving a message from a writer (concept of reading). After the teacher decides to develop these outcomes through indirect instruction using a language experience activity, the teacher might plan and conduct a lesson like the one shown in Figure 12.2. Such indirect instruction helps students feel knowledgeable as a result of reading (they learned how to make the apple sauce) and helps them understand that reading involves a writer who has a message to send (they were the writers with a message of thanks to send to the apple farmer).

ACTIVITIES TO DEVELOP ATTITUDE OUTCOMES

Many activities have the potential to develop the conceptual and emotional outcomes associated with positive reading attitudes. The following storehouse of activities provides a resource for you.

1. Develop a continuing contact with the expressive writing of skilled authors.
2. Place interesting pictures with a word or two about them in very

simple language on the bulletin board. Colorful book jackets from children's literature are also good bulletin board material. These types of bulletin boards help develop positive attitudes.

3. Have students read or recite favorite poems to help develop positive attitudes toward reading and language and to stimulate further poetry reading by the group.

4. Hold informal conferences with students to stimulate continued reading. This can include student-authored books and library books. Circulate during their attitude-development time to conduct these conferences.

5. Plan a field trip to the public library to develop positive attitudes to the lively world of books. Most librarians will conduct the field trip and will present a book.

6. Develop a class book in which each child has one page to review from his or her favorite book. Each page should include a brief statement about what it is about, why it is a favorite, and the title and author. Encourage students to include an illustration of the best part.

7. Pair the students and let each pair read to each other from books they choose. A buddy system is a good way to encourage students to use library books.

8. Have each student write or dictate a story that is typed in primary type. The student may then read this story and exchange it with the other children. These stories may be bound into books and placed in the classroom or the school library.

9. Have the students read and dramatize conversation.

10. Trace or draw cutouts of favorite characters from illustrations. These drawings can provide a constantly changing population of book friends for a display.

11. Draw life-sized figures of favorite characters on mural paper and display them in the classroom or the hall. Primary-grade students like to draw the animals they have read about including Paddington, Curious George, and other well-known animal characters.

12. Make a class list of favorite books in chart form to offer primary students an opportunity to express their interests and preferences. Such a list should be revised periodically as the children's tastes and interests develop.

13. Create a library corner, which is essential to development of positive attitudes. Responsibility for managment can be a buffer's role or a teacher's helper role. Types of books should include fairy tales, poetry, picture books, and concept books.

14. Introduce new books to the class. A few words telling what is special about each new book will help develop students' interest.

15. Model reading and writing often for the students to see. If students never see adults write, an attitude outcome is difficult to develop. What you do is just as important as what you say. Have students see you writing notes to friends, business letters, and expressive stories and poems to share. During nook-and-cranny time read aloud what has been written and ask the students to comment on it. Let students be a part of the revision process for all types of writing, but expecially expressive.

16. Encourage students to write for free samples and information. Many books and magazines include sections that list companies and addresses.

17. Be alert to occasions when the students can be involved in writing and reading: Adding notes at the end of letters to parents, making and sending holiday and birthday cards, writing notes to friends, and drafting school notes for parental signature.

TEACHING PROCESS OUTCOMES

Two process outcomes are emphasized at every grade level: helping students understand how the reading system works and helping them to repair blockages when meaning getting does not proceed smoothly. These process outcomes are then applied when students try to get meaning from content.

In the primary grades curricular outcomes in the process category focus on (1) developing comprehension through knowledge of words, topic, purpose, and text structure and on (2) word meanings, instant identification of those words, and how to figure out words that are not instantly recognized. Fix-it strategies are introduced at the primary-grade level. Consequently, the process emphasis in this chapter is on word meaning, sight words, and how to figure out unknown words. Strategies associated with other aspects of process are discussed in detail in Chapters 13 and 14.

HOW THE READING SYSTEM WORKS

Primary-grade students should be taught an overall strategy for using words, topic, purpose, and text structure to predict meaning. From the very beginning they should be given real text to read and should be directly taught that reading involves making predictions about the meaning of text. They should be shown how words signal meaning, what we know about a topic helps us predict meaning, how knowledge about an author's purpose helps us predict the message, and how the text structure can be used to predict the author's message. For instance, during nook-and-cranny time, or when guiding students' story reading, teachers can discuss how to activate knowledge about a topic and how to con-

Figure 12.3 **An example of how to develop knowledge about how the reading system works**

Background You have previously read two books to the class about hermit crabs, one written as a narrative story that gives a hermit crab human characteristics and another written as expository text that provides factual information about hermit crabs. During nook-and-cranny time, you might do the following:

Lesson Sequence

Introduction Initiate a discussion about the two books with a purpose-setting statement such as, "Let's see how you can figure out the author's message in these two books so you can use this knowledge to make sense out of other text."

Modeling Show how in one of the two texts you used the words to identify the topic, activated what you know about crabs generally and hermit crabs in particular, analyzed the text structure and its implications for meaning, analyzed the author's purpose and its implication for meaning, and used these knowledge sources to make predictions about the author's message.

Interaction with students Using the second of the two texts, have students follow your model and describe how they used words, prior knowledge, type of text and author's purpose to construct meaning for the text.

Closure Summarize the discussion by having students state what they have learned about how the reading system works and what readers do to construct meaning from text.

Desired Outcome When reading text students should be able to comprehend the author's message and should be able to explain how they used the various knowledge sources to determine that message.

Figure 12.4 **An example of how to teach word meaning**

Background Word meaning is crucial to comprehension. The more words people know about a topic, the greater their prior knowledge of that topic, and the better they are at constructing meaning about that topic in text. Good reading teachers teach their students lots of new words, especially in conjunction with the text being read in class. You decide which words need to be taught by asking a student to use a word in a sentence; if the word is used correctly, the student has a concept for the word; if it is used incorrectly or not at all, the student does not have a concept for the word.

Lesson Sequence

Introduction State what word meaning is to be learned and why it is important to have a meaning for the word at this time (in preparation for a particular discussion or for a story that is to be read).

Background experience Provide the students with a concrete or vicarious experience with the word as a basis for identifying the concept's distinguishing characteristics.

Developing characteristics Illustrate the conceptual characteristics of the word using a chart such as the following:

What is it?
part of a train

What are not
examples?
a steam locomotive ◄— **diesel locomotive** —► powered by
a caboose
a diesel truck

What is it like?
pulls the train
powered by
diesel fuel
big

What are some examples?
the one you saw at the
train station
the one in this picture

Engage the students in a discussion of the distinguishing characteristics of diesel locomotives.

Closure Have students use the word in a sentence. Assign guided reading in which the new word appears.

Desired Outcome When students encounter the word in real text they will have an accurate mental picture of the word and will be able to use this prior knowledge to help construct the author's message.

nect this knowledge with what is being said in the text. They can teach students to predict whether the author's purpose is one of entertaining or informing and to use this knowledge to help predict the meaning. They can also teach them to use their knowledge of story structure to predict what will happen next. The aim is to make students aware of how they use their knowlege of topic, purpose, and text to construct meaning so that they can be in control of the meaning-getting process. (See Figure 12.3).

Much time is also spent in the primary grades teaching students about words and the role they play in making the reading system work. The first emphasis is on developing meanings for words, which is done in two ways: by teaching specific word meanings and by teaching about words. To teach specific word meanings, a teacher must determine what words students do not

---

Figure 12.5 An example of how to teach sight words

Background	Decide what words need to be taught as sight words by either noting which frequently appearing words are not instantly recognized or by anticipating which words in the text are not known as sight words. When conducting instruction be sure students have concepts for the following words if you intend to use them when teaching sight words: *letter, word, first, last, left, right, alphabet, sight word, instantly.*
Lesson Sequence	
Introduction	Begin the lesson by showing students a text they are going to read and telling them what words they are going to learn to recognize instantly so that they can read the story fluently. Tell them that they must attend to both the visual form of the words (what it looks like) and the name of the words. Show students where they will encounter the words in the forthcoming text.
Modeling	Present the words one at a time on cards. Point to a word, say its name, and use it in a sentence.
Interaction with students	Have the students do what you did (point to the word, say its name, and use it in a sentence). Write the sentence containing the word on the back of the card, underlining the sight word. Then have the students read the sentence containing the word, read the underlined sight word, write the sight word, look at it, and say its name. Repeat this procedure (with variations) until the students instantly recognize the word.
Closure	Have the students demonstrate what sight words they have learned by flashing them the words and having the students name them. Also have students state why it is important to know these words on sight and when these words will be used in the story to be read. Then guide the reading of the story that contains these new words.
Desired Outcome	When reading text students will instantly recognize the words in print and will be able to state why it is important to instantly recognize such words.

know by asking them to use specific words in a sentence. If they cannot, the teacher provides either real or vicarious background experiences as a concept base, then develops the distinguishing characteristics of the concept using examples of what the word is and is not, and finally, asks the students again to use the words correctly in a sentence. For instance, if a teacher were teaching first graders the meaning of the word *locomotive*, the teacher would first ask them to use the word correctly in a sentence. If the students could not, the teacher would show them a real locomotive, or pictures of a locomotive, identify its distinguishing characteristics (it pulls trains, is powered by diesel fuel, is large), cite examples of what is and is not a locomotive (a diesel truck, for instance, is not a locomotive) and then have the students use the word *locomotive* in a sentence once again. Figure 12.4 shows an example of how to teach word meaning.

When teachers teach *about* words in the primary grades, they focus mainly on the fact that words can have multiple meanings. For instance, the word *strike* can be associated with unions, clocks, baseball, bowling, fishing, and matches. The correct meaning in a particular sentence depends upon the context of the message in which it is embedded. Teachers want primary-grade students to know that words have multiple meanings and that the correct meaning is determined by the context of the message.

It is also important to teach students to be automatic in *identifying* words in print. When a reader instantly identifies words, the reading is smooth and uninterrupted. To achieve fluency, the words that are read must be *sight words*. That is, they must be firmly embedded in a student's memory and when they appear in the text they must be identified immediately and without conscious effort. Efforts to build a sight-word vocabulary begin with the print awareness tasks (letter naming, visual discrimination, and visual memory) described in the previous chapter. Once a student can discriminate among letters and words and remember their visual form, individual sight words are taught. Normally, the first words taught are the most utilitarian ones, such as *a, the, in, are, is,* and other high-frequency words. Because such words appear so frequently, they must be among the first sight words taught if the student is to read real text. The list provided in Figure 7.3 is an example of such high-utility words.

Also among the first sight words taught are those that are less utilitarian but appear in the particular text to be read. If the text is about going to school, the sight words to be taught in conjunction with that text may include *school, teacher, desk,* and *chalkboard.* As students learn to recognize more and more words, teachers begin teaching easily confused words. For instance, some students confuse *was* and *saw* because they examine the words from right to left instead of from left to right; some confuse *where* and *there* because they fail to descriminate the initial letter; and some confuse words such as *after* and *father* because of hasty and partial visual examination. As students progress through

Figure 12.6 **An example of how to teach easily confused sight words**

Background   It is not uncommon for primary-grade students to confuse look-alike words. When reading, for instance, they may say *was* for *saw* or *where* for *there* or *them* for *then*. Such miscues are not disastrous when reading for meaning since a reader will detect the dissonance, look back, and make a correction. However, repeated miscues of this kind disrupt fluency and should be corrected. The cause is failure to examine the word carefully for its distinctive visual characteristics, so instruction focuses on the distinctive graphic characteristics of the two words being confused, as in the following example using *was* and *saw*. When conducting instruction, be sure the student has concepts for the following words if you intend to use them in your teaching: *letter, word, first, last, top, bottom, left, right.*

Lesson Sequence

Introduction   Start by stating what two words are to be learned, why they are being taught together, your evidence that a student is indeed confusing the words, and why it is important to fluent reading that they not be confused. In the case of *was* and *saw,* the student must be sure to visually examine the word from left to right.

Modeling   Present the two words simultaneously on separate cards. Point to each word, say its name, and use it in a sentence. Then show how, by approaching *was* and *saw* from left to right, they do not look alike. Model moving across the page from left to right encountering the first letter, visually examining the word from first letter to last letter, and saying the word.

Interaction with students   Have the student do what you did (moving across the page from left to right, visually examining the word from first letter to last letter, and saying the word). Present the word repeatedly in various contexts and have the student visually examine the word and say its name until the two words are no longer confused.

Closure   Have the students state what words they have learned, what they have learned about visually examining words that will prevent similar miscues in the future, and when they will use what they have learned in real text. Then guide reading that contains these easily confused words.

Desired Outcome   When reading text students will instantly recognize look-alike words that were previously confused and will be able to state how to visually examine such words to avoid confusion.

the grades, more and more sight words are taught. Teachers decide what words to teach by examining the next selection to be read and by determining which of the words used in a particular selection need to be taught. Figures 12.5 and 12.6 show examples of how to teach sight words.

When teaching how the reading system works, then, the emphasis is on teaching students to get meaning by using the multiple knowledge sources (words, topic, purpose, and text structure) and on understanding that readers must know many words, both in terms of meaning and in terms of instant recognition.

FIX-IT STRATEGIES

Because of the emphasis in primary grades on word meaning and word identification, fix-it strategies focus on what students can do when they come to a word that they do not recognize. This category of fix-it strategy is called *word attack* or *word analysis* because when a student does not instantly know a word, the student must attack it or analyze it to figure it out. There are three major ways for figuring out unrecognized words.

First, teachers should teach students to use context to predict an unrecognized word. For instance, if students do not recognize the printed word *engine* in the sentence, "The airplane's engine stopped and it crash landed in a field," they can use their knowledge of airplane crashes to predict that the unrecognized word is either *engine* or *propeller*. This strategy is the most efficient way to solve word identification problems because it is fast and it emphasizes meaning getting. Even if a student predicts *propeller* in this example, the essential meaning of the message remains intact. Consequently, students are taught to turn first to the strategy of contextual prediction when they encounter words they do not recognize. Teachers develop the ability to use context even before formal reading begins by teaching students to supply endings for sentences they say out loud such as, "I went to the store and bought a pound of _____"; or "I went to the store and bought a pair of _____." Later, more difficult predictions are required, such as filling in the blanks in an exercise such as the following:

> The elephant went around the circus _____, performing his tricks and entertaining the _____. He did not seem very happy. _____ master was whipping him and he _____ slowly through one trick after another.

Examples of the various kinds of context clues are provided in Figure 7.4.

Instruction in context emphasizes how students think about use of context. This includes monitoring their meaning getting so that they know when they encounter an unrecognized word and understanding why they first use context to identify a word, as well as knowing how to analyze context to predict an unknown word. Later, when they have also learned to use phonics and word structure to figure out unknown words, they are taught to combine these strategies with context. For instance, in the airplane example, students who are taught to use context in combination with phonics would not predict that the unknown word is *propeller* because, although it makes sense in the sentence, it does not begin with the sound of the letter *e* as does the unknown word. Consequently, the reader searches for a word that makes sense *and* fits the phonic and structural characteristics of the unknown word. (See Figure 12.7.)

A second way to figure out an unrecognized word is to use *structural analysis*. This involves teaching students to examine an unknown word for

---

Figure 12.7 **An example of how to teach context clues as a strategy for figuring out unrecognized words**

Background	When students encounter an unrecognized word in print you want them to first use context as a means for figuring out the word. This strategy is based on the language principle that words in text are related through meaning and through syntactical relationships. When conducting instruction be sure the students have concepts for these words if you intend to use them when teaching context: *predict, identified words, unidentified words, context, relationships*
Lesson Sequence	
Introduction	Begin by stating what kind of reading problem you are trying to fix, the specific kind of context strategy to be used, why context is a preferred strategy, and the situation in which it will be used. Also stress the need to attend to the unknown word and its particular syntactic and/or meaning relationship to the known words around it. Show students where the strategy will be used in forthcoming text.
Modeling	Present an example in which you encounter an unknown word when reading. Explain how you encountered the problem while reading, how you decided to use context to fix it, how you examined the context for the particular syntactic or meaning relationship you are teaching, how that relationship gave you clues to what the unidentified word was, how you tested the predicted word to see if it made sense, and how, if it did fit the context, you then continued reading for meaning.
Interaction with students	Give students similar examples of text containing unknown words and have them explain as you did. At first, provide directives in the form of verbal and/or visual cues to aid the

students, but gradually reduce these in successive attempts as the students become more successful. Be prepared to reexplain and remodel if student responses indicate confusion regarding how to use the strategy.

Closure   Have the students state what they have learned, when it will be used, and the mental process one goes through when using it. Then assign guided reading in which the context strategy can be used in real text.

Desired Outcome   Given real text and a blockage in meaning getting caused by a word unknown in print, students will use a context strategy (or a context strategy combined with other kinds of cues) to figure out the unknown words, remove the blockage, and continue getting meaning.

structural meaning units and root words that, when broken apart, make it easier to figure out the word. For instance, when readers encounter the unknown word *unneeded*, they can separate the root word *need* from the prefix *un-* and the inflectional ending *-ed* and pronounce each part in turn. This strategy is more efficient than phonics because it focuses on meaning units rather than on sound units and is faster than phonics (there are normally fewer meaning units in a word than sound units). However, for this strategy to be usable the unknown word must contain structural units. In teaching structural analysis the progression is from the most common structural units to the less common ones. Consequently, instruction usually begins with analyzing compound words, then common inflectional endings (such as the plural *s, -ed,* and *-ing*), contractions, common prefixes and suffixes, less common prefixes and suffixes, and Greek and Latin roots. A list of common structural units is provided in Figure 7.5.

Students are taught to examine unknown words for recognizable structural units, to break the units apart, to pronounce the units in turn, and to check the results with the sentence context to see if the word makes sense. To use this strategy, readers must be aware of the various kinds of structural units so they can recognize them, and they must not confuse structural analysis with syllabication (which is analysis by sound unit or phonics, not analysis by meaning unit). Also, structural analysis must not be confused with "looking for the little word in the big word," which does not always work (sometimes it does, as with the *at* in the unknown word *chat*, and sometimes it does not, as with the *at* in the unknown words *father* and *plate*). (See Figure 12.8.)

The third strategy for word attack is *phonics.* Students are taught the sound of each letter (or letter combination) and how to blend those sounds

Figure 12.8 **An example of how to teach structural analysis as a strategy for figuring out unrecognized words**

Background   When students encounter a word unknown in print that has a root and affixes, you want them to use these structural elements as an aid in identifying the word. Structural analysis is based on the principle that the meaning of many English words are changed by adding prefixes, suffixes, and inflectional endings. By separating these affixes from the root, an unrecognized word sometimes becomes recognizable. When conducting instruction be sure the students have concepts for these words if you intend to use them when teaching structural analysis: *prefix, suffix, inflectional endings, roots, structural analysis.*

Lesson Sequence

Introduction   Begin by stating what kind of reading problem you are trying to fix and the specific kind of structural analysis to be used to fix it. Describe when this strategy would be used and state that the students must attend to the affix in question and separate it from the root. Show students where the strategy will be used in forthcoming text.

Modeling   Present an example in which you encounter an unknown word when reading. Explain about how you decided to use structural analysis to fix this blockage, examined the unknown word for the affix in question, separated the affix from the root, pronounced the two separate parts, pronounced them together, tested the newly pronounced word to see if it made sense, and continued reading if it did make sense.

Interaction with students   Give students similar examples of text containing unknown words made up from structural units. Have them explain their mental processing in figuring out the word. Assist them at the early stages with verbal and visual directives, but gradually diminish these as students demonstrate success. Reexplain and remodel as dictated by the quality of student response.

Closure   Have students state what they have learned, when they will use it, and how to do it. Assign guided reading containing unknown words that can be figured out using structural analysis and have students apply the strategy in this real reading situation.

Desired Outcome   Given real text and a blockage in meaning getting caused by an unknown word composed of structural units, students will use a structural-analysis strategy in combination with context to figure out the unknown word, remove the blockage, and continue getting meaning.

together to pronounce an unknown word. In the word *umbrella*, for instance, teachers teach students to divide the word into its three syllables (*um-brel-la*) and to pronounce each syllable by saying the letter sounds individually and then blending them together. So, the reader would say the short *u* and the consonant *m* to get *um*, the consonant blend *br*, the short *e*, and the consonant *l* to get *brel*, and the consonant sound for *l* and the schwa sound to pronounce the unaccented final *a*. Then the three syllables would be said one after another, blended together, and the unknown word identified (assuming that the reader's pronunciation is accurate enough and that *umbrella* is a word they have heard and/or used before).

It is easy to see, however, that phonic analysis normally requires more time and effort than either context or structural analysis. Consequently, phonics is the least efficient of the strategies for attacking unknown words. Also, it is sometimes inaccurate since, unless people know virtually all there is to know about phonics, they may produce an approximation of the unknown word rather than an exact reproduction. Finally, phonics is difficult to teach because there are so many letter sounds, letter–sound combinations, generalizations, and exceptions to be learned. However, despite these disadvantages, phonics is an important word-attack strategy because using it, readers can come up with a close approximation of the pronunciation of almost all words. Consequently, when a sentence does not provide enough context clues to make an accurate prediction about a word, and the word does not contain meaning units for structural analysis, readers can turn to phonics and expect that a reasonable facsimile of the word's pronunciation will result. For this reason, considerable time is spent teaching students to use phonics to attack and sound out unknown words.

Instruction begins in the prereading stage with emphasis on auditory discrimination of sounds and letter–sound associations (see Chapter 11). Students are taught the various sound elements beginning with single-consonant letter sounds, consonant blends and digraphs, letter substitution in common phonogram patterns (such as substituting initial consonants in *mat, bat, fat,* and *sat*), short vowel sounds, long vowel sounds, vowel combinations, vowel generalizations, and syllabication. As students progress through the grades, more and more of these phonic units are presented. The focus is on examining words for specific phonic elements (to determine, for instance, whether the unknown word *chow* should be attacked as *c-h-o-w* or as *ch-ow*), breaking the word apart by these units, applying the appropriate sounds to the units, pronouncing the separate sounds, blending them together, and checking to see if the resulting pronunciation makes sense in the context of the sentence.

Phonics is a time-consuming, laborious way to figure out an unknown word. Despite this, phonics must be thoroughly taught since, as a last resort, students can count on it to solve a problem when all other strategies have failed. See Figure 12.9 for an example of how to teach phonics as a strategy.

Figure 12.9 **An example of how to teach phonics as a strategy for figuring out unrecognized words**

Background   When an unrecognized word cannot be figured out using context or structural analysis you want students to use phonics. Phonics is based on the language principle that alphabetic letters and phonogram units have assigned sounds that can be blended together to approximate the sound of the unknown word. When conducting instruction be sure the students have concepts for these words if you intend to use them when teaching phonics: *letters, words, sounds, first, last, middle, same, different, blending, phonogram.*

Lesson Sequence

Introduction   Begin by stating what kind of reading problem you are trying to fix, the specific phonic element to be used, and when it would be used. State that the students must attend to the visual form of the phonic element and its associated sound. Show students where this strategy will be used in forthcoming text.

Modeling   Present an example in which you encounter an unknown word while reading. Explain about how you decided to use phonics to fix the blockage, examined the word to find the phonic elements you knew how to use, supplied the appropriate sound and blended it with other letter sounds, tested the approximation that resulted to see if it made sense, and if it did, continued reading.

Interaction with students   Give students similar examples of text containing unknown words made up from the phonic element being taught. Have them explain the mental processing they used to figure out the word. Assist them at the early stages with verbal and visual cues, but diminish these gradually until they are doing the task independently. Be prepared to reexplain and remodel if student responses indicate confusion.

Closure   Have students state what they have learned, when they would use it, and how to do it. Assign guided reading containing unknown words that can be figured out using the phonic element being taught and have students apply the strategy.

Desired Outcome   Given real text and a blockage to meaning getting caused by an unknown word composed of known phonic elements, students will figure out the word using phonics (in combination with context) and continue getting meaning.

To be good readers, students must understand the relationship between sight words and word analysis. Most words in any given text must be recognized on sight. In fact, the rule of thumb used by most teachers is that unless 95 percent of the words are sight words, a text is too difficult for a student. Only the 5 percent that are not instantly recognized should require attack using context, structure, and phonics. Readers must also monitor their own word identification as they read. They must determine if they recognize a word visually, if they require attack skills, and if so, how to select the appropriate strategy. Strategy use must be preceded by self-monitoring. Good reading ultimately demands that readers use these strategies in combination. Good readers use visual characteristics, contextual meaning, structural units, *and* phonics when all these strategies are available because using them together is more efficient than using them separately.

Word identification, then, involves a four-step procedure. First, a reader examines a word visually and tries to identify it as a sight word. If this does not work, the reader turns to context and tries to predict the unknown word by reference to meaning cues. Then, the unknown word is examined for structural

A primary-grade teacher directs learning about strategies.

units, and if they are present, these are used in combination with context to figure out the word. Finally, the word can be sounded out and the pronunciation confirmed by referring to the sentence context (if it makes sense, it is probably the right word). As each identification procedure is taught, students are urged to use them in combination with procedures already learned.

One other strategy for word identification not mentioned here is the dictionary. Students are frequently told to look the word up in the dictionary when they encounter an unknown word. This book does not recommend this strategy for word identification problems for three reasons. First, hardly anybody really does it. Even when people know how to use the dictionary, they will usually ask someone what an unrecognized word is before they will take the time to look it up in a dictionary. Second, using a dictionary for word pronunciation requires so many skills (alphabetizing, guide words, entry words, pronunciation keys, and so forth) that it is usually impossible to teach students to be proficient dictionary users prior to sixth grade, by which time fewer words need to be attacked because so many are known on sight. Third, it just takes too much time. When meaning getting in text is disrupted because of an unrecognized word, to look up the unrecognized word in a dictionary takes so much time that the text's message is forgotten or the reader's train of thought has been seriously disrupted. Consequently, using dictionaries is taught as a study skill in the later grades (see Chapter 14) and not as a word-analysis strategy.

THE ROLE OF BASALS

As noted in earlier chapters, basal textbooks emphasize many process outcomes and, therefore, frequently become the basis for instruction in this area. Teachers often follow basal prescriptions for skill instruction on the assumption that close adherence to these recommendations will ensure student learning of process outcomes. However, this is not necessarily the case for two reasons.

First, what the basals recommend is not necessarily what needs to be taught. Few current basal texts recommend any instruction in using prior knowledge, purpose, and type of text in combination to construct meaning. Similarly, not all basals have carefully structured programs of word meaning and sight word vocabulary. Some do not make a distinction between instant word recognition and word analysis or teach word analysis techniques as skills to be memorized rather than as strategies to be consciously applied. Others emphasize phonics rather than context as a word-attack technique.

Second, the intention of process instruction is that students will *apply* process knowledge when reading real text. Many basal texts, however, make little attempt to transfer skills from the instructional context of the workbook to the application context of real books read for recreational and functional purposes.

In fact, some basals do not even recommend that skill taught in a particular lesson be applied in the selection read in that lesson.

Consequently, teachers should modify basal text prescriptions to ensure that what needs to be taught is indeed taught and what is taught is actually applied by students in real text. The recommendations made in Chapter 6 should be used to guide decision making when making these modifications.

ACTIVITIES TO DEVELOP
PROCESS OUTCOMES

Although basal textbooks suggest some process-oriented activities, the suggestions are sometimes inadequate. The following list of supplemental activities is provided for you.

Knowledge Activities

1. Writing headlines can help develop an understanding of how reading works. Popular primary books may lead to such headlines as "Dinosaur Missing from Museum," "Fish Saves Family," or "Sharing is Fun."
2. Read three or four lines of a story not known to the students, who then create an ending. Later the students can compare their version with the original.
3. Hold up familiar objects in order to elicit descriptive words such as *round, heavy, square,* and so forth. As the object is shown ask questions such as: "What is this?" "What shape is it?" You can also use pictures. Oral vocabularies are essential for the development of the reading process.
4. You (or a student) start off with a word, such as *Wilbur.* A student adds a new word until a complete sentence is created. The game continues along this general theme until the group tells a complete story about the initial word. These types of stories show how the reading system works.
5. Line up a series of objects for the students to see. They are told to look carefully and to remember the objects from left to right. While their eyes are closed, you (or a student) shift the order of one or two objects; then ask some of the other students to recreate the original order.
6. When the students begin to read they need to recognize certain words for directions. This includes such concepts as *same, different; smaller, larger; big, bigger,* and *biggest; up* and *down; circle* and *underline;*

right and *left*. Games are good for this purpose. For example, to develop correct ideas for *left* and *right*, students may play the game "Simon says, turn left, turn right" and dramatize or give directions as they say the nursery rhyme "Jack and Jill."

7. Say to a small group:

> Sugar is sweet but pickles are _____?
> A jet is fast but a bicycle is _____?
> The clouds are above, the dirt is _____?

This type of procedure begins comparisons. It can also be used to develop relationships. For example:

> Bread is made by a baker; boats are made by a _____?
> A dog runs on its legs but a car moves on its _____?
> In the morning the sun rises; at night the sun _____?

8. The following activities can be used to help students develop sight words:

a. Make up racing games in which students progress in the race by pronouncing on sight the words to be learned. For instance, construct an auto racing course, dividing the track into equal squares. Give each student a toy racing car and provide yourself with a pack of cards upon which are printed the words you want the class to learn. Flash one word to each student in turn. Students who pronounce a word instantly move their racing car one square closer to the finish line. Students who are unable to pronounce the word do not move their car. The first student to get his or her car to the finish line wins.

b. Help students construct self-help references for the words they find difficult. For instance, each student can be provided with a 3 × 5 inch file box and a supply of file cards. Students write every word that is difficult to learn on a file card together with a picture or other aid to help remember the word. Students refer to the file frequently to study the words and to remind themselves of it when they are unable to identify it in reading.

c. Place the words to be learned on sight on the chalkboard. Send one student into the hall and another to the board to point to one of the words. The rest of the class pronounces the word to be sure that all the students know it. Then bring the first student back into the room to try to guess the target word. The student points to one word and says,

"Is it _____?" The student continues this way until he or she identifies the word.

d. Construct ladder games in which a paper ladder leads to a place where a reward of some kind is waiting. For instance, the ladder can be leading to the upper branches of a paper apple tree that has many paper apples on it. Each rung of the ladder has a sight word attached to it. A student must instantly pronounce the word on each rung of the ladder in order to reach the top. The reward is knowing all those words. Other rewards can be used, such as a real apple or a check on a progress chart.

e. A multitude of games for building sight words can be based on the idea of a trip. This trip may be a reconstruction of the adventures of some famous story character (such as Peter Rabbit); it may be a trip on which the students are actually going; or it may be a trip that is completely imaginary (such as a trip to the moon or a trip to a distant city). In any case, construct a game board upon which is drawn the path to be followed in reaching the destination and the hazards to be overcome along the way. Each student progresses on the trip by correctly pronouncing the words that are flashed. The first student to complete the trip wins the game.

f. Play a fishing game in which students are given a pole constructed of a stick and a string having a magnet tied to the end. Place paper fish with target words printed on them in a box or in some other object that will serve as a pond. Attach a paper clip to each fish. Students drop their line into the pond until the magnet attracts a paper clip on a fish. They pull the fish out and get to keep it if they can correctly pronounce the word printed on its side. Each student tries to increase the amount of fish caught each time the game is played.

g. Make nine packs of 10 cards each. The nine packs represent the nine holes of a golf course, and the word printed on the cards are the words to be learned on sight. A player shuffles the cards and puts the pack for the first hole face down on the desk. The player turns each card over in turn, pronounces it, and goes on. Every time the player pronounces a word incorrectly, a mark is placed on the score card. The number the student gets wrong on the first hole (first pack of cards) is his or her score for that hole. The player continues in this manner through the nine packs of word cards, trying to get as small a score as possible. Encourage the students to keep a record of their scores so that they can note their progress in mastering the course. Construct new courses offering new challenges as new words need to be learned.

h. Put the target words on cards, placing a numerical value in the upper right-hand corner of each card in signaling the degree of memorization difficulty. For instance, *dinosaur* is a fairly easy word for learners to identify so is given the value *1,* but *the* is very difficult for young students to recognize so is given the value *3.* Students take turns drawing the cards, reading the words, and noting their scores. If they pronounce the word correctly, their score is the numerical value noted on the corner of the card. Each student tries to increase the number of points each time the game is played.

i. Play a treasure hunt game in which several packets of 10 or more words each are hidden around the classroom. Give each student the first packet and direct them to read each word. The students go through the words as quickly as possible, and the last card tells them where the next packet is hidden. They go to that packet and repeat the process. The final packet will direct them to a spot where each student will receive a reward for having completed the game.

j. Play a variation of the television game Concentration. Place the words to be learned on cards and put them face down on the table. The student must remember where there are two cards exactly alike and try to pick up matching pairs. As the players turn over each card, they must pronounce the word on the card. If they succeed in picking up a card that matches the first word, they get another turn. All students try to increase the number of pairs each time the game is played.

Fix-It Activities Using Context

1. Once students develop a sight-word vocabulary, you can use these words to create sentences where you ask them to read a sentence and to provide the missing word. If the students cannot yet read independently, you can do the same thing as a listening activity, with the sentences on tape or provided by another student, an aide, or you.

2. Read a paragraph to the students and state that you will stop reading every once in a while and hold up a letter card. Direct them to keep the paragraph in mind, to look at the letter on the card, to think of the sound associated with that letter, and to say a word that both begins with that letter sound and fits the sense of the paragraph.

3. Play games with the students that require them to use both context and sound–symbol connections. For instance, direct them to listen to a sentence such as "I went to the store and bought a mouse, a _____, a _____, and a _____." Hold up a letter card to indicate the beginning letter of the word to fill the missing space. The students expand the sentence by adding words that begin with the letter sound you showed.

4. Group your students in pairs. Give each pair a supply of letter cards. Let each take a turn at making up a sentence in which one word is left out. One student must hold up the beginning letter of the missing word at the appropriate spot in the sentence while the other uses the sense of the sentence and the sound–symbol connection of the letter card to guess what word goes in the space. After correctly identifying the missing word, that student must make up a sentence.

5. Give students riddles in which the context supplies only a minimum outline of the missing word. For instance, you could provide the sentence, "The swimmer dived into the _____." Elicit student response encouraging a variety of answers, such as *water, pool, lake, river.* Then place a letter card (such as the letter *w*) at the left of the blank space and say, "What word must go in the blank space?"

Fix-It Activities Using Structural Analysis Activities

1. The word wheel and word slips techniques can be adapted to teach the blending of structural elements to known words. Simply use structural elements instead of sound elements.

2. Context activities can be used to develop this skill. Provide students with sentences in which one word is missing, giving them a choice of a root word or a root and its structural ending to fill the space. For instance, a sample sentence might be, "The two _____ *(boy, boys)* went to the store." Students choose the correct word to fill the blank, pronounce it, and tell why that word is the correct one. *Caution:* The successful use of this technique presupposes that students already know orally the correct form of the word. Certain dialects will not contain many of these inflected and derived forms of words. Teach these as oral responses prior to the activity.

3. It is sometimes helpful to reverse the decoding process. That is, ask students to create words having prefixes and suffixes, or that are compound words. In such a case you should print the known words and word parts on separate cards, scramble them up, and have the students choose one. Then the students must choose another word card that goes with the first choice, making it either a prefixed word, a suffixed word, or a compound word. Be sure have students pronounce the word they have created.

4. Make a chart or a worksheet in which root words or the first part of a compound are listed down the left side and suffixes or the second part of a compound are listed down the right side. Attach strings to the words on the left hand column and direct students to connect the string to the suffix or other part of the compound listed at the right to make a new word.

5. Make up crossword puzzles in which only compound words and/or prefixed and suffixed words can be used as answers.

6. Play a card game in which each player is dealt cards with root words written on them. Place the deck containing just prefixes and/or suffixes in the center of the table. The students take turns drawing cards from the deck and trying to match the drawn card with one of the root words to form a new word. If they can do so, they lay the two cards down together and pronounce the new word. If students draw a card they cannot use, they put it back on the bottom of the pile. The first player to get rid of all his or her cards is the winner.

7. Give context experiences in which students must complete a series of sentences using the same root word in each. For instance, provide them with the root word *play* and tell them to use it together with suffixes to complete the following sentences (see caution in Activity 2):

> He is a baseball _____.
> He is _____ in the game.
> Yesterday he _____ football.
> When he _____ he is happy.

Fix-It Activities Using Phonics

1. Make a shutter device out of tagboard in which you control the opening of the shutter. Insert a card that has the letter to be learned at the left, followed by a picture of an object with the sound of that letter at the beginning. Open the shutter to reveal first the letter and then the picture. Have the students form the

letter sound with their mouths and blend that sound into the picture name as it is exposed.

2. Use the same device as described in Activity 1, but this time insert a picture first, then the letter, then the picture again. Have a student say the picture name, then its beginning letter sound, and then blend that sound into the picture name as it is exposed the second time.

3. Use flashcards containing the letters to be learned. Flash a letter to students and direct them to respond with a word that begins (or ends) with that letter sound.

4. To help students connect letters and sounds, display pictures of common objects (dogs, money, and so on) with the letter the object begins with printed at the left. Encourage students to use these pictures when trying to remember the sound of a particular letter.

5. Make a box and label it with a large printed form of the letter you are teaching. Place in the box pictures and objects whose names begin (or end) with the letter to be practiced. Direct students to reach into the box, draw out a picture or object, name it, and tell what letter it begins with. Make sure students look at the letter on the box while saying the object's name.

6. For students who need review on a number of letters and their sounds, you may modify Activity 5 by putting several letters on the outside of the box and placing objects that begin with all these letters in the box. The students then draw an object, name it, and point to the letter on the box that begins the object's name.

7. Give each student a group of pictures, some of which begin with the letter to be worked on and some of which do not. Hold up a letter card and direct students to hold up any picture they have that begins (or ends) with the sound associated with that letter.

8. Using a flannel board or a pocket chart, place a letter card to the left and a row of three pictures to the right. Two of the pictures should begin with the sound associated with the letter and one should not. Have students select the beginning sound of the two pictures that begin the same.

9. Make a bulletin board or a large chart showing the letters to be learned in one part and next to each one, under a flap, a picture whose name begins with the sound associated with that letter. When students cannot remember the sound of *m,* for instance, they can go to the bulletin board, look under the flap next to *m* and say, "Oh, the sound of *m* is what we hear at the beginning of *money*" (or whatever the picture is under the flap).

10. Make a tagboard chart with the letters to be learned listed down

one side and pictures beginning (or ending) with the sounds of these letters listed down the other. Attach pieces of string to the letters and have a student connect the string to an object that begins with the attached letter sound.

11. Provide students with a number of letters. Play a game in which you say, for example, "I see a letter whose sound we hear at the beginning of the word *money*. What letter do I see?" The students respond by holding up the *m* letter card, looking at it, and saying, "*Money* begins with the letter *m*."

12. Make a set of picture cards for each letter sound. Teach students to play a card game in which several cards are dealt to each player. The students try to pair picture cards beginning with the same letter sound. Each player takes turns asking their opponent, "Do you have a picture card beginning with the letter *m*?" If a student has such a card, he or she gives the picture card to the student requesting it and then has the opportunity to draw a card from the student's hand in return. All students should keep track of the number of pairs they possess.

13. Give the students a group of letter cards. Each student takes turns saying, "I have a letter. *Money* starts with the sound of my letter. What letter do I have?" The student who responds correctly is the next one to select a letter.

14. Play a dramatization game with students in which you hold up a letter card and ask them to act out something that begins with the sound of that letter. Those who are not acting must try to guess what begins with the letter sound being dramatized.

15. Use activities in which you provide the student with a key word and a sentence in which one word is missing. Direct them to supply a word to fill the blank. This word must be related to the key word. For instance, give the key word *cat* and the sentence, "Hit the ball with the _____." Students must supply and pronounce the word *bat*.

16. Play games in which you start with a common spelling pattern written on the board. Students change either the initial or final letter, substitute another, and pronounce the new word. The next student must change it again and pronounce the new word. The pattern of words might look something like this:

> *cat* is changed to *bat*
> *bat* is changed to *bag*
> *bag* is changed to *bad*
> *bad* is changed to *had*
> *had* is changed to *has*

17. Have one student write on the chalkboard a word illustrating a common phonogram pattern. The student must then pronounce the word and make up a sentence using that word. The next student goes to the chalkboard, changes either the initial or final consonant in the word, pronounces the new word, and uses it in a new sentence. At first, you may want to accept any sentence the students produce. As they become more skillful, however, you can modify the activity by having them produce successive sentences that are related to each other and that tell a story. For instance, the sentences might proceed in this manner:

> The cat is in the house.
> He is sleeping near the bat.
> A man put the cat in a bag.
> He must be a bad man.

18. Make word cards using words incorporating the common phonogram patterns you have been working on. Include also a number of cards that have the word *changeover* written on them. Deal each player five cards. One student starts by laying down any word card and naming it. If students cannot play, they draw from the deck until they find a word to play or draw three cards. If a student has a changeover card the student can play that and name the new related word that can be played on it. The first person out of cards wins the game.

19. Play a variation of Crazy Eights by making a deck of 40 cards that have printed on them words containing the phonogram patterns you have been working on. Make six cards with the numeral *8* on them. Each student gets four cards, and the rest of the cards are placed in the center of the table. The first student lays down a card that contains the same word element or an *8* card. The students who have neither a word card that fits nor an *8* card, they must draw a card from the deck. The first person out of cards is the winner.

DEVELOPING CONTENT OUTCOMES

Ultimately, the ability to read is measured by noting how much of the content of particular texts is understood by a reader. Reading for such content understanding begins in the primary grades, building from the listening comprehension activities initiated at the preschool and kindergarten level (see Chapter 11).

Recreational and functional text are used widely at the primary level. Recreational texts are usually short stories following a simple story structure. Typically, they include a character, a setting, a problem the character must solve, a brief series of incidents relating to the character's problem, and a resolution of the problem. Many stories of this type appear in primary-grade basal textbooks. However, recreational reading in the primary grades is not limited to basal text stories. Trade books (picture books and easy-to-read stories) and magazines (*Jack and Jill, Humpty-Dumpty*) are also read recreationally.

The most predominant kind of functional texts are simple expository articles conveying factual information. These are usually brief and straight forward, following a format of introduction–body–conclusion. Many times such functional text will be presented as a story; that is, expository text about hermit crabs may convey factual information by personifying a hermit crab and telling a story about it. Some functional text of this kind is found in basal textbooks, and examples are also found in current events magazines and newspapers designed for primary-grade students (i.e., *Weekly Reader* and *Scholastic Magazine*).

At the primary level, teachers want students to comprehend the content of both kinds of text. Consequently, the teacher plans instruction that guides students to the acquisition of text content.

A primary-grade teacher developing word meaning as part of a content lesson.

INSTRUCTION TO DEVELOP CONTENT OUTCOMES

As noted in Chapter 11, instruction for comprehension of recreational and functional text begins in the preschool and kindergarten years. At that time virtually all comprehension is *listening* comprehension, since so few students at the readiness level can read. The major technique to guide student comprehension in the preschool and kindergarten years is the directed listening activity (see Figure 11.7).

In the primary grades teachers continue to develop listening comprehension using directed listening activities. However, after students have begun to develop a sight-word vocabulary, teachers can guide their reading of recreational and functional text typically found in basals and in trade books designed for primary-grade use. The most frequently used technique for guiding such reading in Grades 1 and 2 is the directed reading lesson, which has been described previously in Chapters 4 and 9.

The directed reading lesson can be used with either recreational or functional text. In either case, the focus is clearly communicated in the purpose-setting section prior to the beginning of reading. Although teachers often specify the purposes, it is also helpful to involve students in this step. Doing so guarantees more student involvement in the reading (and, hence, more comprehension) while also establishing the importance of having clear purposes for reading. Figure 12.10 illustrates how a directed reading lesson can be used with a basal text selection.

APPLICATION OF PROCESS AND THE ROLE OF BASALS

It is important to make connections between process outcomes and the content outcomes associated with recreational and functional text. Process outcomes should not be taught in isolation; in fact, the lessons on teaching process outcomes should be directed toward the reading of recreational and functional text found in basals and other sources (see Chapter 9). Consequently, there are times when both process and content are taught together, with the intention of helping students apply process knowledge while reading for content information.

Part of a teacher's responsibility involves deciding whether a particular lesson is being conducted only for content knowledge or to help students consciously use process knowledge. If the lesson is just to ensure comprehension of content, the directed reading lesson can be used in the way described in Figure 12.10. If the lesson is for applying process knowledge to content, the modified DRL described in Chapter 6 should be used (see Figure 6.2).

Both forms of the DRL are typically used with basal textbooks. That is, basal text selections can be used for content outcomes alone or for applying process knowledge to content. In either case, however, the teacher must "override" the basal text prescriptions, make a decision regarding what the selection is to be used for, and then plan the lesson to achieve that objective. By making such decisions, teachers maintain cognitive control of instruction.

Figure 12.10 **An example of how to teach a directed reading lesson for content outcomes in the primary grades**

Background   You want to have the students read the next selection in the basal textbook. You want to make sure that they comprehend the content of the story. To do so you guide the reading following the steps of the directed reading lesson. At the primary level the selection to be read will almost always be a story narrative.

Lesson Sequence

Introduction   Introduce the story in a manner designed to activate the students' prior knowledge about the topic and/or problem encountered. Extend the students' schema for the topic and/or problem by teaching the meaning of new words that appear in the story, using a technique similar to that described in Figure 12.9. When appropriate also activate student knowledge about text structure and how this knowledge is used to predict meaning.

Purpose setting   There are many ways to comprehend a story. You may wish students to focus on certain causal relationships, on how story problems are reflected in real life, or on broad themes. To insure that students are focusing on the type and level of comprehension you intend, the purposes for reading the selection are stated. At this time it is also helpful to point out the author's purpose for writing the selection and how that purpose and the stated purpose for reading the selection are compatible.

Reading   Have students read the selection. At the early primary level this reading will often be oral, since students may not yet know how to read silently. Also you may ask students to discuss the story in sections as it is being used.

Discussion   The discussion usually follows a question–answer format. You base the questions on the purposes stated at the outset and guide the discussion to ensure that students comprehend the story in the intended way.

Closure   Have students review what was learned from the selection, particularly in terms of the purposes set earlier. Usually you will also plan some type of follow-up activity that will extend and enrich the content knowledge. Frequently such follow-up activities involve writing or otherwise emphasize the integrative nature of reading.

Desired Outcome   Students will be able to state what content knowledge has been gained from reading the selection.

ACTIVITIES TO DEVELOP CONTENT OUTCOMES

Many activities are provided as a supplemental resource in teaching attitude and process outcomes. However, the activities for content outcomes are less extensive. This is because instructional activities for content outcomes are limited by the choice of text. If you limit the students to selections found in basal texts, instructional variety is sparse; if you use a variety of text (including trade books, student-written stories, and children's magazines), instructional variety is richer. The task, therefore, is not to collect different activities but to collect and use different kinds of text.

1. Have students find an action picture in a newspaper or magazine and discuss how the picture helps develop the information in the text.
2. Have students cut out questions from the *Weekly Reader* newspaper. They can exchange questions and then provide answers. Students can compare answers given by the newspaper to their own.
3. Have students choose an advertisement that intrigues them. Have them discuss what might have happened before the advertisement was placed as well as the uses of advertisements.
4. Have students read orally the "most interesting" or "most exciting" parts of a story. This helps them develop and comprehend the meaning of recreational text.
5. Have students sell some toys they no longer want. Have them examine some advertisements for toys and then write one that will help sell the toys. This will illustrate the functional use of newspapers.
6. Discuss a news article. Divide the class into groups of four or five and have each group recount the article. Ask them to rewrite the article as if they had been an eyewitness. Members of the group then share their stories with one another.

A student engaged in a writing activity (courtesy of Michigan State University).

INTEGRATING READING AND WRITING

The language experience approach provides endless opportunities for primary-grade teachers to integrate reading, writing, and oral language. Such integrated activities provide opportunities to meet not only the three outcomes of reading but similar outcomes in writing. Students can develop positive attitudes about both reading and writing during the same integrated unit. During an integrated unit where students first read and then write their own books, an understanding of the reading and writing systems can be directly taught and used. While students are involved in activities leading to content outcomes, functional information (such as how the local government works) can be developed through reading and writing activities. When integrated activities are used, time is not only used efficiently but is used effectively, since integrated instruction more closely represents how writing and reading are used in everyday life.

The following is an example of one integrated language unit at the primary level. *Warm-up activities* are used to get things started, *focusing activities* direct attention to the specific task, *reading–writing activities* and *thinking activities* provide the main focus, and *assessment* is the data collected to determine the effectiveness of the instruction. This particular unit is designed to help students learn how to allocate time in order to complete tasks.

SAMPLE TEACHING UNIT

Allocating Time

Grade Level: Initial Mastery

Day 1   Objectives:

1. To identify behaviors that lead to task completion.
2. To develop taking turns in discussions.
3. To orally express ideas.
4. To increase behaviors that assist in completion of work.

Focusing activity: Set the purpose that the tortoise has correct behavior for completing work. Read aloud the story "The Tortoise and the Hare."

Thinking–speaking activity: Discuss the outcome of the race, why the tortoise won, how people can act like a tortoise or a hare, who it would be better to be like, consequences of being a tortoise or a hare, and so forth. Make use of opportunities to assess listening skills, taking turns, and oral expression.

Thinking–speaking activity: Have students "try on" the behaviors discussed in the previous activity. As the story is read, make space available for students to act out the behaviors. Discuss tortoise behaviors seen during the story.

Assessment: Record the behaviors that were discussed. Note both expressive and receptive behaviors. Record students who orally communicated ideas and took turns. Note students who need instruction in skills and teach them.

Day 2   Objectives:

1. To become aware of time.
2. To estimate time needed for a task.

Warm-up activity: Review the behaviors of the tortoise that led to completing the race. Introduce tortoise bulletin board. Have pictures of desired behaviors. Have students label the pictures and put them on the bulletin board.

Focusing activity: Decide how long it takes to complete some unit of work. Have students close their eyes and estimate how long a minute is. Have students raise their hands when they think a minute is up. Discuss whether a minute was longer or shorter than they thought. Decide on the time needed to do an activity, and discuss whether it takes longer or shorter than they thought. Estimate the time needed to do the first independent task.

Reading–writing activity: Do the independent task and record the time used. Check to see if the estimate was correct. Discuss why the estimate was correct or incorrect. Repeat this sequence of estimating time and then doing a task until the students are fairly accurate. Use a clock and a timer to help set times. As students complete their tasks, have them place a tortoise figure with their name on it on the tortoise bulletin board next to the behaviors they exhibited most.

Assessment: Note those students who were accurate in estimating time and those who need further assistance. Reteach those needing assistance.

Day 3 **Objectives:**

1. To use the following steps in completing a task: (1) listen, (2) look at what needs to be done, (3) check understanding, (4) do the task, (5) check over work, and (6) give self-praise.

2. To follow oral directions.

Warm-up activity: Discuss how well time estimating is going. Review behaviors that lead to task completion and any additional behaviors to the tortoise bulletin board. Act out those behaviors.

Focusing activity: Introduce a chart of the steps needed to finish a job. Uncover Step 1: Listen to what you need to do.

Thinking–speaking activity: Give students simple oral directions like "Go to the blackboard," and "sit up straight." Start with one direction and increase to two or more. Have the students give each other directions.

Assessment: Note students who are following directions and those who need further assistance. Reteach those needing assistance.

Day 4 **Objective:**
To use the following steps in completing a task: (1) listen, (2) look at what needs to be done, (3) check understanding, (4) do the task (5) check over work, and (6) give self-praise.
Warm-up activity: Discuss what a scout for a wagon train does. Have students act like scouts.
Focusing activity: Review Step 1 of the chart. Uncover Steps 2 and 3: Look at what you need to do and check understanding. Discuss why people need to be like scouts.
Thinking–speaking activity: Play a game where you present a number of objects on a tray. Students observe the tray and then close their eyes. Remove an object. Students observe the tray and decide what was removed. After the tray is removed, students list what was there. Have students state the purposes of the activity in order to verify understanding.
Assessment: Note which students were and were not successful in observing. Provide other activities for those that were not successful.

Day 5 **Objective:**
To use the following steps in completing a task: (1) listen (2) look at what needs to be done, (3) check understanding, (4) do the task, (5) check over work, and (6) give self-praise.
Warm-up activity: Discuss Steps 1, 2, and 3. Note the number of tortoise figures on the bulletin board beside each behavior. Estimate the time for the next activity.
Focusing activity: Uncover Steps 4 and 5 of the chart. Discuss how to work, being a good worker, finishing the job, and so forth. Emphasize doing a job right rather than fast. Discuss how to check over work, what to check for (i.e., any unanswered questions, right answers).
Thinking activity: Have students use the steps in independent work.
Assessment: Note students who are successful and unsuccessful at following the steps and give further assistance to those who need it.

Day 6 **Objectives:**
1. To complete the five steps in working through a task.

2. To listen to a story.

3. To draw behaviors that are like an ant or the tortoise.

Warm-up activity: Review the work behaviors by having students act them out. Include specific behaviors from the tortoise bulletin board.

Focusing activity: Review Steps 1–5. Discuss how it feels to finish and know you've done a good job. Uncover Step 6—tell yourself you did a great job. Read the story, "The Grasshopper and the Ant."

Thinking–doing activity: Discuss how the grasshopper would do his work if he were in the room and what the ant would do. Then ask students if they would be like ants or grasshoppers. Have students draw themselves being an ant or a grasshopper. Label the pictures.

Expressive activity: Have students give self-praise by pinning a "good job" badge on themselves as they complete a task using the six steps.

Assessment: Note the students who still need help on task estimating and task completion.

ADDITIONAL INTEGRATED READING–WRITING ACTIVITIES

1. Provide pictures from magazines and other sources. Have students discuss what led up to the events in the pictures. Have students write a story about an event. Put their stories in books to be added to the classroom library.

2. Have the students write riddles and place them in riddle books to be read during free time or nook-and-cranny time.

3. Have students share a story and retell it using rebuses (pictures that stand for words).

    Examples: 3 little 🐷🐷🐷 s built 🏠🏠🏠 s.

4. Instead of "show and tell," have students periodically do "write and read." Start by presenting concrete examples of how to do the activity.

5. Write comparison books with a variety of comparisons. Examples: As big as a _____, as little as a _____; as warm as _____, as cold as _____; as light as _____, as heavy as _____. Group books for each set of comparisons can be added to the classroom library.

6. Have students discuss a sport they are knowledgeable about such as

soccer, basketball, or hockey. As a group, have the students write one line about how it feels to play, then one line about how it feels to watch.

7. Have students think like a vendor at a baseball or football game. Discuss how vendors might sell their products, then have students write a chant about selling them. During nook-and-cranny time, have students read their chants.

8. Have students select their favorite story and rewrite it in playscript. Students can read the new stories, each taking a character role.

9. Have students select their favorite food and create the recipe for its preparation. Place all recipes in a book, duplicate it, and send each parent a copy to read and enjoy.

10. Have students create recipes for a "good kid" cookie. Discuss all the important ingredients by starting with the statement, "A good kid is . . . ." Have students write individually or in groups their recipes for a "good kid" cookie.

CHARACTERISTICS OF AN INSTRUCTIONAL DAY

Primary-grade reading instruction has a number of unique characteristics. One of the most obvious is the allocating of so much time to reading instruction. In most primary grades there are two designated times for reading instruction, one in the morning and another in the afternoon. This allocation of extra instructional time for reading is yet another example of how crucial reading is at this level.

Another distinguishing characteristic is the way in which the time is used. First, time tends to be planned in large blocks. For instance, it is more typical to find reading being conducted for one and one-half hours than for the 50 minutes normally associated with instructional periods. Second, most first- and second-grade teachers tend to integrate reading with language arts. Hence, reading periods generally include listening comprehension, writing, language experience activities, oral ideas and experience sharing, creative drama, and teacher oral reading of stories, as well as the typical basal text activities associated with reading instruction.

This difference in time usage reflects the curricular emphasis in the primary grades. Because attitude outcomes are so important at the primary-grade level, teachers plan many diverse activities to develop concepts and positive responses. This diversity is also a reflection of the shift from listening comprehension to reading comprehension that accompanies the move from the Readiness Stage to the Initial Mastery Stage.

Another distinctive characteristic is the self-contained instructional day in which one teacher is responsible for teaching virtually all subjects. For instance, primary teachers usually will place more emphasis on the classroom library than on the school library, will do much more of their own art and music instruction, and will integrate such activities into on-going reading instruction.

In sum, the first and second grades often have a highly integrated curriculum that includes many diverse activities with little evidence of different subjects being taught. Within this framework, reading is greatly emphasized. However, the emphasis is not just on skills — it is also on developing conceptual understanding and positive responses. Consequently, instruction in the first and second grades is much more language dominated, in that all modes of communication (listening, speaking, and writing, as well as reading) are in evidence.

CONCLUSION

Although reading instruction is crucial at all levels, it is especially important in the first and second grades. It is at this level that students actually begin reading text. This early experience with reading often determines future reading progress.

Primary-grade reading is particularly difficult to teach. Teachers must simultaneously build the accurate concepts and positive feelings that lead to desired attitudes and build the linguistic skills needed to make sense out of print. One of the things that makes this difficult is the fact that most basal textbooks and assessment tests tend to only emphasize linguistic competence, thereby giving teachers the impression that process outcomes should receive more emphasis than attitude outcomes.

Despite the difficulties, however, teachers can give instruction in the first and second grades that will provide the foundation students need to become competent readers. The suggestions contained in this chapter should support your efforts. However, instructional success ultimately depends on your willingness to assume cognitive control of instruction by modifying suggestions to meet the needs of particular instructional situations.

CHECK YOUR UNDERSTANDING

Now that you have read the chapter, check your understanding by answering the Focus Questions presented at the beginning of the chapter. If you are unable to answer one or more of the questions, return to the chapter, find the section which corresponds to the question, and reread.

SUGGESTED READINGS

Bridge, C. (1979). Predictable materials for beginning readers. *Language Arts, 56*(5), 503–507.

Carr, K. S. (1983). The importance of inference skills in the primary grades. *Reading Teacher, 36*(6), 518–522.

Clymer, T. (1963). The utility of phonics generalization in the primary grades. *Reading Teacher, 41*, 252–258.

Culyer, III, R. C. (1979). Guidelines for skill development: Work attack. *Reading Teacher, 32*(4), 425–433.

Cunningham, J. W. (1979). An automatic pilot for decoding. *Reading Teacher, 32*(4), 420–424.

Cunningham, P. M. (1980). Teaching were, with, what, and other "four-letter" words. *Reading Teacher, 34*(2), 160–163.

Dickerson, D. P. (1982). A study of use of games to reinforce sight vocabulary. *Reading Teacher, 36*(1), 46–49.

Dyson, A. H. (1982). Reading, writing and language: Young children solving the written language puzzle. *Language Arts, 59*(8), 829–839.

Eeds, M. (1985). Bookwords: Using a beginning word list of high frequency words from children's literature K–3. *Reading Teacher, 38*(4), 418–423.

Fowler, G. L. (1982). Developing comprehension skills in primary students through the use of story frames. *Reading Teacher, 36*(2), 176–184.

Gipe, J. P. (1980). Use of relevant context helps kids learn new word meanings. *Reading Teacher, 33*(4), 398–402.

Marzano, R. J. (1984). A cluster approach to vocabulary instruction: A new direction from the research literature. *Reading Teacher, 38*(2), 168–173.

Miller, R. (1982). Reading instruction and primary school education. *Reading Teacher, 35*(8), 890–894.

Morris, D. (1982). "Word sort:" A categorization strategy for improving word recognition ability. *Reading Psychology, 3*(3), 247–259.

Ribovich, J. K. (1979). A methodology for teaching concepts. *Reading Teacher, 33*(3), 285–289.

Spache, E. B. (1982). *Reading activities for child involvement* (3d ed.). Boston: Allyn & Bacon.

Spiegel, D. L. (1978). Meaning-seeking strategies for the beginning reader. *Reading Teacher, 31*, 772–776.

Stauffer, R. G., & Cramer, R. (1968). *Teaching critical reading at the primary level.* Newark, DE: International Reading Association.

Taylor, B. M., & Nosbush, L. (1983). Oral reading for meaning: A technique for improving word identification skills. *Reading Teacher, 37*(3), 234–237.

Tompkins, G. E., & Webeler, M. (1983). What will happen next? Using predictable books with young children. *Reading Teacher*, *36*(6), 498–502.

Tyson, E. S., & Mountain, L. (1982). A riddle or pun makes learning words fun. *Reading Teacher*, *36*(2), 170–175.

CHAPTER **13**

Teaching Middle-Grade Reading

GETTING READY

If things go well in Grades 1 and 2, young readers come to Grades 3 and 4 with an accurate conception of reading, positive feelings about reading, an understanding of what the squiggles on the page mean, a basic sight-word vocabulary, various strategies to figure out unrecognized words, and the understanding that words, topic, purpose, and text type are used to predict an author's message. The unique function of Grades 3 and 4 is to expand upon these fundamentals. This expansion focuses particularly on comprehension and on establishing the habit of reading, both for enjoyment and for functional reasons.

This chapter focuses on how a second- or third-grade teacher can expand upon the fundamentals developed in the primary grades. It describes the characteristics, the curricular emphases, and the instructional techniques that you will need to know to teach reading in the third and fourth grades.

FOCUS QUESTIONS

As you read this chapter use the following questions to guide your understanding about middle-grade reading.

1. What particular characteristics are associated with teaching middle-grade reading?
2. What can you do in the middle grades to develop attitude outcomes?
3. What can you do in the middle grades to teach process outcomes?
4. What can you do in the middle grades to teach content outcomes?

5. How would you would integrate reading and writing in the middle grades?
6. What does a typical instructional day look like in the middle grades?

OVERVIEW OF MIDDLE-GRADE READING

The middle grades are unique because they represent the bridging years between learning the fundamentals of reading (the Initial Mastery Stage) and applying these fundamentals in a variety of specialized content areas (the Application Stage). Hence, reading instruction in the middle grades expands upon the fundamentals taught in Grades 1 and 2 while preparing students to handle the heavier reading demands of the middle school.

Because of the unique function of the middle grades, the reading curriculum at the Expanded Fundamentals Stage is different. The emphasis in the attitude area shifts from introductory experiences designed to build accurate concepts and positive feelings to getting students to perceive themselves as readers who understand its function and engage in it enthusiastically. The focus in the process area shifts from an emphasis on print to an emphasis on comprehension strategies. Although the overall goal remains unchanged—getting meaning from text—the emphasis changes. The focus in the content area shifts from simple narrative stories and simple expository text to various forms of expressive literature and to the kind of expository text typically found in content area texts.

Because the curricular emphasis shifts, the instructional emphasis also shifts. For instance, group language experiences that are relied upon heavily in the primary grades begin to give way to individual language experiences and collaborative grouping. In the process area direct instruction activities shift for both knowledge and strategy outcomes. Knowledge outcomes focus less on words and more on how knowledge about topic, purpose, and text types are used to make predictions about meaning and to achieve fluency. Strategy outcomes shift from word-analysis strategies to comprehension strategies, and study strategies are introduced.

In the content area the type of texts used become more complex. Simple story narratives are supplemented by more complex story forms, more poetry, and more folk literature, and teachers guide reading using techniques that are a bit more complex than the standard directed reading lesson. The simple expository text forms used in the primary grades are supplemented by specialized social studies, science, and mathematics texts. Also, teachers introduce study techniques and analysis of question–answer relationships to guide students through this more complex material. The relative emphasis in curriculum and in instructional activities in the middle grades is shown in Figure 13.1.

The bridging function of Grades 3 and 4 not only makes these grades unique but also provides a special challenge for the teacher. As Chapter 3 indicated, different students progress at different rates. The implication for the middle grades is that virtually every child is at a different point in "crossing the bridge" from beginning reading to upper–grade reading. Some are still trying to make sense out of the print whereas others are eagerly demanding more challenging texts. This diversity is common in the middle grades and is a major instructional challenge for teachers at these levels.

DEVELOPING ATTITUDE OUTCOMES

Developing positive attitudes is always a major goal of reading instruction because without good attitudes students are unlikely to become literate people who control the language system and use it for functional and recreational reading. The great emphasis given attitude outcomes in the primary grades continues to be developed at the middle-grade level. For instance, there is continued development of concepts regarding the communicative nature of

Getting middle-grade students involved in meaningful reading is an important aspect of indirect instruction.

Figure 13.1 **Instructional emphasis at the Expanded Fundamentals Stage**

Outcome	Relative Instructional Emphasis	Major Instructional Activity
Attitude Outcomes		
Concepts about reading	_Stress:_ Reading is communication between writer and reader Reading is predicting meaning Reading is sense making Reading is a tool _Continued Development:_ Previously developed concepts	Indirect instruction using projects, language experience, USSR activities, and writing
Positive responses to reading	_Stress:_ Reading is a source of power _Continued Development:_ Previously developed positive feelings about reading	Indirect instruction involving projects, language experience, USSR activities, and writing
Process Outcomes		
Knowledge about how reading works	_Stress:_ Reading fluently and with expression _Continued Development:_ Word meanings Sight words Using words, prior knowledge, purpose, and text to predict meaning	Direct instruction in reading fluently with expression Direct instruction using basal text recommendations
Fix-it strategies	_Stress:_ Generating new predictions to remove meaning blockages Using visible cues to remove meaning blockages Using invisible cues to remove meaning blockages _Continued Development:_ Word-analysis strategies for figuring out words unknown in print	Direct instruction in comprehension strategies using basal text recommendations Direct instruction using basal text recommendations

Figure 13.1 **Instructional emphasis at the Expanded Fundamentals Stage** (continued)

Outcome	Relative Instructional Emphasis	Major Instructional Activity
	Introduce: Study skills used to locate and organize information and to read efficiently	Direct instruction in study skills using basal text recommendations
Content Outcome		
Recreational	*Stress:* Getting meaning from various types of expressive text	Directed reading lessons
	Continued Development: Getting meaning from story narratives	Directed guidance in interpreting literary devices
	Introduce: Understanding various literary devices used by authors	
Functional	*Stress:* Getting meaning from expository texts found in content-area textbooks	Guided reading of content-area texts using SQ3R
	Introduce: Using QARs to get meaning from expository text	Guidance in the relationship between questions posed and the content of the text

reading and its recreational and functional purposes. There is also continued emphasis on making reading exciting and satisfying. These attitude outcomes are stressed at the middle-grade level so that students begin perceiving themselves as readers and begin developing a lifelong reading habit. Both of these outcomes develop, in part, because the students are very involved in reading real materials for real reasons.

CREATING A LITERATE ENVIRONMENT

The attitude outcomes at the middle-grade level focus on getting students to be readers. Much of the responsibility for achieving this outcome lies with the literate environment created in the classroom, which must encourage students

Figure 13.2 **An example of how to use indirect instruction
to teach attitudes in the middle grades**

Background   You want to develop in your students the feeling that reading
makes you powerful. You establish a situation in which the
students are unable to do what they want to do because they
lack information.

Activity 1   As part of the literate environment you establish an activity
that the students very much want to pursue (such as setting up
an aquarium). Although you know they do not have enough information to complete the task, you allow them to work on it.
When frustration occurs because they lack the necessary information you initiate a discussion.

Discussion   You discuss the problem with the students and identify lack of
information as the source of the frustration. You then help
them locate the needed information and point out that reading
provided them with the power to complete a task which had
previously frustrated them.

Activity 2   You have the students return to the original activity and complete it.

to become involved in real reading. To accomplish this, middle-grade teachers
structure the physical, intellectual, and social-emotional environment to encourage the development of these attitudes.

The physical environment in middle-grade classrooms is designed to look
like a place where literate people live and work. There should be a room library
consisting of a large selection of children's books (about three or four books per
student, representing a variety of genre and topic). This library should be
prominently located, attractively decorated, and comfortable looking (some
teachers use throw pillows and beanbag chairs to entice students to settle down
with a book). The idea, of course, is to create the image that reading is a
natural part of life. This image is reinforced by other aspects of the physical environment. For instance, the room should include a variety of projects — many
of which require written directions — and much evidence of student writing, as
well as expository descriptions of various projects in which the class is engaged.
In short, the physical environment should look like an exciting place where
literate people are pursuing interesting, language-oriented tasks.

The intellectual environment created by teachers stimulates many of the
reading and writing activities that are so evident in the physical environment.
Teachers set up the room library, encourage various projects and written com-

munications, establish collaborative groups to exchange ideas, and generally establish the expectation that students in this particular classroom participate in language in real ways. These expectations are the intellectual stimulation that helps develop attitude outcomes.

Similarly, the social-emotional environment should help students perceive themselves as readers and develop the habit of reading. The teacher creates an environment in which students work together, usually in collaborative groups, to achieve goals. Because reading and writing are a natural part of such cooperative learning situations, it is easier for students to develop the desired concepts and responses.

In the middle grades, then, the literate environment helps students see themselves as readers and gives them the opportunity to develop the habit of reading.

INSTRUCTIONAL APPROACHES

As with all grade levels, basal textbooks play a relatively minor role in the development of attitude outcomes in the middle grades. Instead, teachers use language experience and personalized reading activities to develop instruction for attitude outcomes.

Personalized reading plays a particularly important role in the middle grades. Uninterrupted sustained silent reading is an integral part of every instructional day, as it is at all grade levels. In addition, teachers look for other ways to involve students in "free reading." There is a big emphasis on sharing books, and collaborative groups are frequently used to plan and organize puppet shows, skits, creative drama, simulated newscasts, and other related activities. These kinds of activities help students see themselves as readers and develop the reading habit.

Whereas personalized reading is emphasized in the middle grades, language experience also plays a role. In contrast to the primary level, however, much of the language experience at this level is completed individually rather than in groups. Students may use their reading experiences as the basis for an imaginary story, or they may use a field trip as the basis for writing a poem. Teachers continue to create the opportunities for such writing and encourage students to make use of them. However, instead of a jointly produced language experience story such as those typically found in the primary grades, the product is typically produced by an individual.

These efforts are not necessarily unstructured. Indeed, teachers often use the three-step format for indirect instruction (see Chapter 9) to give structure to these activities. This format might be used to plan and conduct a lesson like the one shown in Figure 13.2. Such instruction helps students derive a sense of power from reading while also building the concept that reading is a useful tool.

ACTIVITIES TO DEVELOP
ATTITUDE OUTCOMES

The following is a sample of activities that you can use in the middle grades to
develop attitude outcomes.

1. Acting as evaluators for first- and second-grade books helps middle
   graders develop a positive attitude toward reading. Have students
   present their evaluations to the first and second graders.
2. Present radio shows using a tape recorder. By writing, reading,
   and speaking favorite stories students develop the concept of the
   integrative nature of language.
3. Quiz shows, patterned after "What's My Line?" or "I've Got a
   Secret" offer an opportunity for middle-grade students to become
   acquainted with book characters. This type of activity helps
   develop the concept that reading is life captured in print.
4. Newpaper and magazine articles about children's books, authors,
   or illustrators stimulate the development of a positive attitude
   toward reading. Have students bring these articles to class for
   discussion.
5. Collaborative group reporting of children's literature provides an
   opportunity for comparisons and contrasts of similar books. Make
   books about animals, family life, periods of history, and so forth
   the basis for these discussions.
6. Felt-board characters provide an excellent opportunity for storytelling and the development of positive attitudes. Favorite stories can
   be developed and presented to younger children.
7. Questions in envelope pockets on the bulletin board help students
   develop a positive attitude toward reading. An envelope labeled
   "Who am I?" might present clues about popular characters.
   Another labeled "Where did it happen?" might include clues about
   events in various books. Have students add their own questions
   about books they have read.
8. Have students make bookmarks illustrated with "the part I liked
   best" or "my favorite character." They make lasting mementoes of
   enjoyable reading experiences and help to develop positive attitudes toward reading.
9. Have students make a video of a book by illustrating and connecting scenes. The series of scenes, rolled on a wooden rod, may be
   passed through a frame cut from a box. You can also use an
   opaque projector.

10. Use student-developed book jackets, illustrations, or advertising posters to illustrate a book that has been read. These make excellent bulletin board displays and develop positive attitudes toward reading.

11. Illustrated maps showing a character's travels or the area encompassed by a story offer a good way of sharing a book. Historical fiction books are especially effective.

12. Have students conduct interviews on selected topics with an adult or students from upper classes. Use them in activities where positive attitudes toward reading are being developed.

13. Have students prepare and make appeals before another class on behalf of school or community drives that can be related to selected reading topics.

14. Have students correspond with hospitalized children and adults sharing interesting information about reading topics. This helps to develop the concept of the interrelatedness of language.

15. Have students take characters from books such as *Charlotte's Web* or *Pippi Longstocking* and rewrite the story in a setting suitable to the present. This activity promotes the concept of integrated language usage.

16. Have students write and then display a letter from one character in a book to another. Suggest they tell about something that might have happened had they both lived at the same time and place.

17. Have students create a magazine for the classroom by compiling voluntary artwork and writing projects composition completed during reading. The magazine should be published for classroom distribution.

18. A book fair is an ideal device for getting middle-grade children involved in book reviewing. The class can assume responsibility for reviewing important books prior to the fair. Have representatives travel to other classes to review the books prior to the exhibit.

19. Students can take the responsibility for reviewing Caldecott Award winners for the primary graders. Present these reviews orally.

20. A library corner, complete with bulletin board display, is essential to the development of positive attitudes toward reading. Relate themes for the displays to popular authors (Cleary, Wilder), genre of books (realistic fiction, mysteries, informational), or topics (animal, sports).

21. New books in the classroom library deserve recognition. A few well-chosen words about selected books will help keep them circulating.

TEACHING PROCESS OUTCOMES

Because the middle grades are bridging years, they assume a major responsibility for process outcomes. There is a continued emphasis on knowing word meanings, sight words, and how to use fix-it strategies to figure out unrecognized words, and how to use various knowledge sources to get meaning from text. In addition, however, there is a particularly heavy emphasis in the middle grades on reading fluently and on fix-it strategies to repair breaks in comprehension (such as how to generate new predictions and how to use visible and invisible cues to meaning). Finally, study skills are introduced and used to locate and organize information and to increase reading efficiency. In short, middle-grade teachers must (1) continue the development of primary-grade outcomes, (2) begin placing special emphasis on comprehension and fluency, and (3) introduce new skills that are stressed at the Application Stage of developmental reading growth.

HOW THE READING SYSTEM WORKS

Primary-grade outcomes are continued and expanded in the middle grades. Students continue to be given real text to read and are shown how knowledge about words, topic, author, and type of text all combine to help the reader predict what meaning is being conveyed. Since this has already been introduced in the primary grades, it often takes the form of a reminder in the middle grades. Nevertheless, teachers must be conscious of the need to keep meaning getting in the forefront and to illustrate for students how the various knowledge sources can be used to predict what the author is conveying.

In addition, the middle grades emphasize fluency; that is, how smoothly and accurately the text is interpreted in oral reading. If students read a text with no hesitations or miscues and use intonation patterns consistent with the text's meaning, they are reading fluently. If, on the other hand, they read in a slow, choppy manner characterized by many errors and poor intonation patterns, they are not fluent.

Fluency is a concern in both oral and silent reading. However, it tends to get emphasized in oral reading situations because the easiest way to observe fluency is to listen to students read out loud. Teachers can observe exactly where in the text fluency began to break down, can generate hypotheses regarding causes, and can plan instruction to repair the problem. However, fluency can be assessed during silent reading by timing students. If, for instance, a student takes twice as long to read a particular text as other students, it is reasonable to assume that the student's fluency is not good and that help is needed.

Poor fluency is often associated with poor sight-word recognition because when students instantly recognize all the words in a selection, they tend to read it smoothly. Similarly, fluency is associated with general language competence because it is reasonable to assume that students who have limited oral-language backgrounds, limited exposure to oral reading, or recently learned English as a second language would have difficulty reading fluently.

When these problems are at the root of fluency difficulties, the remedy is straightforward. If the problem stems from unfamiliar words that cause the reader to hesitate, a teacher can teach needed words as sight words prior to the reading of the text. If the problem stems from inadequate general language competence, a teacher can establish a strong oral-language program that includes listening frequently to oral reading and participating in other forms of oral language.

Many times, however, students evidencing no difficulty with sight words or general language ability nevertheless have difficulty reading text fluently. These students need direct instruction beyond the teaching of more sight words and the provision for more oral language. Such fluency instruction must begin with the concept that authors expect their text to have a certain sound when read—that it should sound the way it would be said. In order to "say" the text

A teacher provides guidance on learning strategies.

Figure 13.3 **An example of how to develop fluency**

Background   Some of your students read in a choppy, hesitant manner despite knowing the words on sight and having strong language backgrounds. You might provide a lesson like the following.

Lesson Sequence

Introduction   Begin by setting a purpose for reading a particular text orally. For instance, involve the students in reading a book to a group of first graders. Explain that they must read fluently in order to enjoy their reading. Give examples of fluent and nonfluent reading.

Modeling   Put yourself in the place of a student who is not reading a text fluently. Explain how the meaning of the passage signals what the intonation should be. For instance say, "This is a dangerous situation. The story character must be scared. I need to read it like I'm scared." Then read it that way.

Interaction with students   Give the students sample pieces of text and ask them to do the same kind of thinking that you did. At first help them by pointing out what is happening and how that helps them say it. Gradually diminish the amount of help until students are independently making the decisions about how to say the text passage.

Closure   Have the students apply what they have learned about fluency to the text they are to read to the first graders. Guide their practice of the oral reading and then have them read to the first grade.

Desired Outcome   When reading a text students will monitor the meaning of the text and use this meaning to decide how to say the words in the text.

properly, one must know what it means. Therefore, fluency is dependent upon understanding the author's message; if it doesn't sound right it probably is not the message intended by the author. In that case readers should use the four knowledge sources (words, topic, purpose, and type of text) to make predictions. Sense making, then, is the first instructional emphasis in helping nonfluent readers become more fluent.

Teachers can aid sense making of this kind by encouraging students to think about intonation patterns when they are reading. For instance, teachers can encourage students to say the text as if they were the author. They can then be shown how to draw lines under the meaning units in the text that should be said together and how to change these boundaries until the text sounds right. Similarly, students can improve their fluency by attending to the typographic cues imbedded in the text, particularly the punctuation cues. These cues are direct aids to intonation and, hence, to fluency.

Another frequently used technique is *repeated readings*. To use this technique, teachers have students read a text until understanding is established. Then they direct the students to read it over and over again until it sounds the way they would say it orally. This technique works because it sets the expectation that reading should sound like real language and because it challenges students to strive for natural sounding reading until it becomes almost second nature to them.

Fluency is a major process outcome in the middle grades. It is closely tied to comprehension since appropriate voice intonation depends on understanding the meaning of the text. An example of how to teach fluency is illustrated in Figure 13.3.

FIX-IT STRATEGIES

There is a major emphasis on fix-it strategies in the middle grades. The word-attack strategies initiated in the primary grades continue to be developed, and study skills used to locate and organize information and to increase reading efficiency are introduced. However, the main emphasis in the middle grades is on comprehension strategies.

Just as fluent word identification is the smooth, automatic recognition of words in print, fluent comprehension is the smooth, automatic processing of text message. Fluent comprehension occurs when readers can use the words, topic, purpose, and type of text to predict meaning. Consequently, teachers generally want students to read material for which they have rich backgrounds; that is, they know the words, are familiar with the topic and text structure, and understand their purpose for reading the selection and the author's purpose for writing it. However, sometimes students must read unfamiliar material and when they do, there are occasional breakdowns in comprehension. In such cases they need fix-it strategies to repair the blockage. Three types of strategies are useful here.

The first type of strategy focuses on helping students generate new predictions. When reading text, good readers use the words, topic, purpose, and text structure to generate predictions about meaning. When these predictions are confirmed in the subsequent text, they continue to process the text smoothly and automatically. However, when a prediction is not confirmed, readers must repair the comprehension break.

The first thing to be done in this situation is to look back in the text. Most readers first look for words that they may have mispronounced, and, if found, they use the word-attack strategies discussed in the previous chapter to repair the break. However, if the look-back reveals that the words were all correctly pronounced, the reader begins to look for syntactic and semantic cues that might suggest alternative predictions. Such alternative predictions were demonstrated in Chapter 2 with the "Rotation" and the "Time flies" examples. In these situations, the reader thinks, "Am I thinking of the wrong grammatical relationship here, or the wrong meaning of one of the words? Is there a different schema that I could activate in this situation?"

By thinking about how the message is represented syntactically and about alternative meanings for the words, readers can generate alternative predic-

---

Figure 13.4 **An example of how to teach students to generate new predictions**

Background	You have a group of students who do not monitor their sense making when reading and who do not look back to generate new predictions when meaning getting breaks down. You could teach a lesson such as the following:
Lesson Sequence	
Introduction	Using a basal text selection the students are to read, locate an ambiguous passage that might generate an erroneous prediction. State that you are going to show them how to go back and generate new predictions until a sensible one is found.
Modeling	As you read explain your thinking to the students. Model your continuous monitoring of the meaning, your initial prediction, your puzzlement when the prediction no longer fits the subsequent text, your looking back for clues, your examination of both the semantic and the syntactic text elements that could produce new predictions (such as words having multiple meanings or reversals in the usual word order), your generation of a new prediction, and your testing of this prediction in the text.
Interaction with students	Give the students examples of ambiguous text so that they can do as you did. Have them also explain their thinking so that you can evaluate it. Gradually reduce the help you provide until students are generating new predictions without assistance.
Closure	Return to the basal text selection. Set the purpose for reading the selection, including the reminder to use their strategy for generating new predictions if they encounter situations where their initial prediction is not confirmed.
Desired Outcome	When reading text students will monitor their meaning getting, look back when sense making breaks down, and use semantic and syntactic cues as a basis for generating new predictions.

tions that can be tested within the context of the text. However, students must first be taught that alternative predictions must be made when breakdowns occur and then to use syntactic and semantic cues to generate these predictions. This means that teachers need to provide direct instruction that shows students how to do such thinking. Figure 13.4 is an illustration of how such a lesson might be conducted.

The second type of strategy focuses on visible cues present on the printed page. For instance, when meaning getting breaks down, it can often be repaired by looking back for the typographic cues (punctuation, italics, bold print, and so forth), for key words or word elements such as prefixes and suffixes, or for certain context clues. These cues are all visible in the sense that they are physically present on the page, and if one knows what to look for, they can be used to repair disrupted comprehension. For instance, by looking back for visible cues a reader may note that a disrupted meaning can be repaired by attending to a previously ignored comma, a misread prefix or suffix, the sequence of key words, or missed "relational" word such as *finally*, *since*, or *but*. An example of how to teach students to attend to such visible cues when breakdowns occur is provided in Figure 13.5.

The third type of fix-it strategy for comprehension makes use of invisible cues to meaning. Unlike visible cues, which are imbedded in the text and are therefore physically accessible, invisible cues are imbedded in the mind of the reader. This kind of strategy, therefore, relies heavily on inference. Rather than looking at the page for cues, readers look inside themselves for knowledge about the topic, the purpose, or the text type in order to make inferences about meaning. For instance, readers can often determine the gist of a written message by *classifying*, that is, by grouping together similar words or ideas and using them to make an inference regarding the meaning. Similarly, readers can use their own experience in situations similar to those being described in the text to predict an author's implied meaning. Readers can also make inferences about relationships in text (chronological, causal, compare–contrast) by thinking of a similar situation from their own experience, determining the similarities between it and the text situation, and then inferring on the basis of their personal experience.

Sometimes readers can use previous experience with similar reading or similar types of text to help repair meaning breakdowns. For instance, when reading a newspaper editorial, previous experience with editorials will help readers make inferences about the meaning of the one currently being read. The same is true when reading stories that follow a common structure. Similarly, readers use personal experiences to draw conclusions and to make judgments about the text validity. In short, breaks in comprehension can often be repaired by referring students to knowledge they already have about the topic, the text structure, or the author's purpose. An example of how to conduct instruction about invisible cues is presented in Figure 13.6.

Figure 13.5 **An example of how to teach students
to use visible clues to comprehension**

Background   You have a group of students who, although they monitor their meaning getting, do not know how to look for meaning through visible cues embedded in the text. For instance, when they lose track of the story sequence they do not know that you can look for key sequence words used by the author. The following is an illustrative lesson you can teach in this area.

Lesson Sequence

Introduction   Find a basal text selection in which the author uses visible cues to sequence, such as *first, next, then,* and *finally.* Tell the students you will teach them a look-back strategy to use if they lose track of the story sequence.

Modeling   Show the students how after losing track of story sequence to look back for key sequence words. Explain what you think about as you encounter the problem, as you search for cues, and as you find the cues.

Interaction with students   Provide a series of similar textual examples for the students and have them do as you did in determining story sequence by using key words. Provide help at first, but gradually decrease assistance as students' explanations provide evidence that they understand how to use the strategy.

Closure   Have the students read the basal text selection. In addition to learning about the content of the selection, have them use the key-word strategy if they lose track of the sequence.

Desired Outcome   Given a real text containing sequential events signaled by key words, students will be able to use key words as a strategy for determining sequence.

Figure 13.6 **An example of how to teach students
to use invisible clues to comprehension**

Background   You are teaching a group of students and you note that they are unable to use invisible knowledge about topic, purpose, or text structure to make inferences. For instance, the students are unable to draw conclusions about events in the author's story. The following is an illustrative lesson you can teach in this area.

Lesson Sequence

Introduction   Use a basal text selection that poses questions that require
students to draw conclusions. Note the need to answer such
questions at the outset and state that you are going to show
them how to answer these kinds of questions.

Modeling   Using the basal selection, explain the thinking in drawing conclusions. Show how you attend to the meaning of the text while also
thinking of similar situations with which you are familiar. Talk
about how you relate the text information to your own experience and use it as a basis for drawing conclusions about
the text.

Interaction with students   Using similar text passages, have students follow your model in
drawing conclusions. Provide much help initially, but gradually
reduce this assistance. Be sure that you have them talk out loud
in order to determine whether they are using a viable strategy.

Closure   Have the students read the basal text selection using their
strategy to answer questions that require drawing conclusions.

Desired Outcome   Given a real text to read, students will use their experience to
answer content questions that require drawing conclusions.

Breaks in comprehension, then, can be repaired just as breaks in word
identification can be repaired. As always, however, students must know that the
purpose of reading is to make sense of the author's message and that, if the
message in the text ceases to make sense, they should look back to determine how
to repair the blockage. If the blockage relates to a comprehension difficulty,
readers can do one of three things: (1) they can generate new predictions that are
triggered by reviewing the syntactic and semantic cues in the text; (2) they can
revise a predicted meaning by attending to explicit cues that are physically present on the page; or (3) they can revise predictions by using their previous experience with similar topics, purposes, and text structures. In any case, the
ability to use such strategies depends on whether middle-grade teachers directly
instruct students in the use of these strategies.

THE ROLE OF BASALS

Most comprehension strategies are taught in conjunction with basal textbooks.
However, teachers must use considerable caution in following basal prescriptions for two reasons. First, most basal texts do not present comprehension
strategies as they are presented in this book. The reason for this is that most

basals do not reflect the latest research, only research that has been widely accepted by the buying public. Since the strategies presented here reflect current research findings, they are seldom found in basal texts. What is found instead is reference to the more traditional "skills" of comprehension, such as main idea, cause–effect relationships, looking for details, and so on. Consequently, teachers must modify the prescriptions of the basal texts and recast them as strategies (see Chapters 6 and 9).

Second, as has been previously mentioned, the basal textbooks tend to isolate skills and strategies, teaching them in association with workbooks and ditto sheets. Seldom are the comprehension skills applied to real text. Consequently, teachers must make the necessary modifications so that fix-it strategies are taught in real contexts.

In sum, while most of the comprehension strategies will be taught in direct instruction situations employing basal textbooks, teachers must be prepared to modify basal text prescriptions regarding comprehension, in terms of both *what* strategies to teach and *how* to teach them.

ACTIVITIES TO DEVELOP PROCESS OUTCOMES

Instructional activities that can be used to supplement your teaching of process outcomes in the middle grades are provided below.

Knowledge Activities

1. Have students find five examples of connotative words. Students should group words according to where they found them (newspaper editorial, news article, magazine article, and so forth). Discuss the relationship between the words and their source.
2. Have students choose two sports writers, then analyze and discuss the structure each writer uses. Let students try to develop their own sports articles based on either structure.
3. Draw a runway with a hangar at the end of it. Divide the runway into sections on which sight words are printed. Two students each have an object representing an airplane. The game begins with both planes in the hangar. The first player spins and can move the number of spaces that the spinner signals if he or she can say each word. The players take turns until one plane reaches the end of the runway.
4. Using the newspaper, have students select an article and list

all the pronouns in it. Next to the pronouns have them write the nouns they refer to in the article.

5. Use exercises in which words are replaced with synonyms. Encourage each student to supply another word that means about the same thing. The appropriateness of the synonyms can be judged by group discussion.

6. Teach word opposites. One way to discriminate a concept is by knowing not only what it is but what it is not. It is appropriate at all stages of reading development to play word games in which students supply words that are opposite in meaning.

7. Encourage students to associate content words with mental pictures of that concept. Let them draw or describe their mental pictures.

8. Have students note on 3 × 5 inch cards the word meanings they have learned and the key characteristics and/or synonyms they have created. This builds not only a meaning vocabulary but also a synonym source for use in writing assignments.

9. Begin a sentence with a function word. Students complete the sentence, using words appropriate to the relationship signaled by the function word. For instance, provide sentences such as the following:

> The book is on _____
> Because Tommy was late _____

10. Have students work in pairs with concrete objects. One student manipulates the objects and makes a sentence. The other student restates the sentence changing some of the word positions. The first student corrects the restated sentence.

11. Use exercises in which a string of words is presented orally to the students. They then create sentences using those words. Appropriateness is determined by correct positioning of the words in the created sentences.

12. Use the "telegram" technique. Direct your students to read a paragraph and decide what words could be omitted without losing the meaning. Explain that they are going to send the paragraph as a telegram and will have to pay for each word. What is left will be the main idea and essential supporting details.

13. Make "stand-up" paragraphs. They can be fun and they can teach main idea and detail skills. Select a student to stand in

front of the class and think up a key topic sentence. (This might have to supplied at first.) Other members of the class think up details that elaborate on the topic sentence. As each student adds an important detail, he or she stands behind the student who made the topic sentence. The paragraph becomes a row of students starting at the front of the room. When all the "sentences" have taken their places, have them repeat their sentences one after the other and then construct the paragraph. Do not be afraid to have sentences rearranged or even omitted if they do not belong.

Fix-It Activities

1. Have students find 10 words in a newspaper or a magazine that have double vowels, write them down, and compare them with another student.
2. Have students find five words with suffixes in a newspaper or magazine and write new sentences using each one of them.
3. Have students find five words with prefixes in a newspaper or magazine and write them on their paper indicating what the word is without the prefix.
4. Have students find examples of a blend in a story or article. Using these blends, have the students create tongue twisters.
5. Have students find as many phonograms of *cake* as they can in an article or story. Have them look for other examples of phonograms.
6. Have students combine simple, known words to create either real or new compound words, then discuss the new concepts created when two simple words are made into one compound word.
7. Put words on the chalkboard that signal certain relationships and have students think up sentences using these function words.
8. Say words or show objects to the students who must tell how they are alike or which one does not belong.
9. Have one student call out a category (such as *groceries*) and another student supply as many things that would go in that category as possible.
10. Select a well-written informational paragraph. Put the paragraph's individual phrases on the chalkboard, and direct the students to examine each phrase and use their classifying skills to make their own similar phrase, as in the following example.

Brushing teeth regularly
Bathing frequently
Eating well-balanced meals
Getting enough rest
Getting regular exercise

The main idea might be good health habits.

11. Have one student create a sentence and another change one word or phrase to indicate a change in emotion.

12. Provide unpunctuated sentences for the students. Have them punctuate each sentence several times, using different punctuation each time. Then have the student read each sentence, using the correct intonation according to the punctuation supplied.

13. Before directing a student to read a selection, set a purpose by asking how many things he or she can learn while reading. Direct the student to make tally marks while reading, each mark standing for something learned. Each mark will usually stand for a factual detail in the selection.

14. Before reading a selection from a textbook or reader, put the following purpose-setting formula on the board:

Who? Where? When? How many? What happens?

Ask the students to use this formula as a guide in their reading. Such a guide invariably will produce the details of the selection.

DEVELOPING CONTENT OUTCOMES

In the primary grades two kinds of text tend to be used: simple story narratives and simple expository articles. In the middle grades, however, various types of text are introduced and the content outcomes become more complex. In terms of recreational text, students in the third and fourth grades will not only read increasingly complex stories but also will read biographies, autobiographies, plays, poems, diaries, cartoons, and riddles. Of the stories they read, there will be great variety, including folk literature, fantasy, realistic fiction, and humorous stories.

Functional text also becomes more complex. In addition to the simple expository articles found in the primary grades, middle-grade students encounter content-area textbooks dealing with academic fields. The expectation is that middle-grade students will be able to apply their prior experience with simple expository text to the more complex material found in content-area textbooks.

The middle grades, then, carry a heavy load regarding the development of content outcomes. First, they must continue working with the simple story narratives and expository text found in the primary grades. In addition, there is particular emphasis on more complex forms of recreational and functional text found in content-area textbooks. Finally, middle-grade students are introduced to some of the literary devices that authors use and to the relationship between the questions and answers in content-area textbooks. Middle-grade content, attitude, and process outcomes are bridging experiences from the relatively simple reading required at the primary level to the increasingly more complex and diversified reading demanded at the Application Stage of developmental reading growth.

INSTRUCTION TO DEVELOP CONTENT OUTCOMES

Because content outcomes focus on getting a message that is being conveyed by an author, middle-grade teachers guide students' reading in order to help ensure that they do comprehend a text. This guidance deals with knowledge about the various kinds of recreational text (biographies, autobiographies, poetry, and drama) and the various kinds of increasingly complex functional text (social studies, science, and other textbook materials). However, teachers go beyond requiring students to know about the text forms and structure the reading activity itself to ensure that they will understand the message of the text.

With recreational reading, for instance, middle-grade teachers will often use a technique called the directed reading and thinking lesson (DRTL). In many ways it is similar to the directed reading lesson described in the previous chapter. It begins, just as the directed reading lesson does, by activating student knowledge about a topic and by building concepts for the new words that will be encountered. However, the purpose setting is handled differently in the directed reading and thinking lesson. Instead of simply stating the purposes for reading the selection, teachers have pupils look over the selection to examine the title, the pictures, and any other aspects of the text that might give them clues to the author's message. These clues are then used by the students to make predictions regarding what the text is about, what is going to happen, and so on. The predictions then become the purpose setters for the reading of the text—students read the text to see if their predictions were accurate. The discussion section then focuses on what actually happened in the text, how accurately the students predicted, and how the predictions could have been improved given the clues available in the text.

This technique helps students comprehend the content of a text because (1) it focuses their attention on the special features of the text that provide clues to meaning, and (2) it involves them in making predictions that can be confirmed or reevaluated. Additionally, of course, the directed reading and thinking lesson has the advantage of helping students develop a habit of making predictions an important part of meaning getting. An example of how to teach using the directed reading and thinking lesson is provided in Figure 13.7.

The directed reading and thinking lesson can be used with functional text also. The same format would be followed, but instead of making predictions about what is going to happen in the story or to the main character, predictions focus on the expository information. For instance, in a text about the pyramids of Egypt, the students examine the text, note the clues in the form of titles, headings, subheadings, photographs, and so on and then make predictions regarding what they are going to learn about the pyramids.

Another guidance technique that is particularly useful with functional text is survey, question, read, recite, and review (SQ3R), a five-step process designed to improve comprehension. It works like this. First, students survey the material to be read, noting titles, headings, subheadings, pictures, and other clues to text content. Next, they list questions that they should be able to answer after reading the text. They can get the questions from the teacher or from the end of the chapter, but it is most effective if students formulate their own questions by turning the information they surveyed into questions. For in-

Students reporting on the content of what they have learned.

Figure 13.7 An example of how to teach a directed reading and thinking lesson to ensure comprehension of recreational text

Background   You want your students to read the next selection in the basal text. Your major objective is that they comprehend the content of the story. You decide to use a directed readingthinking activity. An illustration of the procedure follows.

Lesson Sequence

Introduction   Provide a story introduction designed to activate students' background knowledge about topic, purpose, and type of text. Teach new vocabulary words as needed.

Purpose setting   Direct the students to survey the selection examining illustrations, headings, and other clues to story content. Have them use these clues to make predictions about what they are going to encounter in the story. List their predictions on the board, then direct them to read the story to see if their predictions were accurate.

Reading   The students read the selection for the story content and to check their predictions.

Discussion   Discuss with students the story content and the accuracy of their predictions.

Closure   Review the content of the selection. Sometimes, you can follow up the story with an enriching activity that calls for using the knowledge gained from the story.

Desired Outcome   Students will be able to state what has happened in the story selection.

Figure 13.8 An example of how to use SQ3R to ensure comprehension of functional text

Background   Your students are reading a selection from a science textbook on photosynthesis. To help them understand this difficult scientific content you decide to guide their reading with SQ3R. The following lesson is illustrative.

Lesson Sequence

Survey   Introduce the selection by activating student experience with leaves and trees and by eliciting their conceptions of how trees

	get food. Have them look over the chapter to determine what the content is about.
Question	Have the students examine the headings, subheadings, illustrations, and end-of-chapter discussion points. Have them pose a question for each. These questions become the purpose setters for reading the chapter.
Read	Have the students read the chapter to determine the answers to their questions.
Recite	Discuss their answers for each of the questions.
Reread	For questions that have not been answered direct the students to the appropriate place in the text and have them try again to answer them.

stance, a text on the pyramids of Egypt might include a subheading such as "The Pyramids: An Engineering Marvel," which the students could turn into the question: Why are the pyramids an engineering marvel? Once the questions are listed, students read the text to answer the questions. When they finish reading, they look at the questions again and recite the answers. Finally, if they find one or more questions they still cannot answer, they go back into the material and review it again.

The SQ3R technique is very systematic and works well for many of the same reasons as the directed reading and thinking lesson. It involves the readers in establishing purposes for reading, allows them to get a feel for the text through an initial survey, encourages reading to confirm or disprove the predictions embodied in the questions, and promotes the habit of checking to make sure that predictions have indeed been confirmed. An example of how SQ3R can be used is provided in Figure 13.8.

THE ROLE OF BASALS

Basal textbooks often provide an excellent place to teach and apply techniques such as the DRTL and SQ3R. In the middle grades they typically include a variety of recreational and functional text. If a teacher's major goal is for students to comprehend these samples of text, then the use of the DRTL and SQ3R are appropriate.

The important thing to remember about using basal texts, however, is that they serve two purposes: they contain samples of recreational and functional text that can be used for content value or for applying reading knowledge and fix-it strategies. Consequently, when using basal texts, a teacher must consciously decide whether a particular selection is to be used primarily for process application or primarily as a selection for comprehension. Both are viable goals, but teachers must know when they are teaching for one goal and when they are teaching for another.

ACTIVITIES TO DEVELOP CONTENT OUTCOMES

Unlike attitude and process outcomes for which a variety of middle-grade activities can be offered, the activities for content outcomes are more limited. This is because specific content activities are keyed to specific texts, and the particulars of the activity must be decided after you select the text. However, the following examples are illustrative of some middle-grade activities associated with content outcomes.

1. Have students sell a book to the class as a new way of presenting an oral report. The reader–salesman must convince the rest of the class that the book is the best book of its kind. Have the students categorize the book as recreational or informational.
2. A book tree is a way to develop both informational and recreational reading. As a book is read, label a leaf with the title and author and place it on the informational or the recreational side. The goal is to keep the tree balanced in terms of number of leaves.
3. Pantomime is an interesting means of sharing the content of a story that has proved especially popular with the class. Have one or more students put on a pantomime while the rest of the class try to guess who or what the performers represent and/or the type of content represented.
4. Puppets are as much fun to make as they are to operate and are an excellent way of sharing content. Make puppets using clay or papier-mâché for heads and simple cloth squares for bodies.
5. Construct mobiles in the form of major characters from a story. Settings or illustrations of major content can also be used.
6. Make dioramas and shadow boxes to illustrate content from a book. Again, either recreational or functional books can be the basis. Students can indicate their purpose for reading the book.
7. Have students make a miniature stage setting with pipe-cleaner figures to describe part of the information learned from a book. Have them display the stage setting and figures and give a 2-minute talk explaining the content they represent and why they were selected.
8. Have students write following the patterns employed in favorite books. Mercer Mayer's books can lead to original stories, and the

Just So Stories can be used to generate fanciful explanation. The poems on color in O'Neil's *Hailstones and Halibut Bones* can stimulate poems about sounds, smells, and so on.

9. Have students turn to the food advertisements in a newspaper and pick four items they would want for dinner. Write down how much each of these items will cost and the total food costs for preparing dinner.

10. Using advertisements, have students find at least seven things they drink. Have them note their favorites and the cost for a week's supply.

11. The class or school newspaper should have a good feature section devoted to children's books. The sections can classify books as recreational or functional and highlight their novel aspects. Have a different theme for each issue, such as Pioneers, Life in Other Lands, Science Fiction, Magic and Fantasy, Biography, and Natural Science. The class or classes responsible for this section ought to concentrate on novel ways of stimulating interest in the books presented.

12. Original posters, illustrations, or book jackets can be used to illustrate the contents of a book. These become excellent displays and can be used also to develop positive attitudes to reading.

13. Illustrated maps showing a character's travels or the area encompassed by a story offer a new way to show the content of a book. This helps students decide whether to read the book for recreation or information.

14. Murals make excellent group activities for your students. Have students depict either informational content or recreational content. Either should be labeled.

15. Have the class publish booklets about various subjects (science, ecology, World War II). Contributors should do research and then write their portion of the booklet.

16. Have students who have read a similar topic present a "You are There" show where they enact the content.

17. Have students who have read a similar topic present a talk show where central characters are interviewed.

INTEGRATING READING AND WRITING

There are many opportunities to integrate subject matter and the various language modes when teaching the middle grades. The following sample unit is one example.

SAMPLE TEACHING UNIT

Egyptian Mummies

Grade Level: Expanded Fundamentals
Overall Purpose:
To learn about the rituals of ancient Egypt and compare them with rituals of today by gathering information through reading, listening, and interviewing.
Objectives:
1. After reading about Egyptian mummies, students will generate questions to ask a museum curator.
2. After gathering information about the burial ritual, students will enact the ritual and the subsequent discovery of the tombs.
3. Students will list the personal artifacts they would choose to have buried with them as the Egyptian kings did and will share with the class why those objects are important to them.
4. Students will paint a time line of important events in their own lives and will represent each class member in the time line, as if it were a picture inside a pyramid.
5. Students will infer from the objects found in Egyptian tombs (e.g., King Tut's tomb) what life was like in that time.
6. Students will discuss what objects have been placed in well-known American time capsules (e.g., on top of the John Hancock Building in Chicago) and will create a time capsule representing their time.
7. Students will research and write reports about different cultures' death rituals. These reports may be given orally to the class.

> **Day 1** *Warm-up activity:* Using a model, a film strip, or pictures of mummies, motivate students to develop questions about mummies. Write generated questions on a blackboard. Stimulate students with the following questions or comments. What is a mummy? How many people have seen a mummy on television? in a museum? Who knows how mummies were preserved? Are mummies created today? How do our burial procedures differ from the Egyptians? (Assess group knowledge about mummies and the students' ability to generate and state questions.)
> *Focusing activity:* Read aloud and show pictures from *Mummies Made in Egypt,* by Aliki (New York: Thomas Y. Crowell, 1979). The students will

listen and observe to answer questions (information gathering) that have been generated in the warm-up activity and will generate additional questions.

Reading–writing activity: Have students discuss questions that can be answered from the text. Have them also list questions that should have been asked. Following the discussion, classify questions into answered and unanswered categories. Have the students then generate sources for answering the unanswered questions (library, museum, guest speaker, and so on). Assess students' repertoire for finding information.

Assessment: Assess students' knowledge about mummies, ability to develop and state questions, and knowledge of where to go for information. Teach students who couldn't develop questions or locate information these skills.

Days 2 and 3 *Warm-up activity:* Using the questions generated in the prior lesson, have students play the game, Pick and Seek. Place each question on a card with enough duplication for each student to have at least one question to sort. Each student decides where to look for the answer to his or her question. Have one student stationed at each location (library, *Mummies Made in Egypt,* museum, speaker) verify the choice. By the end of the activity questions will be classified for further research *(classification).*

Focusing activity: Library researchers go to the library to gather information regarding the art, artifacts, pyramids, rituals of the ancient Egyptians and the process of mummifying and burying their Pharoahs, as well as the discovery of such famous tombs as Tutenkhamen *(information gathering and reading).*

Reading–writing activity: Students share the information found in the library with one or more students acting as recorders during the discussion. The recorders write a report of the discussion that will be shared and verified by their classmates.

Assessment: Assess student's knowledge about ancient Egypt, some students' abilities to record and report an oral discussion, and all students' abilities to participate in oral discussions. (If a skill lesson for locating information has been taught previously check it during the focusing activity.)

Day 4 *Warm-up activity:* Have students read the written record of the previous day's discussion and alter or approve it. Give each student an approved copy of the written record.

Focusing activity: Have students revise and update the questions generated for the guest speaker. Generate new questions at this time.

Reading–writing activity: In groups of four or five, have students interview another student who is role playing a guest speaker knowledgeable about ancient Egypt. Have students check their own knowledge of ancient Egypt and the validity and form of their questions. Students will give their questions to the guest speaker.

Assessment: With the students, assess their knowledge of ancient Egypt, the ability to record and report oral discussions, and the skill of interviewing. (If a skill lesson has been taught earlier on questions, evaluate it during the focusing activity. All needed skills should have been taught.)

Day 5 *Warm-up activity:* Have students brainstorm all the words they can think of that relate to ancient Egypt. Students then classify words according to the questions prepared for the guest speaker. Have them put words that cannot be classified under a question into a separate group.

Focusing activity: Give each student the responsibility of asking one question. The speaker presents knowledge of ancient Egypt.

Reading–writing activity: Following the oral presentation, students ask their questions individually. Encourage additional questions. Have students write an answer to their question. Duplicate questions and answers and give them to each member of the class.

Assessment: Evaluate knowledge of Egypt (brain storming or written answer to questions), ability to classify, skill in careful listening, skill in interviewing.

Day 6   *Warm-up activity:* After listing sources of information, (book presented in class, library, speaker) have students use each source to locate knowledge about Egyptian burials.

Focusing activity: Have students sort and discuss their questions and answers about burials in ancient Egypt.

Reading–writing activity: Have students select parts to play in reenacting the burial of an Egyptian king and the later discovery of his tomb. Some students may be artists who create jewelry, others may be embalmers, others discoverers, etc. They will then enact the ritual, using the information they have gathered. After the tomb in the pyramid is secured, have the modern day discoverers find the tomb and carefully dismantle it, telling of the artifacts they find.

Assessment: Assess students' ability to classify, to recall information about Egyptian burials, and to dramatize Egyptian burials.

Days 7 and 8   *Warm-up activity:* Have students create their own time line with 12 inches of string and five cards. Each student selects five important events in his or her life and puts one event on each card. Hieroglyphics may be used but they should tell a story to people who might find it many years later. Tape each card on the line in sequential order so that each student has a time line *(informing)*. Have students read each other's time lines.

Focusing activity: Discuss how the kings of Egypt, like the students themselves, would also have five important events in their lives. Discuss how those events could be illustrated with hieroglyphics. Lead the discussion to Egyptian burials of the kings where personal artifacts represented in the time lines might be buried with them.

Reading–writing activity: Have students list the personal artifacts they would choose to have buried with them if they were kings of Egypt. Share these lists with other classmates. Discuss the similarities and differences of the items selected, as well as their implied values. Students should not be allowed to criticize another's selection. Students orally compare and contrast the artifacts and pictures they would have in their tomb with the artifacts shown in the tomb of King Tut.

Assessment: Assess students' ability to sequence events and enumerate similarities and differences of items selected for burial with King Tut's burial.

Day 9   *Warm-up activity:* Brainstorm items that have been discussed so far in the unit and that people would consider important. List items by people.

Focusing activity: In a way the Egyptian tombs are like time capsules. Identify a local time capsule (i.e., cornerstone of a school, church, or court house) that has been opened recently, or a famous time capsule such as the one on top of the John Hancock Building in Chicago. How are the items included in their time capsules reflective of their society? What items would students put in a time capsule to reflect their society for those who open it in 100 years?

Assessment: Assess classification skills, justified-choice skills, and abilities to recall, inform, and imagine.

Follow-up activity: There are many rituals in every culture and they are usually different across cultures. In small groups have students research and write reports about ritualizing a death in different cultures throughout history (including America today). Have students these reports give orally to the class by group.

ADDITIONAL INTEGRATED READING–WRITING ACTIVITIES

1. Provide pictures of action. Have students discuss what might have happened earlier to cause this action. Have students write a story of the events that led to the action. Have students read the stories to each other or to younger students for enjoyment.

2. Have students write riddles and place them in riddle books to be read during free time.

3. Have students share a book about a space ship. Then direct the students by saying, "If you could turn your chair into a spaceship, what would you do?" Have students write their answers.

4. Have students read a well-known story (fairy tale, tall tale, and so on). Then have them discuss how the story would change if told from another point of view (Hansel & Gretel from the witch's view, Paul Bunyan from the Blue Ox's view, *It's Like This Cat* from the cat's view). Have the students write a new version of the story from a different view.

5. Have students discuss what new inventions might occur in the future. Have them illustrate their inventions and write a paragraph to explain its use. Place a compiled book in the classroom library. *Examples:* an automatic surf board, a robot hair dresser, a plane-boat-helicopter, an automatic comb, a pencil that knows all the answers.

6. Have students discuss nicknames such as *Slim, Bones,* and *Speedy.* Have them select a nickname and write a paragraph on how some person got the name. File paragraphs in the writing center to be used in future stories.

7. Have students read a humorous story such as those about Pippi Longstocking or Amelia Bidelia. Have them select one incident and create a cartoon strip for it. Share the cartoon strips with another room.

8. Have students create a What If book. Topics include: *What if there were no cards? What if you were the teacher? What if you were asked to travel on the space shuttle? What if you were invited to the White House to receive a bravery award? What if you were asked to show the Queen of England around your school?* The students can create one classbook or their own book. Books can be shared with other classes or schools.

9. Have students create a Liar's Club with a *biggest whopper* award. Students write on topics such as heroic deeds, family, travel, funniest event, strangest event. All whoppers are placed in the classroom newspaper. The winners are placed in the school newspaper.

10. Have students think like a football player getting ready to begin a play. Students write what the player would say to a player on the other team. Students write what the player's response would be. Keep dialogues for future stories.

CHARACTERISTICS OF AN INSTRUCTIONAL DAY

Because the middle grades are bridging years between the primary and the upper grades, the instructional day takes on some characteristics associated with both. For instance, the middle grades in many schools retain the self-contained classroom arrangement typically found in the primary grades. That is, the students remain with one teacher all day rather than having different teachers for different subjects as is typically the case in the middle school. At the same time, however, the middle grades do have a sharper distinction among school subjects. Whereas the school day at the primary-grade level is primarily devoted to language (especially reading), reading is but one of several subjects taught in the middle grades. For instance, most middle grades will have a period designated for reading, the language arts other than reading (usually emphasizing writing but including elements of listening and speaking), mathematics, social studies, and science, with special subjects (such as art, music, and physical education) taught once in a while, usually by specialists in these areas. Hence, the school day at the middle grades is often a combination of the self-contained classroom unit found in the primary grades and the subject-by-subject arrangement found in the middle school.

Similarly, the time allocation in the middle grades is different from that found in the primary grades. Instead of teaching reading twice a day as is typically the case in Grades 1 and 2, reading is only taught once a day by typical third- and fourth-grade teachers. Also, it is often harder to integrate the various language arts in the middle grades than in the primary grades. In a typical

Middle-grade students often work independently during an instructional day.

first and second grade, reading is often taught in conjunction with listening, speaking, and writing, as well as being integrated into various other activities. At the middle grades, however, the shift in emphasis to subjects tends to make such integration more difficult. There is a tendency to teach only reading during reading period, only social studies during social studies period, and so on. Such a tendency is regrettable, of course, since all these subjects offer opportunities for genuine communication using all the language modes.

The best middle-grade teachers strive to integrate subject matter that promotes genuine language uses. Consequently, there will be students reading for content outcomes during social studies, being reminded of how to apply certain fix-it strategies during science, reviewing reading content during mathematical story problems, being shown how certain reading strategies can be converted into writing strategies, and so on.

Also typical of the middle grades are attempts to involve students in individual reading and writing efforts. Because students in the first and second grades are just beginning to read, many of their activities are group oriented and result in group products. The language experience story is one example. In the middle grades, however, the emphasis shifts to individual efforts and individual products. For instance, third and fourth graders are expected to do much more independent silent reading and individual writing.

This does not mean that there is no place for groups in the middle grades. Indeed, many of the individual projects designed to develop attitude outcomes are preceded by collaborative group activities in which students help one another prior to working alone. Similarly, process and content outcomes are often initiated in basal text reading groups and then move to individual work.

The middle grades, then, retain many of the characteristics of the primary grades while also adapting some of the characteristics that students will encounter when they get to Grades 5, 6, 7, and 8. Although reading usually becomes a separate subject that gets taught in a certain time slot, teachers strive to integrate it into the other subjects, thereby encouraging student involvement in real language activities

CONCLUSION

Because reading in the middle grades comes between the beginning stages of reading encountered in Grades 1 and 2 and the more sophisticated reading found in junior high school, there is much to teach. Additionally, because some children learn more quickly than others, reading levels range from prereading to eighth-grade levels. Finally, the movement to a more structured school day with designated periods for designated subjects restricts teachers' options in terms of integrating activities.

The thrust of middle-grade reading instruction moves from letter and word analysis to an emphasis on comprehension. Because the foundation of understanding print has already been laid, the emphasis can move almost entirely to sense making. Hence, it is in the middle grades that you help students solidify their understanding of what reading is and their perception of themselves as readers; it is here that they gain sophistication in monitoring their own comprehension and in applying strategies to repair breaks in comprehension; and it is here that you help them move away from the relatively simplistic, primary-grade texts and into the variety of literature and expository texts that more accurately represents real-world reading.

CHECK YOUR UNDERSTANDING

Now that you have read the chapter, check your understanding by answering the Focus Questions presented at the beginning of the chapter. If you cannot answer one or more questions, return to the chapter, find the section that corresponds to the question, and reread.

SUGGESTED READINGS

Allington, R. L. (1983). Fluency: The neglected reading goal. *Reading Teacher*, *36*(6), 556–561.

Arnold, R. D., & Wilcox, E. (1982). Comparing types of comprehension questions found in fourth grade readers. *Reading Psychology*, *3*(1), 43–49.

Babbs, P. J. (1984). Monitoring cards help improve comprehension. *Reading Teacher*, *38*(2), 200–204.

Baker, D. T. (1982), What happened when? Activities for teaching sequence skills. *Reading Teacher*, *36*(2), 216–218.

Beck, I. L., & McKeown, M. G. (1983). Learning words well—A program to enhance vocabulary and comprehension. *Reading Teacher*, *36*(7), 622–625.

Bergquist, L. (1984). Rapid silent reading: Techniques for improving rate in intermediate grades. *Reading Teacher*, *38*(1), 50–53.

Burke, E. M. (1978). Using trade books to intrigue children with words. *Reading Teacher*, *32*(2), 144–148.

Chapman, J. (1979). Confirming children's use of cohesive ties in text: Pronouns. *Reading Teacher*, *33*(3), 317–322.

Cohen, R. (1983). Self-generated questions as an aid to reading comprehension. *Reading Teacher*, *36*(8), 770–775.

Crowhurst, M. (1979). Developing syntactic skill: Doing what comes naturally. *Language Arts*, *56*(5), 522–525.

Farrar, M. T. (1984). Why do we ask comprehension questions? A new conception of comprehension instruction. *Reading Teacher, 37*(6), 452–456.

Garner, R. (1982). Resolving comprehension failure through text lookbacks: Direct training and practice effects among good and poor comprehenders in grades six and seven. *Reading Psychology, 3*(3), 221–231.

Gordon, C. J., & Braun, C. (1983). Using story schema as an aid to reading and writing. *Reading Teacher, 37*(2), 116–121.

Hoffman, J. V. (1979). Developing flexibility through reflex action. *Reading Teacher, 33*(3), 323–329.

Kimmel, S., & MacGinitie, W. (1985). Helping students revise hypotheses while reading. *Reading Teacher, 38*(8), 768–771.

Martinez, M., & Roser, N. (1985). Read it again: The value of repeated readings during story time. *Reading Teacher, 38*(8), 782–786.

Mason, J. M. (1983). An examination of reading instruction in third and fourth grades. *Reading Teacher, 36*(9), 906–913.

McGea, L., & Richgels, D. (1985). Teaching expository text structure to elementary students. *Reading Teacher, 38*(8), 739–749.

McIntosh, M. (1985). What do practitioners need to know about current inference research. *Reading Teacher, 38*(8), 755–761.

McKeown, M. G. (1979). Developing language awareness or why leg was once a dirty word. *Language Arts, 56*(2), 175–180.

Moldofsky, P. B. (1983). Teaching students to determine the central story problem: A practical application of schema theory. *Reading Teacher, 36*(8), 740–745.

Reutzel, D. R. (1985). Story maps improve comprehension. *Reading Teacher, 38*(4), 400–404.

Samuels, S. J. (1979). The method of repeated readings. *Reading Teacher, 32*(4), 403–408.

Schwartz, R., & Raphael, T. (in press). Concept of definition: A key to improving students' vocabulary. *Reading Teacher.*

Smith, M., & Bean, T. W. (1983). Four strategies that develop children's story comprehension and writing. *Reading Teacher, 37*(3), 295–301.

Stauffer, R. G., & Harrel, M. M. ((1975). Individualized reading-thinking activities. *Reading Teacher, 28*(8), 765–769.

Taylor, B. M. (1982). A summarizing strategy to improve middle grade students' reading and writing skills. *Reading Teacher, 36*(2), 202–205.

Wong, J. A., & Hu-pei Au, K. (1985). The concept-text-application approach: Helping elementary students comprehend expository text. *Reading Teacher, 38*(7), 612–618.

Wood, K. D., & Robinson, N. (1983). Vocabulary, language and prediction: A prereading strategy. *Reading Teacher, 36*(4), 392–395.

CHAPTER 14

Teaching Upper-Grade Reading

GETTING READY

The upper grades are a significant time in the lives of students. It is here that they move from elementary school to middle school or junior high school and, in so doing, take a major step toward high school and eventually adulthood.

It is also an important time in their reading development. In the upper grades students move from learning how to read to using their reading abilities to learn in other content areas. Because of the emphasis on "reading to learn" as opposed to "learning to read," this stage of reading growth is called the Application Stage—students apply what they know about reading when studying content subjects.

Unfortunately, students are not always helped to make this crucial transition from learning to read to reading to learn. That is, formal instruction in reading is often terminated at the end of the fifth grade, and students are left to fend for themselves in applying their reading skills to such fields as social studies, science, and mathematics.

This tradition, as well as other unique aspects of the upper grades, makes it difficult to teach reading in Grades 5 through 8. This chapter describes those difficulties and then makes suggestions to help you teach reading in the upper grades.

FOCUS QUESTIONS

As you read this chapter use the following questions to guide your understanding about upper-grade reading.

1. What are the unique difficulties of teaching reading in the upper grades?
2. What can you do in the upper grades to develop attitude outcomes?
3. What can you do in the upper grades to teach process outcomes?
4. What can you do in the upper grades to teach content outcomes?
5. How would you would integrate reading and writing when teaching content areas in the upper grades?
6. How would you describe a typical instructional day in the upper grades?

OVERVIEW OF UPPER-GRADE READING

The shift from middle-grade to upper-grade reading is almost as dramatic as the shift from kindergarten to the primary grades for four reasons.

First, the shift from middle grades to upper grades often means a physical move from one school building to another. Typically, American students attend Grades 1 through 4 or 5 in an elementary school and then move to a middle school or junior high school at the fifth- or sixth-grade level. This shift to a new, unfamiliar physical environment is dramatic for children, making it a significant time in their lives.

Second, the shift heralds important organizational changes in the way schooling is conducted. In elementary school students typically have one homeroom teacher for most of the school day and receive almost all instruction from that person. In grades 5 through 8, however, the homeroom teacher is the person to whom students report to at the beginning of the day, but they may go to as many as five or six other teachers over the course of the day to receive instruction in specific subjects. Hence, instead of one teacher providing most of the instruction, specialists teach one subject to five different groups of students each day.

Third, the upper grades represent a dramatic psychological change for students. Whereas the environment in the first four or five grades is consistent and stable, the environment in the upper grades is diverse and requires more flexibility. The upper grades are a bridge from the lower grades to high school and, as such, are designed to ease students into high school behaviors. The change to the upper grades can be a dramatic one for many students.

Finally, the upper grades have traditionally taken a different approach to curriculum and instruction, especially as it relates to reading. Whereas reading is a major curricular thrust in the earlier grades, it often is not a formal part of the upper-grade curriculum. Similarly, there is usually a specialist for reading as there is for each of the subject areas. The assumption has been that reading is mastered in the first five grades and does not need to be taught thereafter.

Recently, however, there has been a growing awareness that reading instruction should continue into the upper grades and that subject matter teachers must show students how to read the specialized content-area materials. Basal texts, however, are not nearly so prevalent in the upper-grades as they are in the earlier grades because reading is not normally taught as a separate subject.

All these characteristics make the teaching of reading in the upper grades a unique and challenging endeavor. The building is different, the school organization is different, the students themselves are at a unique psychological stage, and the context in which reading is taught is different. As a result, upper-grade teachers feel a pressure unlike that felt by teachers at any other level. They are in a unique position between the elementary school and the high school, charged with bridging the gap from learning how to read to applying reading knowledge to the learning of specialized subject matter. The task is not an easy one.

Despite these differences, however, the overall instructional goal in reading remains the same — to develop students who control their meaning getting as they read functional and recreational text. However, reading instruction is taught in the various content areas with their specialized textbooks. There is also a growing emphasis on (1) critical reading — teaching students to make judgements about what is read, (2) study skills — guiding the efficient handling of more complex reading materials, and (3) providing guidance in reading difficult text.

These curricular emphases are reflected in upper-grade instruction. The activities of the literate environment include experiences that encourage critical reading, whereas direct instruction focuses on how to read critically and how to use study skills and study guides to efficiently comprehend content-area textbooks. The curricular and instructional emphasis in the upper grades is shown in Figure 14.1.

DEVELOPING ATTITUDE OUTCOMES

Because reading in the upper grades is so closely associated with the content areas, attitude outcomes often receive less attention than they should. Teachers emphasize learning the content, and they often assume that the students' learned all they needed to know about reading attitudes in elementary school. Such is not the case. The development of the concepts and responses that make positive attitudes toward reading is as important in the upper grades as it was in the earlier ones.

One of the major tasks of upper-grade teachers is to maintain the earlier emphasis on attitudes. This is done by providing reading experiences that reinforce both the conceptual understanding of reading and the positive responses developed in previous years. For instance, upper-grade teachers should provide reading experiences that reinforce the concepts that reading is communication, a functional tool, and a medium for enrichment and enjoyment. Similarly, upper-grade teachers should provide enjoyable reading experiences that develop positive responses to reading.

In addition to reinforcing previously developed concepts and responses, upper-grade teachers should try to develop more sophisticated concepts about the nature of reading. The best example is critical reading. Critical reading involves making judgments about what is read, and it assumes that readers understand that something is not necessarily true just because it appears in print, and that writers compose text to persuade readers to do or to believe something. Consequently, upper-grade teachers should provide reading experiences that teach or reinforce these two concepts.

Figure 14.1 **Instructional emphasis at the Application Stage**

Outcome	Relative Instructional Emphasis	Major Instructional Activity
Attitude Outcomes		
Concepts about reading	*Stress:* Print can be used to convince or persuade	Indirect instruction using integrated reading-writing activities, free reading, and other similar activities
	Continued Development: Previously developed concepts	
Positive responses to reading	*Stress:* Feelings associated with using language to convince others	Indirect instruction using integrated reading-writing activities, free reading, and other similar activities
	Continued Development: Previously developed positive feelings about reading	
Process Outcomes		
Knowledge about how the reading system works	*Stress:* Critical reading	Direct instruction in using knowledge of reading to construct meaning
	Continued Development: Use of words, prior knowledge, purpose, and text to predict meaning	

Figure 14.1 **Instructional emphasis at the Application Stage** (continued)

Outcome	Relative Instructional Emphasis	Major Instructional Activity
	Using meaning to achieve fluency in interpreting text orally	
Fix-it strategies	*Stress:* Study skills used to locate and organize information and to read efficiently	Direct instruction in how to locate and organize information and how to read efficiently
	Continued Development: Comprehension strategies	Direct instruction in comprehension strategies
Content Outcome Recreational	*Stress:* Getting meaning from various literary genre	Directed guidance in interpreting literary devices
	Continued Development: Getting meaning from story narratives and various forms of expressive text	Directed reading lessons and directed reading and thinking lessons
Functional	*Stress:* Using QARs to get meaning from content-area text Getting meaning from text having heavy conceptual loads	Direct guidance in the relationship between questions and answers
	Continued Development: Getting meaning from expository and content-area texts	Guided reading based on various kinds of study guides
		Guidance using structured overviews
		Reading guided by SQ3R

Because of the concern for critical reading, teachers try to develop emotional responses to what is read. For instance, they want students to be enthusiastic about what they agree with, to get angry at writers they disagree with, to feel justified about modifying positions with which they disagree, and so on. These emotional responses motivate and support the development of critical reading.

Hence, there is at the upper-grade level an attempt not only to maintain the concepts and responses developed at the earlier grades but also to develop new concepts and responses associated with critical reading. The attitudes associated with these concepts and responses are the basis for teaching students how to make judgements when they read, which is developed as a process outcome at this level.

CREATING A LITERATE ENVIRONMENT

Because of academic departmentalization in the upper grades, students encounter various environments on any given day. This departmentalization often makes it difficult to establish a literate environment, especially regarding physical arrangements. For instance, it is difficult to physically arrange a classroom when teachers switch classrooms each period. To one degree or another, this is the situation faced by many teachers in the upper grades. They, like their students, move from classroom to classroom during the day. In such situations it is difficult to establish a preferred physical arrangement because each classroom is the homeroom of a colleague.

Despite the organization patterns of the upper grades, teachers can create a literate environment by relying more on intellectual and social–emotional characteristics than on physical characteristics. Intellectually, teachers create a literate environment by involving students in meaningful reading and writing tasks and by setting the expectation that they will pursue these tasks in literate ways. Socially and emotionally teachers involve students in collaborative groupings that encourage intellectual diversity and cooperation in pursuing assigned language tasks. Some teachers counter the changing physical environment by creating posters that can be carried from classroom to classroom. Others create units in transportable cartons that contain needed physical print.

Because upper-grade teachers are so often teachers of a particular content area, the tasks associated with a literate environment usually reflect that content. For instance, an eighth-grade social studies teacher who is teaching a unit on the Civil War may involve students in examining real documents from that era and in drawing conclusions about how people in various parts of the country felt about the morality of the war. Although such reading tasks are closely associated with the content being studied, they nevertheless help students to conceptualize reading accurately and to feel positive about it.

INSTRUCTIONAL APPROACHES

At the earlier grade levels both language experience activities and personalized reading activities are used within a literate environment to develop attitude outcomes. Later, however, both the departmentalized nature of the middle or junior high school and the maturity of the students mitigate against the heavy use of these techniques.

Instead, upper-grade teachers plan units of instruction that are characterized by unifying projects or culminating activities. For instance, students in an English class studying various forms of free verse poetry may study them in preparation for a "Write-In;" or students in a social studies class may study state government in preparation for holding a mock govenment in their school.

For the unit approach to work, teachers must choose a project that is motivating to students and necessitates the learning of the targeted content. Such projects can be done within the departmentalized organization typically found in the upper grades and are enjoyed by students at this age level. Sample projects are listed in Figure 14.2.

Within units, teachers plan indirect instruction designed to develop particular concepts about reading and particular responses to reading. For instance, a unit on newspapers may have as its culminating activity the publication of a student newspaper. During this unit the teacher may wish to develop the concept that newspaper editorials represent an attempt to persuade readers to the paper's view on some issue. To develop this concept, the teacher may plan a trip to the local newspaper and a visit with the editorial writer. Instruction to develop this concept would follow the three-step format for indirect instruction. An illustrative example is shown in Figure 14.3.

Figure 14.2 **Sample projects that can be used as a culminating activity for integrated units**

Science and Social Studies

1. After a current events unit where issues related to city, state, or country have been discussed have students list five changes they would make. Have students read each other's lists and create a class list.
2. After a science unit on health needs have students select what they feel was the most important point and illustrate this point with a poster. Place posters in prominent spots in the school.
3. After a unit on budgets provide students with a budget, a family, and local newspaper advertisements from grocery stores. Have students buy food for a week's time.

4. During election year have students conduct a mock election of those running for office. Conduct the actual election.
5. After a science unit on ecology have students select an important point and create an editorial to be placed in the class or school newspaper.
6. End a science unit on weather with daily written forecasts that include maps. Record and graph the accuracy of the forecasts.

Mathematics

1. After a travel unit have students plan an itinerary for a motor trip in the United States. Given mileage, meal, and hotel costs, have students develop the costs for the trip.
2. After a unit on mapping have students measure and map the school, the neighborhood, or their route from home to school.
3. After a unit on measurement have students measure and record the weights of unknown rocks. Using the sizes and the weights, have students predict in writing the types of rocks they have.

Figure 14.3 **An example of how to develop attitudes in the upper grades**

Background   As part of an English unit on newspapers you want the students to learn that newspaper editorials are written by persons trying to influence readers to share the same viewpoint as the publisher of the paper. To develop this concept indirectly, plan a trip to the local newspaper and schedule an interview with the editorial writer.

Activity 1   Arrange to take students on a field trip to the local newspaper office. In preparation for the interview with the editorial writer, prepare the students to ask questions about how the topics are chosen, why certain positions are taken, and what the writer's techniques are in composing the editorials.

Activity 2   Upon returning to the classroom discuss with students what they found out about the editorial writer and the purpose of editorials. Organize students into collaborative groups where they analyze recent editorials written by the writer they interviewed and where they draw conclusions regarding the persuasive nature of editorials.

Activity 3   Have the students produce their own newspaper, including editorials. Establish an editorial policy to determine the positions to be taken by the newspaper and assign someone the task of writing editorials that will convince others to share the views of the students.

Figure 14.9 **An example of how to teach students to organize and remember what they read**

Background	You are teaching a unit on the lives of famous American presidents. The students have been assigned to read short biographies of selected presidents and you want them to remember the essential points through summarizing.
Lesson Sequence	
Introduction	When students have finished reading the biographies set the purpose for remembering what they have read so that they can use it as the unit progresses.
Modeling	Show the students how you remember the main events and themes in the life of some person you read about by creating a summary in which you put all the details into categories and then label the categories.
Interaction with students	Have the students demonstrate the same mental steps in summarizing what they have read. Have them talk out loud about their reasoning so you have a window into their thinking and can provide appropriate assistance if they get off track.
Closure	Use their summaries as the next step in the unit.
Desired Outcome	When students are trying to remember content information they will summarize it using a strategy that calls for categorizing.

Figure 14.10 **An example of how to teach students to read and study efficiently**

Background	You are teaching an English unit on various forms of written communication. You have asked students to read several different kinds of text in preparation for the next lesson. The kinds of text include encyclopedia articles, newspaper articles, fiction books, magazine articles, and speeches written by politicians.
Lesson Sequence	
Introduction	Make a reading assignment, making sure that every student gets at least two different types of text to read. Emphasize the need to read both while also using study time efficiently.

Modeling	Demonstrate how you tie your reading speed to your purpose for reading and to the difficulty of the material. Explain how you make this decision and how you think about your reading rate as you read the text.
Interaction with students	Have the students examine their texts and talk out loud about deciding how fast to read and how they will monitor their reading.
Closure	Have the students use various reading rates when reading the various forms of written communication.
Desired Outcome	When students have assignments to read they will examine the difficulty of the text and the purpose of the assignment and then select an appropriate reading rate.

remembering information. The format for organizing such lessons is basically the same as for other fix-it strategies, as is illustrated in the sample lesson in Figure 14.9.

Skills of Efficient Study. Skills of efficient study include adjusting reading rates and organizing time to study. The answer to the question, What is causing me to fall behind everybody else? may lie in the fact that everybody else is making more efficient use of study time. Since the study load is typically light in elementary school and students are not routinely expected to spend their free time studying until they get to the upper grades, it is not unusual that this kind of problem arises. Students can control the problem by learning to use a variety of reading rates and by organizing their free time.

Using a variety of reading rates is not the same as speed reading. In fact, speed reading has no real place in the elementary reading curriculum because it is highly specialized and of limited use. Adjusting the rate of reading, however, is something all students can learn to do, and it is applicable to many content-area reading situations. It involves teaching students to read (1) at a brisk pace if the materials are easy and are being read for recreational purposes, (2) at a slow pace if the materials are difficult and are being read for factual information, (3) at a rapid, skimming rate when looking for a key word or key idea, and (4) at a very rapid scanning pace when previewing material. In short, by adjusting the reading rate to the purpose for reading and to the difficulty of the material, readers can make much better use of their study time.

Similarly, students can be taught to use their free time efficiently. Instruction here involves estimating available study time, prioritizing study assignments, and making a "time budget" that distributes available time according to priorities. This category of study skills, like the others, is best taught through direct instruction. An illustration of how direct instruction can be used to develop efficiency in study is found in Figure 14.10.

THE ROLE OF BASALS

As was noted earlier, reading in the upper grades is seldom taught during a separate period as it is in the earlier grades. Instead, reading instruction is integrated into the content areas (and, sometimes, is associated with literature studies conducted in English class). The prevalent textbook is not a basal reading text but, rather, a content-area textbook (a social studies text, a science text, a literature text).

Consequently, upper-grade teachers seldom use a basal reading textbook. Instead they teach reading skills such as critical reading or study skills in a content-area textbook. However, the decision making is much the same as when you use a modified directed reading lesson (see Figure 6.2). The only difference is that the strategy is applied not to a basal selection but to a content-area textbook.

ACTIVITIES TO DEVELOP PROCESS OUTCOMES

There are many activities that you can use in developing the process outcomes noted above. The following are illustrative.

1. Have students compile a reading notebook containing excerpts from their reading that are unusually expressive and make use of similes, metaphors, or alliterations. Have them use these figures of speech in their writing.
2. Have students compare the language of an editorial column with that of a news article on the same topic. Note the use of connotative words.
3. Have students find an article that arouses emotional response and rewrite it in their own style as a straight newspaper article.
4. Have students compare the quality of advertised goods by noting what is omitted from various ads. Note the use of propaganda devices.
5. Have students identify examples of technical vocabulary used in various types of articles (e.g., foreign policy, sports, business news).

6. Have students write an article persuading people to their point of view by using biased words and appropriate propoganda devices. Have them analyze words with similar meanings to differentiate shades of meaning.

7. Give students an entire page from a newspaper. Have them find, as quickly as possible, an article about some subject you have discussed in a story. Time them. To increase their ability to quickly spot articles in which they are interested, have them select a subject and then list as many key words as possible for that subject that might help them identify articles on it.

8. At these grade levels it is useful to study homonyms, or pairs of words that sound and look alike but have different meanings. Present students with a list of words that are frequently confused. Have them look up meanings and use the words in sentences. Give such words as these:

alleys, allies	*aloud, allowed*	*bare, bear*
board, bored	*borough, burrow*	*bough, bow*
bridal, bridle	*cell, sell*	*break, brake*
course, coarse	*desert, dessert*	*except, accept*
lose, loose	*lesson, lessen*	*peace, piece*
cue, queue	*quiet, quite*	*receipt, recipe*
rein, rain	*sensible, sensitive*	*site, sight*
tide, tied		

9. To develop sensitivity to word choice in conveying meaning, have students list words found in their reading that they think may someday disappear from our language. Examples: *pullover, skillet.* They may also list new words or phrases that are coming into common use. Example: *A-ok, roughneck* and manufactured words including *Kleenex* and *Kodak.*

10. Give directions and sentences such as the following to develop sensitivity to word order and other syntactic cues: "Rearrange the following sentences and then indicate whether the sentence is true or false: *For gasoline use fuel autos. Trees on grow oak apples.*"

11. Have students locate news articles that relate to guaranteed freedoms of the United States Constitution. Group the articles and have students discuss them.

12. Have students list and evaluate the advantages and disadvantages of various types of taxes (income, property, value added, excise) as described in news articles, features, and editorials.

13. Help students understand the behavior of characters in a book by analyzing possible causes of their behavior. Have them evaluate

the choices made by the characters and then think through possible alternative choices. Have them write a one- or two-sentence description of the character, a short description of the character's behavior, and three possible alternative behaviors the character might have shown.

14. Have students read three or four authorities on a given subject and then list the various facts that they advance to support their opinions. Use this exercise with history and civics. Current periodicals often provide diverse opinions on the same subject.

15. Have students evaluate the reliability of articles by judging the source (e.g., the President said, the White House announced, an informed spokesman said, all Washington believes). Prioritize the reliability of the sources.

16. Have students pick an editorial and list all the persuasive language used. Have them write their own editorial for some subject covered on the editorial page.

17. Have students pick an editorial and list the following: the nature of the problem, facts supporting and contradicting the writer's position, and opinions supporting and contradicting the writer's position.

18. To be complete, a news story should answer each of the five Ws: *why, where, who, what, when*, and sometimes *how*. Have students pick a news story and try to answer all these questions. Have them write their own news story covering each of the questions.

19. Have students choose two sports writers and analyze and compare their styles of writing. Have them note the special language they use to capture attention.

20. Give students a list of questions in each of which one word is underlined. This is the key word. Have them draw a line under another word in each question that they would look for in the index. For example:

    1. What percentage of the industry in Kentucky is devoted to coal mining?
    2. What is the value of the annual orange crop in the state of Florida?
    3. Do the seasons affect the formation of icebergs in the North Atlantic Ocean?

21. To teach prefixes and suffixes write a stem word on the board and have the students make as many words from it as they can by adding prefixes and suffixes. Example:

port

report	porter
support	reporter
transport	supporter
deport	transportation
import	deportment
export	importer

22. Have students compare advertised prices for the same items in two stores in contrasting areas of the city. Then have them list reasons for the variations.
23. Have students predict the response of a governmental official or agency to a current news event.
24. Have students compare the platforms or policies of two competing candidates by analyzing their reported statements.
25. Have students open their books to the table of contents. Ask questions that may be answered from it, such as: "Is there a chapter in this book about mammals?" "On what page is the chapter?" "How many pages are there in the chapter?"
26. Have students compare explanations of causation in news articles with appropriate social science generalizations about human behavior.

DEVELOPING CONTENT OUTCOMES

Content outcomes are greatly emphasized in the upper grades because the curriculum focuses on content-area subjects such as social studies, English, and science. Indeed, the purpose of reading the textbooks in these areas is to understand and to be able to answer a teacher's questions about this content.

Since most of the reading in the upper grades occurs in the subject-area classrooms, reading instruction is often referred to as content-area reading. Content-area reading is the instruction provided by subject-matter teachers (a social studies teacher, a science teacher) to help students understand the content of the textbooks being read in those areas. Content-area reading, as with content outcomes, can be divided into two major categories: recreational and functional. Recreational reading occurs mostly in English classes where students read and study literature, whereas functional reading occurs mostly in subjects such as social studies and science where students read textbooks loaded with factual information. In both types of classes teachers use various guided reading techniques to ensure that students comprehend their texts. These techniques are described below for each kind of text.

TECHNIQUES FOR GUIDING RECREATIONAL READING

The major techniques for guiding recreational reading in upper-grade English literature texts are the directed reading lesson and the directed reading and thinking lesson described in Chapters 12 and 13 respectively. As noted in those discussions, the DRL and the DRTL have much in common despite having distinctive characteristics. They both gradually guide students from an introduction, to the reading, to a discussion of a selection. They are different because the DRL is more teacher directed, with the teacher specifying the questions to be answered and the purposes for reading, and the DRTL involves students more in both purpose setting and question asking, so that they think more about what is to be learned from the passage. Both techniques are useful to teachers who wish to guide their students' reading of recreational text in English classes. When more teacher direction is needed, the DRL can be used; when the objective is to make students reflect on the reading task, the DRTL can be used.

A special problem associated with teaching literature in the upper grades is the tendency of good authors to use special literary devices such as foreshadowing, flashbacks, symbolism, and allegory and to employ special

Content reading becomes more complex in the upper grades.

Figure 14.11 **An example of how to teach students to interpret literary devices in comprehending the content of recreational text**

Background	You are teaching a literature unit on *The Island of the Blue Dolphins,* by Scott O'Dell. Since this book contains many idioms that must be understood in order to understand the story, you decide to teach the students how to interpret idioms.
Lesson Sequence	
Introduction	After introducing the novel, point out in the text several examples of idioms (such as *night had fallen*). Tell the students that O'Dell uses several of these in his story and that you are going to show them how to interpret idioms.
Modeling	Give several examples of idioms and model how you use your background experience and the context of the passage to interpret the words figuratively rather than literally. Explain your thinking so that students have an opportunity to use your model when they try a similar passage.
Interaction with students	Provide several more examples of idioms. Have students do as you did in figuring out what the idioms mean.
Closure	Have the students read sections of *The Island of the Blue Dolphins.* As they do, point out the idioms and have them interpret their meaning in the context of the passage.
Desired Outcome	Given an example of literature in which the author uses idioms, students will be able to interpret the author's meaning in that passage.

---

language forms such as idioms, similes, metaphors, and onomatopoeia. These literary devices are best taught while reading the literature. Figure 14.11 illustrates what such a lesson might look like.

There are, then, two major ways of guiding students' reading of the recreational text found in upper-grade literature classes. The first is to use techniques such as the DRL and the DRTL to guide student's interpretation of the literature. The second is to teach students to interpret the special literary devices associated with good literature.

TECHNIQUES FOR GUIDING FUNCTIONAL READING

Content-area textbooks in the upper grades become increasingly packed with conceptual and factual information. Social studies texts introduce more and more terms, names, dates, relationships, abstract ideas, specialized meanings, generalizations and references. Science texts use more technical terms, symbols, formulas, abbreviations, complex classifications, and more subtle relationships. Mathematics texts pack more abstract information into small sections in which the precise meaning is to be extracted. Teachers need to guide students in comprehending content in these functional texts.

The techniques developed in the previous chapter can continue to be used. For instance, SQ3R is an excellent study technique students can continue to use in the upper grades. However, because of the increased complexity of the material, upper-grade teachers often find it necessary to provide additional guidance such as the three specific kinds suggested here.

First, teachers often find it useful to guide functional reading by teaching a technique called question-answer relationships, also known as QARs.* Since much upper-grade reading is guided by author- and/or teacher-made questions, the QAR technique was devised to help students decide where answers to various types of questions might be found. For instance, students are taught that answers can be found in a sentence on the page (right there) or in several sentences or paragraphs (think and search) or in your own prior knowledge (on your own). Hence, when faced with the task of answering questions in functional texts, students think about the question, its relationship to what is said in the text, and where to go to find the answer. A sample lesson on teaching the QAR techinique to upper-grade students is contained in Figure 14.12.

A second technique for guiding students' reading of functional text is to give them study guides. Study guides are precisely what the name implies: guides to the study of the material in the text. As upper-grade functional text gets increasingly complex, its comprehension also gets more complex. Many teachers prepare study guides for students to use as they read a particular chapter or text. For instance, if a science chapter on classifying animals is organized in a particularly complex way, a teacher might provide a study guide that directs students to particularly relevant sections of the text. If a social studies text requires literal thinking at one point, requires thinking about implied relationships at another, and requires generalizations beyond the text at another, a teacher might write a study guide that cues students to the kind of thinking required in various sections of the text. If a teacher wants students to pay particular attention to certain charts and illustrations or certain sections of a text, a study guide could be written directing students to those particular materials. Study guides can take many forms, from lists of questions; to matching tasks; to simple directions for what to do first, second, and third; to complex charts that students must complete as they read. Whatever their form, their purpose is to help students comprehend functional text.

* Raphael, T. Question-answering strategies for children. *Reading Teacher, 36*(2), 186–191.

A third technique for guiding reading of functional text is the structured overview. Structured overviews are particularly useful for text that introduces many new words. They usually consist of a picture or a schematic diagram of the important words in the text that shows how they are related to one another. Figures 2.1 and 2.4, which describe the reading curriculum, are a type of structured overview. The idea is to show a picture of the important words and how they relate to each other. Structured overviews enable students to preview and relate the major ideas that will be covered in their reading, thereby creating expectations that are helpful in comprehending the text. An example of a lesson using structured overviews is seen in Figure 14.13.

There are many modifications of QARs, study guides, and structured overviews that teachers develop and use when teaching content-area subjects using functional text. All these modifications have one thing in common, however—they are all attempts by the teacher to steer students' comprehension of targeted content.

Figure 14.12 **An example of how to teach students to use QARS to comprehend the context of functional text**

Background	You are teaching a science unit "Systems of the Body." The students have been directed to read a chapter in their science text and answer the questions found at the end of the chapter. You want your students to use QARs as an aid in finding the correct answer.
Lesson Sequence	
Introduction	After the purposes of the science unit have been set explain to students that they will more easily find the answers to the questions if they use a technique called QARs.
Modeling	Demonstrate for students how you identify whether a question is a "right there" (the answer is found right on the page), a "think and search" (the answer requires information from more than one sentence or paragraph), or an "on my own" (the answer is not in the selection, but instead, is found in the reader's own knowledge) question. Explain how you thought about the question, the information in the text, and where to find the answer.
Interaction with students	Give students samples of text and related questions. Have them talk out loud about how they looked through the information provided in the text and then decided how to answer the question. Gradually increase the complexity of the text material as students become more proficient at question answering.

Closure   Have students apply their understanding of QARs in answering the questions at the end of the science chapter "Systems of the Body."

Desired Outcome   When required to answer questions about text material the students will first analyze the question in terms of where the answer can be obtained (right in the sentence, within several sentences or paragraphs, or from background experience).

Figure 14.13 **An example of how to use structural overviews to ensure student comprehension of functional text**

Background   You are teaching a unit on the branches of the federal government and how the system of checks and balances works. You want the students to read the appropriate chapter in the textbook, but you are concerned about the heavy conceptual load.

Lesson Sequence

Introduction   Select those words in the chapter that represent the key concepts about how the branches of the federal government work and arrange them into a conceptual diagram that shows their relationship to each other and to previously learned ideas. Encourage students to add related ideas from their own prior knowledge.

Modeling   While showing the structured overview talk about the concepts, their relationship to each other, and how these concepts are the framework for the chapter to be read.

Interaction with students   As students begin reading sections of the chapter and encounter the various concepts in the structured overview, have them discuss how one concept is tied to another, how new information is added to old information, and how their prior knowledge is expanded.

Closure   After the chapter has been read modify the diagram of the structured overview to reflect the new ideas that emerged during the discussion. Display this modified overview and discuss it as a means for summarizing the chapter.

Desired Outcome   Given a content-area text on a given topic, students will understand the relationships among the various concepts discussed in the chapter.

ACTIVITIES TO DEVELOP
CONTENT OUTCOMES

The following are some illustrative activities that you can use when developing content outcomes in the upper grades.

1. Have students locate current examples of how humans modify their geographic environment.
2. Have students follow published weather reports for their location for an extended period and then try to account for the weather reports by applying meteorological theories. Have them try forecasting the weather.
3. Have students identify examples of social and technological changes by comparing historical accounts of an event with its contemporary counterparts. Some examples of issues that have persisted in American history are:

   Isolationism vs. foreign involvement
   How wealth is distributed
   Race relations
   Civil liberties
   Industrialization vs. conservation
   The balance of power between state and federal governments

4. Have students choose an item of current interest or concern and write an article on it. Encourage them to write an eye-catching caption for their article.
5. Have students read all the editorials on an editorial page. Have them write a letter to the editor on an editorial with which they disagree and another on an editorial with which they agree. Have them read and critique each other's letters.
6. Divide the class into collaborative groups of four or five and assign a newspaper story to each group. One member of each group reads their story aloud. Then each group rewrites the story as if they had been eyewitnesses. Have members of the group share their stories with other groups.
7. Have students collect folklore such as rope-jumping rhymes, counting-out rhymes, legends, or folk songs related to the area. Create a "Foxfire" book to be shared with other classes.
8. Have students make a collection of myths, legends, interesting

mottoes, and proverbs. Have them create a book with an attractive jacket and place the book in the library.

9. Have students plan an automobile trip they would like to take. Use road maps so they can determine their exact route.

10. Have students create travel brochures for the road trips planned in Activity 9.

11. Analogous stories written in the manner of old favorites offer a challenge to older students. Edward Lear's nonsense limericks can lead to original limericks and Rudyard Kipling's *Just So Stories* to other how-it-happened reports.

12. Panel discussions of various kinds can occur even though no two members of the panel have read the same book. Have students discuss stories in terms of the problems faced by the main characters. They can compare stories with one another and react in terms of the kind of solution presented in each story: did it involve magic, accident, or effort on the part of the particular character who is being discussed? Would the students have handled the problem in a different way if they had been there? Why or why not? How is each solution different from (or the same as) solutions mentioned by other members of the panel?

13. Have students identify the beliefs, attitudes, and values that constitute the so-called generation gap by keeping a file of articles and editorials written by representative younger and older people.

14. From newspaper accounts, have students identify a community problem that can be solved or eased by adolescents. Have them take appropriate social action.

15. Hold a mock press conference. Have the reporters carefully prepare questions beforehand. Two students can be the noted people being interviewed. Have students write articles on the press conference.

16. Select a topic and search for original manuscripts, old page proofs, first editions of books, book jackets, taped interviews with authors and other interesting persons in the community, or any other documentation related to the topic. Have students write history from original sources.

17. Have students keep diaries about memorable historical experiences as if they had lived through the period being read about. Add the diaries to the resources available to other people who are studying the topic.

18. Have students compare stock market behavior with news events reported on the front page of a newspaper.

INTEGRATING READING AND WRITING

Upper-grade English, social studies, and science teachers should involve students in writing activities associated with their content area. Most of the reading and writing that occurs in upper-grade content areas is embedded in topical units from the content area. For instance, social studies teachers may have units on the Civil War, or the development of laws, or the relationship between geography and economics, whereas science teachers may have units on simple machines, electricity, or photosynthesis. Although these units primarily focus on content outcomes associated with social studies and science, they can include reading and writing outcomes if teachers intentionally structure their content-area units to include reading and writing.

The following is an example of one such unit. It was taught as a social studies unit using the book *My Brother Sam Is Dead*, and it includes both reading and writing.

Reading and writing are closely integrated in the upper grades.

SAMPLE TEACHING UNIT

Resolution of Conflicts

Grade Level: Application
Overall Goal:
To learn how conflicts can be resolved.
Materials:
Students read a book that focuses on conflict and resolutions such as *My Brother Sam is Dead*, by James Lincoln Collier and Christopher Collier (New York: Fourwinder Press, 1974).

Objective 1 Students will recognize varying points of view in the story.

Warm-up discussion activity: Have the students discuss their feelings about the book, especially those that relate to the characters.

Reading–writing activity: Have the students categorize the feelings that were expressed and group those feelings according to various characters' (father, Tim) points of view. Students conclude with written statements of the varying points of view.

Assessment: Teach the students who cannot determine point of view with pronoun usage and connotative words usage.

Objective 2 Students will develop a point of view.

Discussion activity: Sam's brother, Tim, was often asked to state publicly which side he was on. Using this as a springboard, have the class generate other areas of conflict they are familiar with (weekend privileges, propositions to be voted on, school rules). For each topic provided, create an affirmative statement and a negative statement. Assign students to collaborative groups, one group taking the affirmative position, the other the negative position.

Collaborative group activity: Have the students collaborate to develop their position using examples and elaborations to support their position.

Objective 3 Students will defend their point of view.

Discussion activity: Have the students discuss how Tim had to defend his point of view. Using the examples generated, instruct students in persuasive writing.

Strategy Instruction: Instruct students in components of persuasive writing, that is, persuasive writing contains a statement indicating the importance of the audience, examples, and elaborations that support the positions and an appeal for the audience to act regarding the position.

Writing–reading activity: Have the students collaborate to write a position paper using the components of persuasive writing.

Objective 4   Given the story *My Brother Sam is Dead*, students state how varying points of view created conflict.

Discussion Activity: Have the students will review the varying points of view and how these led to intrapersonal conflicts within the characters.

Reading–writing activity: Have the students list the conflicts in the story *My Brother Sam is Dead* and support each stated conflict with examples.

Objective 5   Given information about conflict, students will develop strategies for resolving conflict.

Discussion activity: The story *My Brother Sam is Dead* contains three types of conflict: (1) intrapersonal conflicts within individuals who are torn between different points of view; (2) personal conflicts among family members who believe differently; and (3) national conflict among those who want linkage with England and those who want to separate. Have students discuss these conflicts in terms of how people try to persuade others to their view, including appeals to authority (credibility or power of the source); motivational appeals (needs, fears, of the receiver); and substantive appeals (relations between phenomenon such as cause and effect, analogy, deductive or inductive reasoning). For instance, on page 6 Sam's father says, "In my house I will decide what constitutes treason." His argument is dependent upon his perceived authority. Center discussion around questions such as: When can conflict be handled by talk? How many of the conflicts in the book could have been resolved by talk? What parallel examples of national, intra-

personal, or interpersonal conflict can be identified? Which of these can be resolved through
talk?

Reading–writing activity: Have students in collaborative groups write a scenario of a conflict they
have observed that includes needed background information to explain the conflict. Have the students
then read the scenarios and try to resolve the conflict through role playing. As the students observe
the role play have them assess the effectiveness of
the resolution and critique the ways used to resolve
the conflict. Finally, have the students brainstorm
alternative methods of resolving conflicts based on
the three methods of persuasion.

ADDITIONAL INTEGRATED
READING–WRITING ACTIVITIES

1. Provide pictures where an emotion is clearly illustrated (exhaltation, anger, happiness). Have the students discuss what events led to the emotion and then write a story that climaxes with this emotion. Students read in collaborative groups to judge if story line is appropriate and to provide feedback about the best sections.

2. Have students write think-pinks (two one-syllable words that rhyme such as *sad lad*) and provide definitions (What is an unhappy boy?). Place them in books with questions on one page and answers on the following page. Thinky-pinkies (two-syllable words) can also be written (What is an angry devil? *steamin' demon*). Thinkity-pinkities can also be written (What is an exact car accident? a *precision collision*).

3. Have students read a mystery story such as the ones about Encyclopedia Brown (*Encylopedia Brown and the Case of the Dead Eagles,* by Donald J. Sobal) individually or in groups. Discuss different endings that could have occurred by having students answer what-if questions. Have students write their new endings for the story.

4. Have students read a number of ghost stories (*The Haunted Trailer,* by Robert Arthur, *Ghost Story,* by Genevieve Gray, *Hex House,* by Betty Levine). Have them discuss what makes ghost stories scary and then write ghost stories using the results of the discussion.

5. Have students discuss sayings such as: Sometimes you get more by giv-ing. It's better to give than receive. Grass is greener on the other side of the fence. You only get what you take for yourself. Students select a

saying and write a short critical essay about it. Other students read and critique the essay.

6. After sharing a book together, have students write a letter from one of the book's characters to another that shares what happened after the story ended. Example: Using the character Kit in *Witch of Blackberry Pond* (by Elizabeth Speare) a student might write to a cousin about what happened after the witch trial.

7. Have students create lists of things to do before they finish school. Compile the lists in a book and note when each item is completed. The list can be added to.

8. Have students create poems and compile concrete poem books made up of poetry formatted to visually reflect the subject of the poem. Example:

m
erry
Christma
shappynewye
armerrychristmas
happynewyearmerrych
ris
tmas
happ
ynew
year

9. Have students place themselves in the role of a famous sports person (a tennis player, a gymnast, a runner) who drops his or her racket, falls off the parallel bars, or trips during the last 10 yards. Discuss what the player might do, think, and say. Have students write a poem using these circumstances.

10. Read the book *The King Who Rained,* then discuss figures of speech. Brainstorm figures of speech like *frog in my throat, I'm a little hoarse* (horse)*, I'm playing bridge.* Have students write and illustrate their own books and then read them to younger children.

CHARACTERISTICS OF AN INSTRUCTIONAL DAY

As noted in the overview at the beginning of this chapter, an instructional day at the upper-grade level is often quite different from the instructional day in elementary school. In the upper grades school is usually departmentalized according to subject-matter areas and students are often grouped by ability. Consequently, rather than spending all day with one teacher and a heterogeneous group of students, upper-grade students see several different teachers each day and are often homogeneously grouped with other students of similar ability. All this is further complicated by the fact that in many school districts there is no formal reading instruction in the upper grades except for those students who are reading well below grade level. Each content-area teacher provides instruction in attitude, process, and content outcomes. The heaviest emphasis, however, is on content outcomes, because content-area teachers are responsible for teaching the subject matter of their field.

CONCLUSION

The unique characteristics of the upper grades greatly influences the reading instruction provided there. Students are grouped by ability, teachers only teach a single subject, and no one has overall responsibility for reading instruction. As a result, reading instruction is often confined to content-area textbooks. It is not unusual, therefore, for both students and teachers to ignore reading.

However, if students are to move through the Application Stage of developmental reading growth and go on to the Power Stage, reading instruc-

An instructional day includes collaborative efforts.

tion in the upper grades must be deliberate and systematic. If you teach content-area subjects, you must consciously try to integrate into content instruction the reading instruction associated with attitude, process, and content outcomes. In the end, it is the demands of teaching these reading outcomes within the framework of the content areas that is the distinctive aspect of upper-grade reading.

CHECK YOUR UNDERSTANDING

Now that you have read the chapter, check your understanding by answering the Focus Questions presented at the beginning of the chapter. If you cannot answer one or more of the questions, return to the chapter, find the section that corresponds to the question, and reread.

SUGGESTED READINGS

Barrow, L. H., Kristo, J. V., & Andrew. B. (1984). Building bridges between science and reading. *Reading Teacher, 38*(2), 188–192.

Bromley, K. D. (1985). Precise writing and outlining enhance content learning. *Reading Teacher, 38*(4), 406–411.

Degler, L. S. (1978). Using the newspaper to develop reading comprehension skills. *Journal of Reading, 21*(4), 339–342.

Dwyer, E. J. (1982). Guided reading in poetry: Combining aesthetic appreciation and development of essential skills. *Reading Psychology, 3*(3), 261–270.

Freeman, R. H. (1983). Poetry writing in the upper elementary grades. *Reading Teacher, 37*(3), 238–242.

Holbrook, H. T. (1985). The quality of textbooks. *Reading Teacher, 38*(7), 680–683.

Lange, J. T. (1983). Using S2RAT to improve reading skills in the content areas. *Reading Teacher, 36*(4), 402–404.

Poostay, E. J. (1984). Show me your underlines: A strategy to teach comprehension. *Reading Teacher, 37*(9), 828–830.

Raphael, T. E. (1984). Teaching learners about sources of information for answering comprehension questions. *Journal of Reading, 27*(4), 303–311.

Richgels, D. J., & Hansen, R. (1984). Gloss: Helping students apply both skills and strategies in reading content texts. *Journal of Reading, 27*(4), 312–317.

Rogers, D. G. (1984). Assessing study skills. *Journal of Reading, 27*(4), 346–354.

Steward, O., & Green, D. S. (1983). Test-taking skills for standardized tests of reading. *Reading Teacher, 36*(7), 634–638.

Stott, J. C. (1982). A structuralist approach to teaching novels in the elementary grades. *Reading Teacher, 36*(2), 136–143.

Widmann, V. F. (1978). Developing oral reading ability in teenagers through the presentation of children's stories. *Journal of Reading, 21*(4), 329–334.

Wood, K. D., & Mateja, J. A. (1983). Adapting secondary level strategies for use in elementary classrooms. *Reading Teacher, 36*(6), 492–496.

Wrights, J. P., & Andreasen, N. L. (1980). Practice in using location skills in a content area. *Reading Teacher, 34*(2), 184–186.

PART V

SPECIAL INSTRUCTIONAL PROBLEMS

Throughout this book the point is made that classroom reading instruction is complex and difficult. One reason for this is the unique problems encountered when teaching reading.

Part 5 presents three special instructional problems. To ensure that you receive the best information about each, we have asked experts in each area to write the respective chapters. Chapter 15 focuses on the role of computers in classroom reading instruction and is written by Dr. Michael Kamil of the University of Illinois at Chicago; Chapter 16 focuses on mainstreaming and working with gifted and handicapped students and is written by Dr. Sandra Michelsen of Valparaiso University; and Chapter 17 focuses on special language problems and is written by Dr. Maria Torres of Michigan State University.

At the end of this unit you should be able to describe the decisions you will be faced with regarding the special instructional problems discussed in the unit, and you should be able to answer questions such as the following:

1. What is the role of computers in classroom reading instruction?
2. How will you approach the problems of teaching mainstreamed students, both gifted and handicapped?

3. What instructional modifications will you make to account for special language problems encountered in your classroom?

CHAPTER **15**

Computers and Classroom Reading Instruction

Michael L. Kamil

GETTING READY

In this chapter you will learn what a computer is and what it can do. You will also learn how computers can and cannot (or should not) be used in reading and reading instruction. Finally, a list of sources for information about computers and their uses in reading and language arts will be provided.

FOCUS QUESTIONS

As you read this chapter use the following questions to guide your understanding of computers and how they relate to reading instruction.

1. What are the potential relationships between computers and language instruction?
2. How do computers work?
3. How are computers being applied to classroom instruction in reading and language arts?
4. How do you evaluate computer software designed for use with reading and language arts?
5. How do you evaluate computer hardware?
6. What are some cautions to keep in mind when using computers for classroom reading instruction?
7. What can you expect to be future classroom uses of computers?

USES OF COMPUTERS IN
READING AND LANGUAGE ARTS

There are three distinct ways in which computers impinge on reading and language arts instruction. The first is the relatively new area of *computer literacy*. Traditionally, literacy has been conceived of as being wholly related to reading and writing. With the development of electronic computers (beginning around 1945) and the ultimate development of home microcomputers, there has been a growing need to teach students about the uses of computers. Thus, the concept of computer literacy has evolved with the growing prevalence of computers.

There is little agreement on just what constitutes computer literacy, just as there is dispute over definitions of conventional literacy. The major issue is usually whether or not computer literacy should include knowledge of how to program. It is often argued that knowledge of programming computers is analogous to learning arithmetic. That is, hand calculators make the performance of the mechanics of arithmetic obsolete, but computational knowledge is viewed as important for conceptual understanding. Those who urge that programming be taught as part of computer literacy often suggest that this

Computers can be used for reading and writing.

knowledge is important to understanding computers even though the user may never apply it.

Other aspects of computer literacy include familiarization with operating a computer, the uses one can make of computers, and the social consequences of computers. Some good sources for extended discussions of computer literacy are included in the reference sources at the end of this chapter.

The second way in which computers relate to reading and language arts is in the use of computers to deliver instruction for reading and writing. These uses can be further classified as drill and practice, computer-assisted learning (CAI), simulations, and uses as aids in instructional management. These are the computer uses most people consider central to reading and language arts. Each of these will be discussed in a separate section.

A third way in which a computer can be used is as an extremely powerful tool for writing, particularly when it is coupled with word-processing software. Whereas this is also an instructional use of computers, it is becoming more prevalent as an indispensable aid in composition. A word-processing program can allow a student to revise, edit, correct, and manipulate a text before printing a final copy. It can eliminate the repetitious work of copying when incorporating changes in a manuscript.

Another use of computers is for retrieval of information from centralized data bases. Many libraries have card catalog systems that can be viewed from a computer terminal. Commercial computer services like Dow Jones, Compuserve, and The Source have information banks that can also be accessed by computers that are appropriately equipped.

Before proceeding to examine the uses of computers in education in greater detail, it is important to consider what a computer is and what it can do as well as the strengths and limitations of using computers for educational applications.

A BRIEF INTRODUCTION TO COMPUTERS

The question most often asked about computers is, What is a computer? This is also one of the most difficult questions to answer in terms that are meaningful to the average person. At the simplest level it is easy to say that a computer is an automatic electronic device that processes information. However, there are few elements in that definition that make it easy for one to incorporate the concept of *computer* into a schema.

Computers process information that is stored electronically in codes. These codes are represented by *bits* (short for *bi*nary dig*it*), the smallest unit of information a computer can process. A bit can be thought of as something similar to a switch. That is, each bit is either on or off. Mathematically, this is represented as either a 1 or a 0. For most microcomputers, groups of eight bits are used to represent a *byte,* often referred to as a computer *word.* When the memory capacity of a computer is described as 48K or 256K, for example, the units are bytes of memory.

Every letter, number, or other symbol used in written English is assigned a code, called an ASCII code (for American Standard Code for Information Interchange). Each code can be stored in a single byte. Every character displayed including spaces, periods, and so forth has to be represented in a single byte of memory. Text storage uses up large amounts of memory; 64K of memory, without any other considerations, could hold the equivalent of about 35 pages of typewritten text (assuming about 300 words to a page).

COMPONENTS OF COMPUTERS

Every computer must have a *central processing unit* (CPU), memory, and peripheral devices to allow information to be *input* to the computer and *output* from it. The CPU is like an executive, making decisions about how to handle information coming into and going out of a computer. It is the CPU that does the real work of the computer.

Memory is generally divided into two sorts: RAM and ROM. *RAM* stands for *random access memory.* The contents of RAM are said to be volatile — they disappear when the power is turned off. The user of a computer can change the contents of RAM at any time and can tell the computer to read the contents or write into any part of it. Conversely, *ROM* stands for *read only memory.* It is memory that cannot be changed and is nonvolatile. It always remains the same, even when the power is off. ROM memory is usually reserved for special instructions that the CPU needs; for example, when the computer is first turned on.

When describing the memory size of a computer, it is customary to refer only to the RAM memory, since this is the only portion of memory that the user can control. When a computer has, for example, 64K of memory, it actualy has 65,236 words or bytes of RAM memory. (*K* stands for 2^{10}, or 1,024.) RAM memory is critical since it is the working memory of the computer. If a program cannot fit in the amount of RAM, it cannot be run on the computer.

The normal input device for microcomputers is a keyboard. Output is usually accomplished by a VDT, or *video display terminal.* Other output devices can include printers, voice synthesizers (to allow the computer to be understood, for example, by someone who could not read), and a range of other machinery the computer can control.

To be really useful, a computer has to be connected to some sort of storage device, typically a tape recorder or a disk drive. With these storage devices any program can be stored and kept for use at a later time. When the computer is turned on, it can be instructed to read a program from one of its storage devices into RAM. After the program is loaded into memory, it can be "run." The storage capacity of tape and disk drives is very large — many programs can be stored on a single cassette or diskette. However, each of the programs stored on the diskette or tape must be small enough to fit into the amount of RAM available to the computer.

A printer is another important peripheral device that is often attached to computers. For some instructional computing, printed output *(hardcopy)* is not often needed. However, when a student must be able to take along a copy of an assignment, worksheet, or even a composition, a printer is indispensable. There are two categories of printers, dot matrix and letter quality. Dot matrix printers are so named because they form each printed character by making impressions of appropriate dots in locations in a matrix. This accounts for some of the poor legibility in computer-printed text. The greater the number of dots in the matrix, the better the quality of the individual letters.

Letter quality printers often use *daisy wheels* to form the characters by impacting a ribbon with a wheel containing the individual characters. This is similar to the way in which typewriters operate, and the resulting print is usually indistinguishable from typed text.

Some microcomputers come equipped with what is called a *hard disk* drive. This is a storage device that is similar to a diskette, but with far greater capacity. Floppy diskettes are so named because they can easily bend. Hard disks cannot; they come in sealed cases and the data stored on them is less likely to be subject to accidental loss. The major advantage of a hard disk is the amount of storage. Whereas a floppy diskette can store from about 100K to 400K of programs or data, a hard disk has the capacity to store upward of about 5MB (5 million bytes). Note that the smallest figure for a hard disk represents the equivalent of approximately 50 floppy diskettes.

Hard disks are relatively expensive and cannot be used easily with all microcomputers. They are most beneficial when the tasks the computer will perform requires access to a large amount of data or the need to store a large number of programs or records.

HARDWARE, SOFTWARE, AND COURSEWARE

A very common distinction when dealing with computers is that between hardware and software. *Hardware* refers to all of the physical components of a computer. The CPU, the disk drives, the monitor, the memory chips, and the like are all hardware. The computer itself and all of its peripherals fall into the hardware category. In contrast, *software* is the term for all of the instructions that are used to tell the computer what to do. Some of these instructions can be stored in ROM so that the computer will, for example, automatically know what to do when the power is turned on. Other examples of software are the commercial programs that are sets of instructions that tell the computer what to do and the order in which to do them. A computer cannot do anything without software; that is, computers must be instructed to perform tasks, and those tasks must be described in explicit detail in the software.

For educational materials, there is a third category called *courseware*. Courseware represents all of the supplemental materials that can be used to help integrate the computer-based instruction into a curriculum. Courseware might include teachers' manuals, additional readings for students, follow-up activities, or cross-references to other materials that might be used to teach related skills or content. In short, courseware explains to teachers how the software can or should be used educationally.

WHAT IS NEEDED TO USE A COMPUTER FOR EDUCATIONAL PURPOSES?

There is no simple answer to this question because the type of computer that one needs for a specific educational purpose will depend entirely on what the purpose is. Many educational programs can be run on small-capacity, inexpensive computers. Some applications that will involve a great deal of record keeping or other management activity can only be accomplished on computers that have greater capacity and are more expensive. This limitation is only one of the reasons why the prospective user of computers in education must carefully determine the purpose and goals of the computer-based instruction.

EXAMPLES OF APPLICATIONS IN READING AND LANGUAGE ARTS

Software for drill and practice is, at its simplest, merely a translation of ordinary workbook pages into electronic form. Thus, the computer might simply be used to present a large number of similar exercises to teach, for example, how to match words and the graphic representations of them. The key here is that the software does not do more than give students an opportunity to practice a skill that has been previously taught by the teachers. As will be seen in the section on evaluating software, the value of this type of software is dependent on the curriculum into which it is placed. However, since it is easy to produce drill and practice software, a large proportion of the available software is of this type. The best of drill and practice software can be a substantial improvement over conventional drill and practice worksheets.

Computer-assisted instruction, or tutorial software, involves using the computer to present material for learning. Any explanations that a teacher might present to a class, small group, or individual can be incorporated into this format. A program might present explanations of syllabication rules, methods for locating the main idea of a passage, or techniques for clarifying pronoun references. For reading, the computer might also be used to teach spelling–sound correspondences. The distinguishing characteristic of this type of software is that it attempts to *explain* the material, even though practice may be a part of the lesson.

Simulations are not so common as the other types of software. The idea behind a simulation is that it artificially reproduces a situation that would be otherwise difficult to create. Examples of these programs are not so common in reading and language arts as they are in science. One example allows the student to interact with a computer in a conversationlike dialogue, with the aim of improving language skills. Similarly, adventure games simulate real situations of danger—moon walks, desert islands, haunted houses, and so forth. These programs help develop problem-solving skills and can be incorporated directly into reading curricula.

Another class of software is designed to be used as tools in other language arts instruction. Word-processing software is the best example of this. Students can use a word processor as a facilitating tool for writing and editing. Many software packages allow students to use a word processor to create messages that can be sent to other students. Most of these systems could be used by an instructor to provide informative feedback to students on their compositions. Current practices in teaching writing stress the importance of editing. The real value of word processors over conventional methods of composing is that it allows for fast, easy, and efficient editing.

Finally, there is a great deal of software that is designed to help in the management of instruction. There are two kinds of computer-managed instruction (CMI) systems: program dependent and program independent. The program dependent management systems are designed to work with a specific program. They can often help teachers organize a class for instruction, assist in grading, and even produce individualized educational plans. The program independent systems allow a teacher to specify the curriculum objectives to be used with *any* instruction. An important issue must be raised here: the use of CMI systems does not guarantee better instruction. At best, it probably only relieves a teacher of a great deal of manual record keeping. The ultimate responsibility for student learning, aside from being with the student, will be on the teacher or on other types of computer software.

EVALUATING READING AND LANGUAGE ARTS SOFTWARE

There are some considerations in the evalution of software that are common to all educational fields. There are also some unique considerations in the evaluation of reading and language arts software.

GENERAL CONSIDERATIONS IN EVALUATING SOFTWARE

The primary concern in evaluating software for any area of instruction should be its consistency with the rest of the curriculum. That is, whatever else enters into an evaluation, the software must deliver instruction that is consistent with the other forms of instruction a student will receive. For example, software that presents individual skill-based drill and practice exercises would be useless in an environment in which the remainder of reading instruction was done from a whole-language perspective. In other words, the teaching goals of computer-based instruction should be the same as, or similar to, those for the other types of instruction in the school setting.

A second concern is that the software should do its task better than could be done in another instructional mode. If the computer-based instruction has no advantage over other instruction, it should be rejected. "Better" is not a precise criterion. Its meaning will depend on the type of software and the particular school in which the evaluation is conducted. Better, as a criterion, should serve primarily to remind an evaluator that a piece of software must have some advantage over other instruction before it is implemented.

Because curricular goals are critical in assessing the value of computer software, the very first step in conducting an evaluation is to specify those goals as completely as possible. This entails specifying (1) the beginning state of student knowledge, (2) the desired outcomes of instruction, and (3) the resources (e.g., amount of time, number of teachers) available for accomplishing the task. Only when all of these are specified can software be selected for individual school or classroom needs.

The diversity of curricular goals and types of computer software means that each type of software may have to be evaluated according to a different set of criteria. This means simply that there is no single evaluation form that will be appropriate for all software. Each evaluation should be tailored to local and individual needs. However, all software of a given type for a given purpose should be evaluated according to the same set of criteria.

SPECIFIC CRITERIA FOR READING AND LANGUAGE ARTS SOFTWARE

There is an important characteristic that is often overlooked when evaluating reading and language arts software. It is important to assess the readability level of the text that is presented on the screen. While this is almost never overlooked in evaluations of conventional materials, it is almost always overlooked in software evaluations.

Similarly, one should be careful to assess the level of prior knowledge and cognitive abilities that are assumed by the program. These will be critical to a student's success in using the program, and the time to find out about them is during the evaluation, not during instruction.

For drill and practice software, the criteria that are important include the appropriateness of feedback. Does the program let the student know what was right and wrong at the appropriate time? Do the exercises get easier if the student misses a few and harder if the student succeeds? In general, software, to be most effective, should go beyond simple drill and practice and include elements of explanation when the student is not performing at acceptable levels. However, much of the drill and practice software is an improvement over conventional forms. If your teaching style incorporates drill and practice, computers may help you do it more effectively.

Evaluating CAI software requires examination of the instructional strategies and the presentation modes, as well as all the other criteria discussed above. The clarity of the instruction is important. Does the program teach, rather than just talk about or mention content? Does the instruction adjust to the level of the students by branching to segments that are either easier or harder? Feedback should, as in other programs, be appropriate. It should neither demean the student nor be unrealistically optimistic (particularly when the student has not done well).

In addition, the program should help maintain the student's attention by using sound, graphics, or animation where appropriate. These elements should not distract from the basic goal of the program, however. Good software will allow the user to select options like sound on or off.

Students should be able to leave the program in the middle of it and return at a later time (e.g., after recess!). They should also be able to get help by asking for it (usually by pressing a special key). Furthermore, they should not have to spend an inordinate amount of time reviewing instructions if they already know them.

Good CAI software will incorporate a management system so that both students and teachers will know what progress has been made and what remains to be done. This can encourage students to work at an optimum pace. The management system should be easy to use and understand. It should also be consistent with what is done in noncomputer contexts.

Finally, the CAI software should be factually accurate. Whereas this seems obvious, even conventional textbooks have been published with errors in them. The programs should also be examined for appropriate grammar, syntax, spelling, and the like. It is desirable that the programs be modifiable, but at the very least, a good evaluation will make the user aware of limitations that have to be considered. Teachers may have to go so far as to produce auxiliary materials to correct deficiencies in software.

Simulations are the most difficult sort of software to evaluate. The important criteria to remember in evaluating simulations is that they must actually accomplish the purpose for which they are being used. Often the simulation is only partly relevant to the curriculum goal. In this case it may be more work to incorporate the simulation into your instruction than to teach without it.

A second consideration is the amount of time it takes to participate in a simulation compared to the amount of learning. Whereas it may be enjoyable for students to simulate certain aspects of their learning, an alternative approach might be more sensible if the achievement is not commensurate with the time.

Evaluating software as tools for other tasks can take almost as many forms as there are tools or pieces of software. As an example, the evaluation of a word processor should be done in light of the students' abilities and time they will have available for using it. Ideally, word processors should be easy to use, require little or no specialized computer knowledge, be able to produce all of the effects the user wants, and make editing simpler than it otherwise would be. Optional but desirable features include spelling checkers and even some sort of stylistic analyses. Again, the importance of these features will depend to a large degree on the particular aims of an individual teacher in a given classroom environment.

These criteria for evaluating reading and language arts software are meant to be merely examples. As indicated previously, there is no one evaluation. Each situation is different, and the evaluation must ultimately be based on the students, the teaching environment, the resources, and the curricular goals.

After you find good software, *then* try to find a machine that can run it. If you do not find software that meets your needs, it is reasonable to use it *if you can adapt it (or your other instruction) to make up for the deficiencies.* Most importantly, though, do not use poor software simply because there is nothing better.

HARDWARE

In an ideal situation, users would first make decisions about the software they want and *then* make a decision about what hardware would be best for running the software. However, the realities of most situations are that the user often finds the hardware in place. The next section describes what to do in either case.

EVALUATING HARDWARE

If a teacher has examined software and has decided that there are pieces of it that are really critical to implementation, the hardware decision is very simple: find a computer or computers that will run the selected software. Remember, the primary goal is to teach students. The hardware will only deliver the instruction. If teachers do not concentrate on the instructional aspects, their efforts will be doomed from the beginning.

However, many computer users find that they already have hardware. If that is the case, the situation should be reversed from that described in the previous paragraph. A teacher should examine all of the pieces of software that are available for the available hardware and determine whether any of it is worth using. Teachers must not be afraid to reach a negative decision. There may be times when curricular needs are not met by the available software.

In the event teachers are lucky enough to choose their own hardware, they must evaluate it along many dimensions, much the same as they did for software. The relative importance of each dimension will differ for each educational environment, just as the importance of software criteria varied for different situations.

Price is always an important consideration, particularly in times of tight fiscal policy. However, what is available for the money is equally important. In an evaluation, a teacher must consider what the hardware will be able to do: How much memory does the machine have? Is it expandable? Can peripherals be added a few at a time? Does the machine have color and/or graphics capabilities? Can it produce sound, voice, or music? How legible is the screen display? (Note how important this last is for the teaching of reading and language arts!) How compatible is the hardware with other hardware in the same schools or in schools nearby? What kind of repair or service facilities will be available for the machines? Finally, the question of how much software support is available is important. That is, teachers must ask how much new soft-

Computer hardware being used by a student.

ware is likely to be produced for the machines. This last can only be estimated, but it is important.

To gather data, teachers should examine the hardware themselves — in the configuration they want to use, not a simpler or a more sophisticated version. They should also try to find users of the hardware and determine what their experiences have been. There are also reviews of hardware published by many of the resources listed at the end of this chapter.

CAUTIONS AND LIMITATIONS
OF COMPUTERS

When using computers in reading and language arts instruction, there are several important limitations and cautions. One of the most basic of these limitations is that, at the present time, the capacity of computers to speak and listen is relatively primitive. That means that those students who have not achieved at least a minimum reading and writing level will not be able to use much of the available software.

PROBLEMS OF SPEECH INPUT AND OUTPUT

There are also problems with the speech production element of CAI for reading. Several approaches to speech production have been used. The simplest technique has been to tape-record whatever speech or language the program is going to present. A computer then can control the tape and play the appropriate segments during the lesson. However, there are some difficulties in searching back or skipping ahead on the tape.

A second alternative has been to synthesize speech so that a computer can produce any segment at any point in the program. Votrax technology has been used for a long time in the PLATO computer system, even though the voice quality is not so good as would often be required. Another more recent development with better voice quality is the Borg-Warner Ufonic device for Apple computers. Another version has been developed by IBM for use with its *Write To Read* software.

A third speech production alternative has been to "digitize" speech. That is, speech is converted to computer codes (0's and 1's) and is reconstructed when needed. The voice quality of the best digitized speech is as good as a tape recording. The limitation is that the codes for digitizing speech take up a great deal of storage space in the computer and space is usually at a premium in the microcomputers commonly used in educational environments.

Speech input (or talking to the computer) is much more limited than speech output. Technology has provided us with computers that are capable of recognizing small, limited sets of words. However, it is not possible, at present, for computers to recognize any word by any student with 100 percent accuracy. If there is a training phase during which the computer can "listen" to a student speak the words to be used, accuracy for a small set of words can be as high or higher than 90 percent.

Thus, for most practical purposes, it is not possible at present for a computer to listen to a student read and make consistently accurate judgments about fluency and accuracy. It is only possible to have a computer speak to a student and then only with relatively sophisticated microcomputers. Advances in technology may make dramatic improvements in this area.

PROBLEMS WITH VISUAL DISPLAY

Another critical problem for reading instruction with computers is the quality of the displays. That is, many computer users report that they have visual problems, fatigue, headaches, and other ailments after working with and reading from a computer video display. Some research has shown that the speed of reading from computer displays may be as much as 25 percent slower than from a similar but conventionally printed hardcopy. These problems may be accentuated by the tendency for less expensive microcomputers to use television displays rather that higher resolution monitors.

TRANSFER PROBLEMS

An important problem concerns whether instruction given by computer transfers to other, noncomputer situations. That is, students who learn material in CAI settings may not make the conection between performance during the CAI lesson and applying that learning when reading books. Although transfer of learning is critical for sound teaching, students rarely transfer learning spontaneously. Because many studies show only moderate achievement gains in CAI programs, it is essential that teachers using CAI constantly evaluate and monitor student progress in transferring learning.

WHAT ABOUT THE FUTURE?

For the novice computer user, the array of equipment, software, possible uses, and choices to be made is overwhelming. Beginning computer users are also overwhelmed by the rate of introduction of new hardware and software. It will take a great deal of effort to keep up with new developments while learning about those that already exist.

What is in store for the future? In terms of hardware, teachers can expect

Good instruction is an important part of learning to use computers.

to see better sound quality integrated into computer software. Speech input capabilities are likely to be added to microcomputers as well. In short, teachers may soon see computers that can listen as well as speak to students during reading instruction. The development of the video disk will allow more realistic graphic displays to be presented. The amount of information that can be stored on video disks will allow far more realistic simulations and more extensive lesson activities for CAI. Of course, computers will become cheaper, have more memory capacity, and have more flexibility. Most of the limitations mentioned previously should be overcome shortly. Once the hardware limitations are gone, it will be up to software developers to provide sound instructional programs that can make use of the capabilities of the computer.

In software teachers should see the development of improved instructional programs that are closely related to curriculum concerns. Computers will be used to enhance certain instructional tasks, like word processing, and will be restricted in others. As greater hardware capacity becomes available, software will take advantage of it. Programs will be able to provide a greater range of instruction, remediation, and management than before. As computer networks develop, students will have easy access to data bases, other computer users, and instruction that would not normally be available at a local site.

Input for software content will be sought from teachers and students with an emphasis on curricular unity rather than on isolated bits of software. Learning in the ultimate computer environment will be free from many of the constraints of the conventional classroom. Teachers will be able to deal with many of the more difficult instructional problems like teaching cultural appreciation, values, and the like. Whereas this attractive goal is possible, it is still some distance in the future and requires even better technology, both hardware and software, than is available today. It is important that teachers prepare for the proliferation of computers by learning what they are and by using them when and where they are appropriate.

CHECK YOUR UNDERSTANDING

Now that you have read the chapter, check your understanding by answering the Focus Questions presented at the beginning of the chapter. If you cannot answer one of more questions, return to the chapter, find the section that corresponds to the question, and reread.

SUGGESTED READINGS

Auten, A. (1982). Computer literacy, Part III: CRT graphics. *Reading Teacher, 35*(8), 966–969.

Balajthy, E. (1984). Reinforcement and drill by microcomputer. *Reading Teacher, 37*(6), 490–494.

Balajthy, E. (1984). Computer simulations and reading. *Reading Teacher, 37*(7), 590–593.

D'Angelo, K. (1983). Computer books for young students: Diverse and difficult. *Reading Teacher, 36*(7), 626–633.

Dudley-Marling, C. C. (1985). Microcomputers, reading, and writing: Alternatives to drill and practice. *Reading Teacher, 38*(4), 388–391.

Krause, K. C. (1984). Choosing computer software that works. *Journal of Reading, 28*(1), 24–27.

Mason, G. E. (1983). The computer in the reading clinic. *Reading Teacher, 36*(6), 504–507.

O'Donnell, H. (1982). Computer literacy, part II: Classroom applications. *Reading Teacher, 35*(5), 614–617.

Phenix, J., & Hannon, E. (1984). Word processing in the grade one classroom. *Language Arts, 61*(8), 804–812.

SUGGESTED RESOURCES REGARDING COMPUTERS

PERIODICALS

The following periodicals are general computer publications that contain information on a wide variety of computers. The articles range in difficulty from novice level to advanced-user level.

Byte
Creative Computing
Commodore: The Microcomputer Magazine.
80 Micro
InCider
InfoWorld
Popular Computing
PC World
PC

The following periodicals are specifically designed to cover educational topics as they relate to computers:

Computers, Reading and Language Arts
Educational Computer
Electronic Learning
The Computing Teacher
Classroom Computer News
Teaching and Computing
Electronic Education

The following periodicals deal with theory and research in computers and education:

AEDS Journals
AEDS Monitor
Educational Technology
Journal of Computer-based Instruction
T.H.E. Journal

BOOKS

Coburn, P. et al. (1982). *Practical guide to computers in education.* Reading, MA: Addison-Wesley.

Dennis, J., & Kansky, R. (1984). *Instructional computing: An action guide for educators.* Glenview, IL: Scott, Foresman.

Federick, F. (1980). *Guide to microcomputers.* Washington, D.C.: Association for Educational Communications and Technology.

Geoffrion, L., & Geoffrion, O. (1982). *Computers and reading instruction.* Reading, MA: Addison-Wesley.

Grady, T., & Gawronski, J. (1983). *Computers in curriculum and instruction. Alexandria, VA: ASCD.*

Mason, G., Blanchard, J., & Daniel, D. (1983). *Computer applications in reading.* Newark, DE: International Reading Association.

Pantiel, M., & Petersen, B. (1984). *Kids, teachers and computers.* Englewood Cliffs, NJ: Prentice-Hall.

Peterson, D. (1984). *Intelligent schoolhouse.* Reston, VA: Reston.

Spencer, D. (1983). *An introduction to computers: Developing computer literacy.* Columbus, OH: Charles E. Merrill.

OTHER SOURCES OF INFORMATION

These sources provide information, in-service education, assistance for computer users, and often, co-op buying services for computer hardware and software. Not all of these organizations provide all of these functions.

Conduit, P.O. Box 338, Iowa City, IA 52240
Epie Institute, P.O. Box 620, Stony Brook, NY 11790
Micro-Ideas, 2941 Linneman St., Glenview, IL 60025
Microsift, Northwest Regional Educational Laboratory, 710 Second Avenue Southwest, Portland, OR 97204
Minnesota Educational Computer Consortiun (MECC), 2520 Broadway Drive, St. Paul, MN 55113
Technical Education Research Centers (TERC), Computer Resource Center, 8 Eliot Street, Cambridge, MA 02138

CHAPTER **16**_____

Exceptional Children and Mainstreaming

Sandra Michelsen

GETTING READY

As discussed in Chapter 3, it is a classroom reality that not all students have "normal" developmental reading growth. A related reality is mainstreaming, in which students with diverse needs are integrated into a regular classroom environment. This chapter provides you with background information concerning students who do not progress at a normal rate of developmental reading growth and offers suggestions about reading instruction for these students when they are mainstreamed with normal students.

FOCUS QUESTIONS

As you read this chapter use the following questions to guide your understanding about reading instruction for students with diverse needs.

1. What is PL 94–142?
2. What are the implications of this law for the classroom teacher?
3. What are the categories of diversity that you may encounter in your classroom?

INTRODUCTION

Exceptional, diverse needs, normal, and *gifted* are very difficult terms to define. From a broad perspective, all children are exceptional and have diverse needs. For the purposes of this chapter, however, an exceptional child is one who requires special education services in addition to those offered in a regular classroom environment. More than 1 out of 10 children required such extra educational service during some or all of their years in school and are considered exceptional. An exceptional child is a legally identified student whose needs require special educational services. Children whose needs are above that offered in the regular school curriculum are known as gifted. They, too, required special instructional consideration even though many states do not require that they be legally identified.

Thus, in this chapter: (1) a normal student receives regular educational instruction and has not been legally identified for special education services; (2) an exceptional, or special education, student has diverse needs to the degree that special educational services have legally been identified as required; and (3) a gifted child is an exceptional child with diverse needs requiring educational services beyond the regular curriculum despite the absence of legal identification.

Diversity enhances classroom life.

STUDENTS WITH DIVERSE NEEDS

To appreciate how a student with a diverse learning need views a regular classroom environment, imagine the following situations:

Rub cold cream on a pair of eyeglasses and try to read with them. Imagine sitting in a small reading group taking turns reading aloud. Your turn comes, you hesitate between words, and you even skip some. The teacher tells you to hurry up while other students begin calling out the words before you can identify them. Then some giggles erupt within the group, and you hear whispers of "stupid," and "dummy." How would you feel at this time? Would you like to read?

Imagine you are a second grader. You are asked to read a list of vocabulary words that includes: *chersonese, exuvial,* and *syzygy.* You can actually read words like *cat, bed,* and *deep.* When you hesitate or make a mistake, the teacher chastises you and accuses you of not really trying. Imagine how you would feel. Would you want to continue to try? Would you be eager for reading group tomorrow?

Turn down the volume on the television so that you cannot quite hear every word. Pretend this is your reading lesson and the teacher is introducing a strategy to identify words using context clues. Listen for 5 to 10 minutes. Would you be able to explain the strategy when the teacher called on you? Due to your inability to do this task successfully, you are told that you did not listen hard enough and you cannot go out for recess. How do you feel about reading? Was reading group a successful experience for you?

Imagine that your reading group meets from 10:00 A.M. to 10:30 A.M. At that time you always have a difficult time concentrating. Your blood sugar is very low because you are a diabetic. You really need a snack. You cannot answer some of the teacher's comprehension questions about the story. You are told that you need to think harder. You must answer the next three questions before you can go down to the office to get your orange juice. How would you feel about reading?

Imagine you are asked to read a story with sentences like *The cat sat on a fat rat.* At home you are currently engrossed in a book about how to write a trigonometry program on your microcomputer. How would you feel about attending reading group? Would you be eager to find out what happened when the cat sat on the fat rat?

These five instances highlight some diversities found in many regular classrooms. Teachers must recognize these needs, be sensitive to them, and deal with the reading instruction for each particular need. This chapter assists in this.

HISTORICAL BACKGROUND OF SPECIAL EDUCATION

Early in our nation's history, residential schools were established for the physically handicapped and mentally impaired to provide for housing, care, and education. Prior to this time, these citizens had been largely ignored by society. The residential placement kept the handicapped out of the mainstream of everyday life. Some individuals with milder handicaps were taught the skills to cope with their handicaps. The aim was to return this group of individuals back to society. For the most part, instituationalization meant a lifetime placement without reprieve.

Around the turn of the century a trend to establish special public school classrooms for handicapped children emerged. This eliminated the need for full-time institutional placement for such children. These special classes within

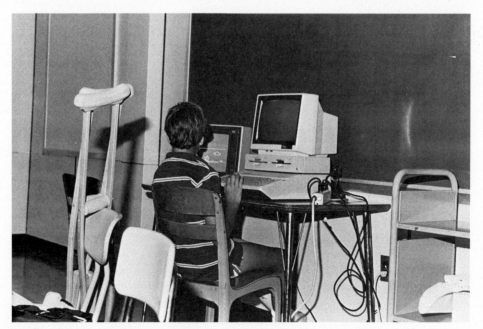

Equal access is an important principle of mainstreaming.

the public education framework were not immediately accepted or successful. It was at this time that the classes for the mentally handicapped became known as *special education*. Although this stigma remains today, special education now serves a much broader population than just the mentally handicapped.

Following World Wars I and II, a new feeling about handicapped citizens began to emerge. Normal young adults returned from the wars handicapped. The general public became more accepting and willing to provide for these people. Also, parents of handicapped chidren created lobbies and brought the issue of educating handicapped persons to the forefront. The number of special education classes increased.

Until the 1960s these classes were generally self-contained. A handicapped child placed in a special education classroom remained there for the entire school day. They did not associate with the regular classrooms in the same building even for lunch or recess. With the civil and human rights movements in the 1960s and 1970s, a new concept of the educational plight of the handicapped emerged. Equality of education became a major theme of educational planning. The strengths of learners were emphasized instead of their handicaps, with educational experiences and materials adapted to the learner. Every attempt was to be made to have the special learner take part in as much education as possible. Important state and federal court decisions required that mentally, physically, and emotionally handicapped children be educated in regular classrooms. This led to the congresional passage of the Education for All Handicapped Children Act in 1975, known as Public Law 94–142. This law became effective in 1977 and dramatically changed the education experiences of special education students.

PL 94–142

The Education for All Handicapped Children Act requires an appropriate public and free education for all children in the United States between the ages of 3 and 21 years of age. The key word is *appropriate*. The most suitable education for children with diverse needs is sought. A classroom teacher should be familiar with four of the major aspects of PL 94–142.

1. An important aspect of PL 94–142 is "the least restrictive environment." This phrase means that students must be placed in the regular classroom unless the total evaluation of the student indicates otherwise. At times a combination of special classes and regular classroom instruction more appropriately fits a student's needs.
2. The law mandates certain requirements for testing measures and evaluation. Placement testing must be free from racial and cultural

bias and must be appropriate for the handicapped student. No single testing instrument or evaluation can be used as the sole determiner of placement.

3. A statement must be written regarding a child's educational needs and a plan to meet these needs. This statement is developed through the combined efforts of specialized personnel, the classroom teacher, and the parents and is known as an Individualized Education Program (IEP). The IEP must be reviewed and updated annually. Although the exact format of the IEP form is not specifically mandated, it must include: (1) a child's current educational levels, (2) short-term objectives and annual goals, (3) the special services and personnel required, (4) programs or methods to be used, (5) the initiation date of special services and expected termination dates, and (6) tests, measurement, and other information to be used to assess progress.

4. To protect the students' rights, parents have access to a student's records. If the parents desire, they can request other evaluations. Parents also have the right to appeal decisions regarding placement of a student.

IMPAIRMENTS COVERED UNDER PL 92–142

About 12 percent of the school-age population fall within the guidelines of PL 92–142. The emotional, physical, and mentally handicapped guidelines include the mentally impaired, the hard of hearing or deaf, the speech impaired, the visually impaired, the orthopedically and health impaired, and the learning disabled.

Mentally Impaired. Mental impairment refers to a general intelligence level that is not within the average IQ range of 90 to 110. The term *educable mentally impaired* (EMI) and *trainable mentally impaired* (TMI) are educational labels. Educable mentally impaired children are thought to have IQs within the 75 to 50 range and TMI children are considered to have the IQ range of 25 to 50. Generally, a TMI child is not placed in a regular classroom. Despite the tendency to use IQ scores, it must be emphasized that no specific IQ number determines classroom placement. According to the guidelines of PL 94–142, the whole child must be evaluated.

Hearing Impaired. A hearing-impaired child is deaf or hard of hearing. A hard-of-hearing student has defective hearing, but is functional with or without the use of a hearing aid. A deaf student's disability makes successful language learning difficult. Testing for intensity or loudness of sounds measured by decibels determines placement for the hearing-impaired child.

Visually Impaired. A visually impaired child is partially sighted or blind. A partially sighted student has a visual acuity of 20/70 after correction, and a blind student has a visual acuity of 20/200 or less after correction. The partially sighted student usually is able to read regular or large print; a blind student usually will read only braille.

Speech Impaired. This category is also called *communication disorders.* A child with a disorder of this nature has difficulty with oral communication that may be linked to other handicaps such as mental retardation. Speech impairments can result from a physical problem, such as a cleft palate, a disease, such as cerebral palsy, or from other functional factors. Impairments fall within three categories: (1) articulation disorders that consist of errors in production, (2) voice disorders that include difficulties in pitch, intensity, quality, and flexibility, and (3) functional disorders that involve the interruption of the flow of speech, such as stuttering.

Physically or Health Impaired. This category includes many orthopedic, neurological, and health impairments. An orthopedic disability also includes congenital malformations. Physical impairments encompass chronic ailments, such as diabetes, and terminal diseases, such as cancer.

Learning Disabled. The category of learning disabled includes a whole range of disorders that affect a student's ability to learn. These problems include difficulty in listening, thinking, talking, reading, writing, or doing mathematics. Learning disability conditions include brain dysfunctions. A student may have a learning disability despite a normal or above-average IQ range. In essence, learning disability refers to students who are not achieving their academic potential.

In summary, PL 92–142 means that a classroom teacher may be required to teach students with these diverse educational needs because they will be mainstreamed into the classroom. Consequently, a classroom teacher must be knowledgeable about general principles and specific instructional strategies in order to assist these students. Since gifted students are not specifically included within PL 92–142 they are discussed later in this chapter.

GENERAL SUGGESTIONS FOR HELPING MAINSTREAMED STUDENTS

The following suggestions are useful when instructing mainstreamed students:

1. Do not worry about how many children will be mainstreamed into your classroom. The hearing impaired, visually impaired, learning disabled,

and physically handicapped are not all placed in the same classroom. Generally, only one or two mainstreamed children are placed in a particular classroom.

2. Most mainstreamed students are more like normal students than they are different from them. The students have more similarities with other students in a regular classroom and need to be treated as such.

3. Maintain high student expectations. High expectations and positive attitudes are particularly important for diverse learners.

4. PL 94–142 mandates that teachers must participate in the planning of the annual IEP. However, teachers should exceed this requirement and work on a day-to-day basis with the specialized personnel and parents regarding a student's diverse needs and the suggested methods to be used in the classroom. Teachers should coordinate instructional materials or procedures with specialized personnel who helped develop the particular IEP so the child does not get confused. A simple principle such as the silent e rule can confuse a student if it is referred to in different ways by different personnel.

5. Teachers need not change their view of reading instruction and reading outcomes when instructing a child with diverse needs. They should still instruct students to work out their own problems when blockages in comprehension occur and to have them enjoy reading. Teachers must, however, set high expectations for their developmental reading growth no matter what a student's disability.

SPECIFIC SUGGESTIONS FOR READING INSTRUCTION

The following suggestions for reading instruction are useful in pursuing the reading outcomes specified earlier in this book.

MENTALLY IMPAIRED

When planning reading instruction for a mentally impaired student, teachers need to realize that the student probably will have a low tolerance and get frustrated easily. Also, it is likely that the student will have a short attention span, a below-average language ability, a below-average ability to generalize and to conceptualize, and a poor self-concept. Teachers must plan for the student to reach his or her highest potential but also be aware of the student's role in the classroom in relationship to his or her self-concept. Thus, teachers should plan individually for the child so that instruction is at the appropriate level. Since these students do not learn at the same pace as others, they need systematic instruction. A teacher also must include them in large-group reading activities so they can share reading experiences with other members of the class.

When instructing mentally impaired students in reading real–life reading materials, such as telephone books and magazines, should be used as much as possible to remind them of the holistic and meaning-getting features of reading. Also, they should listen to tape recordings of textbook chapters and of other groups' stories so they can participate in subsequent discussions. Language experience activities are also useful with mentally impaired students because they emphasize that reading is connected with background experience and is holistic and meaningful.

HEARING IMPAIRED

A hearing-impaired student placed in a regular classroom will communicate by speech (lip) reading or through the use of a hearing aid, or a combination of a hearing aid and speech reading. Teachers need to know what the student is using. If the student is watching the teacher's lips, then it is critical to place this student always within sight and to remember to speak slowly and distinctly. If the student is using a hearing aid, it is necessary to place the student near the teacher and away from distracting sounds.

All mainstreamed students need special attention.

Since a hearing-impaired child has difficulty with sounds, a phonics approach to reading instruction is not very helpful. Emphasis should be placed on a strong sight-word vocabulary and contextual meaning should be emphasized. Many visual materials and teaching aids should be used. Teachers should make sure that the steps of a reading strategy are listed on the board for the student to read. Directions should be written as well as spoken. Since a hearing-impaired child generally has a language disability also, practice with various kinds of speaking activities is helpful.

VISUALLY IMPAIRED

For students with low vision, teachers can use a multi-sensory approach to reading instruction. A child with impaired vision needs to feel objects and how words and letters are formed. The students should be placed in the reading group and in the classroom so that the teacher or other students can read to them. Tape recordings of text also may be used. As with any other student with a diverse need, teachers must be aware of the extent of the student's disability and make sure that the child properly uses any special devices and/or materials suggested in the IEP. Similarly, they need to know if regular reading materials are appropriate or if the child should use large-print books. In the case of a blind child, braille is needed. A pair of glasses that is in a desk will not assist a low-vision student to read.

SPEECH IMPAIRED

Regarding speech-impaired students, teachers must find out from the student's speech pathologist what assistance the child is receiving. It is very important that the student be encouraged and reminded, but not badgered, to use appropriate speech in reading class. Teachers should consistently require that the child read and answer questions like any other child in the reading group, and should encourage the student to read and talk without interruption. It is important to develop an attitude of acceptance among the child's peers. For instance, if a student's disability is stuttering, do not eliminate the child's turn during oral reading. The rest of the group should be encouraged to listen to the child and to refrain from calling out the words before the stuttering student has time to speak. For other speech disabilities, a teacher can be an important model in emphasizing correct speech. Again, the frequent use of the tape recorder is an excellent instructional tool to reinforce correct speech and speech patterns.

PHYSICALLY OR HEALTH IMPAIRED

Since this category covers many diverse needs, it is very difficult to offer specific instructional methods for teaching these children to read. Many health impairments will not affect a student's learning ability in any way. Others, such as cerebral palsy, can affect a child's ability to communicate and to interact with text. In this regard, teachers need to be acquainted with the rate of deterioration accompanying the physical condition and to modify expectations accordingly.

Remember that a student with an orthopedic disability must not be excluded from a reading group just for convenience sake. Every possible effort should be made to physically include that child in the reading group. These children may not spend as much time in active play as others and may actually have more time to read than normal children. Use this as an opportunity to suggest many different and interesting books for the child to read. A child who does not participate in physical education, however, should not be expected to do extra work sheets during that period of the day.

A student with a health impairment such as diabetes involving highs and lows of efficiency levels should receive reading-group instruction during one of the high-efficiency periods. Thus, if a child with diabetes needs nourishment at 10:30 A.M., 10:00 A.M. would not be a good time for the reading group to meet. If the child's physical impairment decreases his skill in communicating, such as being unable to write, certain technological devices or a tape recorder may be used for oral responses. Remember that because a child has difficulty communicating what he or she knows, or what he or she is thinking, does not necessarily mean that the cognitive processes are impaired or that reading developmental growth is impeded.

LEARNING DISABLED

Students classified as learning disabled (LD) exhibit a discrepancy between potential ability and what is actually being achieved. There are many conditions that account for this disability, including perceptual handicaps and brain injury. A learning-disabled child most likely has one or more problems in perceptual motor-skills, thought processes, communication problems, or general learning difficulties. There is no single reading method or technique that can be uniformly applied to a learning-disabled child. There are, however, some general guidelines that can assist in planning a reading instructional program for such a student.

1. Since the student usually has some confusion in learning, tasks need to be simplified and broken down into small steps. Shorter assignments can be given and less work put on a page. Instead of 10 fill-in sentences on a page, a teacher could divide this in half and only give 5 at a time.
2. A teacher should structure the environment for the student. The child needs to know specifically where the materials are located,

what procedures to follow, and how the tasks are to be completed.

3. A teacher should give more frequent feedback to a learning disabled student. Such students often have a failure syndrome and need to feel more positive in their learning efforts. A star or sticker can be given for each correct answer instead of one for an entire page.

4. To reduce learning confusion and to establish a more structured environment, teachers can establish a specific, quiet, private place for the child to do his or her reading. This will help eliminate minor distractions. This does not mean segregation from the reading group. As with other mainstreamed students, the learning disabled should be included in disabled in group-reading activities whenever possible.

A learning disabled student's main problem is one of learning confusion. The more a classroom teacher can do to eliminate that confusion, the more the LD student is assisted. A classroom teacher also needs to communicate frequently with the specialized personnel involved in this child's IEP and use suggestions from them for reading instruction.

THE GIFTED CHILD

This section of the chapter discusses historical influences upon gifted education and characteristics of giftedness and makes instructional suggestions to assist in planning reading experiences for gifted students.

THE HISTORY OF GIFTED EDUCATION

Attention to gifted education has been sporadic during the past 60 years, depending upon the social and political climate of the time. For example, during World Wars I and II, interest in gifted education declined. With attention focused on Sputnik in the 1950s, there was renewed interest in developing intellectually superior students. Concern about the space race led to many special programs for intellectually endowed children in the areas of math and science. Even though it is generally thought that the top 2 to 5 percent of the nation's school population is gifted, these children are not always identified.

With the move toward equity during the 1960s, gifted education again declined. The problem of elitism was a major difficulty in gifted instruction. It was thought that a gifted child should be educated as a normal child and should not be given anything extra. It was also felt that gifted children could make it on their own and that they did not need any additional attention in school. In the early 1970s interest was rekindled with the establishment of a Directorship of Gifted Education in the United States Office of Education.

PL 94–142 does not especially mandate programs for gifted children. However, by the early 1980s many states had authorized gifted education as a requirement for high-ability students. Some states even authorize IEPs for their gifted children. Most states now have guidelines for gifted programs.

In summary, opponents of gifted education believe that (1) it is elitism education; (2) teachers cannot be prepared adequately to deal with gifted students; (3) there is not enough funding; (4) students are too difficult to identify; and (5) gifted students can make it on their own. Proponents of gifted education, in contrast, believe that gifted learners are the most retarded of our school population if one considers the difference between their potential and their actual achievement level. Supporters of gifted education feel that an important national resource is being lost by failing to provide appropriate education for gifted children.

IDENTIFYING GIFTED STUDENTS

Identification of giftedness varies. There is not single set of characteristics to identify a child as gifted. There are, however, accepted areas that are usually used. These include: general intellectual ability, specific academic aptitude, aptitude in the visual and performing arts, creative or productive thinking, and leadership ability. Many data need to be considered to identify gifted students, including a student's past performance, standardized test scores, teacher evaluation and progress reports, parent reports, and language ability. All this information may be assembled into three areas: intellectual ability, task commitment, and creativity.

A classroom teacher does not have the responsibility for singularly deciding if a student is gifted or not. Usually, other educators and specialized personnel assist in this recommendation.

READING INSTRUCTION FOR THE GIFTED

The foremost principle in planning reading instruction for gifted students is to differentiate instruction and not just give more work. A student who has already mastered a reading skill does not need to be given a second worksheet on that same skill. The gifted child needs something different. A classroom teacher should plan a combination of enriched and accelerated experiences following the three stages described later in the chapter.

Enrichment experiences involve going deeper and more thoroughly into what is presently being studied. If a reading group is studying Mexico in a basal reading text, a gifted student can go to the library and do a research report on certain aspects of Mexico. Acceleration involves going ahead of the grade level. If a third grader is reading at at fifth-grade level, then that child may go on and read higher-grade-level materials. It is important for classroom

Gifted students profit from enriched environments.

teachers to realize that pure acceleration for the high-ability child is not totally appropriate. A third-grader reading an eighth-grade-level novel may not find the subject matter relevant or suitable. Thus, a classroom teacher needs to seek a balance between providing experiences that enrich at a gifted child's present grade level and experiences that offer acceleration into a higher ability level.

When providing differentiated learning experiences, teachers must attend to a student's higher level of cognitive ability. There are six levels of thinking: knowledge, comprehension, application, analysis, synthesis, and evaluation. Most normal children are taught and learn predominantly at the levels of knowledge, comprehension, and application. These levels involve convergent thinking and center around finding an answer. Gifted students need to be provided with instruction at the levels of analysis, synthesis, and evaluation. These levels emphasize divergent thinking rather than simply finding an answer. At the analysis level, a student discusses information implicit in the reading. To synthesize, a student compares and contrasts subject areas using a number of materials and/or media. At the evaluation level, a student makes judgements about the information. Remember that gifted education needs to emphasize the depth and quality of thinking and learning, rather than the quantity of work completed. Too many times gifted children become unmotivated because they are expected to do more of the same.

Just as earlier chapters stress the importance of direct instruction, differentiated instruction for the gifted also must include direct instruction. Gifted students do not get everything on their own. They need instruction in how to analyze, synthesize, and evaluate. A classroom teacher cannot confuse practice and drill, which the gifted student usually does not need, with direct instruction.

Literature presents a wide range of opportunities for classroom teachers to plan differentiated learning experiences for gifted students. One good children's literature book can provide access into many different subject areas and several modes of language — speaking, listening, and writing. Teachers must not have gifted students read just for the sake of reading or to occupy time.

Reading experiences for the gifted should also include critical and creative reading. A student is reading critically when the higher-level thinking skills are being used. A student is reading creatively when he or she reorganizes what has been read. The student may rewrite or elaborate upon a story, or transform a story into a puppet show or a musical.

As with other special education students in the classroom, there should be a balance between including a gifted child in normal reading-group activities and in individual independent activities that meet the diverse instructional needs of the gifted.

INSTRUCTIONAL STAGES IN THE EDUCATION OF THE GIFTED

To plan for gifted students, a systematic model is needed. The one recommended here* consists of three stages of learning. Type 1 is called exploratory. At this stage a student learns at the lower levels of knowledge acquisition. Type 2 includes higher-level thinking skills and a more openended involvement for the student. Type 3 is the stage at which an individual applies this knowledge to a real-life purpose with the ultimate goal of a real product and a real audience.

For instance, a student at the Type 1 stage may read a book of poetry. At the Type 2 stage, the student might analyze the meaning of selected poems, compare and contrast types of poems, and make personal judgements about them. The student then could write original poetry and send it to a children's newspaper or magazine for possible publication. This would be the Type 3 stage. The student also could make an entire collection of poetry, put the poems into book form, and place it in the school's library. This also would be

* Renzulli, J. (1977). *Enrichment triad model.* Mansfield Center, CT: Creative Learning Center Press.

an example of a Type 3 activity. With these three stages of experiences, a student explores and reads poetry at the Type 1 stage, examines it at stages of higher levels of thinking at the Type 2 stage, and produces a real product with a real audience at the Type 3 stage.

CONCLUSION

This chapter provided background concerning students with diverse needs in reading instruction and offered suggestions about planning reading experiences to meet these students' unique instructional needs. PL 94–142 has many implications for you as a classroom teacher. You should know the different categories included within this law and how to modify your reading instruction for each category of diverse learners. Also, you should know what is included to identify a gifted student and how to plan differentiated instruction for this special learner.

CHECK YOUR UNDERSTANDING

Now that you have read the chapter, check your understanding by answering the Focus Questions presented at the beginning of the chapter. If you cannot anwer one or more of the questions, return to the chapter, find the section that corresponds to the question, and reread.

SUGGESTED READINGS

Burg, L., & Kaufman, M. (1980). Laws about special education: Their impact on the use of reading specialists. *Reading Teacher, 34*(2), 187–191.

Carlsen, J. M. (1985). Between the deaf child and reading: The language connection. *Reading Teacher, 38*(4), 424–426.

Carr, K. S. (1984). What gifted readers need from reading instruction. *Reading Teacher, 38*(2), 144–146.

Gaug, M. A. (1984). Reading acceleration and enrichment in the elementary grades. *Reading Teacher, 37*(4), 372–376.

Greenbaum, J., Varas, M., & Markel, G. (1980). Using books about handicapped children. *Reading Teacher, 33*(4), 416–419.

Guthrie, F. M., & Cunningham, P. M. (1982) Teaching decoding skills to educable mentally handicapped children. *Reading Teacher, 35*(5), 554–559.

Hansen, J., & Hubbard, R. (1984). Poor readers can draw inferences. *Reading Teacher, 37*(7), 386–589.

Lanquetot, R. (1984). Autistic children and reading. *Reading Teacher, 38*(2), 182–186.

Lukasevich, A. (1983). Three dozen useful information sources on reading for the gifted. *Reading Teacher, 36*(6), 542–548.

Moller, B. W. (1984). An instructional model for gifted advanced readers. *Journal of Reading, 27*(4), 324–327.

Monson, D., & Shurtleff, C. (1979). Altering attitudes toward the physically handicapped through print and non-print media. *Language Arts, 56*(2), 163–170.

Price, E. H. (1976). How thirty-seven gifted children learned to read. *Reading Teacher, 30*(1), 44–49.

Sinatra, R. C., Gemake-Stahl, J., & Berg, D. N. (1984). Improving reading comprehension of disabled readers through semantic mapping. *Reading Teacher, 38*(1), 22–34.

Smith, J. P. (1982). Writing in a remedial reading program: A case study. *Language Arts, 59*(3), 245-253.

Speckels, J. (1980). "Poor" readers can learn phonics. *Reading Teacher, 34*(1), 22–26

REFERENCES

Cartwright, G., Cartwright, C., & Ward, M. (1984). *Educating special learners* (2d ed.). Belmont CA: Wadsworth.

Gearheart, B. R. (1983). *Education of the exception child: History, present practices, and trends.* Lanhorn, MD: University Press of America.

Gearheart, W. (1984). *The exceptional student in the regular classroom* (2d ed.). St. Louis, MO: Times Mirror/Mosby.

Geass, R. M., Christiansen, J., & Christiansen, J. L. (1982). *Teaching exceptional students in the regular classroom.* Boston: Little, Brown.

Henninger, M. L., & Nellserood, E. M. (Eds.) (1984). *Working with parents of handicapped children: A book of readings for school personnel.* Lanhorn, MD: University Press of America.

Morsink, C. V. (1984). *Teaching special needs students in the regular classrooms.* Boston: Little, Brown.

CHAPTER **17**_____

Special Language Issues

Maria Torres

GETTING READY

Teachers must become aware of bilingualism and black English because more than one fourth (27 percent) of the total enrollment in United States public elementary and secondary schools represents a racial or ethnic minority. Nineteen of the 50 states in the United States have a minority population of 25 percent or more, and 12 states increased in minority student populations by 6 percent or more between 1970 and 1980. Specifically, the black population accounted for 16 percent of the total public school enrollment in 1980. Between 1976 and 1982 the number of language minorities between 5 and 14 years of age who spoke a language other than English at home increased by 27 percent. Thus, at some point in your career, you will be faced with students who are bilingual and/or Black English speakers. Whether you make a difference in such students' chances to blossom into fully literate individuals may well depend on what you know about special language issues.

FOCUS QUESTIONS

As you read this chapter use the following questions to guide your understanding of bilingualism, Black English as a social dialect, and the instructional implications these situations pose.

1. What is a social dialect? How is the concept of social dialect different from regional dialect?
2. How is bilingualism defined? Will bilingualism confuse a student?

3. Is more standard English the solution to success in reading for Black English-speaking students?
4. What are the four major goals of bilingual education program?
5. What instructional strategies can you use to adapt instruction to meet the needs of Black English-speaking students? Of a language minority student?

MAJOR TYPES OF
LANGUAGE DIFFERENCES

When people speak, it is like choosing the right outfit from their wardrobe for a special occasion. They choose what to wear depending on whether they want to impress someone or want to feel comfortable. Each situation calls for a series of choices. Furthermore, what a person wears for one occasion is not necessarily the best choice for another. Thus, people change clothes to fit new situations. It is all right to be different, but if someone wore evening clothes to go skiing, he or she would stick out like a sore thumb. Thus, there are limits, or a range, of appropriateness of dress.

Teachers need to attend to special language needs.

This is also so when people are speaking. There are choices about the manner of speaking, the words to use, the emphasis, and the intonation. Choice of language can be influenced by the formality of a situation. Imagine how students would speak in response to a classmate's question in a formal presentation as opposed to the way they would speak to that same classmate if they met casually in the hall. Everybody can recall a similar case in which formality prompted a change in how they spoke. The person one is speaking to can also modify the way one talks. For example, talking to a minister is different from talking to one's sister. Talk can also be affected by what is talked about or where the conversation takes place. The choices people make are not often made consciously, but it is possible to trace the patterns of how they speak and why they intuitively know when it is appropriate or not. People learn all this by acquiring natural language as they are growing up.

Variations in language can also be connected to social group membership. These are called varieties or dialects. For example, at a national conference in the Midwest, a person may immediately notice how the pronunciation or choice of words differs among the persons present. Midwesterners speak differently from New Yorkers or Texans. These different ways of speaking are called regional varieties or dialects. Differences in racial or ethnic background, in social class background, in whether a person is male or female, or in what kind of job the person holds may also result in different ways of speaking.

This chapter concentrates on two language situations that have been the focus of discussion and inquiry, particularly as they relate to educational attainment and achievement of racial and ethnic minorities in the United States. Specifically, this chapter focuses on Black English and bilingualism, some of the myths and realities associated with these language situations, and the implications these have organizing and planning for instruction.

BLACK ENGLISH

In 1979 Judge Joiner concluded in the landmark *King vs. Ann Arbor* decision that schools did not recognize the differences in dialects between standard English and Black English; that Black English was a consistent, systematic, rule-governed, and different form of speech; that the problem was not that black children possessed a different speech but that the schools did not take speech into account in teaching black students the literacy skills needed to achieve in school; and that it was the schools' obligation to make teachers knowledgeable about Black English and to train them to use this knowledge in the instruction of black children. How these conclusions were reached is discussed here.

Black English is a name given to a variety of dialects. In general, Black English speakers across the United States are said to use the same features when speaking; the pronunciation, the sentence structure, and the vocabulary are generally the same. However, there are differences across regions, social class, and educational experience. In this sense it is not very different from the standard English varieties mentioned earlier. New Yorkers who speak a Black English speak differently than Black English speakers from New Orleans or Atlanta.

Not all black Americans speak Black English, although the majority may be familiar with it. Some individuals use only one or two features of Black English. Some blacks use Black English features as they speak, but feel very comfortable with reading and writing in standard English. Yet again, some blacks speak Black English in some circumstances and standard English in others. Furthermore, Black English is spoken by Puerto Rican and other children in many urban settings. Thus, it is important for teachers to be aware of such possibilities when assessing the language needs of black children, in particular, and Black English speakers in general.

Various interpretations have been offered regarding the origin of Black English. What does this have to do with teaching? The way teachers look at the origin of Black English may have an impact on what they do in their classrooms. One such interpretation is that Black English is a corruption of standard English. From this perspective, the Black English features found in standard English are stressed. Another more recent view is based on the strong links between Black English in the United States and on the African continent. A third perspective takes aspects of both views and looks at the interactional nature of Black English development.

There are incidents supporting each of these views. The first perspective, also known as the *deficit model*, presents the following evidence: (1) there are similarities between Black English features and "errors" made by foreigners in their attempt to learn standard English; (2) the "noise" level in homes of black Americans prevent children from hearing certain sounds, (3) black mothers have been found to speak to their children with less frequency when compared to white middle-class mothers, and (4) blacks consistently score low in verbal sections of standardized tests.

The counter argument is guided by what is known as the *difference theory*. This theory assumes equality of languages. It holds that the African slaves brought to the United States did not have a common African language that facilitated communication across tribal languages. Faced with the need to communicate among themselves as well as with whites, a common language was established. The development of this common language follows the same kinds of stages as the language development of the African creoles. The first phase is a simplified language that contains elements of the several languages of its speakers, also known as *pidgen*. The second phase, the development of a creole, is a result of the acquisition of the simplified language as a native language by a new generation. In other words, the language of communication between the slaves and their children was the simplified common language of slaves. However, the children who spoke this common language as their native language expanded its use and transformed it into a bonafide communication system. It differs systematically from the language from which it originates, but it continues to share many of its original features.

The third perspective emphasizes that the simplified language system and its development interacted with a foreigner's type of English to produce what today is known as Black English. Because there is a common core in syntax, vocabulary, and sound system, it may appear solely as a corruption of the first, but it is actually a different language system from English. Furthermore, it has been found that many researchers had not taken into account the fact that when parents and children are taken out of their homes and put in a laboratory situation they are inhibited and speak less. In fact, tremendously elaborate use of language can be found in oral rituals of Black English speakers. For instance, *the dozens* is an exchange of verbal insults that usually takes place among young black males who know each other well and frequently involves the mother as a target of insults although it can, and does, focus on other topics as well. Whether one agrees with the appropriateness of this language or not, it counters the deficit theory and testifies to the high verbal performance of blacks.

One of the major points Judge Joiner made was that Black English was not inferior, but was a consistent, systematic, rule-governed form of communication. Such findings are important for instruction because the way teachers act toward the use of Black English in the classroom, consciously or unconsciously, can be the result of thinking about Black English as an imperfect acquisition of English resulting from a nonsupportive home environment. Some teachers immediately correct a student who uses a final possessive *s*, such as "I sees," without stopping to think that this is a feature of Black English. Rather than correct the student the teacher should use a context in which the final possessive *s* is deleted to determine whether the meaning of the sentence conveys the same message in spite of the deletion of possessive *s* and whether pointing out the difference between standard English and Black English is essential to the lesson.

It is possible to agree that Black English is a bonafide communication form but to be convinced that a distinction needs to be made about when Black English is appropriate and when it is not. This is indeed a different matter and will be treated as a distinct concern at a later point in the chapter.

BILINGUALISM

Bilingual language situations in the United States result when an individual speaks a language other than English — such as Chinese, Japanese, French,

Spanish, or Croatian—some or all of the time at home or in the community and, either through formal or informal schooling, is proficient at some level in English. The home or community language is the native language and English is the second language.

Individuals are usually categorized in groups according to the language spoken; these groups are called *language minorities*. Any one of the many language minority populations in the United States must be considered within the context of their sociohistorical conditions and, more specifically, in relation to the language attitudes of the community. Both the historical conditions and the attitudes have implications for determining how to deal with language diversity in your classroom. For example, some of the language minority groups are also historically disenfranchised racial or ethnic minorities, such as the Puerto Ricans. Not only may the native language be instructionally appropriate for the individual child but it may also be culturally and politically symbolic of ethnic identification for the group. However, not all language minorities share the same historical conditions nor are language issues equally important across ethnic groups. However, the fact is that a student with another language brings greater complexity to a classroom. Under these circumstances, how well the student knows the native language or the second language are specific educational questions that teachers must learn to deal with.

One can also find differences in the degree of bilingualism. At the individual level, for example, a teacher may find that one child responds when told in English to get in line, but that same child has a blank expression during most of the reading lesson. Another child of the same language minority may be in the high reading group and be as engaged as any other student in the group. What causes this? Although there may be more than one explanation, consider the following. The first child is probably non- or limited-English proficient, and the other, although possibly bilingual, is not limited in his or her knowledge of and use of English. In other words, not all members of a language minority group have equal difficulty in understanding, speaking, reading, and writing English. As a matter of fact, English may be the dominant language for individuals of a language minority group.

How well individuals know the language can be explained by thinking of bilingualism as a continuum. Chinese offers a good illustration. At one extreme, there is the monolingual Chinese speaker who has just arrived in the United States and does not have a working knowledge of English. At the other extreme, although less likely to occur, there is a monolingual English-speaking person of Chinese descent. In between these two extremes there are many possibilities, including a person of Chinese descent who uses a mixture of English and Chinese to communicate with others on a daily basis. Furthermore, it is possible that the degree of bilingualism is related to an individual's ability to understand or speak the language or to their ability to read and write it. Many United States–born Hispanics, for example, understand and speak Spanish well, but are less proficient in reading and writing Spanish. On the other hand, there are individuals who can read and write Spanish comfortably in church or at home, but are unable to do so when faced with the task of translating in a courtroom or teaching a lesson in science. Not only are they at a loss for words, but they cannot understand or write the specialized language of these fields.

HISPANICS—THE LARGEST LANGUAGE MINORITY

The number of language minority speakers who are limited in their proficiency of English is estimated to be as high as 8,034,000 in the United States. Approximately 60 percent of the language minority school-age children are from a Spanish-language background. Thus, most of the knowledge about bilingualism in the United States is drawn from Hispanic children. Where appropriate, examples of other language minorities will be noted. However, Hispanics will be the primary examples used.

Hispanic is an umbrella term that refers to Spanish-speaking populations that come from 21 different countries, including the Mexican–Spanish-origin population that originally resided within the boundaries of what once was Mexican territory and today is the southwestern United States. Hispanic is not a well-received term by some groups because it is a political term associated with government funding and does not originate from the people themselves. The term, and the degree of its acceptance, is subject to regional and ethnic variation. Some people prefer terms such as *Latino* or *La Raza*. Suffice it to say that teachers should ask a student or the parents to self-identify. For our purpose, the term Hispanic will be used interchangeably with Spanish speaking, although not all Hispanics are Spanish speaking or vice versa.

There is a richness of cultural diversity among Hispanics. At a national level, the largest Hispanic groups are Mexican–Mexican Americans, Puerto Ricans, and Cubans. The largest concentration of Mexican–Mexican Americans is in the southwest, the largest concentration of Puerto Ricans is on the East Coast, and the largest concentration of Cubans is in the Florida area. Each group has a history, a political perspective, a literary tradition, and a language and cultural style that is different and unique. Hispanics draw from these rich traditions as they interact with the institutional mandates of everyday life in the United States. However, the interaction tends to reinforce the use of oral language more than the written form.

Many Hispanics are not first generation, but they speak Spanish in their home or community. Is this any different from Italian, Polish, or other ethnic groups in the United States? The answer is yes and no. The affirmative aspect is that, as with the Italians and the Polish, there is a loss of the native language with each passing generation. What then accounts for the continued maintenance of Spanish, unlike other language groups? There are two reasons. First, the rate of language loss over generations is not only slower than that found in other groups but is coupled with a higher birth rate among Hispanics, meaning that the number of individuals who speak Spanish is growing. Second, the combined effects of the constant flow of immigration from all parts of Latin America, the proximity of the Mexican border, the settlement patterns of Hispanics, and the segregation policies and practices against Hispanics that continue in many American cities also serve to give the impression of enormous growth among the Spanish-speaking population in the last couple of years.

In 1980 a little fewer than one-third of the Spanish-speaking school-age population was estimated to speak only English at home. This suggests the widespread use of the native language among Spanish-speaking children but does not give any indication of their ability to work in a totally English setting. Furthermore, it is recognized that the widespread use of Spanish does not mean that all Spanish-speaking Hispanics do not know English.

In a classroom, then, a teacher cannot assume that a language minority child does not know English well; nor is it safe to assume that they can understand all that is going on when English is the language of instruction. It is important to find out how well they know English, what skills they have, and ultimately, how instruction can be adapted to meet their needs. Furthermore, it is important to understand (1) what they use their native language and second language for, (2) whether they mix the languages, and (3) how they change from one language to the other.

EIGHT MYTHS ASSOCIATED WITH SPECIAL LANGUAGE ISSUES

There are many myths associated with language and the education of blacks and language minorities. The following section compares and contrasts the myths or variants thereof.

1. *Teaching students in their native language will confuse them intellectually.* This is a myth that comes from the language minority children's failure to achieve at the same rate as Anglo children and from a long tradition of studies beginning in the 1920s that hypothesized that bilingual children were at a disadvantage when tested because intelligence tests were so heavily based on language performance. When bilingual children were found to have more grammatical errors, reduced vocabulary, and deficiencies in articulation, it was concluded that bilingualism was a negative condition that should be eliminated. The tests were not questioned, nor was the possibility explored that bilingual people were not only cultured but perhaps more intelligent.

As scholars searched for evidence to demystify this tradition, they began by accounting for the flaws that resulted from how the research was done. The research studies had not taken into account the effects of social class or the complexity of definition posed by bilingualism. Sorting out these factors and looking closely at the phenomena has resulted in the conclusion that bilingual children were more mentally flexible than monolinguals. How could this be, when previous evidence showed deficiencies? Researchers have found that greater mental flexibility was more frequently found when learning a second language did not result in sacrificing the first language. In other words, if an individual learned a second language and became fully proficient in both languages, the ability to use both languages would result in greater mental flexibility. Furthermore, it was found that the existence of bilingualism in an individual is more likely to cause mental flexibility than the reverse.

In addition, literacy skills in a first language appear to help academic achievement in a second language. For example, experience with reading in English gives a student an advantage when faced with a French text. The student knows that a cluster of letters make up a word and that the word means something, the space between a cluster of letters means that it is a word separate and distinct from other words, the capital letter at the beginning of a cluster of letters followed by a space and other clusters of letters that end up with a period at the end indicate a sentence, and thus a thought. A student knows these words convey a message, and once the key to the pronunciation is known, words can be decoded, and so forth. In other words, there are concepts that need not be taught to a child who already knows one language and is learning another. There are, however, some differences depending on the language group being taught. For example, the general notion that one reads from left to right is different for Arab-speaking or Asian groups. However, the point is that teaching someone who has some concepts for the printed word can save a teacher some steps. This is why children who have been in school in their native countries for four or five years come to the United States and learn to read and write at a much more rapid pace than children who did not have school experience in their language.

There is no clear equivalent to this myth in the case of Black English. However, as is true in the bilingual situation, blacks who have poor auditory discrimination or articulation as measured by standardized tests have been labeled as intellectually deficient, immature thinkers, and learning disabled. Very few scholars bothered to look at the biases of the tests until relatively recently. Even present-day tests that include natural writing samples have failed to take into consideration that the tone, organization, and style of written work can be influenced by cultural aspects. What is also similar in both cases is the interference issue. A Black English speaker, when reading orally, may not pronounce a sentence as written in a standard English text. Most of the time, teachers immediately conclude that the speaker does not know how to decode and that the lack of decoding skills affects comprehension. There is no evidence of interference when a child transforms standard English text into Black English. On the contrary, it is evidence of a very sophisticated mental process. Not only do the children demonstrate an understanding of the text by producing sentences that mean the same thing in their dialect but they also demonstrate an act of immediate translation from one dialect to another in order to produce a new sentence.

2. *Students need more English in bilingual education classrooms.* This myth at first glance seems to be logical. If practice makes perfect, then the more students practice English by hearing and speaking it, the more likely they will be to learn it faster. Just think about situations a person is in when listening to a different language radio show while traveling abroad, or when in the presence of two individuals who are speaking a language a person does not know. Does the person understand? Does the person pay very much attention? Probably after noting that what the person was hearing was in an unfamiliar language and not comprehensible, he or she would tune out and not listen anymore. This form of language is called *incomprehensible input*, because what was said could not be understood. Thus, more is not better under all circumstances. In the case of teaching a non- or limited-English–speaking child, it is important to think out *how* to teach English.

A second reason why more English is not better is illustrated in the following example. Teachers very often tell parents that they should stop talking to their children in the native language and should expose their children to more English because they need more practice. Imagine a parent of a child who is limited-English proficient. The probability is very high that the parent is also limited-English proficient. Now, imagine them at home sitting at the kitchen table and the parent putting into practice the teacher's advice. What kind of experience can this parent have with the child? Imagine that the parent has a blue coffee mug in his or her hands. The parent can probably say *cup, blue, coffee,* or *cup blue coffee.* If the parent decides to extend the "lesson," the parent might say *inside coffee* or *inside cup coffee,* and so forth. Very soon, the parent will run out of anything to say. On the other hand, if the parent were to speak in the native language, he or she could make more sophisticated comments about the color and function of the cup, the weight with or without coffee or another liquid, the shape of the cup, the size of the cup relative to other cups, and so forth. The difference in experience is clear. The amount of language exposure in the first situation is limited to approximately 10 words, as opposed to 250 words in the second, and the difference in intellectual and conceptual exposure is like day and night.

There is another practical matter to consider. Previous "sink-or-swim" methods where only English was spoken were not successful in schooling language minorities.

The variant myth for Black English is teach them standard English, or as a teacher from Detroit put it in reference to standard English in a 1982 article, "They need to be taught, corrected, and properly directed in mastering their native tongue."

Again, this stems from failure to recognize Black English as a different language system. It is true that, unlike the bilingual situation, standard and Black English share a common core of syntax and sounds. This makes black speakers proficient in understanding standard English speakers. However, similar to the second-language learner, there is a need to lower what is called *the affective filter*. In other words, there are invisible barriers that create favorable or unfavorable conditions for learning a language. Some teachers have proposed to teach standard English by making blacks feel ashamed of the way they talk. The results for the majority of children have been disastrous. When children are threatened by the feeling that their language and culture are not as good, their defenses arise, creating a barrier for learning. Encouraging greater pride and awareness about the black language and culture has proven to be more successful. As a result of the Civil Rights and Black Power Movements, more and more black youth developed positive views about Black English, and this reinforces its use. This reinforcement seems to have had positive effects. Although not nearly as satisfactory as they should be, there are reports of improvement by blacks in language arts and reading scores at the national level.

3. *Previous generations of immigrants learned English and were successful without school programs.* Early immigrants had bilingual schools in many states. One example was the German population that between 1838 and World War I had what they called German schools. Many laws were passed during this period that provided options for teaching in a language other than English. One such law was passed in Ohio in 1839, stating that:

> In any district when directors keep an English school and do not have branches taught in German, it shall be lawful for youth in such districts who desire to learn in the German language, to attend a district German school.*

It was more the result of the anti-German and antiforeign sentiments than a concern for educational achievement of Germans that later resulted in the prohibition of teaching in a language other than English in public schools.

The second related point is that the immigrants who came to this country in the early part of this century did not "make it" on the basis of education. The most common road to success was through the pooling of family resources to buy a small plot of land or to establish a business. The success rate of im-

---

* Fishman, Joshua. American heritage: Language maintenance in the classroom *4*(1) (1969, September), 18. *Center Forum*. Center for Urban Education.

migrants of first- and second-generation children through schooling may not have been as high as is popularly believed.

A third argument related to this myth is that the labor economy has changed. In the past the nature and amount of the entry jobs were significantly different. Today most jobs require some degree of training. Nonskilled workers from the auto and steel industry are presently faced with the need for retraining to qualify for a job. There are many jobs that still do not require a skilled work force, but these jobs are more scarce than they used to be. Thus, it is more difficult for today's immigrants to find jobs. Furthermore, the job-training opportunities usually require some knowledge of English, again posing a barrier that adds to the complexity of making it.

Many critics bring up the cases of the Vietnamese students who graduate *magna cum laude* today from American schools. They are faced with these same conditions, so why can they make it in schools? Although very few scholars have focused on this phenomena, there are some immediate issues that come to mind. Most of the first wave of Vietnamese to come to the United States were connected with the United States military in Vietnam, were middle class or higher in the Vietnamese context, and had a favorable disposition to English and the United States. In other words, they were political refugees and did not come to the United States for ecomonic survival. Among the Hispanics, the early wave of Cubans, which was a middle-class professional or upper-class group, were very successful in educational attainment, unlike the Puerto Rican or Mexican populations. These differences suggest that factors other than language are at work that account for the failure or success of language minorities in the educational system. Thus, it is important to find out if these outstanding Vietnamese children were first- or second-wave immigrants and whether they reaped the benefits of a middle-class environment. Furthermore, some of these children went to school in Vietnam. It has been found that a strong base in the first language is helpful in learning a second language and promotes successful achievement in that second language. Thus, it would also be important to consider prior schooling of these children.

Third, and closely related to previous schooling, is the age of the child. It has been found that older students are more efficient language learners than younger children. It has been thought in the past that the best time to introduce a second language to children is when they are young because a more nativelike pronunciation and use of the language results. Whereas this is true, older children have more experience as well as conceptual and intellectual knowledge that permits them to learn a new language in relatively less time, although a noticeable accent may remain.

A fourth point is that, when a language learner is highly motivated and unthreatened, language learning is facilitated resulting in a lower affective filter. Furthermore, when individuals are learning a language because it will help integrate them socially, it is more likely that they will be more favorably disposed to the new language than when they feel they have to do it for economic survival.

The last point is that these *magna cum laude* Vietnamese students represent a very small proportion of the Indo-Chinese population that arrived in the United States in the 1970s and 1980s. Though they are the pride and models of the community that many others aspire to imitate, their lot cannot be mistaken for that of the majority of the Indo-Chinese. In addition, these students arrived when there was high awareness of the need to provide responsive educational programs for language minority populations, especially where they are found in greater numbers, such as on the West Coast and in Texas.

A similar notion is that people who speak a foreign dialect have been successful, why are not Black English speakers? The point is that where social mobility is possible, dialects do not make much difference. It didn't for John F. Kennedy, Lyndon B. Johnson, or Jimmy Carter, who all reached the presidency despite their dialects! Although one cannot deny the importance of a dialect, this should not be confused with other sociopolitical issues. Regional dialects are not the same as social dialects. A person speaking a negatively evaluated dialect, such as Black English in the United States, is labeled unintelligent and incompetent. For socioecomonic mobility the speaker of a social dialect must learn to detect when and where each of the dialects is appropriate and how to move from one to the other.

4. *Fostering native language learning will lead to separatism, as with Quebec.* This is the same kind of thinking that led to the elimination of language schools in the United States during the World War I period. The issues of what language the people in power will impose on the people they have power over has its roots in the first people who were conquered. To impose one language over another because the two languages cannot coexist is not a universal solution. There are many other alternatives. In India there are 12 official languages; in Tanzania there are two official languages; in China there are 54 different nationality groups, most of which are educated at an elementary level in their native language in the autonomous regions. In a great majority of the countries of the world, similar language differences exist. Some countries opt for coexistence of languages at a state level, others opt for a language that serves to bridge all other languages, known as a lingua franca. In the case of the Philippines, English and Filipino serve as lingua franca to many other languages; in India, English and Hindi serve as lingua franca. There are cases where minority languages coexist within the boundaries of a region, as is the case of the Yunan province of China, where 22 language groups live side by side. In other cases there are distinct language areas, as in Switzerland where the country is divided into cantons. Each canton has an official language. The case of Quebec is a political, social, and economic situation of which language is only a part. Recognizing language as a symbolic issue in the resolution of the Quebec situa-

tion is correct. However, to boil down the issue of separatism in Quebec to the issue of language is to diminish the sociohistorical conditions that have led to the explosive conditions present today.

5. *Bilingual education is nothing more than a jobs program.* This myth does not focus on students or the instruction a school provides, but on the displacement of white teachers by language minority teachers, a possible side effect of special programs. One of the original claims of ethnic and racial minorities was that there was a lack of teachers who were sensitive to the children's needs. Training and hiring more knowledgeable and sensitive teachers was attempted. In some cases this meant teachers from the language minority group; it also meant teachers trained in teaching language minority populations. It was preferable that a trained language minority teacher who met both conditions be hired. Many teachers have been trained as a consequence. A great number of language minority individuals, including the author, are results of these training programs. But not all the trained teachers are language minority, and the number of trained teachers still does not meet the growing demands for teachers who can meet the language minority children's needs. In 1984 it was estimated that the nation needed 52,000 to 56,000 bilingual teachers. In California, the largest recipient of federal funds for language minority schooling, the proportion of white teachers has remained constant throughout the years, although the actual number of Hispanic teachers has increased tremendously. The need is growing at a much faster rate than the number of graduating teachers. For example, between 1980 and 1981 four out of five teachers who had limited-English-proficient students did not have the basic preparation to meet their needs.

6. *Children are being taught an "incorrect" Spanish.* It is very likely that a professional from a Spanish-speaking country could walk into a bilingual classroom and come out with the impression that the Spanish spoken in the classroom is incorrect. If they were to pick up the materials sent out by the bilingual programs, they would be even more adamant. The concern reflected in this argument is similar to that of the standard English and Black English situation. It is not true for all programs, and it is more true for bilingual programs with a Mexican-American population. Why? First, every language has a variety of dialects. In Spanish there are more than 20 varieties reflecting the number of countries whose official language is Spanish. Each one of these countries has its own standard. Within each country, however, there are varieties associated with the social group membership and from regional, gender, racial, ethnicity, and occupational differences. In the United States, the Mexican-American population claims its own Spanish dialect, which has many varieties including a mixture (code switching) of English and Spanish that has its own system. In other words, this variation puts together English and Spanish words at random that make up a complete thought, but violate the rules used by people who are knowledgeable in this variety.

The second factor is that many teachers were not Spanish-dominant speakers upon entering the bilingual education program and have only had on-the-job training. The teachers who were trained in English-speaking schools know how to talk about their subjects in the language they were taught — English. The language minority children's needs, however, necessitate that teachers learn the language and style appropriate for teaching these subjects in the native tongue as well.

7. *Children of language minority groups are proficient in their native language, therefore content should be taught in the native language.* This is a generalization to which, when applied to individual children, the general truth does not apply. In other words, some language minority children are not proficient in their native language and some do not perform like native speakers in either the native language or the second language, but speak a mixture of the two. The most common proficient native-language speaker is a newly arrived immigrant student.

Assessment is required to find out a student's proficiency level. There are oral-language proficiency tests that take into account the fact that a child may code switch, such as the Bilingual Syntax Measure. Some oral-language tests combine both a natural-language sample with the more traditional ways of measuring language, such as the Language Assessment Scale (LAS). These two tests, when appropriately adminstered, can give a fair understanding of a child's ability to understand and speak English, and in the case of Spanish speakers, the oral-language performance. However, there is some caution to be exercised with any test. For example, it has been found that the scores in Spanish on the LAS may be somewhat depressed. The kind of language measured by the LAS may not reflect that spoken at home or in the community. No matter how much testers try, they face variations of language from area to area. Listening to a child and encouraging a child to write in a purposeful way may give further indications of their ability to produce language as well as the kind of language they produce.

A similar kind of myth can be found in Black English. It is based on the assumption that black children who speak Black English will be able to read texts written in Black English. What is not considered is that white students, when they go to school, must be taught to read in standard English. Why should Black English speakers not require reading instruction in their own dialect? The other related implication is that the sound-symbol correspondence simplification will itself make reading possible. In this regard, the example of the Initial Teaching Alphabet (ITA) is appropriate. Sir James Pitman, who designed the ITA, produced an alphabet of 44 written symbols that corresponded on a one-to-one basis to the sounds in English. His premise was that this simplification would help beginning readers during the early stages of reading and would not interfere in the transfer to traditional orthography. Today this method is no longer used, testifying to the fact that reading is not merely the decoding of written symbols, even when there is instruction in this method.

8. *Parents want their children to learn English, so why put their children in bilingual education program?* There are differences in opinions about how to go about educating children among language minority populations. However, there is no disagreement about parents wanting their children to learn English. This strong desire is anchored in the parents' belief that a better education and better job will result from learning English. However, this does not necessarily mean the parents want the native language eradicated. All surveys of parents done in the last decade have indicated that parents would like their children to maintain the native languages, not only because it helps maintain family and social ties, but increasingly, it has been thought to increase the potential economic opportunity of their children. In other words, there is an advantage to knowing two or more languages when you apply for a job.

Black parents, similar to language minority parents, want their children to obtain a better education and occupation. The knowledge of school language, standard English, is viewed as a prerequisite or at least as potentially leading to educational and economic improvement. However, black parents do not favor teaching Black English as much as language minority parents do, although this often depends on the subgroup one refers to. A more parallel situation is found among Mexican-American parents. They too want their children to learn to speak correctly, not *pocho*. A recent survey of parents in San Jose, California, indicated that nearly 65 percent preferred that standard Spanish be taught in the schools. However, in this same group of parents there were people who expressed some strong opposition because they felt at a loss with standard Spanish. Generally, these parents are second or third generation and do not identify with the Mexican standard Spanish.

MEETING SPECIAL LANGUAGE NEEDS THROUGH BILINGUAL EDUCATION

As teachers, administrators, government officials, parents, and communities began to recognize that many Hispanic school children were not working at grade level and that they dropped out of school at a younger age and more often than their Anglo counterparts, they began to search for alternatives. One such alternative was to teach academic content in the native language. This alternative was labeled *bilingual education*. Bilingual education molded itself to fit the American educational system with the particular aim of educating language minority school children. In other words, it aimed at improving the academic achievements of language minorities and at decreasing the drop-out rate. The way bilingual education proposed to meet these goals was by teaching students English as a second language, teaching academic subjects in the students' native language, developing positive self-concept in the students, and in some instances, maintaining the native language through enrichment activities.

ENGLISH AS A SECOND LANGUAGE

English had been previously taught by the sink-or-swim method, which consisted of putting children in an all-English classroom environment in which they had to learn not only the English language but also the subject matter being taught. English as a second language is viewed as a method for teaching children who have a native language other than English. It is different from the regular English course in that it introduces language in a more systematic and planned way. Additionally, it is different from foreign language learning in that there is a viable context for the use of English in natural settings.

ACADEMIC SUBJECTS

The continuation of academic subjects in a student's native language was based on two premises: (1) when a child is burdened with learning what is being

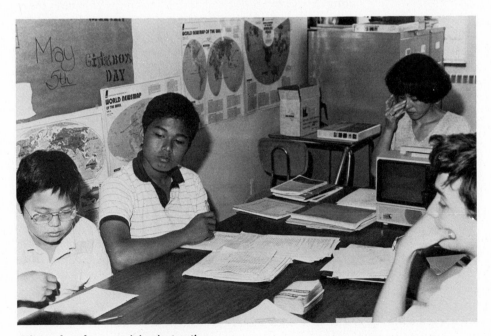

Bilingual students receiving instruction.

Developing self-concept is an important part of helping students with language problems.

taught while at the same time learning the language, there will be considerable loss of content, and (2) the native language is assumed to be the stronger language.

Thus, concepts of math, social studies, science, and other content areas are introduced in the stronger language. The amounts of time in the native language or the form the lesson takes can vary.

SELF-CONCEPT

Why children do well in school subjects or why they continue their education is influenced by the way they feel about themselves, that is, their self-concepts. If Annie likes herself, for example, and if she believes that she can do the work well or go to college, there is greater self-motivation and greater enthusiasm in doing so. Liking themselves or feeling good about themselves is related to how people feel about their families and their cultures. All people belong to a cultural group, and their belongingness partially determines how they act in social situations. In every school classroom, culture is at work. Culture affects how teachers organize their classrooms, how the classroom rules as well as what will be taught in the classroom are developed. Culture also creeps into the way teachers teach and how they look at their students' progress.

When cultures come in contact with each other and rejection or intolerance results, the members of the less powerful group suffer. Thus, in many classrooms the power lies with teachers, and when they are not aware of cultural differences, intentionally or not the clash of cultures may interfere with student learning.

One clear example of culture at work is the preference of Mexican-American children to work in groups. To some teachers, however, cooperation without permission by teachers is cheating. Teachers who are in tune with the Mexican-American culture do not have trouble here. Not only do they perceive nonsanctioned cooperation as an appropriate method of learning but organize their classroom so as to permit such cooperation. Thus, bilingual education not only brings into the classroom knowledge about the child's history, music, dance, foods, and holidays, which is the usual way culture is perceived in the schools, but also provides for children to incorporate their ways of learning into the classroom.

MAINTENANCE

Finally, the maintenance of the native language is seen to be a way to (1) ensure higher levels of literacy in both languages, and (2) to extend positive self-concept arguments by appreciating the language associated with a cultural group. This entails learning subject matter in the native language as well as learning the native language as a subject matter.

There have been many problems of implementation for bilingual education programs. It is easier to state goals than to put them into effect. It is also easier to identify complexities that contribute to the problems of implementation than to find solutions to the problems. It takes time, trial and error, and knowledge resulting from experience, as well as new thinking to get these problems resolved.

MEETING SPECIAL LANGUAGE NEEDS OF BLACK ENGLISH

In the early 1970s some attempts were made to develop programs for Black English speakers that specifically centered on language issues. One was the development of, and implementation of, a black dialect reading program. This program assumed that, if the mismatch between the spoken language and the written language were reduced, greater comprehension and fewer errors in oral reading would result. The goal of this program was to improve the reading of Black English speakers. Another strategy was the development of English as a second dialect program of instruction. This program assumed that the distance

Meeting the special language needs of students (courtesy of Michigan State University).

between standard English and Black English was sufficient to merit the development of a program that would build on the similarities between the two dialects while systematically presenting the differences. The aim of the program was to teach standard English.

One of the strategies was based on the affirmation of Black English as a legitimate instructional language medium and the other recognized Black English as a base for learning standard English, but did not confirm or deny its legitimacy as a language to be used as a means of instruction. Whereas neither one has had wide acceptance, some useful principles can be derived from the experience and incorporated into lesson planning. One of the principles is part of the multicultural education movement that purports to teach students about diversity of cultures and equity. What this has actually meant for teachers is the use of culturally diverse materials in their teaching. This is especially true when the student population itself is from different cultural backgrounds. The limitations of most multicultural programs in this respect is that many have not gone beyond the level of surface culture. The need to incorporate cultural forms more appropriate to black culture still needs to be addressed.

The second principle regards language. Teachers are being taught, as part of their language arts and reading courses, that language dialects exist and that rather than ignore language varieties in the classroom they should think about adaptations in teaching that would encourage expression of concepts, thoughts, ideas, and emotions in whatever languages students bring with them. The degree to which teachers can implement these principles is regulated by their knowledge of the language and culture, the classroom composition, and the curriculum goals. However, at minimum, a teacher should include some materials written in Black English and expose all children to the power of a June Jordon or a James Baldwin as part of the language arts program. Teachers should refrain from correction of Black English features; they should introduce the Black English features as a different way of communicating, when appropriate; and use individual conference periods to point out the differences between the two dialects in a sensitive fashion.

PROVIDING INSTRUCTION FOR SPECIAL LANGUAGE SITUATIONS

Language instruction in schools has been enriched by educators' reflection on the implications of language acquisition research. The following is an illustration of how teachers can begin to think about applying language knowledge to the instruction of Black English-speaking and language minority children. The discussion is organized around three notions: language is a means of communication; language is developmental; and meaning is constructed by verbal and nonverbal cues.

LANGUAGE IS A MEANS OF COMMUNICATION

Language, when spoken in a natural context (as when you talk to your mother, a next-door neighbor, or the store clerk), is governed by the need to communicate. As children grow they acquire the language of their surroundings as a means of conveying their desires and figuring out the meanings of utterances spoken by others. This is true whether the child is learning English, Croatian, or Arabic. Children, as they interact with adults and other children, make many grammatical errors that are ignored. The emphasis is on the meaning. Corrections by adults occur when there is an error in content. As a matter of fact, parents usually attribute meaning to nonsensical utterances a child makes. It is natural, then, that black children speak in the dialect spoken at home and that a transformation from the standard English text to Black English occurs when reading aloud. They are trying to make sense, to construct meaning from the text, and they are using their own language variety to do so. There are implications for teaching. First, literacy, reading, and writing should be primarily organized for making sense of the world. It must be interesting, purposeful, and meaningful and, thus, an act of giving or receiving through a written text. Second, the pronunciation or use of a dialect in oral reading should not be corrected as decoding errors. Emphasis should be placed on meaning.

LANGUAGE IS DEVELOPMENTAL

Before children as infants acquire their native language, there is usually a period of silence. In other words, they are not born today and speaking tomorrow. Usually it takes 12 to 18 months before children start one-word utterances. During the 12 to 18 months before producing an utterance, they acquire what is called *receptive knowledge* of the language. That is to say, they can understand what is spoken to them, but they cannot yet produce language. Receptive knowledge of the language is also found in a second-language situation. When learning second languages, students should not be expected to speak English immediately. You will soon see how their need to communicate with peers and adults will motivate them to speak English or to incorporate standard English features when they speak a nonstandard variety.

Furthermore, the production of language starts out with what is called a *one-word stage*. At this point children produce words that are meaningful in the environment, such as *mama, ball, eat, milk*. At a later point children produce two-word phrases such as *Daddy go* and *pretty boy*. As they continue to engage in the mastery of their language, children go through a process of self-correction and engage in the production of more and more complex utterances.

In a similar way, second-language learners go through various phases of acquisition, producing more complex, longer, and nativelike utterances after systematic exposure to the language. Black English speakers have also been found to incorporate features of standard English into their speech gradually. Thus, teachers' anxiety about the errors produced should be eased by looking at non-nativelike structures as developmental.

MEANING IS CONSTRUCTED BY VERBAL AND NONVERBAL CUES

An adult interprets what a child says by looking around for contextual cues. A smile and a pointing finger from a toddler may be sufficient indicators for an adult to understand that the child wants to draw attention to an object or occurrence of interest. A child learns how to interpret utterances spoken to them by using contextual cues also. For example: to find out whether the command "Come here" really means "I would like you to come here whether you want to come or not" or "You may choose to come here if you want," the child uses facial gestures, tone of voice, and other contextual cues to interpret the meaning of what was said. A very similar situation occurs when learning a second language. The learner tries to make sense about utterances spoken in the second language by using context, gestures, movement, and so forth.

There are a few implications for organizing instruction of students from different dialect or language backgrounds. For example, one such implication is related to auditory discrimination. The contrasts made by standard English speakers may be different for black or language minority students. In Black

Helping students construct meaning is at the heart of instruction provided for students with language needs.

English words such as *pen, pin* and *toll, told* are not as distinguishable from each other as in standard English. Thus, caution is required when planning instruction to determine whether what is to be taught really provides cues for correct interpretation. In second-language learning there is an increasing use of a function (or social purpose) of language as a way of organizing the curriculum. A social situation is developed so that the context provides the basis for interpreting the meaning of the utterances. It also helps organize lessons or units that emphasize communication over grammatical forms.

This in no way exhausts the implications for instruction or the principles of language acquistion that need to be considered in teaching the linguistically different student. Nonetheless, it provides a way of thinking about language teaching–learning processes and the linguistically different child.

RESOURCES

Where do teachers get more information, materials, and experts to help with special language in the classroom? There are a few places that can offer assistance, including university English departments and colleges of education. Local experts are also found through state educational agencies in multicultural and bilingual divisions and among elementary or secondary language arts and reading personnel. Nationally, there are a few networks such as the Title IV National Origin and Race Desegregation Assistance Centers and the Title VII Multifunctional Bilingual Education Centers. A school district can request technical assistance and training and provide searches for materials at minimal cost. A key source for information about these networks and other resources is the National Clearinghouse for Bilingual Education (NCBE), 1555 Wilson Boulevard, Suite 605, Rosslyn, Virginia 22209, (800) 336–4560. The NCBE can provide information about the nearest Title IV and Title VII service center.

Two other sets of people are potentially helpful: students and parents. Children from the same language and cultural background as a student a teacher is concerned about can be great resources as tutors. They can transform an instructional task, making it culturally and linguistically more appropriate for the student needing help. Furthermore, tutoring also allows tutors to review the content of the lesson and improve their own skills. A good peer or cross-age tutoring system in a classroom can help use this resource better.

Parents can also be of great help. They can be used in a way similar to the buffer described in Chapter 8. Although teachers may have to spend some time recruiting parents who will be dependable, the efforts result in great benefits for students. Remember to encourage parents to visit the classroom and to show them that their help is appreciated. Initially, if a teacher does not know their language, search for a bilingual person who can help communication. Elicit from the parents ways they see they can help and encourage them to do so. Remember, parents want a better life for their children. Capitalize on this desire.

CONCLUSION

The increasing numbers of language minority and black students in the American public schools calls for a closer look at special language problems. Although there are numerous bilingual programs throughout the United States that address the needs of language minority populations, there are many schools that do not have the resources to provide the necessary instructional support for students with special language needs. Consequently, teachers must become aware of language varieties, dialects, and language differences. More importantly, teachers must take a serious look at the instructional implications associated with having these students in their classrooms. This chapter does not provide you with a recipe for reading instruction of language minority or black children. Instead, it gives you a perspective from which you can begin to examine and design instruction for these children when you find them in your classroom.

CHECK YOUR UNDERSTANDING

Now that you have read the chapter, check your understanding by answering the Focus Questions presented at the beginning of the chapter. If you cannot answer one or more of the questions, return to the chapter, find the section that corresponds to the question, and reread.

SUGGESTED READINGS

Barnitz, J. G. (1982). Orthographies, bilingualism and learning to read English as a second language. *Reading Teacher, 35*(5), 560–567.

Bresnahan, M. (1976). Selecting sensitive and sensible books about blacks. *Reading Teacher, 30*(1), 16–20.

Downing, J. (1984). A source of cognitive confusion for beginning readers: Learning in a second language. *Reading Teacher, 37*(4),366–372.

Ebel, C. W. (1980). An update: Teaching reading to students of English as a second language. *Reading Teacher, 33*(4), 403–407.

Feeley, J. T. (1983). Help for the reading teacher: Dealing with the Limited English Proficient (LET) child in the elementary classroom. *Reading Teacher, 36*(7), 650–655.

Gamez, G. I. (1979). Reading in a second language: "Native language approach" vs. "direct method." *Reading Teacher, 32*(6), 665–670.

Gillet, J. W., & Gentry, J. R. (1983). Bridges between nonstandard and standard English with extensions of dictated stories. *Reading Teacher, 36*(4), 360–364.

Heathcote, O. D. (1982). Sex stereotyping in Mexican reading primers. *Reading Teacher, 36*(2), 158–165.

Hu-Pei Au, K. (1979). Using the experience–text–relationship method with minority children. *Reading Teacher, 32*(6), 677–679.

Kupinsky, B. Z. (1983). Bilingual reading instruction in kindergarten. *Reading Teacher, 37*(2), 132–137.

Minkoff, D. (1984). Game activities for practicing English as a second language. *Journal of Reading, 28*(1), 40–42.

Moustafa, M., & Penrose, J. (1985). Comprehensible input PLUS the language experience approach: Reading instruction for limited English speaking students. *Reading Teacher, 38*(7), 640–647.

Perez, S. A. (1979). How to effectively teach Spanish-speaking children even if you're not bilingual. *Language Arts, 56*(2), 159–162.

Prewitt Diaz, J. O. (1982). The effects of a dual language reading program on the reading ability of Puerto Rican students. *Reading Psychology, 3*(3), 233–238.

Schon, I. (1985). Remarkable books in Spanish for young readers. *Reading Teacher, 38*(7), 668–670.

Stauffer, R. G. (1979). The language experience approach to reading instruction for deaf and hearing impaired children. *Reading Teacher, 33*(1), 21–24.

Tomkins, G. E., & McGee, L. M. (1983). Launching nonstandard speakers into standard English. *Language Arts, 60*(4), 463–469.

Wheat, T. E., Galen, N. D., & Norwood, M. (1979). Initial reading experiences for linguistically diverse learners. *Reading Teacher, 33*(1), 28–31.

Wiesendanger, K. D., & Birlem, E. D. (1979). Adapting language experience to reading for bilingual pupils. *Reading Teacher, 32*(6), 671–673.

REFERENCES

Ascher C. (1983). Writing instruction for dialectally different youths. *Urban Review, 5,* 69–73.

Barnitz, J. G. (1980). Black English and other dialects: Sociolinguistic implications for reading instruction. *Reading Teacher, 33,* 779–786.

Bongere, M. B. (1981). Dialect and reading disabilities. *Journal of Research and Development, 14,* 67–73.

Bruntress, N. G. (1982). Educational implications of Ann Arbor decision. *Educational Horizons,* 79–82.

Cronwell, B. (1984). Black English influence in writing of 3rd and 6th grade black students. *Educational Research, 77,* 233–236.

Cronnell, B. (1983). Dialect & writing: A review. *Journal of Research and Development in Education, 17,* 58–64.

Davis, B. G., & Armstrong, H. (1981). The impact of teaching Black English on self-image and achievement. *Western Journal of Black Studies, 5,* 208–218.

Dennard, K. (1981). Black educator speaks about Black English. *Reading Teacher, 35,* 133.

Donald, B. (1983). Black English—heritage, help or hindrance? *Principal, 61,* 45.

Durkin, D. (1984). Poor black children who are successful readers: An investigation. *Urban Education, 19,* 53–76.

Edwards, V. (1983). Dialect speakers: Fact and fantasy. *Early Childhood Development and Care, 11,* 79–87.

Eherwein, L. (1982). Do dialect speakers' miscue influence comprehension? *Reading World, 21,* 255–263.

Ferguson, A. M. (1982). Case for teaching standard English to black students. *English Journal, 71,* 38–40.

Freeman, E. (1982). The Ann Arbor decision: The importance of teachers attitudes toward language. *Elementary School Journal, 83,* 41–47.

Gemake, J. S. (1981). Interference of certain dialect elements with reading comprehension for third grade. *Reading Improvement, 18,* 183–189.

Gentry, R. (1983). What reading teachers should know about dialect. *Reading World, 23,* 108–115.

Gillet, J. W., & Gentry, J. R. (1983). Bridges between non-standard and standard English with extensions of dictated stories. *Reading Teacher, 36,* 360–364.

Guillary, S. F., & Clifford, C. S. (1980). What is being done for black children in reading. *Reading Horizons, 21,* 22–27.

Johnson, F. L., & Buttay, R. (1983). White listener's responses to sounding black and sounding white: The effects of message content on judgement about language. *Communications Monographs, 49,* 33–49.

Jones, C. D. (1979). Ebonics and reading. *Journal of Black Studies, 9,* 423–448.

Markham, L. R. (1984). "De dog and de cat": Assisting speakers of Black English as they begin to write. *Young Child, 39,* 15–24.

McPhail, I. P. (1982). Toward an agenda for urban literacy: The study of schools where low income black children read at grade level. *Reading World, 22,*

McPhail, I. P. (1982). Toward an agenda for urban literacy: The study of schools where low income black children read at grade level. *Reading World, 22,* 132–149.

Monteith, M. K. (1980). Implications of Ann Arbor decision: Black English and reading teacher. *Journal of Reading, 23,* 556–559.

Padak, N. D. (1981). Language and educational needs of children who speak Black English. *Reading Teacher, 35,* 144–151.

Palmer, B. C., & Hafner, L. E. (1979). Black students get an edge in reading. *Reading Horizons, 19,* 324–328.

Politzer, R. L. et al. (1981). Teaching standard English in third grade: Classroom functions of language. *Language Learning, 31,* 171–193.

Ramsey, P. A. (1979). Teaching the teacher to teach black dialect writers. *College English, 41,* 197–201. (1981). *Discussion, 43,* 633–638.

Schwartz, J. I. (1982). Dialect interference in attainment of literacy. *Journal of Reading, 25,* 440–446.

Smith, R. P., & Denton, J. J. (1980). Effects of dialect, ethnicity, and orientation of sociolinguistics on perception of teaching candidates. *Educational Research Quarterly, 5,* 70–79.

Smitherman, G. (Ed.). (1981). *Black English and education of black children and youth.* Detroit: Harlo.

Steffersen, M. S. et al. (1982). Black English vernacular and reading comprehension: A close study of 3rd, 6th, and 9th graders. *Journal of Reading Behavior, 14,* 285–298.

Stockman, I. J., & Vaughn Cooke, F. B. (1982). Re-examination of research on language of black children: The need for a new framework. *Journal of Education, 164,* 157–172.

Taylor, J. B. (1983). Influence of speech variety on teacher evaluation of reading comprehension. *Journal of Educational Psychology, 75,* 662–667.

Thomas, G. E. (1983). Deficit, difference and bicultural theories of black dialect & non-standard English. *Urban Review, 15,* 107–118.

Torrey, J. W. (1983). Black children's knowledge of standard English. *American Education Research Journal, 20,* 627–643.

Troutman, D. E., & Falk, J. I. (1982). Speaking Black English and reading: Is there a problem of interference? *Journal of Negro Education, 51,* 123–133.

Wangberg, E. G. (1982). Non-standard speaking students: What should we do? *Clearinghouse, 55,* 305–307.

Yellin, D. J. (1980). Black English controversy: Implications for the Ann Arbor case. *Journal of Reading, 24,* 150–154.

PART VI

CONTINUED PROFESSIONAL GROWTH

This book was written to develop professional teachers rather than technicians. One of the distinguishing characteristics of professionals is that they continue to learn and grow.

This unit, consisting of a single chapter, provides suggestions for how you can continue to learn and grow as a teacher, thereby maintaining your status as a professional. When you finish the chapter, you should have an understanding of what it takes to maintain a sense of professionalism and vitality while working within the reality of classrooms.

CHAPTER **18**

Continued Professional Growth

GETTING READY

This book began by pointing out two truths about reading instruction in today's schools: first, some teachers are more effective than others and, second, many teachers teach more like technicians than professionals. Subsequently, this book has tried to point out what makes teachers effective and how they can become professional decision makers who maintain cognitive control of their instruction rather than technicians who merely follow the directions in a teacher's guide.

Professional teachers are lifelong learners. They make a conscious effort to remain professionally fresh and vibrant. Learning how to continue your professional growth throughout your career is an important part of being a teacher. This chapter describes why continued professional growth is important and makes suggestions about how to ensure that your teaching remains fresh and vital throughout your career.

FOCUS QUESTIONS

As you read this chapter use the following questions to guide your understanding of how to continue your professional growth.

1. What happens when teachers do not make conscious efforts to continue their professional growth?
2. How can you assess your professional growth?
3. What are some professional activities that ensure your continued professional growth?

4. What personal things can you do to maintain your freshness and vibrancy as a teacher?
5. What are the rewards of continuing your professional growth?

ASSESSMENT PLAN

Your continued professional growth depends upon you and your ability to assess your strengths and weaknesses so that you can use your strengths while overcoming your weaknesses. While preparing for a teaching position, you need to ask yourself: What are my strengths and weaknesses? What needs to be worked on now? What needs to be worked on later? This self-assessment can be structured around the following four areas: student needs, curriculum mandates, the role of a teacher, and the classroom environment.

Student Needs. This category involves assessing what you know about reading growth and your ability to apply this knowledge to students' reading needs. Do you feel knowledgeable about developmental reading stages, instructional reading levels, the influence of verbal aptitude on reading growth, student interests, and so forth? Can you effectively use these concepts in classroom teaching? Organize these into two lists, one labeled *Strengths* and one labeled *Needs.*

Curriculum Mandates. This category involves assessing what you know and what you can do regarding the typical reading curriculum. Do you know what you are trying to teach for each of the three outcomes? Do you have objectives and activities for each instructional goal? Are you familiar with the strengths and weaknesses of basal reading materials? Do you understand state assessment tests and standardized tests and their role in the reading curriculum? Can you effectively use these in your instruction? Add these items to your list of strengths and needs.

The Role of a Teacher. This category involves assessing your knowledge of a teacher's role and your ability to perform it. Can you assess students for the three outcomes? Can you provide appropriate direct and/or indirect instruction for the three outcomes? Can you create an environment conducive for learning? Can you find, develop, and organize materials for instruction? Which of the above can you do effectively? Which are you concerned about? Add these to your list of strengths and needs.

The Classroom Environment. Finally, assess your ability to create a classroom environment conducive to teaching and learning. Do you know what constitutes a literate environment? Can you create one? Do you know how to account for and create good social-emotional, physical, and intellectual environments? Add these to your list of strengths and needs. Figure 18.1 is a checklist you can use to assess yourself.

PROFESSIONAL DEVELOPMENT PLAN

Once your self-assessment is completed, use the data to create a professional development plan. Begin your plan by setting goals for yourself. How can you improve your classroom work based on your assessment of yourself? Your planning should include both long- and short-term goals. Both are crucial to lifelong professional growth. Successful completion of short-term goals provides incentives and rewards for continuing the effort, and successful completion of long-term goals provides a pattern of thinking and action that supports lifelong professional growth.

People set goals as they search for ways to improve. In fact, the heart of professional growth is the on-going search for improvement. The best teachers are the ones whose motivation to excel has them constantly looking for ways to improve. In short, they are always experimenting with better ways to do things.

Enrolling in graduate classes stimulates professional growth (courtesy of Michigan State University).

Figure 18.1 **Teacher self-assessment**

	Strength	Need

A. *Student variable*
   1. Did I have knowledge of
      a. reading stages
      b. instructional reading levels
      c. independent reading levels
      d. influences of verbal learning and aptitudes
      e. student interests		

B. *Curriculum variable*
   1. Did I have knowledge of
      a. instructional goals
      b. objectives and activities for goals
      c. strengths and weaknesses of basals
      d. state assessment test
      e. standardized tests
   2. Can I use
      a. reading stages
      b. instructional reading levels
      c. independent reading levels
      d. influences of verbal learning and attitudes
      e. student interests		

C. *Teacher variable*
   1. Did I have knowledge of
      a. student assessment
      b. student instruction
      c. environments conducive to learning
      d. developing and organizing materials
   2. Can I use
      a. student assessment data
      b. instructional strategies
      c. classroom environments conducive to learning
      d. developed and organized materials		

D. *Classroom environment variables*
   1. Do I have knowledge of
      a. literate environment
      b. social–emotional environment
      c. physical environment
      d. intellectual environment
   2. Can I use
      a. literate environment
      b. social–emotional environment
      c. physical environment
      d. intellectual environment		

RESOURCES FOR IMPROVEMENT

The teaching profession offers both formal and informal resources for improvement and updating.

FORMAL RESOURCES

The primary resources in this category include professional organizations, professional journals, and graduate work in universities. Professional organizations tend to divide into ones with an interest in particular kinds of problems (for example, reading problems or early childhood problems) and those with an interest in particular curricular areas (social studies, language, mathematics, and so forth). All of these organizations have annual conferences where teachers gather to exchange ideas and to hear speakers present information on the most recent innovations in the field. These conferences are often highly exciting, intense, and satisfying experiences where teachers obtain many ideas and return to their classrooms stimulated and renewed. A list of organizations that have a particular interest in the teaching of reading is included in Figure 18.2.

Second, teachers can get new ideas and innovations from the various professional journals that are available. Many of these journals are associated with professional organizations such as those noted in Figure 18.2, but others are published independently. In either case, these journals contain teaching and curriculum ideas that have been submitted from all over the country. By subscribing to and reading one or more of them, you are assured of intellectual stimulation and continued growth as a teacher. Figure 18.3 contains a list of journals of particular assistance to teachers interested in improving reading and writing instruction.

Finally, many colleges and universities offer programs of graduate study for teachers. These institutions offer a wide range of course and workshops describing recent trends and research findings about the problems of teaching. Participation in such graduate education is an effective way of pursuing both short-term and long-term goals. It not only broadens your perspective on your classroom work but also serves as the basis for salary increases in many states.

INFORMAL RESOURCES

Helpful ideas can come from a variety of informal sources including students, colleagues, your school district, and your own travel. The most accessible and possibly the most overlooked resource is your students themselves. By listening to students and questioning them about their interests and concerns, you can get many useful ideas for modifying your instruction and for incorporating student interests into your materials and activities.

Figure 18.2 **Professional organizations**

Association for Supervision and Curriculum Development
    225 North Washington Street
    Alexandria, VA 22314

International Reading Association
    800 Barksdale Road
    PO Box 8139
    Newark, NJ 19711

State affiliates of International Reading Association

National Council of Teachers of English
    1111 Kenyon Road
    Urbana, IL 61801

State affiliates of National Council of Teachers of English

Figure 18.3 **Professional journals**

Elementary School Journal
        University of Chicago Press
        PO Box 37005
        Chicago, IL 60637

Instruction
        PO Box 6099
        Duluth, MN 55806–9799

Journal of Reading
        IRA
        800 Barksdale Road
        PO Box 8139
        Newark, NJ 19711

Learning Magazine
        530 University Avenue
        Palo Alto, CA 94301

Reading Psychology
        1010 Vermont Avenue, NW Suite 612
        Washington, DC 20005

Reading Teacher
IRA
800 Barksdale Road
PO Box 8139
Newark, NJ 19711

School Library Journal
PR Bowher Co.
PO Box 67
Whitinsville, MA 01588

A second informal resource is other teachers. Teaching is an isolated profession in which you spend most of your professional time with children and very little with professional colleagues. Yet, colleagial interaction is one of the most helpful ways to maintain professional growth. One way to ensure colleagial interaction is to have a "buddy system" in which you team with another teacher from your school or from other schools in the area. You can periodically exchange ideas, materials, and innovations that have worked. This plan can also include exchange visits to one another's classrooms. Contrary to the publishing business where plagiarism is frowned upon, plagiarism is encouraged in teaching. If somebody else has a good idea, borrow it, and see if you can make it fit your own situation; if you have a good idea, encourage your colleagues to use it with their classes. This kind of exchange promotes the growth essential to teaching.

Similarly, school districts provide informal sources for professional growth. Most school districts, for instance, provide resource centers where the most recent ideas about instructional improvements are cataloged and displayed for the teachers' use. Many districts also have professional days during which teachers can take time off for professional growth. A visit to another teacher's classroom is an excellent way to spend this time because it gives you another perspective on your own work. Finally, school districts offer various in-service programs. Whether attendance is voluntary or mandatory, these programs are another excellent way to develop yourself professionally. Also, many of these in-service programs are backed up by a longitudinal, formal, district-wide staff development program where participation can earn you salary increases or other incentives. All such district-level activities are excellent sources of ideas and innovations.

Finally, your own travel can be a resource for growth. For instance, you could plan your travel around a professional theme, such as traveling in foreign countries to visit and compare school systems or traveling through this country with the goal of collecting local folk lore for use in your classes. In short, there is

A teacher examines new curriculum materials.

an abundance of formal and informal resources available to teachers who want
to grow and get better at their profession.

MONITORING AND EVALUATING PROGRESS

In addition to taking advantage of available resources for professional growth,
teachers need to monitor and evaluate their progress toward the goals they
have set as part of their professional plan. At designated points, you should sit
down and examine the data you have collected regarding how well or how
poorly you are achieving your goals. This data gathering and evaluation need
not be formal. However, it does need to be regular and honest.

RECORD STUDENT PROGRESS

There are many ways to collect data about your impact on students. One way
is to keep careful records of your students' progress toward the goals you have
set and to evaluate yourself in terms of how well your students achieve these
goals. For instance, if you want students to develop certain concepts about
reading, you must keep records of their progress and review these periodically.

Similarly, if you want students to develop certain attitudes or to become more aware of how reading works, you must keep track of this. If you want students to become better writers, you must keep samples of their writing throughout the year and periodically review their progress. By setting goals and then reviewing the data regarding how well your students are achieving these goals, you will find yourself modifying your teaching in order to meet these goals. Such change is evidence of professional vitality and growth.

In addition to keeping track of student progress on academic work, you should also keep track of *their* awareness of lesson content. For instance, it is a good practice to periodically interview students following lessons, asking them what they think you were teaching, why they think you were teaching it, and how to do it. If several students give responses that indicate misconceptions about the lesson, you should reevaluate your teaching and make changes that will improve your students' awareness of what is going on during instruction.

MAINTAIN A REFLECTIVE JOURNAL

A second way to keep track of your professional growth is to keep a reflective journal. Either daily or several times a week, you should write your thoughts about your progress. Note what is going well and what is not going so well. In-

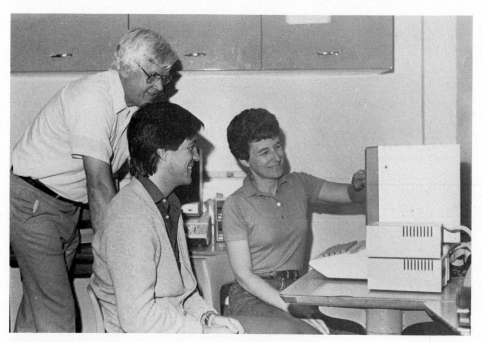

School district in-service programs help keep teachers current.

Professional growth is enhanced through the sharing of ideas.

clude your ideas, thoughts, and feelings and periodically evaluate your journal and yourself. Ask yourself if you are progressing the way you want to or if there is a problem that needs to be resolved. If possible, share this information with another professional and have that person help you evaluate it. Decide with that person whether to continue as you have been or to make changes.

BE SELF-MONITORING

A third way to monitor and evaluate your professional growth is to tape-record (or video-tape) your own instruction. It is very difficult to be aware of what you are doing while engaged in the act of teaching. However, you can be much more objective and perceptive when you listen to or watch yourself. It is particularly helpful if you focus on one thing at a time. For instance, watch or listen to the tape once to determine how many times you were distracted from the main focus of the lesson, another time to determine whether each student was given an equal opportunity to respond, another time to see how explicit you were in showing students how to do the task, and so on. Each time you will become aware of ways to improve your teaching, and once you are aware, you can take steps to improve. If you are not aware, however, you can never improve. Again, sharing and discussing the results of these analyses with a colleague is better than solitary evaluation.

THE IMPORTANCE OF
PERSONAL GROWTH

Teachers should be well-balanced people. They should not only be competent professionals but also be interesting people. This means that professional development is not enough — it must be accompanied by personal development.

Because teaching is such a demanding task, it can become all-absorbing. You can become so devoted to helping students achieve and grow that all of your time is allocated to professional tasks. In short, you can become a highly professional drudge. This must be avoided.

Teaching is person-to-person interaction, and in the final analysis, your impact on students will depend both on your professional competencies and on how interesting you are as a person. Your students' desire to interact with you will depend on how they see you as a person. Attention and respect is not awarded to drudges; it is given to teachers who are alive and vital in their private lives as well as in their professional lives.

To achieve vitality as a person, cultivate interests beyond the classroom. Know what is going on in the world around you, and become involved in com-

Cultivating interests beyond the classroom is an important part of professional growth.

munity, state, and national affairs. This does not necessarily mean that you must be a political activist, merely that you should take an active interest in contemporary affairs. You do this by reading more than professional journals.

Personal development means developing your own interests and aptitudes. Because teaching is stressful and absorbing work, it is particularly important that you have a rich family and social life, that you have hobbies and activities that absorb your energies and attention once school is finished. In short, you should be a multidimensional person who has a variety of interests, someone who paints, or flies airplanes, or refinishes furniture, or runs marathons, or explores caves. These other interests will help balance the professional devotion required to be a classroom teacher.

FACING THE REALITIES

All the plans mentioned for continuing professional growth are helpful. However, one major problem remains. It involves the realities of classroom life, which often force otherwise dedicated teachers to become technicians who follow prescriptions rather than professionals who exercise professional control.

It is alarming that so many teachers act like technicians. At a time when the teaching of reading must be thoughtful, there are too many teachers who are mechanical, routinized, and procedural. The result is students who respond to reading in mechanical ways, who see reading as tasks to be completed rather than genuine communication, and who rarely choose to read once school is over.

It is not that such technical teachers are simply unwilling to put forth the necessary effort. Most teachers try hard and want to do well by their students. However, the complexities of the job simply overwhelm many teachers. There just seems to be too much to attend to and not enough help, too many demands and not enough time, too many pressures and not enough reward, and too many students who have difficulty learning and not enough techniques that work. Eventually some teachers stop trying to be innovative and rely on prescriptions from others that they can follow in routinized ways. This seems to be what many central office administrators, publishers, and school boards want. In short, it is easier to give in and become a technician who lets others do the thinking.

The typical scenario proceeds something like this. A new teacher accepts a position in a school district that uses a mandated basal text program and expects high achievement on the state assessment test. The principal frequently visits the new teacher's classroom to ensure that the basal is being followed and that the students are being prepared for the test. Following the lead of the veteran teachers in the building, the new teacher uses the basal text prescriptions and prepares students for the test. Instruction lacks interest or relevancy, students get bored, the success rate is low, and students become unmotivated. Soon the teacher becomes discouraged and casts about for "the answer." The school district and the state either encourage the use of another prescription or closer adherence to the one already in use. The teacher follows these directions, but the results are the same. Yet another prescription is suggested; the teacher tries to implement it, but has little success. The teacher's frustration and boredom continue, and eventually all signs of freshness, innovation, and vibrancy disappear. The teacher either gives in to mindless technical behavior or gives up the profession entirely.

This is a dim picture. Does it have to be this way? The authors of this book think not. While the source of technical behavior in teachers is rooted in the reality of the workplace, there are ways to deal with these realities and to fight off the pressures to become a technician. Three suggestions follow.

BE REALISTIC

Classroom teaching in this society is difficult. The pressures are great and the rewards (at least in terms of money and prestige) are small. Teachers are expected to work miracles with large numbers of students in a public servant role that provides a minimum of resources. They must have the strength to maintain cognitive control over their own teaching while fighting off the pressures for conformity and regimentation that come from school and society. They are expected to resolve inherently unresolvable problems while working in isolation from their colleagues. The task is difficult.

In the face of this difficulty, you must be realistic. You need to understand that students will not always respond with enthusiasm, not all students make dramatic progress, there is a bureaucracy in teaching, and classroom teachers often seem powerless. You must also understand that there are no panaceas in teaching. There will never be a single right way to teach reading to all students, teachers will always be seeking better ways, and the nature of teaching is to constantly strive to improve.

ACCEPT DILEMMAS

You must also learn that teaching is full of dilemmas. Survival in the classroom demands keeping students busy, but this is not necessarily teaching. Your task is to demonstrate how to cognitively process language even though no one knows for sure how this cognition occurs, only that it is different for different people. You must think in terms of real-world applications of reading even though the school district, the state, and this society seem to place more value on test scores that measure the performance of isolated skills. And you must stress cognition, strategic awareness, and mental processing when the instructional materials you are required to use often stress memory, drill, and accuracy.

MAINTAIN A VISION

Finally, you should have a vision that transcends the constraints of the workplace. You must view reading as more than skills and as more than a subject; you must view it as part of a language communication system. You must think of the outcomes of reading not only as getting the message but also in terms of positive responses and accurate concepts of what reading is. You must see teaching as a person-to-person interaction that no script or machine or prescription will ever replace. And you must realize that (1) the rewards of teaching lie in presiding over nondramatic growth that you witness daily in various kinds of students; (2) no outside authority governs what happens when you close your classroom door and begin teaching; (3) no day will be like any other; (4) no matter how long you teach there will still be new challenges; and (5) the cliché "the youth of America is in the hands of its teachers" is not a cliché at all, but rather, the truth.

In sum, you must love and value teaching, but not romanticize it. It is a demanding and difficult task, and progress results more from diligent planning, reflective application of pedagogical knowledge, and tenacity in making and sticking with decisions than from flashy demonstrations, intuitive interactions, or dramatic confrontations. It is work that guarantees some failure daily while never guaranteeing success. It can demand all your time and effort and still produce few tangible results. Only when these realities are consciously acknowledged and dealt with can teachers fight off the temptation to be technicians. To know what the realities are is to arm against them. You cannot be surprised if your expectations are realistic, and you are prepared to deal with them.

CONCLUSION

Effective teaching is associated with vital teachers who make their own decisions and who are in control of their instruction. They know their profession and are not afraid to modify and change their techniques as they continually search for better ways of doing things. They are, in short, intellectually independent.

Such independence is difficult to achieve in teaching and even more difficult to maintain. The constraints and difficulties of being a classroom teacher conspire against this independence and toward a dependency on scripts and prescriptions that discourage independent thinking.

However, you need not succumb to such pressures. It is not easy, but independence can be maintained. Three strategies are helpful. First, you must have a realistic image of your job and its pressures. No amount of romanticizing will eliminate the constraints that teachers face, which must be acknowledged before being dealt with. Second, you must develop and implement an active program of professional growth. This program should be career long, and should make use of colleagues, the school district, universities, professional organizations, and journals. Finally, you must ensure that your personal growth is not suppressed by an all-out commitment to professional growth. To the contrary, continued personal growth in a profession as demanding as teaching is as important as continued professional growth.

This society needs thoughtful teachers who, despite the difficulties of the task and the absence of panaceas, reflectively improve their instruction year after year. Teachers who have such potential for professional independence and growth discover that teaching is not only important but highly rewarding, exciting, and challenging. The key is cognitive control. Teachers who know what they are doing and make their own decisions on the basis of their professional knowledge discover that teaching is an absorbing and fulfilling profession.

CHECK YOUR UNDERSTANDING

Now that you have read the chapter, check your understanding by answering the Focus Questions presented at the beginning of the chapter. If you cannot answer any of the questions, return to the section that corresponds to the question, and reread.

SUGGESTED READINGS

Bailey, M. H., & Guerra, C. L. (1984). Inservice education in reading: Three points of view. *Reading Teacher, 38*(2), 174–176.

Bean, R. M., & Eichelberger, R. T. (1985). Changing the role of reading specialists: From pull-out to in-class programs. *Reading Teacher, 38*(7), 648–653.

Cassidy, J. (1977). Reporting pupil progress in reading—parents vs. teachers. *Reading Teacher, 31*(3), 294–296.

Charnock, J. (1982). Notes from the reading–language skills teacher. *Reading Teacher, 36*(2), 132–135.

Criscuolo, N. P. (1980). Effective ways to communicate with parents about reading. *Reading Teacher, 34*(2), 164–166.

Cunningham, P. M. (1977). Match informal evaluation to your teaching practices. *Reading Teacher, 31*(1), 51–56.

Dreher, M. J., & Singer, H. (1985). Parents' attitudes toward reports of standardized reading test results. *Reading Teacher, 38*(7), 624–632.

Guthrie, J. T. (1983). TV effects on achievement. *Reading Teacher, 36*(7), 732–734.

Jongsma, E. (1985). Homework: Is it worthwhile? *Reading Teacher, 36*(7), 702–704.

Lapp, D., Flood, J., & Gleckman, G. (1982). Classroom practices can make use of what researchers learn. *Reading Teacher, 35*(5), 578–585.

Rhodes, L. K., & Hill, M. W. (1985). Supporting reading in home—naturally: Selected materials for parents. *Reading Teacher, 38*(7), 619–623.

Sittig, L. H. (1982). Involving parents and children in reading for fun. *Reading Teacher, 36*(2), 166–169.

Vukelich, C. (1984). Parents' role in the reading process: A review of practical suggestions and ways to communicate with parents. *Reading Teacher, 37*(6), 472–477.

Glossary

ability groups. teacher-assigned instructional groups in which student members match in ability.

academic content. the projected areas of study of a lesson.

accountability. holding teachers and student responsible for student achievement; enacted by state legislatures and/or boards of education.

application. the ability to transfer what has been learned from the classroom to the real world; i.e., using reading strategies while reading recreational or functional text.

Application Stage. a stage of developmental reading growth typically associated with Grades 5 through 8; curricular emphasis is on applying basic reading skills and study skills to other curricular content such as social studies and science.

assessment. a collection of data to be used in making decisions; crucial to instruction, especially direct instruction, because good decisions cannot be made about instructional objectives until student performance is assessed.

attitude outcomes. one of the three major reading outcomes; consist of developing a positive response to reading and an accurate concept of what reading is; viewed as the foundation of an effective instructional program because little can be learned unless students have a positive response and an accurate concept.

NOTE: Terms associated with chapters 15, 16, and 17 on computers, mainstreaming, and special language problems are defined by the respective chapter authors within the chapters themselves.

basal textbook. the reading textbook used in most American classrooms; each series consists of a student's edition of stories written to match the average ability level of the grade at which it is to be used, a teacher's edition containing instructional suggestions, and a variety of supplementary materials.

basal text approach. a way to organize an instructional program in reading; instruction is organized around the stories and books in a basal text series; students read each story in each basal text and complete associated workbook and test materials under the supervision of a teacher.

buffer. a person a teacher recruits to assist with routine classroom tasks; can be an adult, an older student, or a student in the class.

classroom complexity. the intricate entanglements of daily classroom life that teachers are expected to monitor and manage, such as the activities of the students, social interactions of the classroom, accountability factors for both teacher and students, and dilemmas.

cognition. the act of knowing; associated with the mental processing a reader does to make sense out of text.

coherence. a characteristic of written text that refers to the consistency and clarity with which the message is conveyed.

cohesion. the act of uniting paragraphs and sections into a whole message through use of signal words and periodic summaries.

collaborative groups. a temporary grouping structure used primarily for developing attitude outcomes; students of varying abilities work together to solve a problem or to complete a project.

combined approach. a way to organize the reading program; instruction occurs both directly (with basal text activities) and indirectly (with language experience and personalized reading activities); a teacher uses each approach to develop specific reading outcomes.

competencies. a series of skills representing the reading act broken down into its component parts; based on the concept that the best way to understand reading is by breaking it down into smaller pieces, i.e., letters progressing to syllables, etc.

composing. the act of creating (or writing) text; an act performed by an author; the author decides on a message to send and creates a text, using conventions of language, that represents that message.

comprehension. the process of making sense of an author's or speaker's message (see also *reading*).

concepts. the understanding a person has of a particular phenomenon; the sum of the person's direct and vicarious experiences with that phenomenon; organized into a network of related understandings (the *schema* for the phenomenon)

connotative language. a technique of persuasive writing, using terms that trigger emotional response; example: the word *arrogant* has negative connotation.

constraints. limits on a teacher's freedom to perform various tasks of teaching; example: society has certain expectations that teachers must take into consideration when making instructional decisions.

content outcomes. one of the three major reading outcomes; consists of understanding the message the author conveys in a text; example: in a text in which an author intends the reader to understand how to assemble a bookcase, the content outcome is that the reader be able to assemble the bookcase.

context. the semantic elements of a text that immediately precede or follow a sentence or word and can be analyzed to predict meaning.

conventions. agreed upon ways of doing things; language conventions are agreed upon ways of interpreting language messages; example: it is a convention of the English language that we read text from top to bottom and from left to right.

critical reading. making a judgment about the meaning an author is conveying in text; requires the reader to go beyond reconstructing the author's message to making a value judgment about the message.

curriculum. that which is to be taught; in reading, it includes the attitude, process, and content outcomes.

decision making. see *instructional decision making.*

decoding. figuring out what an unknown word is; i.e., when a reader uses phonics or context or a combination of these to identify the unknown word *platypus.*

denotative language. neutral terms that tend to be objective in nature; example: to refer to a person as being *thin* rather than *skinny.*

developmental reading. the steady, progressive pattern that most students follow in learning to read; the instruction provided in a particular grade is part of a development progression; the different points along this line of development are called *stages of developmental reading growth.*

developmental stages. see *developmental reading.*

direct instruction. the teacher develops curricular outcomes by overtly interacting with students; often characterized by an abundance of teacher talk.

directed listening activity (DLA). a technique for structuring listening activities to ensure that students understand the content outcomes; includes introduction, purpose setting, listening, discussion, and closure.

directed reading activity (DRA). a technique for structuring reading activities to ensure that students understand the content outcomes; includes introduction, vocabulary development, purpose setting, reading, discussion, and closure.

directed reading-thinking activity (DR-TA). a technique for structuring reading activities; similar to the directed reading activity except that students are involved in making predictions about the purposes for reading.

Expanded Fundamentals Stage. a stage of developmental reading growth typically associated with Grades 3 and 4; curricular emphasis is on learning and applying the fundamental skills of reading, particularly comprehension.

expectancy. the tendency of all humans to do what is expected of them; example: children from homes where reading and learning is valued tend to have positive expectations regarding learning to read.

explanation. the process of providing students with the information and assistance needed to construct a schema about a particular phenomenon; associated with direct instruction; utilizes explicit statements, modeling, and guided practice.

fix-it strategies. see *strategic.*

fluency. the relative smoothness of a person's reading; fluent reading reflects the reader's clear understanding of the words used, the topic, the author's purpose, and the text structure and is evidenced by correct intonation and an absence of interruptions.

frustration reading level. the level of reading materials that is too difficult for a particular student to read; materials are normally too difficult if a student fails to recognize at least 95 percent of the words instantly and/or fails to answer 75 percent of the questions posed about the content of the text.

functional text. text created for a utilitarian or practical purpose; i.e., textbooks, encyclopedias, recipes, application forms, newspapers.

goal. what a student is to learn; the outcome of instruction; in reading, the major goals are described as attitude, process, and content goals.

heterogeneous groups. groups composed of students who vary in several ways; example: collaborative groups may be composed of students who read at a variety of levels.

homogeneous groups. groups composed of students who are alike in one or more ways; example: ability groups are formed by placing together in one group students at approximately the same instructional reading level.

independent activities. activities students do by themselves while the teacher is teaching other students in a reading group; often referred to as *seatwork.*

independent reading level. the level of reading materials that is comfortable for a particular student to read; materials are comfortable if the student recognizes at least 99 percent of the words instantly and answers 90 percent of the questions posed about the content of the text.

indirect instruction. a way of teaching in which a teacher develops curricular outcomes by providing independent activities designed to help students "discover" certain things; often characterized by an absence of direct guidance by the teacher.

inference. the process of constructing meaning that an author implies but does not state explicitly; requires readers to make predictions using a combination of prior knowledge and text-based clues.

Initial Mastery Stage. a stage of developmental reading growth; typically associated with Grades 1 and 2; curricular emphasis is on learning and applying the fundamental skills of reading, particularly word identification.

instruction. a teacher's intentional use of academic work, presentations, and interactive exchanges to provide the information students need to understand and achieve a desired curricular outcome.

instructional decision making. deciding individually what instruction is to be rather than following the prescriptions provided by someone else; based upon professional knowledge; associated with teachers who are not dominated by the classroom environment; competent instructional decision making is the first step toward professionalism in the classroom.

instructional objective. a carefully structured statement with three parts: what the student will be able to do following instruction, the specific conditions for using what is taught, and how often the student has to demonstrate competence for the teacher to accept it as learned; example: given a display of free verse poetry in the classroom, the student will voluntarily select at least one free verse poem to share with the class.

instructional reading level. the level of reading materials that a student can read with teacher assistance; such materials are characterized by a student's recognizing 95 to 99 percent of the words instantly and answering 75 to 90 percent of the questions posed about the content of the text.

integration. to form into a whole all four language modes in the classroom; listening, speaking, reading, and writing are interrelated; an important characteristic of the literate environment.

intellectual environment. part of the classroom environment created by teachers interested in establishing a literate environment; characterized by expectations that language will be used meaningfully and by challenges to get involved with meaningful language communication.

interactive phase. major part of a process lesson; sometimes called guided practice; teacher attempts to move students gradually to a point where they can use strategies independently.

interactive process. the simultaneous interaction of various knowledge sources (topic, author's purpose, and text structure) to get meaning from text.

interest. the student's response to a *topic* being pursued; by arranging instruction to include topics of interest to students, they will be more tenacious in pursuing tasks; example: a student who responds more positively to the topic *dolls* than the topic *race cars* is said to have more interest in dolls.

invisible cues. cues to meaning that are embedded in a reader's mind or background experience or available schema knowledge; example: if meaning blockage is in a story, a reader can think how stories typically follow a structure from a setting to a main character to a problem, etc.

language. the body of words and system of conventions a culture or society employs to communicate messages.

language experience. meaningful encounters with language; using various modes of language to communicate messages; such *language experiences* contribute to an accurate concept of reading and to the building of positive attitudes toward reading.

language experience approach (LEA). a way of organizing an instructional program in reading around materials written by students; students engage in experiences, talk about the experiences, write about the experiences, and then read what they have written.

language modes. the four ways in which language is used; includes listening, speaking, reading, and writing.

literacy. the ability to successfully manipulate the four modes of language (reading, writing, speaking, and listening) in the environment in which one lives.

literary structure. see *text structure.*

literate environment. a classroom permeated with examples of literacy and language in action; various kinds of student communication, both oral and written, are encouraged; integration of the four language modes is emphasized in classroom activities.

locational skills. strategies used to locate information in books, graphic material, or other information storage devices; examples of having efficient locational skills would be knowledge of the Dewey decimal system, Reader's Guide, atlas, etc.

management. patterns and routines used by an instructionally effective teacher to ensure a fluid and efficient school day.

modeling. showing a student how to do a task with the expectation that the student will then emulate the model; in reading, modeling often involves talking about how one thinks through a task since much of reading is cognitive.

modified DRL. a technique for structuring a reading activity so that skills and strategies are taught prior to the story in which they will be applied; includes an introduction of the story, instruction in the skill, purpose setting for both story content and skill application, reading, discussion of story and the skill application, and closure.

motivation. a condition affecting student perseverence; related particularly to a student's response to an *activity* being pursued; by arranging instruction to include activities which motivate students, their perseverance is increased; example: a student who responds more positively to problem-solving activities than to memory activities is said to be more motivated when doing problem-solving activities.

nook-and-cranny time. short periods of time during the school day when no academic tasks are being pursued.

objective. see *instructional objective.*

outcome. what the student is to learn; the goal of instruction; in reading, the major outcomes are described as attitude, process, and content outcomes.

pacing. moving through instructional content briskly enough to keep the students' attention but not so briskly that the students become frustrated; pacing takes into account students' aptitude levels and is adjusted to their needs.

patterns. routine ways to accomplish procedural tasks that tend to occur every school day; for instance, efficient teachers try to establish patterns for how to enter the classroom, how to collect the milk money, how to get the students' attention, etc.

perseverance. the ability to persist in any action undertaken; perseverance explains some differences in the rate of reading growth; four conditions affect perseverance: expectancy, self-concept, motivation, and interest.

personalized reading. a way of organizing an instructional program in reading around materials students select from the school library or from a room library; students select a book of their choice, read at their own pace, and receive individual help from teachers in conferences.

phonics. the process of using letters and letter sounds to sound out an unknown word

phonetic analysis. see *phonics.*

physical environment. part of the classroom environment created by teachers interested in establishing a literate environment; characterized by physical evidences of literacy and by physically attractive areas that entice students to engage in meaningful reading.

positive response. a positive attitude; in this book, a positive response to reading; closely tied to one's concept of reading since it is difficult to feel good about something that is not understood; to create positive responses, reading experiences are provided that are fun and rewarding.

Power Stage. a stage of developmental reading growth typically associated with Grades 9 to 14; curricular emphasis is on the highly technical aspects of reading and studying.

practice. practice is repetition and drill of an act to make it habitual; example: a game that requires repeated recognition of certain words provides practice on those words.

preconception. the understanding one has about a phenomenon prior to encountering a new experience regarding that phenomenon.

prescriptions. directions for teaching skills or strategies; found in basal texts and in other commercially prepared instructional materials.

procedural patterns. part of classroom organization; characterized by predetermined organizational procedures that become classroom routines; example: a teacher has a predetermined pattern so that students automatically know what to do after completing a practice activity.

process outcomes. one of the three major reading outcomes; consists of understanding how the reading system works and how to apply fix-it strategies to remove blockages to meaning when reading; examples of process outcomes include using multiple knowledge source strategies to predict meaning and context strategies to identify a word meaning.

professional. a teacher possessing knowledge about reading and how to instruct; characterized by the ability to make one's own decisions.

Readiness Stage. a stage of developmental reading growth typically associated with preschool and kindergarten; curricular emphasis is on building positive responses to reading and accurate concepts of what reading is.

reading. reconstructing the content of a text using prior knowledge about letters, words, topic, text purpose, and structure.

recreational text. text created to entertain or enrich a reader; examples: stories, poems, and plays.

round-robin reading. a technique for listening to students read orally; each student reads aloud in turn while the teacher listens.

safety valves. learning centers or activities available to students; do not change daily; need not be associated with academic work in the classroom; tend to be viewed by students as fun; examples: vocabulary games, board games, journal writing, and recreational reading.

schema. a mental structure in which a person's experiences with a phenomenon are organized and stored; see also *concept*.

schemata. plural of *schema*.

seatwork. see *independent activities*.

self-concept. the image that people hold of themselves; developed from perceptions of what other people think of them.

self-fulfilling prophecy. a phenomenon of human behavior characterizing the tendency of humans to fulfill the expectations set for them.

semantic. the meaning associated with words or clusters of words.

sight word. a word a reader recognizes instantly when encountered in text.

social-emotional environment. part of the classroom environment created by a teacher interested in establishing a literate environment; characterized by warmth, acceptance, and agreed-upon procedures for the interchange of ideas.

SQ3R. a procedure for reading functional text systematically; S = *survey*, Q = *question*, and the three R's = *read*, *recite*, and *review*; students are taught to use the five steps in sequence when reading functional text.

strategic. the flexible, adaptable, and conscious use of knowledge about reading to remove a blockage to meaning; characterized by applying fix-it strategies in order to repair blockages; examples: substituting different schema, making inferences, etc.

structural analysis. using prefixes, suffixes, inflectional endings, and root words to identify words and their meanings.

study skills. skills associated with improved study; examples: organizational skills (notetaking and outlining), locational skills (indexes and encyclopedias), and efficiency skills (flexible reading rates).

syntactic. the meaning associated with the grammatical structure of the English language; includes word order, function words, etc.

task analysis. the process whereby a teacher decides what steps are involved in performing a particular task; teachers do task analyses in order to know how to explain to students how a task is performed.

teacher effects. the impact a teacher has on students; usually determined by measuring how well students achieve the intended curricular outcomes.

teaching. refers to all the tasks associated with being a classroom teacher; is distinguished from instruction by the fact that the latter refers only to what teachers do to develop intended curricular outcomes.

technician. a teacher who follows the directions of another, particularly as it relates to instruction; characterized by a reluctance (or inability) to make one's own instructional decisions.

text. authors compose text to communicate messages or ideas; the meaning is in the author; the text carries the meaning, but readers must reconstruct the author's meaning from the cues embedded in the text.

text structure. the way a written text is organized; examples: newspaper articles have a particular structure, epic poems have another structure, plays have another structure, etc.

time on task. the amount of time a student attends to an academic task; the more time on task, the more a student tends to learn.

uninterrupted sustained silent reading (USSR). a reading activity during which all classroom participants (including the teacher) read a book of their choice. Often called sustained silent reading or DEAR (drop everything and read).

unit. a unified learning experience that may encompass several days or weeks; develops a variety of related objectives; is characterized by a logical progression of activities moving toward predetermined goals; often offers opportunities for integration of language.

USSR. see *uninterrupted sustained silent reading*.

verbal reasoning. aptitude for learning language; characterized by the ability to understand and respond to instruction; influenced by background experience, culture, and language.

vicarious experience. not a real experience; an experience that replaces a real experience; example: seeing the Empire State Building is a real experience; seeing a picture of the Empire State Building is a vicarious experience.

visible cues. tangible cues visible on the printed page that clarify either syntactic or semantic meaning and lead to new predictions; examples: word order, typographic cues, key function words, structural elements of words, and semantic context.

vital signs. determinants of reading health; reflect the three curricular outcomes; a teacher can monitor students to see if they have accurate concepts of what reading is and if they respond positively to reading (attitude outcomes), understand how reading works and possess fix-it strategies (process outcomes), and get content meaning from functional or recreational text (content outcomes).

word analysis. see *word attack*.

word attack. a category of fix-it strategies that focuses on what to do when a word is not recognizable on sight; three major methods are context, structural analysis, and phonics.

word identification. the process of identifying the words in text; includes both sight-word recognition and word-attack techniques.

Author Index

A

Allen, C., 262
Allen, E. G., 96
Allen, R. V., 96, 262
Allington, R. L., 212, 344
Alexander, J. E., 67
Alvermann, D. E., 18
Andreasen, N. L., 383
Andrew, B., 382
Anselmo, S., 67
Armstrong, H., 450
Arnold, R. D., 344
Artley, A. S., 41
Ascher, C., 450
Ashton-Warner, S., 96
Atwell, A. A., 212
Auten, A., 41, 113, 401

B

Babbs, P. J., 41, 344
Bailey, M. H., 262, 469
Baker, L., 344
Balajthy, E., 401
Barnitz, J. G., 449, 450
Barrow, L. H., 382
Baumann, J. F., 131, 157
Bean, R. M., 469
Bean, T. W., 345
Beck, I. L., 344

Berg, D. N., 420
Berglund, R., 96, 113
Bergquist, L., 344
Birlem, E. D., 450
Blachowicz, C. L., 18, 262
Black, J. K., 156
Blair, T. R., 96
Blanchard, J., 403
Bongere, M. B., 450
Boodt, G. M., 113
Boothby, P. R., 18
Botel, M., 114
Braun, C. P., 345
Brecht, R. D., 158
Bresnahan, M., 449
Bridge, C. A., 96, 307
Bristow, P. S., 158
Brittain, M. M., 96
Bromley, K. D., 382
Bruntress, N. G., 450
Burg, L., 420
Burke, E. M., 344
Burns, M., 177
Burris, N. A., 262

C

Canady, R. J., 41
Carlsen, J. M., 420
Carr, K. S., 307, 340
Cartwright, C., 420

Cartwright, G., 420
Cassidy, J., 469
Casteel, C. P., 177
Chapman, J., 344
Charnock, J., 131, 469
Chernow, C., 177
Chernow, F. B., 177
Christiansen, J., 420
Christiansen, J. L., 420
Chomsky, C., 41, 232
Clymer, T., 307
Coburn, P., 403
Cohen, R., 344
Combs, M., 262
Coody, B., 113
Crafton, L. K., 131
Cramer, R., 307
Cramond, B., 114
Criscuolo, N. P., 67, 469
Cronnell, B., 450
Crowhurst, M., 344
Culyer, III, R. C., 307
Cunningham, J. W., 307
Cunningham, P., 307, 420, 469

D

D'Angelo, K., 401
Daniel, D., 403
Davis, B., 450

Davis, L., 114
Degler, L. S., 262, 382
Dennard, K., 450
Dennis, J., 403
Dickerson, D. P., 307
Dionisio, M., 232
Donald, B., 450
Downing, J., 41, 449
Dreher, M. J., 469
Dudley-Marling, C. C., 401
Duffy, G., 96, 113
Durkin, D., 18, 450
Dwyer, E. J., 382
Dyson, A. H., 207

E

Ebel, C. W., 449
Edwards, V., 450
Eeds, M., 307
Eherwein, L., 450
Eichelberger, R. T., 469
Ellis, D. W., 262
Evans, H. M., 113
Evans, J. R., 67

F

Falk, J. I., 452
Farrar, M. T., 96, 345
Feeley, J. T., 449
Ferguson, A. M., 450
Filmer, H. T., 263
Fitzgerald, J., 41
Fleet, A. C., 177
Flood, J., 469
Forgan, H. W., 177
Fowler, G. L., 307
Frederick, F., 403
Fredericks, A. D., 67
Freeman, E., 451
Freeman, R. H., 382
Friedman, S., 232

G

Galen, N. D., 450
Gambrell, L. B., 212, 232
Gamby, G., 262
Gamez, G. I., 449
Garner, W. I., 41, 35
Gaskins, I. W., 232
Gaug, M. A., 420
Gawronski, J., 403
Gearheart, B. R., 420
Gearheart, W., 420
Geass, R. M., 420
Gemake, J., 41
Gemake, J. S., 451
Gemake-Stahl, J., 420
Gentile, L. M., 113, 262
Gentry, J. R., 449
Gentry, R., 451
Geoffrion, L., 403
Geoffrion, O., 403
Gillet, J. W., 449, 451
Gipe, J. P., 307
Gleckman, G, 469
Golden, J. M., 41
Goodall, M., 263
Gordon, C. J., 345
Gourley, J. W., 131
Grady, T., 403
Green, D. S., 382
Greenbaum, J., 420
Groff, P. J., 262
Guerra, C. L., 469
Guillary, S. F., 451
Guthrie, F. M., 420
Guthrie, J. T., 41, 96, 212,
  232, 469
Guzzetti, B. J., 212

H

Haley, D., 96
Halfacre, J. D., 178
Hall, M., 263

Hall, M. A., 96
Haller, E., 158
Hamilton, M. C., 113
Hamilton, S. F., 113
Hannon, E., 401
Hansen, J., 420
Hansen, R., 382
Hare, V. C., 96
Harrel, M. M., 345
Heald-Taylor, B. G., 232
Heathcote, O. D., 449
Heathington, B. S., 67
Helton, G. B., 131
Henninger, M. L., 420
Hill, M. W., 469
Hill, S. E., 131
Hoffman, J. V., 345
Hoffman, S., 263
Holbrook, H. T., 113, 382
Hoot, J. L., 262
Hubbard, R., 113, 420
Hunt, L. C., 96
Hu-Pei Au, K., 158, 344,
  449
Hurst, A. W., 177

I

Isaac, M. L., 212

J

Jamsa, E., 114
Janney, K. P., 113
Jennings, M., 113
Johns, J. L., 113, 212
Johnson, F. L., 451
Johnson, M. S., 156
Johnson, T. D., 263
Jones, C. D., 451
Jones, C. J., 114
Jones, L. L., 41
Jongsma, E., 469

K

Kansky, R., 403
Kaufman, M., 420
Kimmel, S., 345
King, R. T., 131
Kitagawa, M. M., 212
Klein, M. L., 178
Kopfstein, R. M., 18
Krause, K. C., 401
Kress, R. A., 158
Kristo, J. V., 282
Kupinsky, B. Z., 449

L

Lambie, R. A., 96
Laminack, L. L., 96
Lamme, L. L., 67
Lang, J. B., 67
Lange, J. T., 382
Langer, J. A., 113
Lanquetot, R., 420
Lapp, D., 469
Larrick, N., 263
Lass, B., 263
Lehr, F., 18
Lentz, K. A., 262
Lesiak, J., 263
Lipson, M., 42
Lukasevich, A., 420

M

MacGinitie, W., 345
Mackay, M. E., 177
Mager, R., 114
Mallon, B., 96
Manna, A. L., 114
Markham, L. R., 451
Marshall, N., 158

Martin, C. E., 114
Martinez, M., 345
Marzano, R. J., 212, 307
Mason, G. E., 114, 401, 403
Mason, J., 33, 345
Mass, L. N., 67
Mateja, J. A., 383
McCracken, M. J., 114
McCracken, R. A., 114
McGea, L., 345, 450
McIntosh, M., 345
McKenna, M. C., 158
McKeown, M. G., 344, 345
McMillian, M. M., 113
McPhail, I. P., 451
Mendoza, A., 114
Mikkelsen, N., 114
Miller, D. C., 114
Miller, G. M., 114
Miller, R., 307
Minkoff, D., 449
Moe, A. J., 41
Moldofsky, P. B., 345
Moller, B. W., 420
Monson, D., 420
Monteith, M. K., 451
Moore, J. C., 114
Morris, D., 307
Morris, R. D., 178
Morrow, H. W., 131
Morsink, C. V., 421
Moustafa, M., 449

N

Nellswrood, E. M., 421
Nelson, D., 113
Nessel, D. D., 114
Nevi, C. N., 178
Norwood, M., 450
Nosbush, L., 307
Noyce, R.M., 232

O

Odland, N., 114
O'Donnell, H., 401
Omotoso, S. O., 67
Otto, J., 42

P

Padak, N. D., 451
Palmer, B. C., 451
Pantiel, M., 403
Pearson, P. D., 42, 212
Pelosi, P. L., 158
Penrose, J., 449
Perez, S. A., 449
Petersen, B., 403
Peterson, D., 403
Pflaum, S. W., 158
Phenix, J., 401
Pieronek, F. T., 67
Pikulski, J. J., 158
Politzer, R. L., 451
Poostay, E. J., 382
Preston, F. W., 262
Prewitt-Diaz, J. O., 450
Price, E. H., 420

R

Radencich, M. C., 114
Ramsey, P. A., 451
Rand, M. K., 42
Raphael, T., 345, 382
Reimer, B. L., 263
Reutzel, D. R., 345
Rhodes, L. K., 212, 469
Ribovich, J. K., 307
Richgels, D., 345, 382
Riley, J. D., 212
Robinson, N., 345
Roehler, L., 96
Roettger, D., 67

Rogers, D. G., 382
Roney, R. C., 42
Roser, N., 345

S

Sadow, M. W., 212
Safter, T., 114
Samuels, S. J., 345
Sanacore, J., 42
Schon, I., 450
Schwartz, J., 451
Schwartz, R., 345
Seaver, J. T., 114
Shake, M. C., 212
Shannon, P., 18, 131
Shavelson, R. J., 18
Shurtleff, C., 420
Shuy, R. W., 42
Sides, N. K., 114
Silvaroli, N. J., 158
Sinatra, R. C., 420
Singer, H., 18, 469
Sittig, L. H., 469
Smith, J. P., 420
Smith, L. B., 232
Smith, L. J., 67
Smith, M., 345
Smith, R. P., 451
Smitherman, G., 451
Spache, E. B., 307
Speckels, J., 420
Spencer D., 403
Spiegel, D. L., 307
Stauffer, R. G., 307, 345, 450
Stefferson, M. S., 451
Stern, P., 18
Stevenson, J. A., 157
Steward, O., 382
Stockman, I. J., 452
Stott, J. C., 382
Strange, M., 42, 212

Swaby, B., 131

T

Tatham, S. M., 42
Taylor, B. M., 307, 345
Taylor, J. B., 452
Templeton, S., 263
Thomas, G. E., 452
Tompkins, G. E., 450
Torrey, J. W., 452
Towner, J. C., 113
Troutman, D. E., 452

U

Unsworth, L., 131

V

Vaughn Cooke, F. B., 452
Vukelich, C., 469

W

Wagner, B. J., 114
Wangberg, E. G., 452
Waterman, M., 158
Weeks, T. E., 67
Welch, F. C., 179
Wenzel, N. R., 114
Wheat, T. E., 450
Widmann, V. F., 383
Wiesendanger, K. D., 450
Wilcox, E., 344
Wilde, S. J., 18
Wilson, C. R., 42
Winograd, P. N., 96
Wiseman, D. L., 263
Wixson, K., 67, 212
Wong, J. A., 345
Wood, K. D., 178, 232, 345, 383

Wrights, J. P., 383
Wutz, S. V., 158

Y

Yates, J. R., 131
Yellin, D. J., 452

Z

Zirkelbach, T., 263

Subject Index

A

Ability groups, 134-135, 137
Academic content
  managing, 168-169
Accountability, 9
Activities
  for attitude outcomes, preschool and
    kindergarten, 241-243
  for process outcomes, preschool and
    kindergarten, 248-253
  for content outcomes, preschool and
    kindergarten, 255-256
  for integrating reading and writing,
    preschool and kindergarten, 257-259
  for attitude outcomes, primary grades,
    271-273
  for process outcomes, primary grades,
    287-295
  for content outcomes, primary grades,
    299-300
  for integrating reading and writing,
    primary grades, 300-305
  for attitude outcomes, middle grades,
    316
  for process outcomes, middle grades,
    326-329
  for content outcomes, middle grades,
    334-335
  for integrating reading and writing,
    middle grades, 335-341
  for attitude outcomes, upper grades,
    355-356
  for process outcomes, upper grades,
    365-368
  for content outcomes, upper grades,
    374-375
  for integrating reading and writing,
    upper grades, 376-380
Ann Arbor decision, 425
Application, 80-81
Application Stage
  defined, 48
  curricular emphases, 51, 57
  347-383
Aptitude, 59
Assessment
  developmental stages, 62-66
  defined, 78
  of interests, 138

of attitudes, 137–138
of social relationships, 139
of reading ability level, 139–142
Attitude
outcomes (reading), 27–31
in basal text, 117
assessing, 144–145
outcomes (writing), 216–217
in preschool and kindergarten, 238–243

B

Basal approach, 86–88
Basal reading series, 12–13
Basal textbooks
described, 12–13
approach to instruction, 86–88
strengths and weaknesses, 116–118
in preschool and kindergarten, 237
in primary grades, 286, 297–298
in middle grades, 325–326, 333–334
in upper grades, 365
Bilingual education
meeting special needs, 443
providing instruction, 445–447
resources, 447–448
Bilingualism
defined, 427–429
myths, 430–440
meeting special needs, 440–443
Black English
defined, 425–426
origin, 425–426
myths, 430–438
meeting special needs, 443–445
providing instruction, 445–447
resources, 447–448
Buffer
with interaction patterns, 167

C

Classroom
physical arrangement, 160–161

Coherence in writing, 219, 221
Cohesion in writing, 218–219
Collaborative groups
defined, 134
collaborative sharing, 102–103
reading groups, 134–136
Combined approach to instruction, 93–95
Complexity of classrooms, 9–11
Composing, 214–215
Concepts
about reading, 29–30
about writing, 216–217
in preschool and kindergarten, 44, 238
in primary grades, 46
in middle grades, 49
in upper grades, 51

Connotative language, 358
Constraints
complexity of classrooms, 9–11
in writing, 230–231
Content outcomes
in reading, 37–38
in basal texts, 118
assessing, 150–156
in writing, 217–218
in preschool and kindergarten, 253–255
in primary grades, 295–297
in middle grades, 329–331
in upper grades, 368–373
Context
restoring meaning, 33–35
assessing, 148
types of, 150
oral, 245–247
teaching of, 279–281

Context clues, see *context*
Critical reading, 357–358
Cultural differences, 59–60
Curriculum
reading, 40–41
preschool and kindergarten, 236–238
primary grades, 266–269
middle grades, 310–312
upper grades, 348–351

D

Denotative language, 358
Decision making, see *instructional decision making*
Decisions
    indirect instruction, 186–188
    direct instruction, 196–202
Decoding, see *word analysis*
Developmental reading growth
    stages of, 44–54
    Readiness Stage, 44
    Initial Mastery Stage, 45
    Expanded Fundamentals Stage, 45–46
    Application Stage, 48
    Power Stage, 48
    curricular emphases, 54–58
    conditions affecting, 58–62
Dialect, 424–425
Dilemmas
    classroom complexity, 9–11
    assigned reading levels, 140
Direct instruction
    defined, 76
    reading example, 84–85
    terms, 78–81
    writing, 227–228
    preschool and kindergarten, 243–249, 253–255
    primary grades, 273–286, 295–297
    middle grades, 318–325, 329–333
    upper grades, 357–365, 368–373
Directed listening activity (DLA), 254
Directed reading lesson (DRL)
    steps, 88
    lesson plan, 126
    preschool and kindergarten, 254
    primary grades, 298–299
    middle grades, 330–332
    upper grades, 369–370
Directed reading and thinking lesson (DRTL)
    middle grades, 330–332
    upper grades, 369–370
Drafting in writing, 219, 221–222

E

Editing during writing, 219, 222–223
English as a second language, 441
Expanded Fundamentals Stage
    defined, 45–46
    middle grades, 309–345
Expectation (also expectancy)
    defined, 60–61
    in literate environment, 104–105
Explanation
    defined, 79

F

Fix-it strategies, see *strategies*
Fluency
    as a process outcome, 31–34
    disruption of, 33–34
    assessing, 145
    teaching of, 318–321
Frustration reading level, 140
Functional text
    defined, 37–38
    in preschool and kindergarten, 254
    in primary grades, 296
    in middle grades, 329–330
    in upper grades, 370–373

G

General strategy for comprehension (also how reading works)
    introduced, 39–40
    preschool and kindergarten, 44–45, 243–245
    primary grades, 46, 273–279
    middle grades, 49, 318, 321
    upper grades, 51, 357–358
Goals
    of reading instruction, 4–5
    as outcomes, 27–39
Goal setting, 120–121

Grade level
  characteristics of preschool and
    kindergarten, 44, 236–238, 260–261
  characteristics of primary, 45, 266–267,
    305–306
  characteristics of middle, 45–48,
    310–311, 341–343
  characteristics of upper, 48, 348–349,
    380–381
Grouping
  reading groups, 134–136, 159–177
  collaborative groups, 134–136
  ability groups, 134–136
  heterogeneous groups, 134
  homogeneous groups, 134

H

Heterogeneous groups, 134
Hispanics
  defined, 429
Homogeneous groups, 134
How the reading system works, see *general
strategy for comprehension*

I

Independent activities
  in literate environment, 102–103
  management, 161–163
Independent reading level, 139
Indirect instruction
  defined, 76–77
  reading example, 83–84
  terms, 81–82
  writing, 225–227
  in preschool and kindergarten, 238–241
  in primary grades, 267–271
  in middle grades, 311–315
  in upper grades, 349–353
Individualized reading, see *personalized
reading*

Inferencing
  defined, 24, 321–325
Initial Mastery
  defined, 45
Instruction
  defined, 70–75
  direct, 76–77
    example, 84–85
  indirect, 76–77
    example, 83–84
  planning for indirect, 184–188
  planning for direct, 188–203
  subtleties of, 203–209
  in preschool and kindergarten, 235–264
  in primary grades, 265–308
  in middle grades, 309–346
  in upper grades, 347–383
Instructional decision making
  characteristics of, 14–16
  by reference to vital signs, 62–66
  lesson plan formats (reading), 186–203
  indirect instruction (reading), 186–188
  direct instruction (reading), 196–203
  indirect instruction (writing), 225–227
  direct instruction (writing), 227–228
  subtleties of, 203–209
Instructional objective, 180–183
Instructional practices
  current, 7–8
Instructional reading level, 139
Integration
  literate environment, 180
  reading and writing, 214–215
  in preschool and kindergarten, 256–260
  in primary grades, 300–305
  in middle grades, 335–341
  in upper grades, 376–380
Intellectual environment
  defined, 82
  in literate environment, 104–108
  example, 111–112
  in preschool and kindergarten, 240
  in primary grades, 269
  in middle grades, 314–315
  in upper grades, 353

Interaction patterns, 166–167
Interaction
  during instruction, 79
Interest
  influence on perseverance, 61–62
  in literate environment, 106–107
Invisible cues
  restoring meaning, 36
  assessing of, 149–150
  teaching of, 323–325
  at Readiness Stage, 45
  at Initial Mastery Stage, 46–47
  at Expanded Fundamental Stage, 49
  at Application Stage, 51

J

Junior high school, see *upper grades*

K

Kindergarten
  Readiness Stage, 44
  preschool and kindergarten, 235–264
Knowledge sources
  in reading text, 26–27, 31–33
  assessing use of, 143
  instruction of
    preschool and kindergarten, 243–245
    primary grades, 273–279
    middle grades, 318–319
    upper grades, 357–358

L

Language experience
  approach to instruction, 89–91
  in preschool and kindergarten, 241
  in primary grades, 270–271
  in middle grades, 315

Language use
  formal and informal, 101
Language variations
  verbal reasoning, 59–60
  language variations, 60
  special language problems, 423–452
Large-group instruction, 121–123
Lesson
  organization, 125–129
  formats, 183–203
  examples of
    preschool and kindergarten, 240–254
    primary grades, 270–299
    middle grades, 314–333
    upper grades, 354–373
Lesson plans
  types of, 183–185
  indirect instruction, 185–186
  direct instruction (reading), 189–202
    process outcomes, 189–194
    content outcomes, 194–202
  indirect instruction (writing), 225–227
  direct instruction (writing), 227–228
Letter names, see *print awareness*
Letter sounds
  reading competencies, 22
  fix-it strategy, 35
  in preschool and kindergarten, 45,
    247–248
  in primary grades, 46, 281–284
  in middle grades, 49
Listening
  in preschool and kindergarten, 56, 237
  for teaching process outcomes, 245
  for teaching content outcomes, 253–255
Literacy, see *literate environment*
Literate environment
  characteristics of, 100–103
  components of, 103–109
  creating, 109–112
  in writing, 225
  in preschool and kindergarten, 239–240
  in primary grades, 269–270
  in middle grades, 313–315
  in upper grades, 353

Locational skills
    sample curriculum at Application Stage,
        51–52
    upper grades, 359–361

M

Management
    patterns, 161–168
    of academic content, 168–169
    sustaining student engagement, 169–173
    steps in creating management, 175–177
    record keeping, 166
Middle grades
    Expanded Fundamentals Stage, 49–50
    middle grades, 309–345
Middle school, see *upper grades*
Modeling
    in literate environment, 105–106
    during strategy instruction, 189–194,
        199–200
    in lesson plan, 84, 189–194, 199–200
Modified DRL
    lesson plan, 125–129
Motivation
    influence on perseverance, 60–62
    in literate environment, 107–108

N

Nook-and-cranny time
    defined, 120
Note taking, 360

O

Objectives
    described, 180–182
    student behavior, 181
    condition, 181–182
    criterion, 182
    in writing, 224–225

Organizing
    year-long program, 119–121
    whole-group instruction, 121–123
    small-group instruction, 123–129
Organizing and remembering skills
    sample curriculum at Application Stage,
        51–52
    upper grades, 359–363
Outcome
    of reading instruction, 27–39
    as objectives, 180–182
    in task analysis, 190–192
Outlining, 360–361

P

Pacing, 170
Patterns
    for independent activities, 161–163
    for safety valves, 163–165
    procedural patterns, 164–166
    interaction patterns, 166–167
Perseverance, 60–62
Personalized reading
    approach to instruction, 91–93
    in middle grades, 315
Phonics
    assessing, 148
    common phonic elements, 152–154
    preschool and kindergarten, 45, 245–248
    teaching of, 248, 281–285
    primary grades, 46, 281–285
    middle grades, 49
Physical environment
    defined, 81
    in literate environment, 103–104
    example, 111
    in preschool and kindergarten, 239–240
    in primary grades, 269
    in middle grades, 314
    in upper grades, 353
Positive response
    attitude outcomes, 27, 30–31
    assessing, 144–145

Positive response *(continued)*
  in preschool and kindergarten, 44,
    238–241
  in primary grades, 46, 267–271
  in middle grades, 49, 311–315
  in upper grades, 51, 349–353
Power stage
  defined, 48
  sample curriculum, 53
Practice
  defined, 79–80
  activities for practice, see *activities*
Preschool
  Readiness Stage, 44–45
  preschool and kindergarten, 235–264
Prescriptions
  in the basal text, 12–13
  primary grades, 297–298
  reorganizing, 123–129
  middle grades, 325–326
Primary grades
  Initial Mastery Stage, 45–47
  primary grades, 265–308
Print awareness
  in readiness curriculum, 44
  teaching, 234–245
Prior knowledge, 23–24
Procedural patterns, 164–165
Process
  defined, 27–28
  outcomes, 31–37
  in basal texts, 117
  assessing, 145–150
  instruction of
    in preschool and kindergarten,
      243–253
    in primary grades, 273–295
    in middle grades, 318–329
    in upper grades, 357–368
Propaganda devices, 357–358

Q

Question-answer relationships (QARs), 371

R

Readiness
  as a developmental stage, 44–45
  preschool and kindergarten, 335–364
Reading
  defined, 27
  described, 22–27
  examples of how it works, 25–26, 32–33
Reading aloud to students, 82, 241
Reading rate, 363–365
Recordkeeping, 164–166
Recreational text
  defined, 38
  in preschool and kindergarten, 254
  in primary grades, 295–296
  in middle grades, 329–332
  in upper grades, 369–370
Repeated readings, 321
Round-robin reading, 180

S

Safety valves, 163–165
Schema, 22–23
Seatwork, see *independent activities*
Self-concept
  influence on perseverance, 61
  bilingual education, 442–443
Self-fulfilling prophecy, 60
Semantic
strategies, 35
  assessing, 148–149
  middle grades, 321–325
Sight words
  word knowledge, 143
  basic sight word list, 146–147
  teaching, 276–279
Skills of efficient study, see *study skills*
Small-group instruction, 123–129
Social-emotional environment
  indirect instruction, 81–82
  in literate environment, 108–109
  example, 111–112

Social-emotional environment *(continued)*
  in preschool and kindergarten, 239–240
  in primary grades, 269–270
  in middle grades, 313–314
  in upper grades, 353
Social environment
  as a complexity of classroom life, 9
  in the literate environment, 108–109
  see *social-emotional environment*
Social interactions, see *social-emotional environment*
Socialization outcomes
  preschool and kindergarten, 236–238
Speed reading, see *reading rate*
SQ3R
  middle grades, 331–333
  upper grades, 371
Stages of development, see *developmental reading growth*
Stages of writing, 218–221
Strategic reading, 24–25, 32–33
Strategies
  to restore meaning, 33–37
  assessing, 147–150
  writing, 221–223
  preschool and kindergarten, 245–248
  primary grades, 279–286
  middle grades, 321–325
  upper grades, 359–365
Structural analysis
  restoring meaning, 36
  assessing, 146
  common structural units, 151
  teaching of, 280–282
Structural overview, 372
Student engagement
  defined, 160
  sustaining, 169–174
Study guides, 371
Study skills
  at Expanded Fundamentals Stage, 57
  at Application Stage, 57
  at Power Stage, 58
  upper grades, 359–364
Summarizing, 361–364

Syntactic
  strategy, 35
  assessing, 148–149
  in middle grades, 321–325

T

Task analysis, 190–192
Teaching, 70
Technician, 17
Test taking, 361–363
Text
  defined, 26
  recreational, 38, 150–156
  functional, 38, 150–156
Time
  scarcity of, 115
  allocation of, 119–120
Time on task
  managing, 169

U

Unit
  organization (basal), 123–125
  sample integration unit in preschool and kindergarten, 257–259
  sample integration unit in primary grades, 301–304
  sample integration unit in middle grades, 336–340
  sample integration unit in upper grades, 377–379
  in upper-grade subject areas, 368
Upper grades
  Application Stage, 48, 51
  upper grades, 347–383
USSR, 65
  direct instruction, 83–84
  indirect instruction, 185
  literate environment, 108–109

V

Verbal reasoning, 59–60
Visible cues
  restoring meaning, 36
  assessing, 149–150
  teaching of, 323–325
  at Readiness Stage, 45
  at Initial Mastery Stage, 46–47
  at Expanded Fundamental Stage, 49
    at Application Stage, 51
Vital signs
  defined, 62
  decision making, 63–65
  assessing vital signs, 143–156

W

Word analysis
  as fix-it strategies, 35
  at Readiness Stage, 45
  at Initial Mastery Stage, 46
  at Expanded Fundamental Stage, 49
  at Application Stage, 51
  in preschool and kindergarten, 245–248
  in primary grades, 279–286
Word attack, see *word analysis*
Writing
  in literate environment, 101–102
  relationship to reading, 214–215
  outcomes, 216–224
  curriculum, 216–224
  in preschool and kindergarten, 256–260
  in primary grades, 300–305
  in middle grades, 335–341
  in upper grades, 375–380